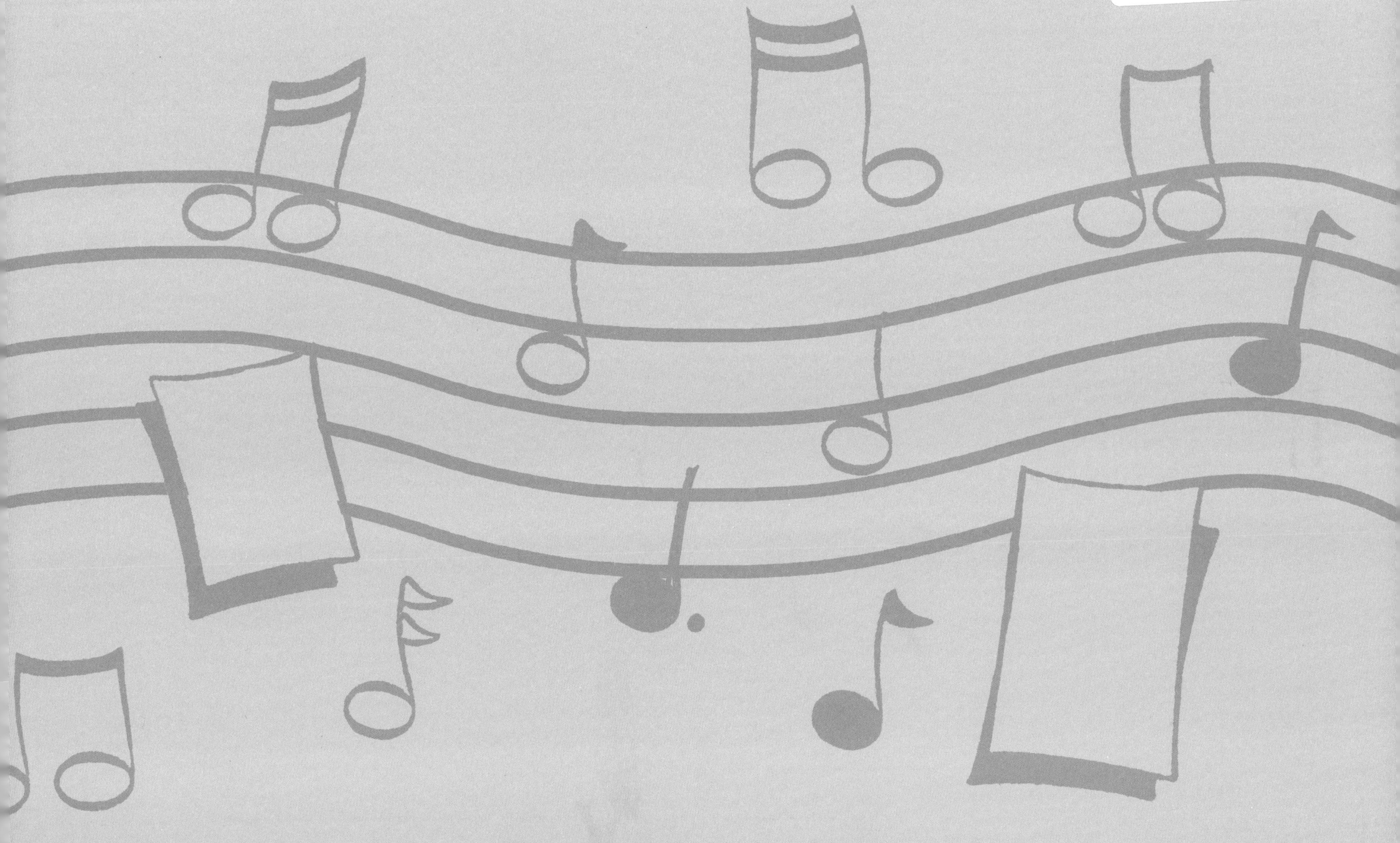

Walt Disney's Silly Symphonies Vol. 2

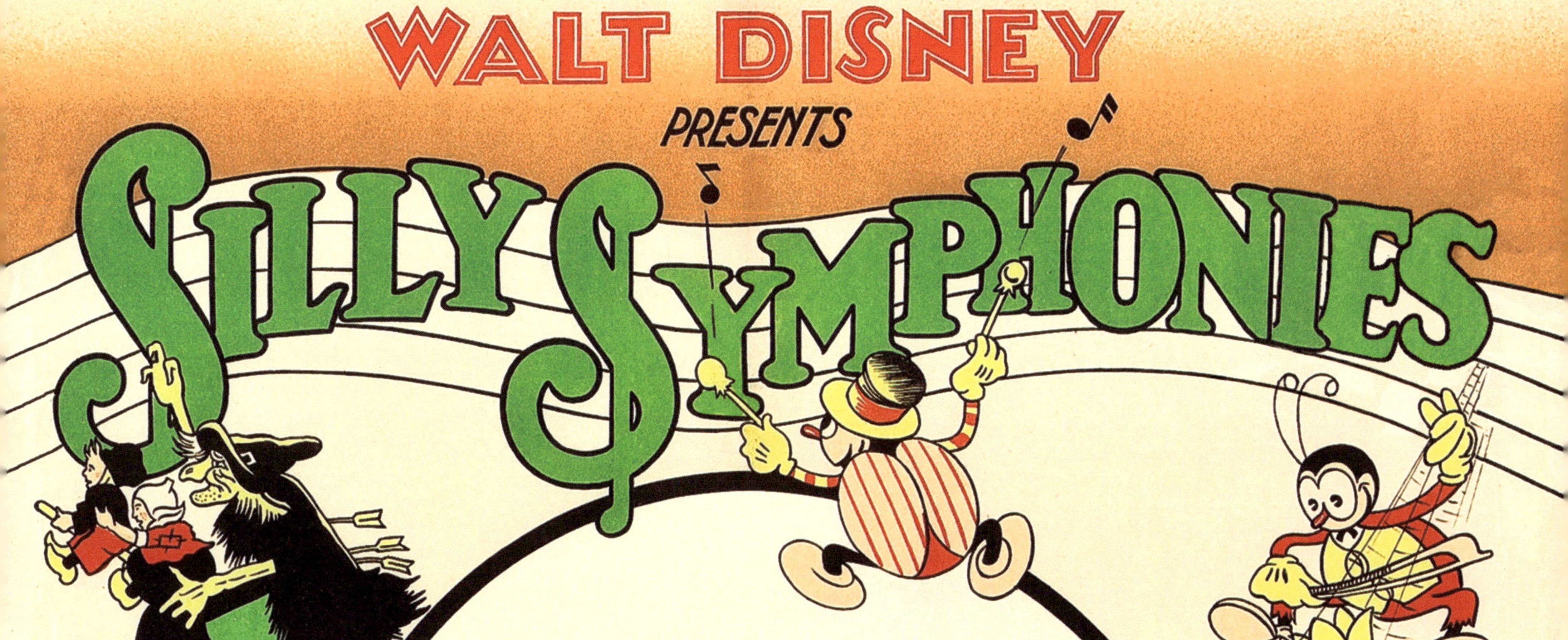
WALT DISNEY
PRESENTS
SILLY SYMPHONIES

THE SUNDAY NEWSPAPER COMICS
VOLUME TWO
1935 TO 1939

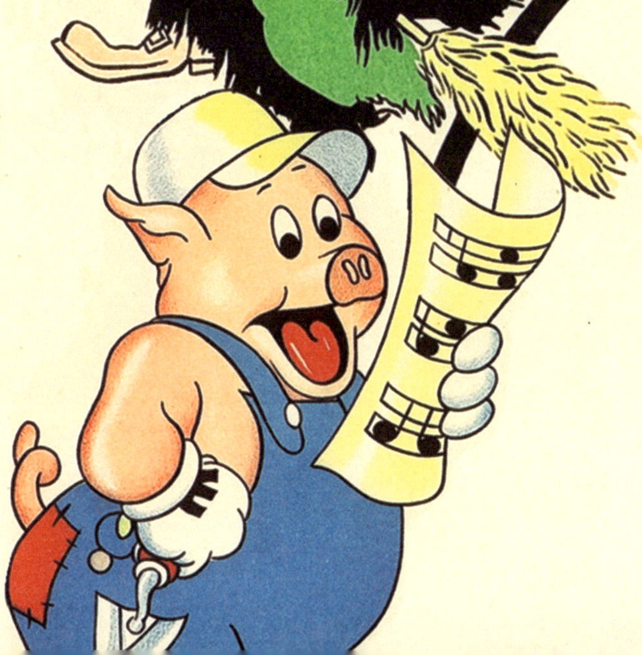
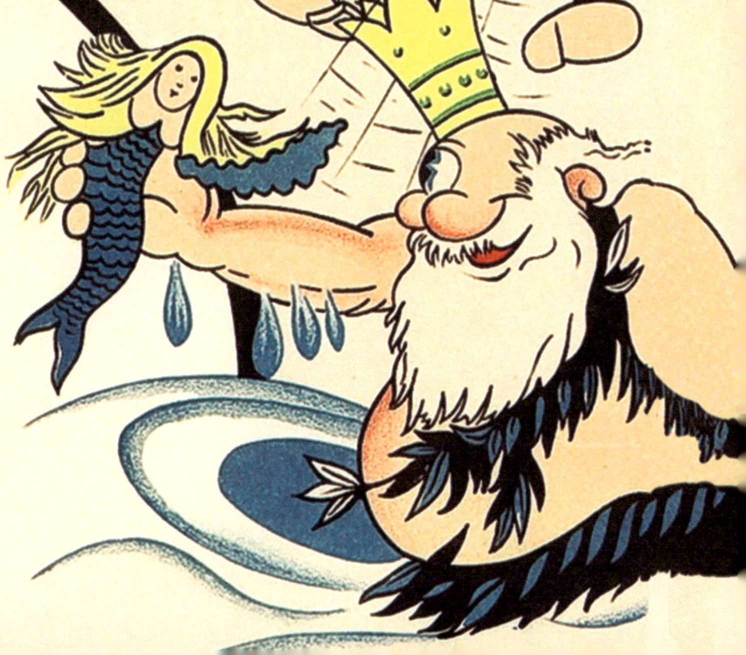

THE LIBRARY OF AMERICAN COMICS

IDW PUBLISHING
San Diego

THE LIBRARY OF AMERICAN COMICS

EDITOR/CO-DESIGNER DEAN MULLANEY   ASSOCIATE EDITOR BRUCE CANWELL
ART DIRECTOR/CO-DESIGNER LORRAINE TURNER   CONSULTING EDITOR DAVID GERSTEIN
COLOR RE-CREATION DIGIKORE STUDIOS   SCANNING REBEKAH CAHALIN
INTRODUCTION J. B. KAUFMAN   PUBLISHED BY TED ADAMS

ISBN: 978-1-63140-804-5   First Printing, December 2016

Published by:
IDW Publishing
a Division of Idea and Design Works, LLC
2765 Truxtun Road, San Diego CA 92106
www.idwpublishing.com
LibraryofAmericanComics.com

Ted Adams, Chief Executive Officer/Publisher
Greg Goldstein, Chief Operating Officer/President
Robbie Robbins, EVP/Sr. Graphic Artist
Chris Ryall, Chief Creative Officer
David Hedgecock, Editor-in-Chief
Matthew Ruzicka, CPA, Chief Financial Officer
Laurie Windrow, Senior VP of Sales and Marketing
Dirk Wood, VP of Marketing
Lorelei Bunjes, VP of Digital Services
Jeff Webber, VP of Licensing, Digital and Subsidiary Rights
Jerry Bennington, VP of New Product Development

Distributed by Diamond Book Distributors
1-410-560-7100

A NOTE ON SOURCE MATERIAL: The black-and-white artwork in this book was scanned from the Disney Licensed Publishing collection. The color reference material was photographed from original bound volumes at the Walt Disney Archives.

Special thanks to:
—Curt Baker, Ken Shue, Iliana Lopez, Julie Dorris, and Danielle Digrado at Disney Licensed Publishing
—Becky Cline, Kevin Kern, and Joanna Pratt at the Walt Disney Archives
—Holly Brobst at the Walt Disney Archives Photo Library

Additional thanks to Sarah Gaydos, Justin Eisinger, Alonzo Simon, and Heritage Auctions.

All contents, unless otherwise specified, copyright © 2016 Disney Enterprises, Inc. All rights reserved. The Library of American Comics is a trademark of Library of American Comics, LLC. All rights reserved. Text Introduction © 2016 J. B. Kaufman. With the exception of artwork used for review purposes, none of the comic strips in this publication may be reprinted without the permission of Disney Enterprises, Inc. No part of this book may be reproduced or transmitted in any form, electronic or mechanical, including photocopying, recording, or by any information and retrieval system, without permission in writing from Disney Enterprises, Inc. Printed in China.

Title page artwork is modified from a 1933 *Silly Symphony* poster released in France.

PUBLISHER'S NOTE: These comic strips were created in an earlier time and may contain cartoon violence and occasional historically-dated content, such as gags about smoking, drinking, gunplay, and racial stereotypes. Needless to say, the characters in these stories wouldn't mix it up with these elements today; we include them here with the understanding that they reflect a bygone era. Enjoy the show!

CONTENTS

SILLY SYMPHONIES

THREE LITTLE KITTENS / 12
July 28 - October 20, 1935
Written by Ted Osborne, drawn by Al Taliaferro

THE LIFE AND ADVENTURES OF ELMER ELEPHANT / 26
October 27, 1935 - January 12, 1936
Written by Ted Osborne, drawn by Al Taliaferro

THE FURTHER ADVENTURES OF THE THREE LITTLE PIGS / 40
January 19 - August 23, 1936
Written by Ted Osborne, drawn by Al Taliaferro

DONALD DUCK / 74
August 30, 1936 - December 5, 1937
Written by Ted Osborne, drawn by Al Taliaferro

SNOW WHITE AND THE SEVEN DWARFS / 142
December 12, 1937 - April 24, 1938
Written by Merrill de Maris,
drawn by Hank Porter, assisted by Bob Grant

THE PRACTICAL PIG / 164
May 1 - August 7, 1938
Written by Merrill de Maris,
drawn by Al Taliaferro

MOTHER PLUTO / 180
August 14 - October 16, 1938
Written by Merrill de Maris,
drawn by Al Taliaferro

THE FARMYARD SYMPHONY / 192
October 23 - November 27, 1938
Written by Merrill de Maris,
drawn by Al Taliaferro

TIMID ELMER / 200
December 4, 1938 - February 12, 1939
Written by Merrill de Maris,
drawn by Al Taliaferro

INTRODUCTION

by J. B. KAUFMAN

It's not difficult to understand why the 1930s and early '40s are widely regarded as the "Golden Age" of the Walt Disney studio. The Disney films of those years were marked by a distinctive, original quality that proved irresistible to audiences of the time, and is no less appealing today. The same quality distinguished the studio's ancillary activities, including its comic strips. Readers of Volume 1 in the present series of reprints can vouch for the early years of the *Silly Symphony* Sunday comics. This newspaper feature, based on an innovative series of animated cartoons with a musical orientation, debuted in 1932. Although its story material was based only loosely on that of the films, the strip mirrored the freshness and charm of the *Silly Symphonies* themselves.

In this second volume, covering a period from the summer of 1935 through early 1939, the *Symphony* comics continue to reflect their cinematic namesakes, the favorites that readers were seeing every week at the movies. At the Disney studio of the 1930s, however, nothing stood still for very long. As the studio continued to pioneer new ideas and techniques and to refine its artistic standards, its films evolved and became radically unlike those of the early years. Inevitably, those changes were reflected in the comics. The progress of the *Silly Symphony* strip in these pages charts the maturation of the Disney studio into new and unfamiliar territory.

The strips reproduced here can be broken down into four distinct phases. They begin where they left off at the end of Volume 1, with discrete continuities based, more or less faithfully, on individual films. Writer Ted Osborne and artist Al Taliaferro had, after working as a team for more than a year, established a pattern: taking a *Silly Symphony*'s plot as a starting point, they would hatch a parallel story of their own. The relationship between the film version and the comics version could be complex and varied, providing no end of intrigue for the latter-day Disney enthusiast who compares the two. The convention of rhyming dialogue, established at the outset of the strip in 1932 (and by this time adopted in many of the films), continued for the moment. Taliaferro maintained his impressive artistic facility, keeping pace with the Disney animators and rendering a variety of characters *exactly* as they appeared in the films—sometimes with poses that seemed to come directly from the screen.

As before, the stories chosen for this treatment were selected from key films in the series. *Three Orphan Kittens*, released in 1935, was notable for the elegant sophistication of its visual effects, and would go on to win the Academy Award as the best cartoon of the year. Its corresponding comic continuity, "Three Little Kittens," retained the bare bones of the film's concept and changed almost everything else. *Elmer Elephant* (1936), about the troubles of a little jungle misfit, likewise inspired a comic continuity that retained the film's setting and characters, but took their story in a new direction. The appearance of a new continuity based on *Three Little Pigs* probably seemed counterintuitive in 1936; the film had been released three years earlier. But, in fact, the new story was a multilayered device. *Three Little Pigs* had been one of the hit movies of 1933—it remains today, arguably, the most successful one-reel cartoon ever produced—and by 1936 it had already inspired two Pig sequels: *The Big Bad Wolf* (1934) and *Three Little Wolves* (1936). Now Osborne and Taliaferro crafted a continuity that

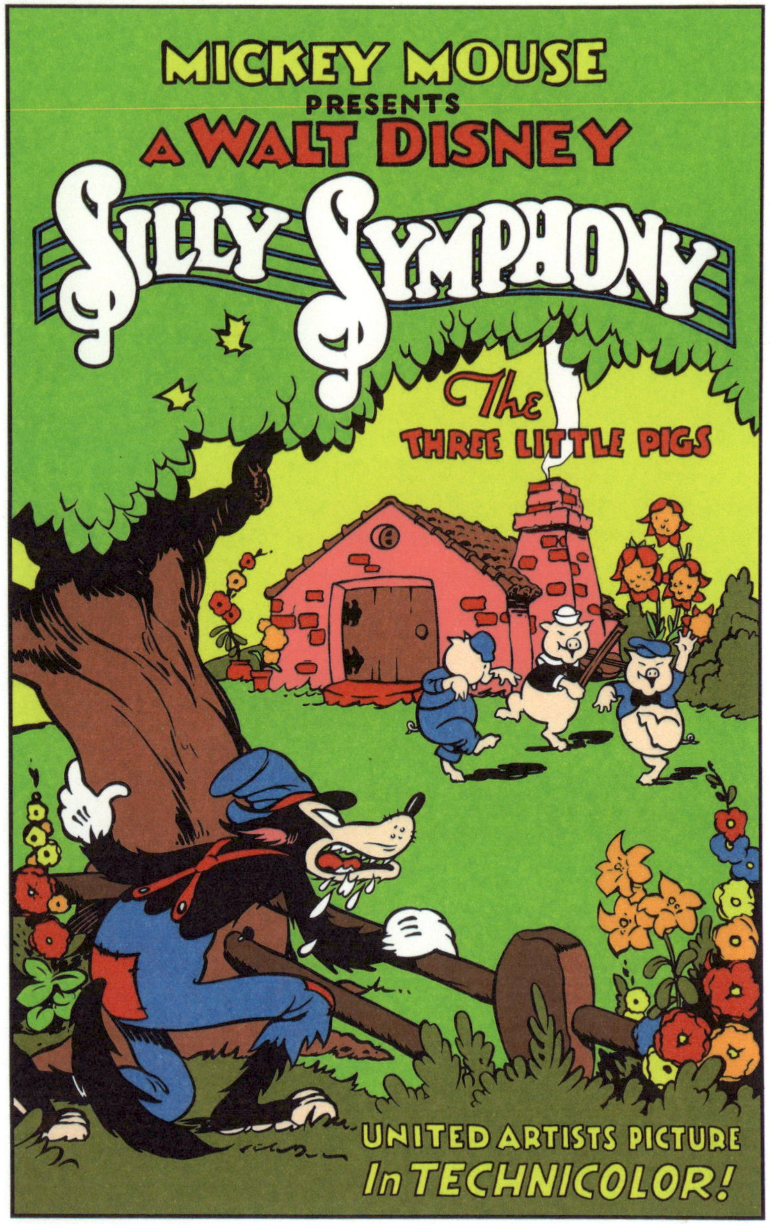
MICKEY MOUSE
PRESENTS
A WALT DISNEY
SILLY SYMPHONY
The
THREE LITTLE PIGS
UNITED ARTISTS PICTURE
In TECHNICOLOR!

ABOVE: A latter-day seriograph reproduction of the 1933 *Silly Symphony* poster for *The Three Little Pigs*.

incorporated elements of the original film and the first sequel, but leaned heavily on the *second* sequel, due for imminent release to movie houses—then topped that with a series of original gags and plot details that were common to *none* of the films.

The *Silly Symphony* comic page marked its first major turning point in the late summer of 1936, launching a new long-running continuity, not built around an individual story, but designed simply as a starring vehicle for Donald Duck. There was a precedent for this departure. Donald's first-ever appearance in the comics had occurred two years earlier on the *Symphony* page, in a continuity based on the film *The Wise Little Hen* (and now preserved in *Silly Symphonies* Volume 1). His role had been intended as a single isolated appearance—but Donald made a strong first impression, and neither the movies nor the comics were about to let him go so easily. Soon he could be seen again, onscreen and on the comic page, as a regular member of Mickey Mouse's supporting cast. The squawking, belligerent Duck quickly developed a fan following, and began to evolve into a major Disney character with star potential of his own.

In the meantime, Al Taliaferro, the artist who had first introduced Donald to the comic page, was developing his own special fondness for the character. Taliaferro had ambitions for a separate comic strip starring the Duck, and pressured Walt Disney for a chance to try out his idea. Walt's answer was to give artist and duck a trial run, turning over the *Silly Symphony* Sunday page to Donald for what amounted to an extended audition. Osborne and Taliaferro, for so long charged with creating episodic pictorial narratives based on the *Silly Symphonies*, now shifted gears to begin producing weekly slapstick comedies for the studio's short-tempered new cartoon star. Ultimately the trial lasted for well over a year, a continuity collected and preserved for the first time in this volume.

This was a significant development in more ways than one. Though observers outside the studio might not have guessed it, the days of the cinematic *Silly Symphonies* were numbered. Once the Disney studio's most prestigious product, they were gradually being replaced in Walt's priorities by a still more ambitious venture: a *feature-length* cartoon. *Snow White and the Seven Dwarfs*, a seemingly impossible undertaking, had been in story development for two years by the autumn of 1936 and was moving inexorably into production. As it did so, it absorbed some of the top animation talent in the studio—talent that had once been reserved for the *Silly Symphonies*.

For the time being, of course, this shift was imperceptible outside the studio walls. *Silly Symphonies*, including some of the best, would continue to appear on movie screens and in the comics for several years to come. But in the meantime the launch of the *Donald Duck* continuity, in what was still nominally the *Silly Symphony* space, had a marked effect on the tenor of the Disney Sunday comic page. The *Symphonies*, with their constantly changing landscape of stories and characters, had held pride of place at the top of the page, with reliable *Mickey Mouse* holding court in the lower portion. Now the page changed course and became, in effect, a showcase for the two most popular *continuing* Disney stars. The convention of rhyming dialogue, a staple of the *Symphony* comics from 1932 on, disappeared in the *Donald* strips—and, in fact, dialogue of *any* kind was drastically curtailed. Although created by the same writer and artist who had produced the earlier *Symphony* stories, the strip now became largely a compendium of sight gags.

The months of the *Donald Duck* continuity, August 1936 to early December 1937, coincided with the Duck's rise to a new prominence in the movies. Now he was no longer simply a member of Mickey Mouse's supporting cast, but the star of his own series of cartoons. In time his popularity would come to surpass that of Mickey himself. The comic continuity built on this new celebrity status and also contributed to it in some ways. One notable event occurred in October 1937, when Osborne and Taliaferro added a group of new characters to the Disney pantheon: Donald's nephews Huey, Dewey, and Louie. Typically, new Disney characters were introduced on the screen, then worked their way into comics, storybooks, and other showcases. This time the influence flowed in the opposite direction: Donald's nephews made such a hit with newspaper readers that they were soon featured in the animated cartoons as well. They went on to take their places among the best-known Disney characters.

In the end, Donald did pass his audition with flying colors. From Taliaferro's viewpoint, the extended newspaper series accomplished its objective, demonstrating that the Duck was more than capable of carrying his own comic strip. Tellingly, during the last months of the run, the original title panel, "Silly Symphony featuring Donald Duck," was replaced by a new panel reading simply "Donald Duck." And, indeed, by this time a new *Donald Duck* daily strip was in the works, to debut in newspapers early in 1938. In the movies, and now in the comics, Donald had arrived.

Simultaneously, many other activities were taking place at the Disney studio—most spectacularly, continuing work on *Snow White and the Seven Dwarfs*. As the challenges of this monumental undertaking mounted, Walt pressed on undaunted, fired by an enthusiasm that spread to the rest of his staff and carried them along with him. Their efforts culminated in a film that would make history, transform the fortunes of the Disney studio, and exercise a powerful influence on the film industry at large. As *Snow White* approached completion during the summer of 1937, the studio and its distributor laid plans to unveil their feature as a special Christmas attraction across the nation. The Disney marketing experts marshaled their

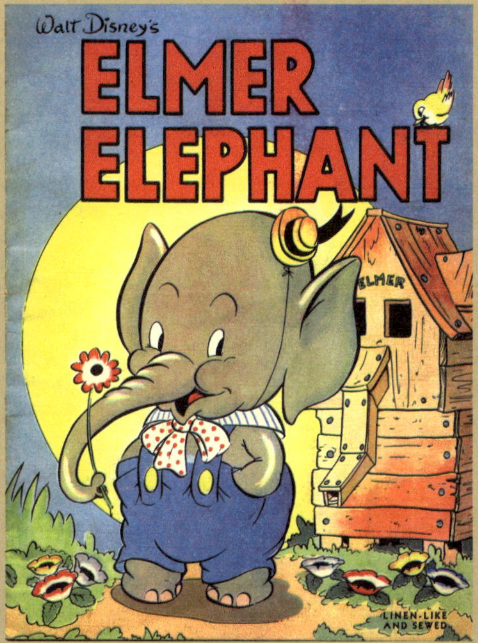

Walt Disney's
ELMER
ELEPHANT
ELMER
LINEN-LIKE
AND SEWED

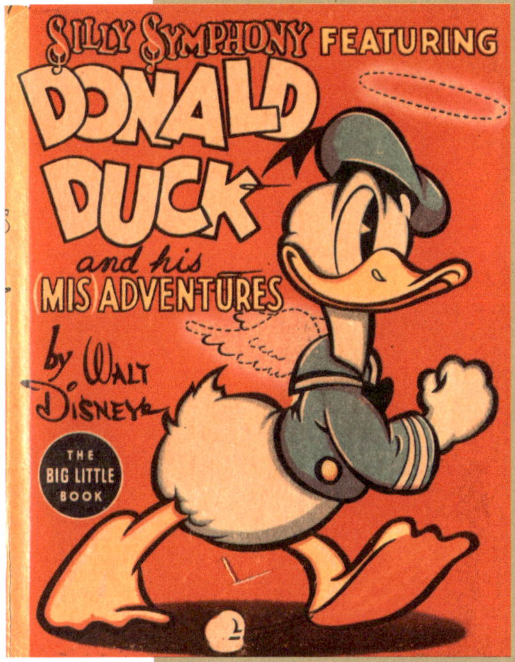

SILLY SYMPHONY FEATURING
DONALD
DUCK
and his
MIS ADVENTURES
by WALT
DISNEY
THE
BIG LITTLE
BOOK

ABOVE: A 1938 *Elmer Elephant* picture book published by Whitman, in which Mickey and Pluto make guest appearances.

LEFT: A 1937 Big Little Book from Whitman featuring Al Taliaferro's art from the "Donald Duck" series in *Silly Symphonies*.

WALT DISNEY'S
The
PRACTICAL PIG
SILLY SYMPHONY
© W.D.P.
R.K.O. RADIO PICTURE IN TECHNICOLOR

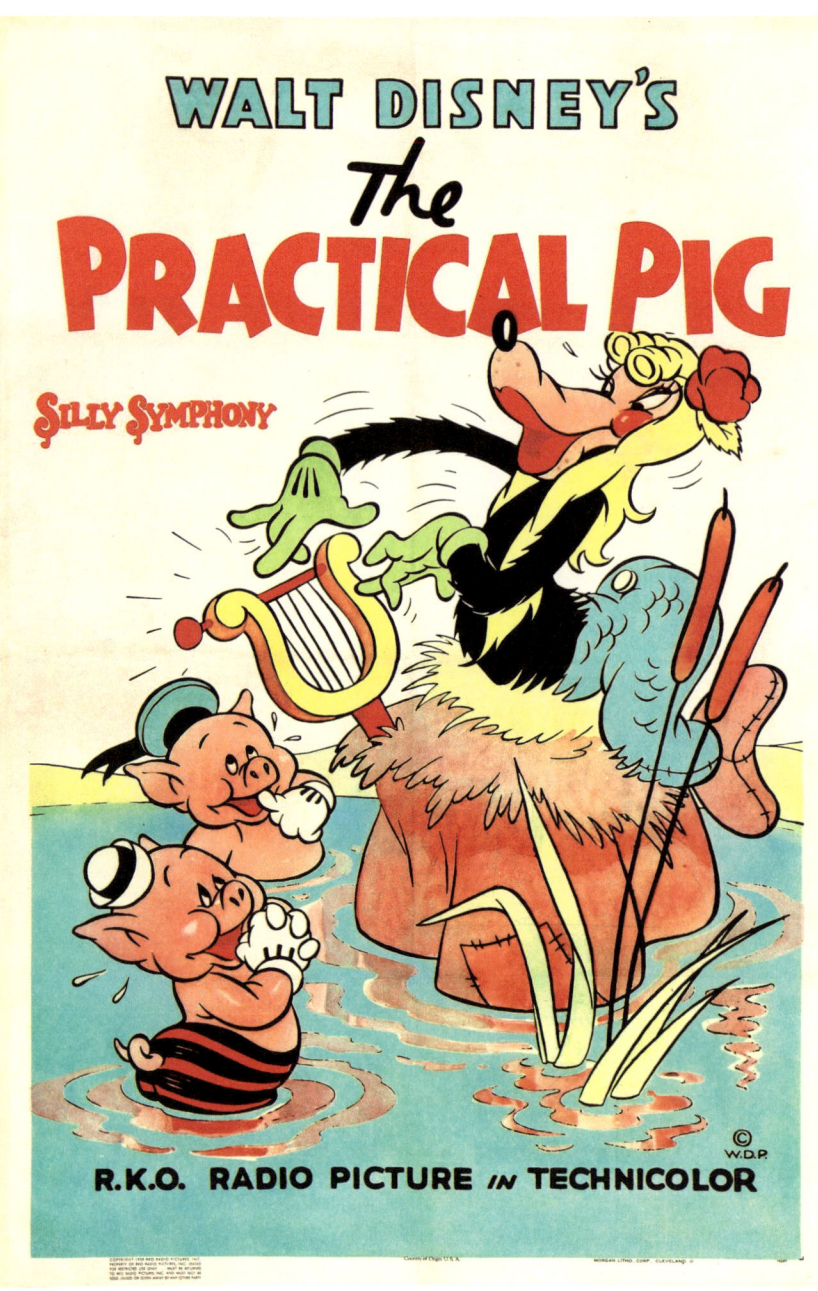

ABOVE: A 1939 one-sheet poster for Disney's *The Practical Pig* theatrical cartoon.

forces, mounting a spectacular promotional campaign. A key element in that campaign was the comics: the *Silly Symphony* comic page, having demonstrated its useful versatility, provided a ready-made showcase for the latest Disney triumph.

Hampered by production delays, *Snow White* ultimately failed to meet its nationwide December opening date. A single theater, Hollywood's Carthay Circle, opened the film before the end of December 1937; the rest of America and the world had to wait until 1938. Nonetheless the carefully coordinated promotional campaign rolled into action on schedule, unleashing a flood of *Snow White*-related press and merchandise. And the *Silly Symphony* comic strip entered the third major phase of its history, giving over its prized position at the top of the comics page to a twenty-week retelling of Snow White's story.

For the first time since 1932, Al Taliaferro relinquished the artistic reins—the *Snow White* continuity was written by Merrill de Maris and drawn by Hank Porter, assisted by Bob Grant. Together they invested the tale with a quaint storybook quality. By the time the film began to open at theaters across America in the early months of 1938, the Sunday comic page had been whetting audiences' appetites for several weeks—as it had routinely done for the *Silly Symphonies*. Just as with the *Symphonies*, the comics adaptation maintained a loose fidelity to the film, at times closely mirroring the screen continuity, at other times veering into unfamiliar story material (including some gags and plot ideas that had originally been developed for the film, but were dropped during pre-production). The full run of the story is reproduced in this volume, where *Snow White* enthusiasts can savor and compare the screen and print versions.

Snow White's adventure came to its happy ending late in April 1938. The Sunday comic feature then shifted gears once again, and, for the first time in nearly two years, returned to its original mission: retelling stories from the *Silly Symphonies.* Merrill de Maris, the writer of the *Snow White* continuity, remained in place as the strip's writer; but Al Taliaferro, now established as the artist behind the new *Donald Duck* comic strip, compounded his workload by returning to the *Silly Symphony* page as well.

So the *Symphonies* were back in their original spot, but with some key differences. By this time it was official: the *Silly Symphony* film series was coming to an end, phased out as Disney's top animation talent was shifted to a multitude of new feature projects. The last of the *Symphonies, The Ugly Duckling*, was completed and in the can by the autumn of 1938. But that and other titles were carefully held back, released to theaters on an intermittent schedule that extended well into 1939. The Sunday comic feature continued as well, adapting storylines from the series—with new title panels that announced each individual story, minus the unifying rubric of "Silly Symphonies." The early convention of rhyming dialogue, dropped for Donald Duck's launch in 1936, likewise did not return. In every way, readers were encouraged to see the new continuities as individual self-contained works, rather than entries in an ongoing series.

As before, these mini-narratives were based on key Disney films. The studio's production of *The Practical Pig*, yet another sequel to *Three Little Pigs*, was complete by May 1938 when its comic continuity appeared, but most movie audiences had not yet seen it; its theatrical release would be delayed for nearly a year. By contrast, *Mother Pluto* and *Farmyard Symphony* had already been released to theaters and were familiar to viewers (*Mother Pluto*, in particular, had been released nearly two years before its comic continuity appeared in newspapers). In all these stories de Maris and Taliaferro followed standard procedure and based their continuities loosely on the films, hewing closely to some elements of the original stories but combining those elements with other ideas that were wholly original to the comics. *Farmyard Symphony*, in its screen form, has practically no plot; the comic version builds on a minor running gag from the film and spins it into a tale with a moralizing twist.

This volume ends with an intriguing anomaly: a story that was *planned* as a movie short, but never completed. On pages 27-38 the reader can see the earlier continuity based on the 1936 short *Elmer Elephant*. By the end of 1936 that film had aroused enough interest that the Disney story department set to work on a sequel to be titled "Timid Elmer." Their story was never realized as a film, but late in 1938 de Maris and Taliaferro adapted "Timid Elmer" to the comics. Its reprinting here provides a rare luxury: a glimpse of an unfinished Disney film story. The comic version doubtlessly varies from the film scenario—given the creative liberties that Taliaferro and the strip's writers routinely took with film stories—but that only adds to the interest of this unique sidelight.

By February 1939 the *Silly Symphony* Sunday page had appeared in newspapers for a full seven years—years in which it had explored, adapted, and generally reflected the wide-ranging activities of the Disney studio itself. The *Silly Symphony* film series would come to an end in 1939, but the comic strip had built up its own momentum and was not about to quit. As the next volume will demonstrate, the strip had become a versatile platform, capable of sustaining its own vein of comic art for years to come. •

WALT DISNEY'S
'THREE LITTLE WOLVES'
895
A WALT DISNEY PICTURE BOOK

Walt Disney's
FIRST FULL LENGTH
FEATURE PRODUCTION
Snow White
and the
Seven Dwarfs
in the Marvelous
MULTIPLANE TECHNICOLOR
Distributed by R K O Radio Pictures Inc.

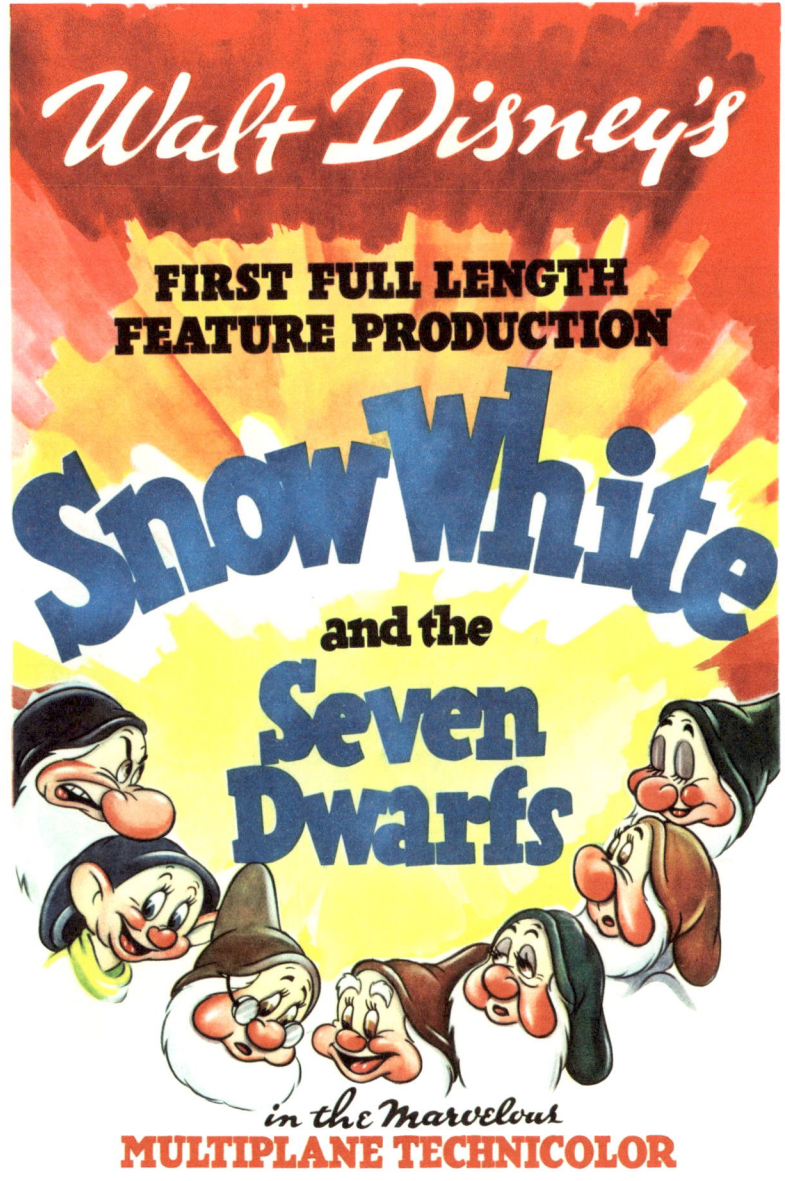

RIGHT: A 1937 one-sheet poster for *Snow White and the Seven Dwarfs.*

ABOVE: A *Three Little Wolves* picture book from Whitman in 1937.

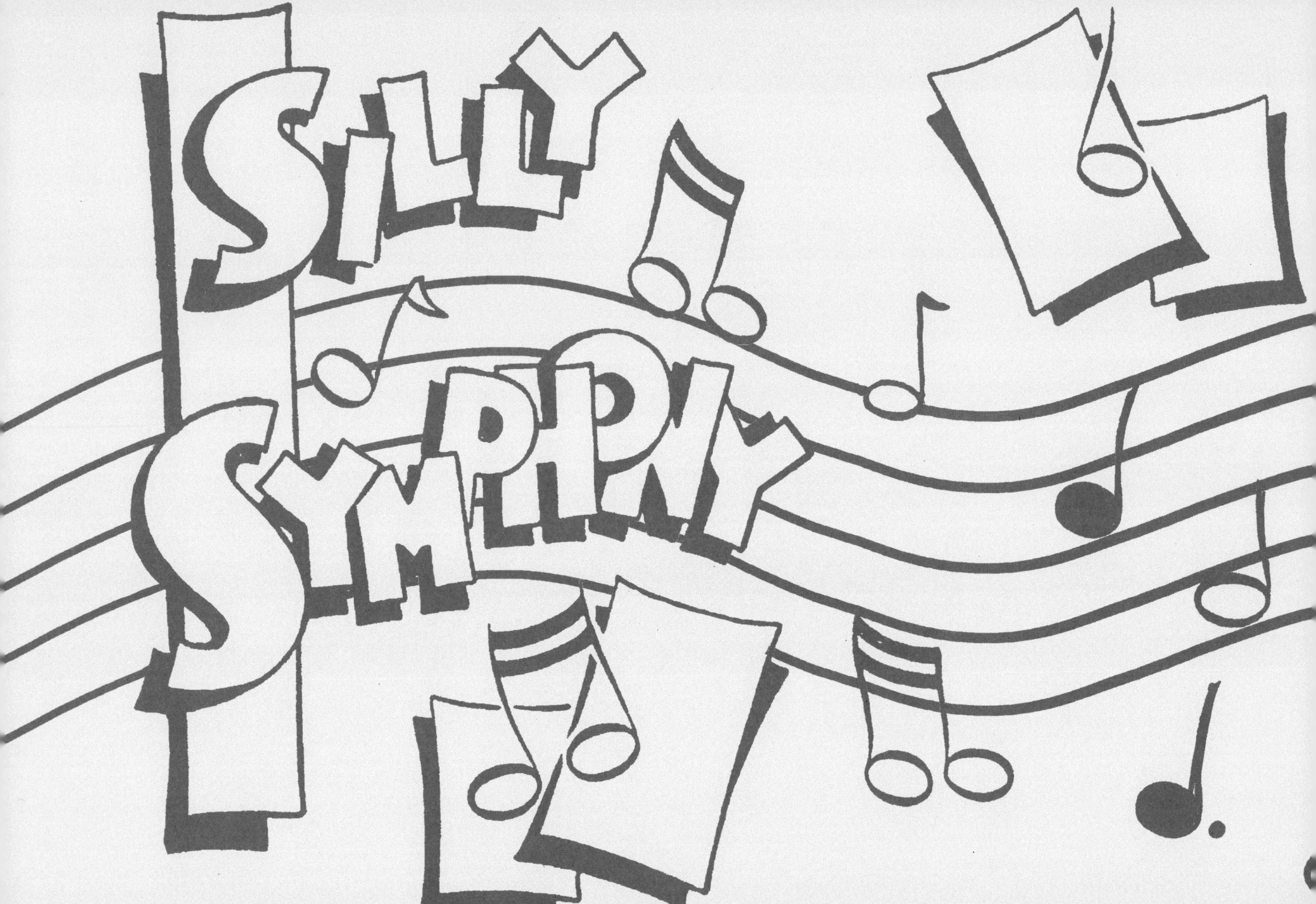
SILLY
SYMPHONY

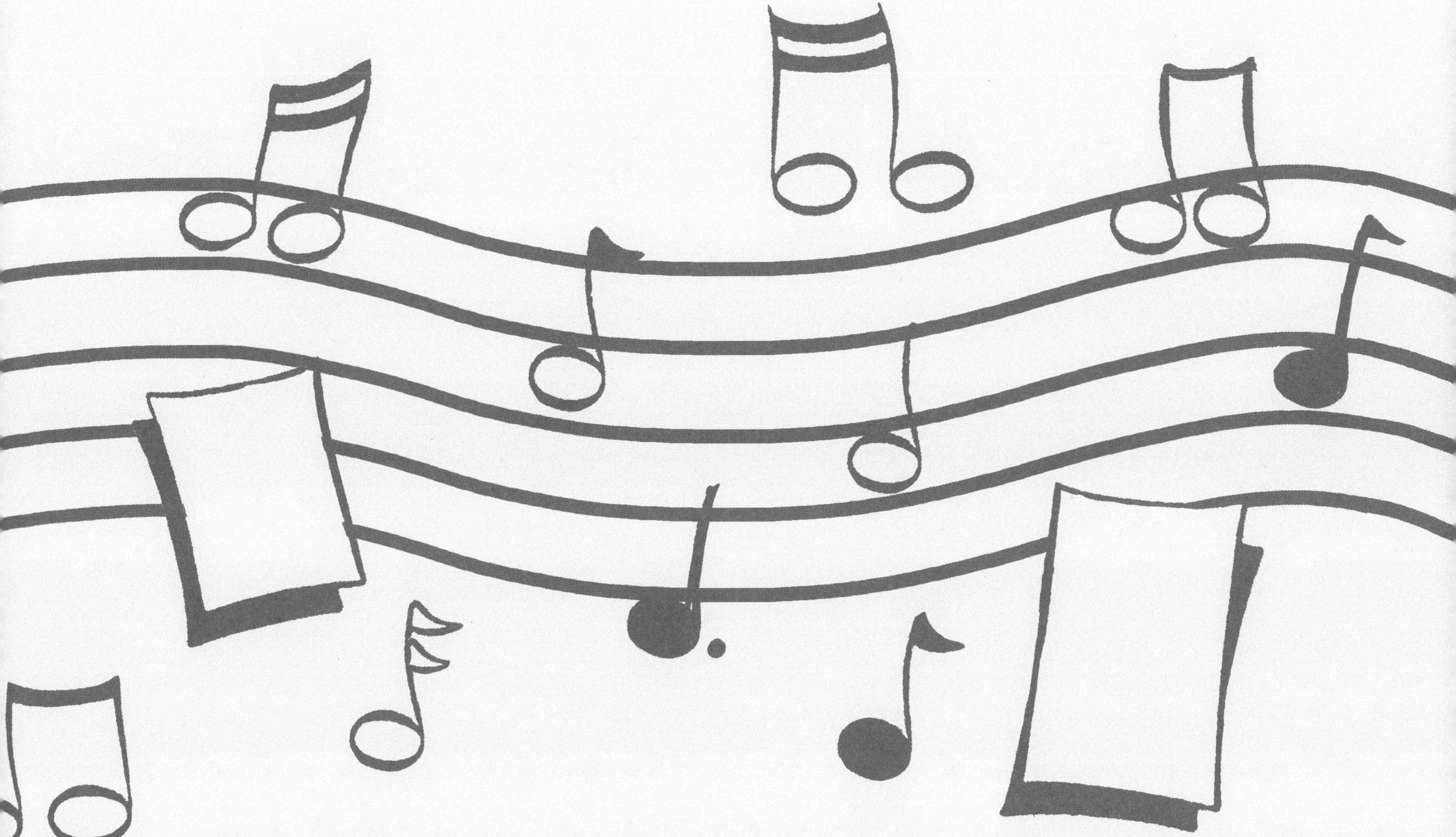

THREE LITTLE KITTENS

July 28 - October 20, 1935
Written by Ted Osborne, drawn by Al Taliaferro

In the Academy Award-winning short *Three Orphan Kittens*, the kittens of the title take refuge in a family home, cause mischief, and are eventually discovered and adopted by the little girl of the household. The comic continuity, "Three Little Kittens," retains that basic concept, but changes almost all the details. The kittens in the film enter the house after being abandoned in a snowstorm in the dead of night; the comic story takes place on a warm, sunny afternoon, and the kittens are merely fleeing neighborhood boys and a watchdog. The movie kittens' mischief in the house includes a creative musical sequence on the keys of a piano; their comics counterparts settle for tangled yarn, broken vases, and other customary destruction. Perhaps most noticeably, the maid featured in the film is nowhere to be seen in the comic continuity and the adult who wants to throw the kittens out is the little girl's father.

The film's story is told from the viewpoint of the kittens. The humans function as incidental players, glimpsed only by way of their feet and hands; their faces are never shown. (This approach was repeated in other animal-centric Disney films, turning up a full twenty years later in *Lady and the Tramp*.) The comic continuity retains this device, and takes it a step further: the humans' dialogue is never heard. Even when one of the kittens floods a box of cigars with water, the father's violent reaction is only *suggested*, and we are left to imagine his colorful language for ourselves.

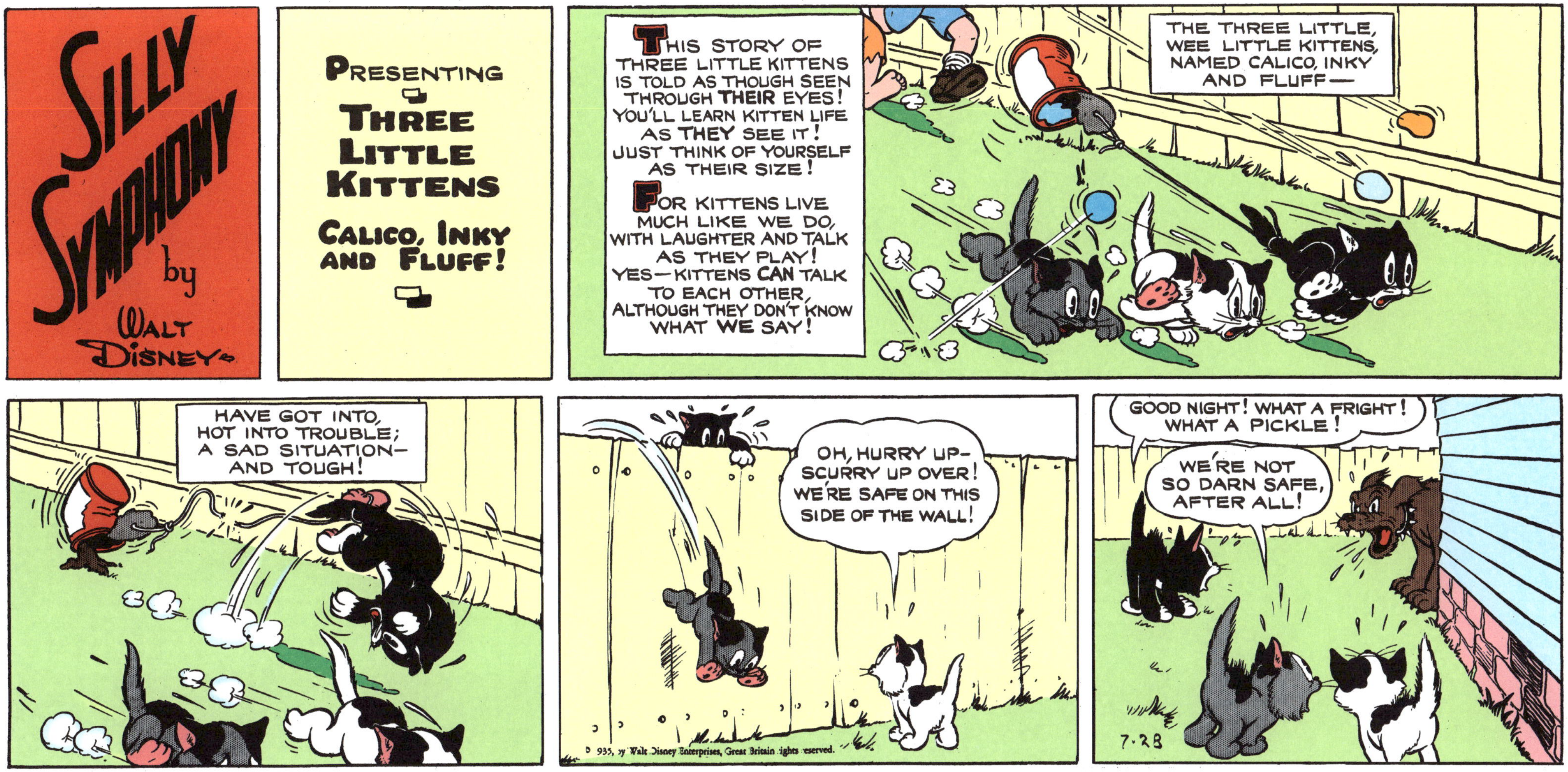
SILLY SYMPHONY
by
WALT DISNEY
PRESENTING
THREE LITTLE KITTENS
CALICO, INKY AND FLUFF!
THIS STORY OF THREE LITTLE KITTENS IS TOLD AS THOUGH SEEN THROUGH THEIR EYES! YOU'LL LEARN KITTEN LIFE AS THEY SEE IT! JUST THINK OF YOURSELF AS THEIR SIZE!
FOR KITTENS LIVE MUCH LIKE WE DO, WITH LAUGHTER AND TALK AS THEY PLAY! YES—KITTENS CAN TALK TO EACH OTHER, ALTHOUGH THEY DON'T KNOW WHAT WE SAY!
THE THREE LITTLE, WEE LITTLE KITTENS, NAMED CALICO, INKY AND FLUFF—
HAVE GOT INTO, HOT INTO TROUBLE; A SAD SITUATION— AND TOUGH!
OH, HURRY UP— SCURRY UP OVER! WE'RE SAFE ON THIS SIDE OF THE WALL!
935, by Walt Disney Enterprises, Great Britain rights reserved.
GOOD NIGHT! WHAT A FRIGHT! WHAT A PICKLE!
WE'RE NOT SO DARN SAFE, AFTER ALL!
7-28

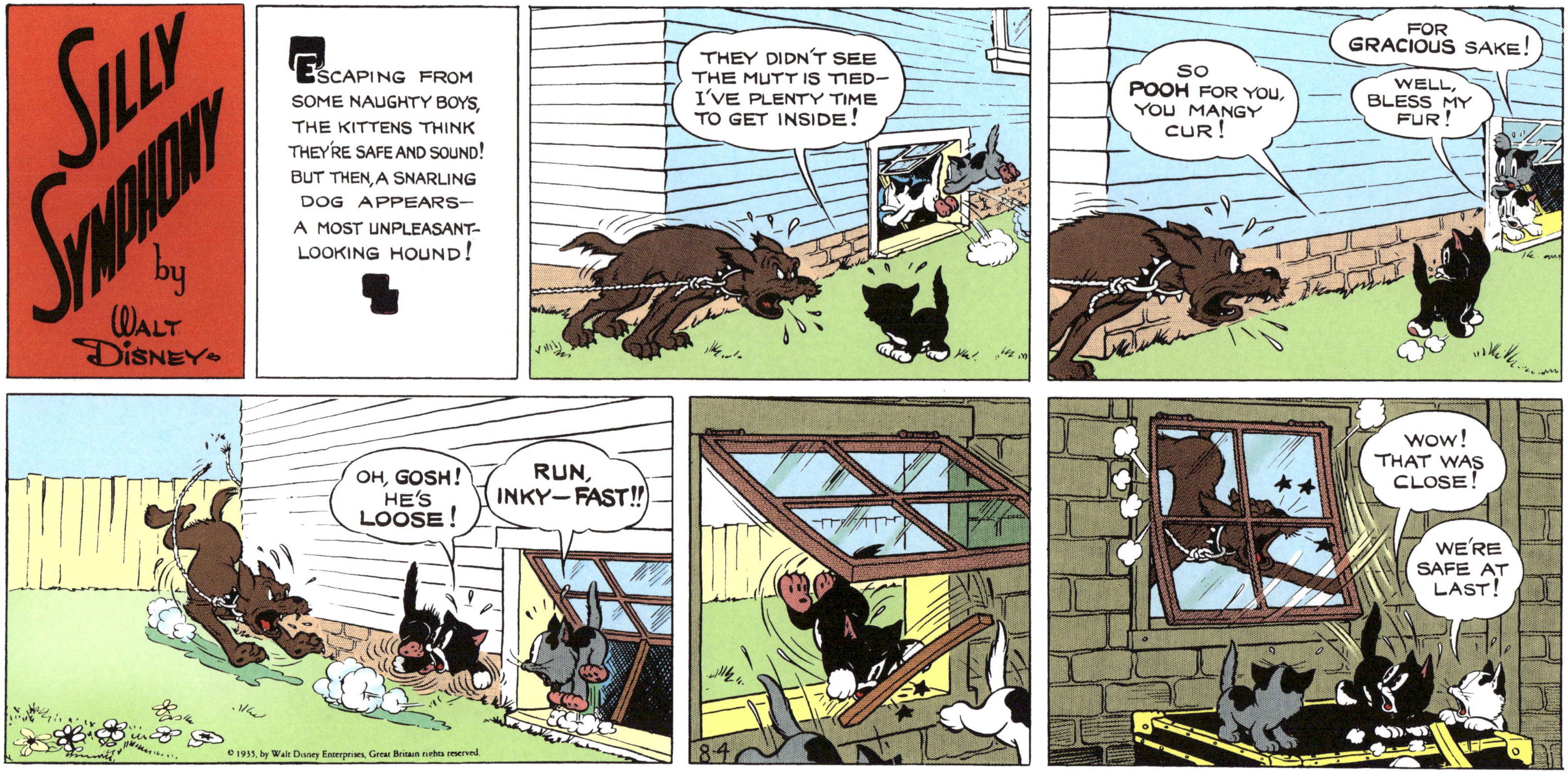

SILLY SYMPHONY by WALT DISNEY
ESCAPING FROM SOME NAUGHTY BOYS, THE KITTENS THINK THEY'RE SAFE AND SOUND! BUT THEN, A SNARLING DOG APPEARS— A MOST UNPLEASANT-LOOKING HOUND!
THEY DIDN'T SEE THE MUTT IS TIED— I'VE PLENTY TIME TO GET INSIDE!
SO POOH FOR YOU, YOU MANGY CUR!
FOR GRACIOUS SAKE!
WELL, BLESS MY FUR!
OH, GOSH! HE'S LOOSE!
RUN, INKY—FAST!!
WOW! THAT WAS CLOSE!
WE'RE SAFE AT LAST!
© 1935, by Walt Disney Enterprises, Great Britain rights reserved.
84

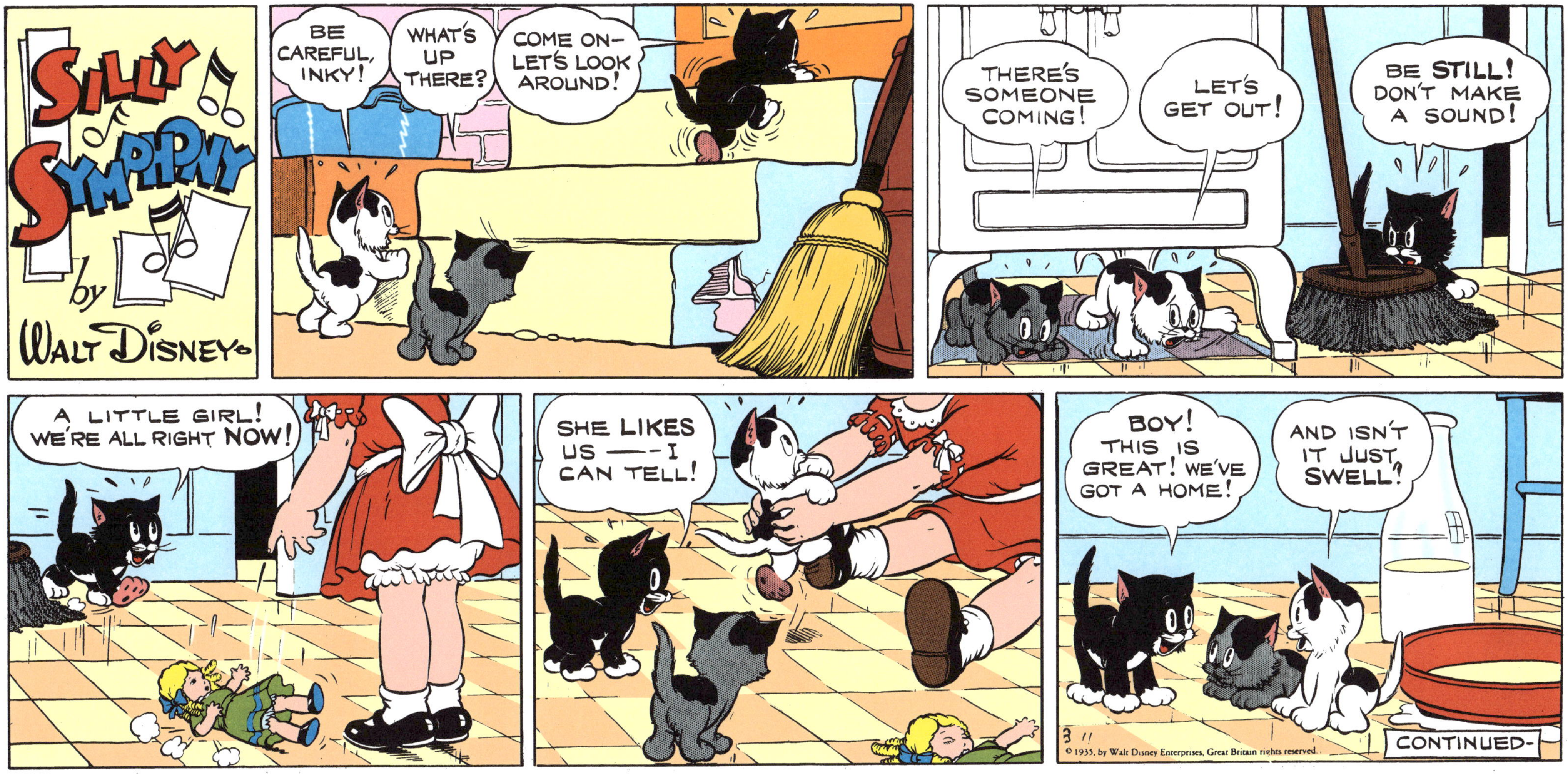
SILLY SYMPHONY
by
WALT DISNEY
BE CAREFUL, INKY!
WHAT'S UP THERE?
COME ON— LET'S LOOK AROUND!
THERE'S SOMEONE COMING!
LET'S GET OUT!
BE STILL! DON'T MAKE A SOUND!
A LITTLE GIRL! WE'RE ALL RIGHT NOW!
SHE LIKES US —- I CAN TELL!
BOY! THIS IS GREAT! WE'VE GOT A HOME!
AND ISN'T IT JUST SWELL?
© 1935, by Walt Disney Enterprises, Great Britain rights reserved.
CONTINUED-

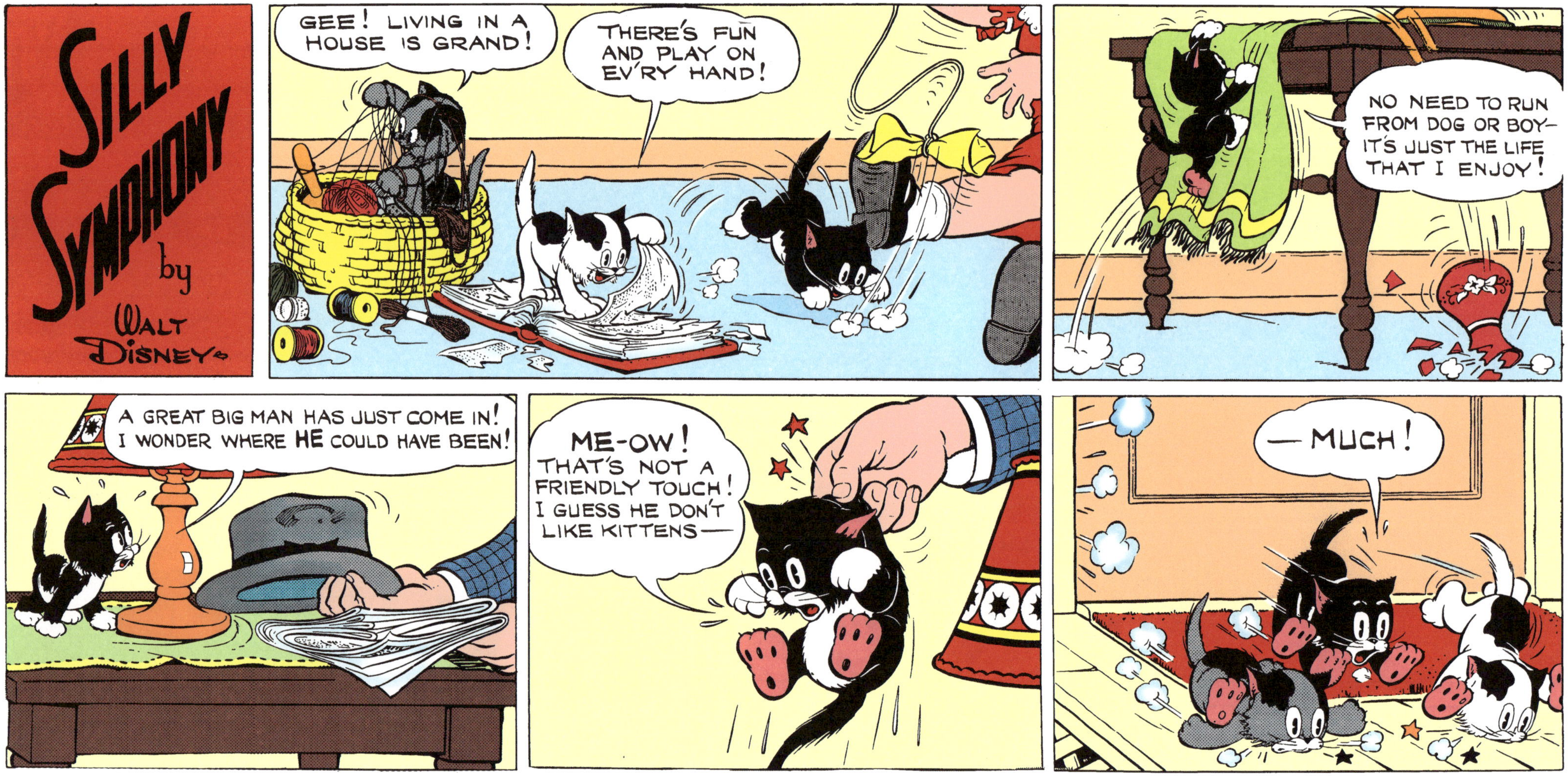

SILLY SYMPHONY
by
WALT DISNEY
GEE! LIVING IN A HOUSE IS GRAND!
THERE'S FUN AND PLAY ON EV'RY HAND!
NO NEED TO RUN FROM DOG OR BOY— IT'S JUST THE LIFE THAT I ENJOY!
A GREAT BIG MAN HAS JUST COME IN! I WONDER WHERE **HE** COULD HAVE BEEN!
ME-OW! THAT'S NOT A FRIENDLY TOUCH! I GUESS HE DON'T LIKE KITTENS—
—MUCH!

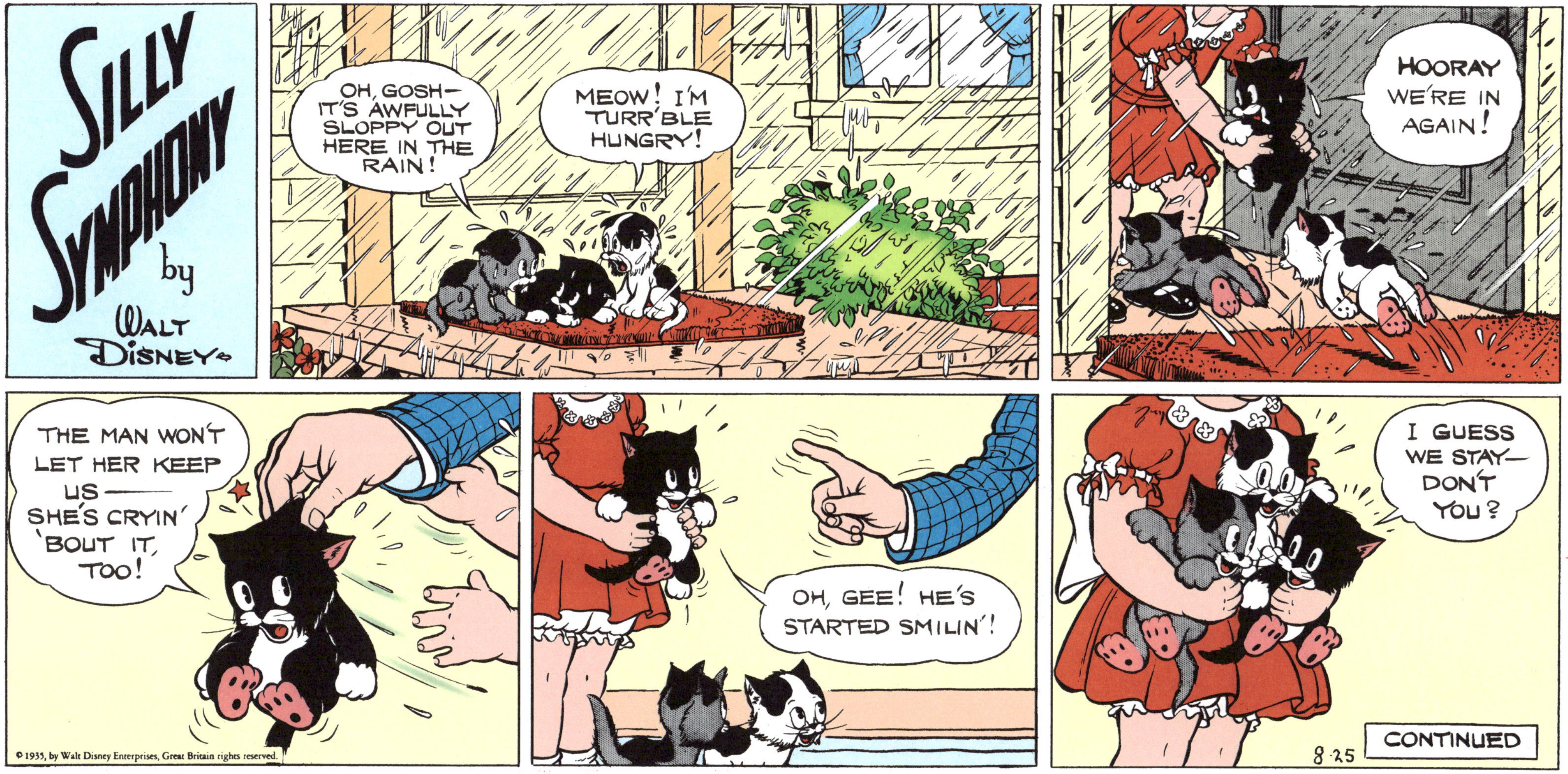
SILLY SYMPHONY
by
WALT DISNEY
OH, GOSH— IT'S AWFULLY SLOPPY OUT HERE IN THE RAIN!
MEOW! I'M TURR'BLE HUNGRY!
HOORAY WE'RE IN AGAIN!
THE MAN WON'T LET HER KEEP US —— SHE'S CRYIN' 'BOUT IT, TOO!
OH, GEE! HE'S STARTED SMILIN'!
I GUESS WE STAY— DON'T YOU?
8-25
CONTINUED

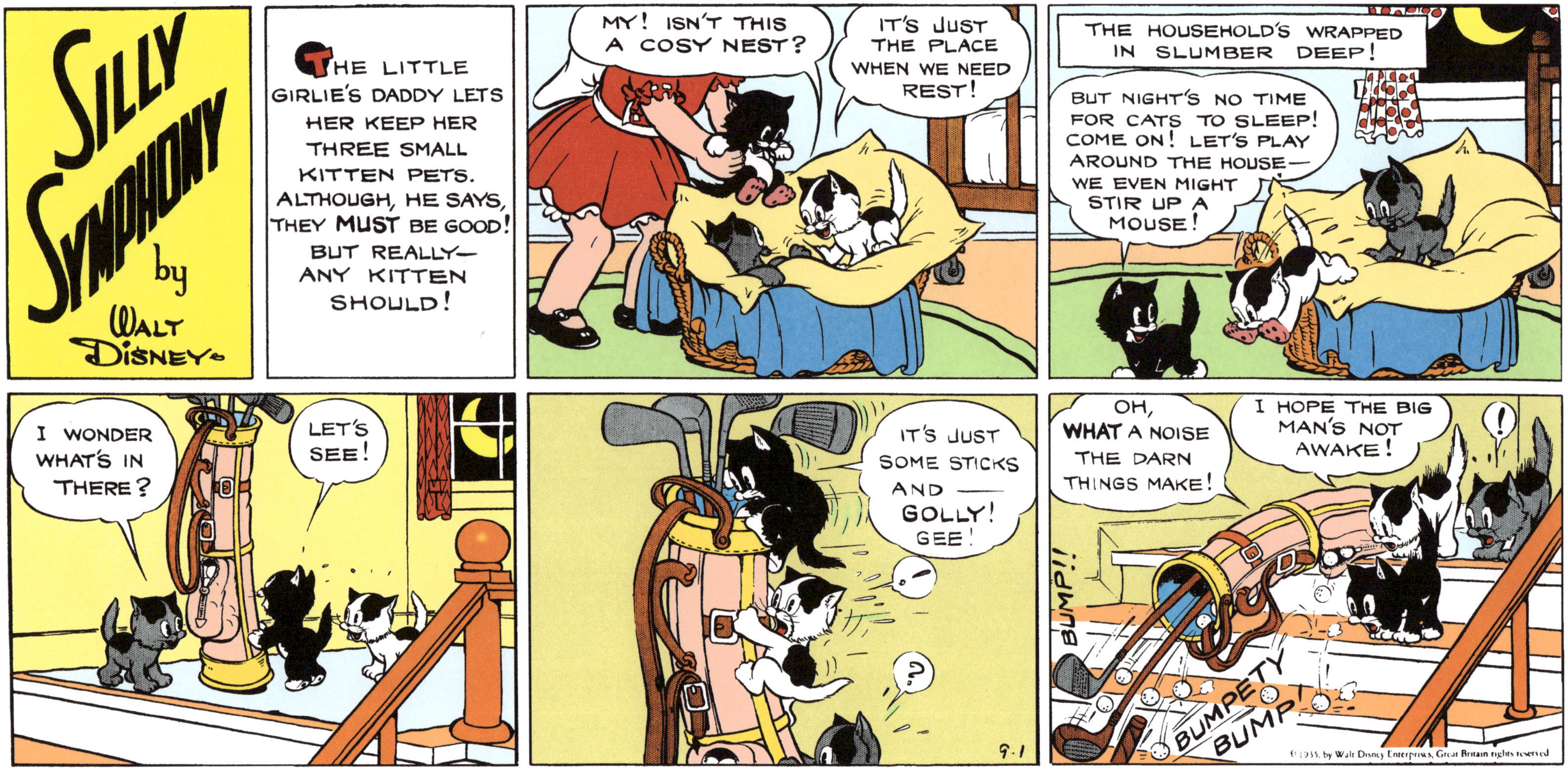
SILLY SYMPHONY by WALT DISNEY
THE LITTLE GIRLIE'S DADDY LETS HER KEEP HER THREE SMALL KITTEN PETS. ALTHOUGH, HE SAYS, THEY MUST BE GOOD! BUT REALLY— ANY KITTEN SHOULD!
MY! ISN'T THIS A COSY NEST?
IT'S JUST THE PLACE WHEN WE NEED REST!
THE HOUSEHOLD'S WRAPPED IN SLUMBER DEEP!
BUT NIGHT'S NO TIME FOR CATS TO SLEEP! COME ON! LET'S PLAY AROUND THE HOUSE— WE EVEN MIGHT STIR UP A MOUSE!
I WONDER WHAT'S IN THERE?
LET'S SEE!
IT'S JUST SOME STICKS AND —— GOLLY! GEE!
?
9-1
OH, WHAT A NOISE THE DARN THINGS MAKE!
I HOPE THE BIG MAN'S NOT AWAKE!
!
BUMP!!
BUMPETY BUMP!
© 1935, by Walt Disney Enterprises, Great Britain rights reserved

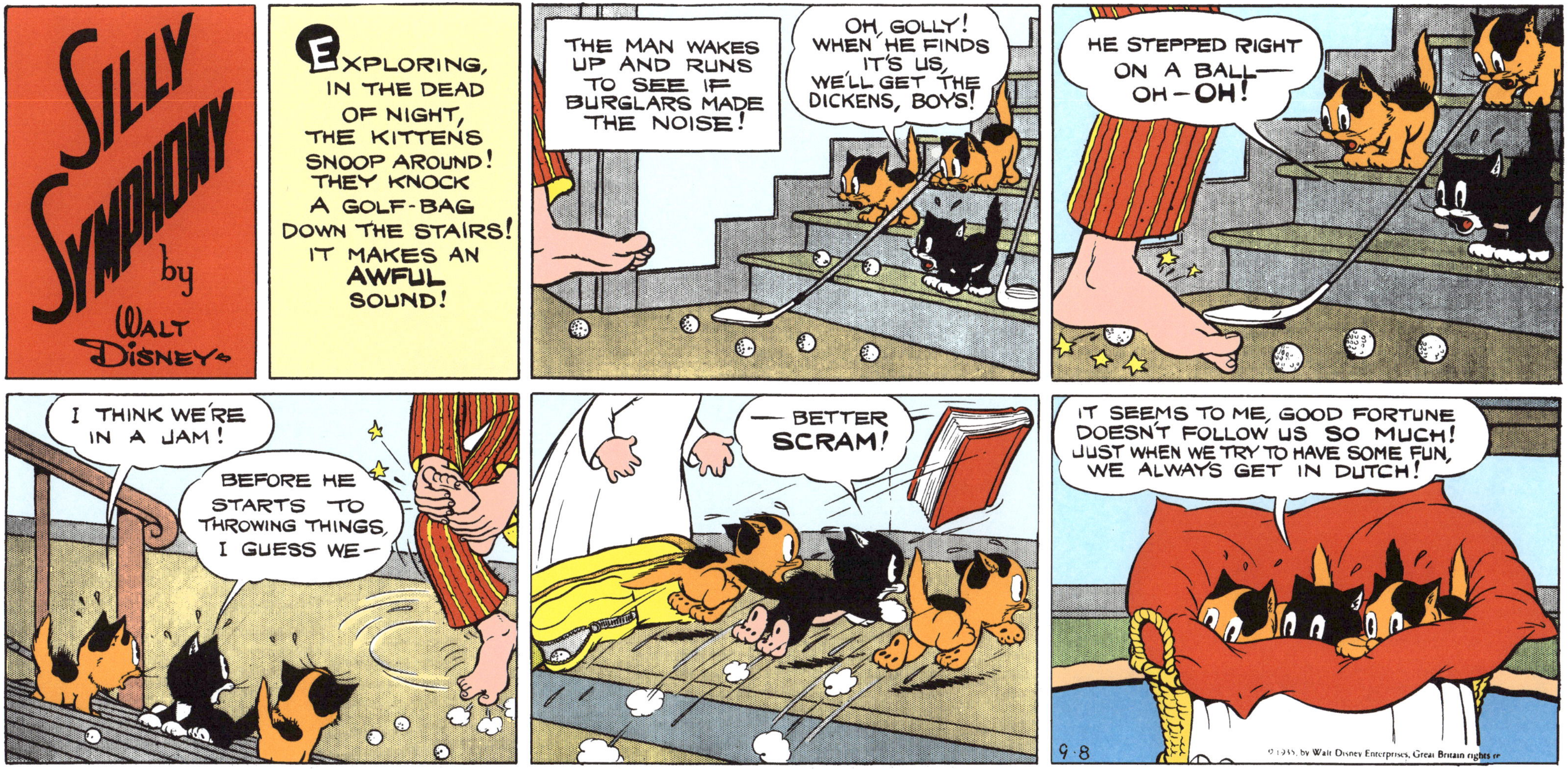
SILLY SYMPHONY
by
WALT DISNEY
EXPLORING, IN THE DEAD OF NIGHT, THE KITTENS SNOOP AROUND! THEY KNOCK A GOLF-BAG DOWN THE STAIRS! IT MAKES AN AWFUL SOUND!
THE MAN WAKES UP AND RUNS TO SEE IF BURGLARS MADE THE NOISE!
OH, GOLLY! WHEN HE FINDS IT'S US, WE'LL GET THE DICKENS, BOYS!
HE STEPPED RIGHT ON A BALL— OH—OH!
I THINK WE'RE IN A JAM!
BEFORE HE STARTS TO THROWING THINGS, I GUESS WE—
—BETTER SCRAM!
IT SEEMS TO ME, GOOD FORTUNE DOESN'T FOLLOW US SO MUCH! JUST WHEN WE TRY TO HAVE SOME FUN, WE ALWAYS GET IN DUTCH!
9-8
1935, by Walt Disney Enterprises, Great Britain rights re

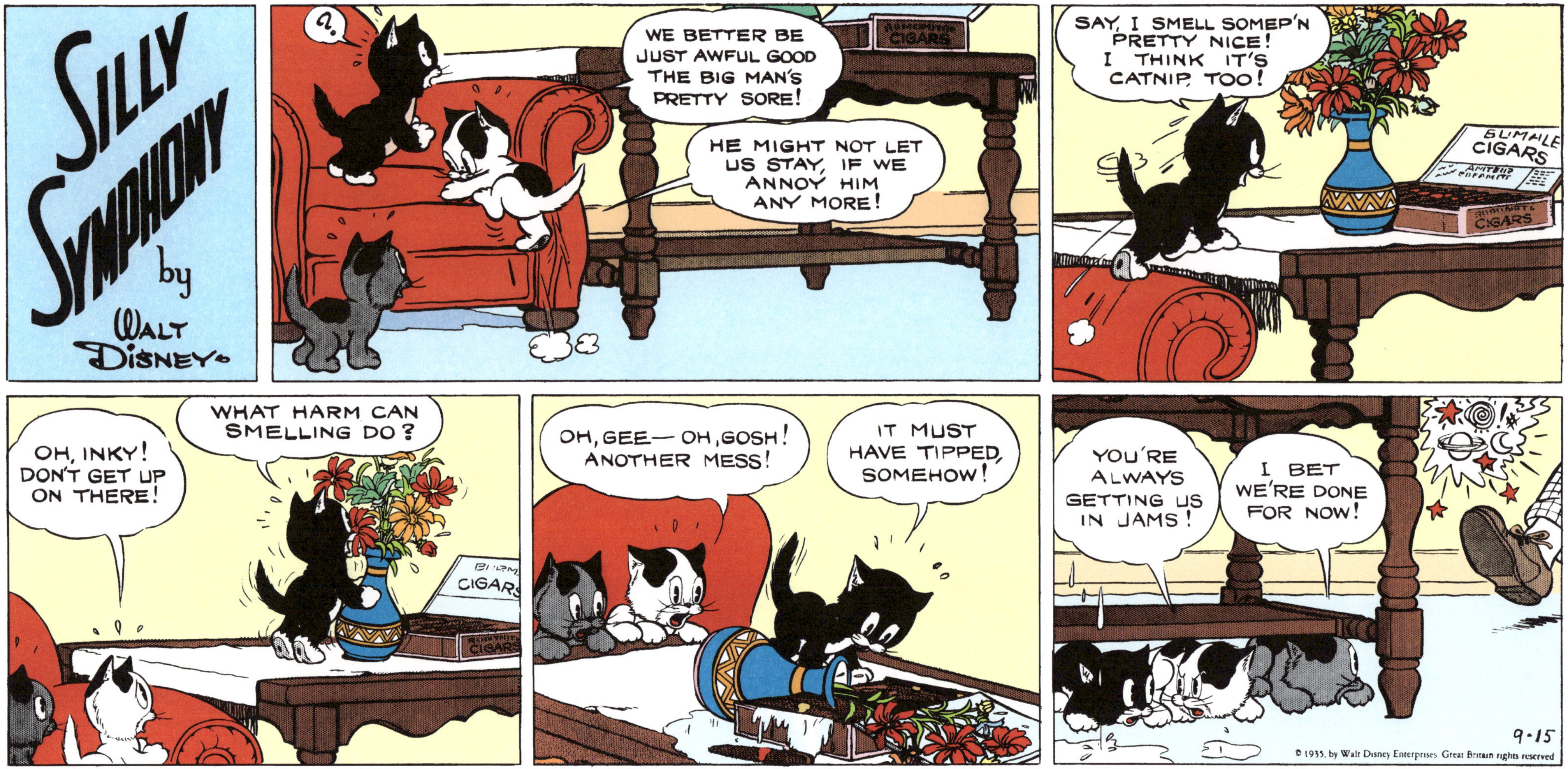

SILLY SYMPHONY
by
WALT DISNEY
?
WE BETTER BE JUST AWFUL GOOD THE BIG MAN'S PRETTY SORE!
HE MIGHT NOT LET US STAY, IF WE ANNOY HIM ANY MORE!
CIGARS
SAY, I SMELL SOMEP'N PRETTY NICE! I THINK IT'S CATNIP, TOO!
CIGARS
CIGARS
OH, INKY! DON'T GET UP ON THERE!
WHAT HARM CAN SMELLING DO?
CIGARS
CIGARS
OH, GEE— OH, GOSH! ANOTHER MESS!
IT MUST HAVE TIPPED, SOMEHOW!
YOU'RE ALWAYS GETTING US IN JAMS!
I BET WE'RE DONE FOR NOW!
9-15
© 1935, by Walt Disney Enterprises. Great Britain rights reserved

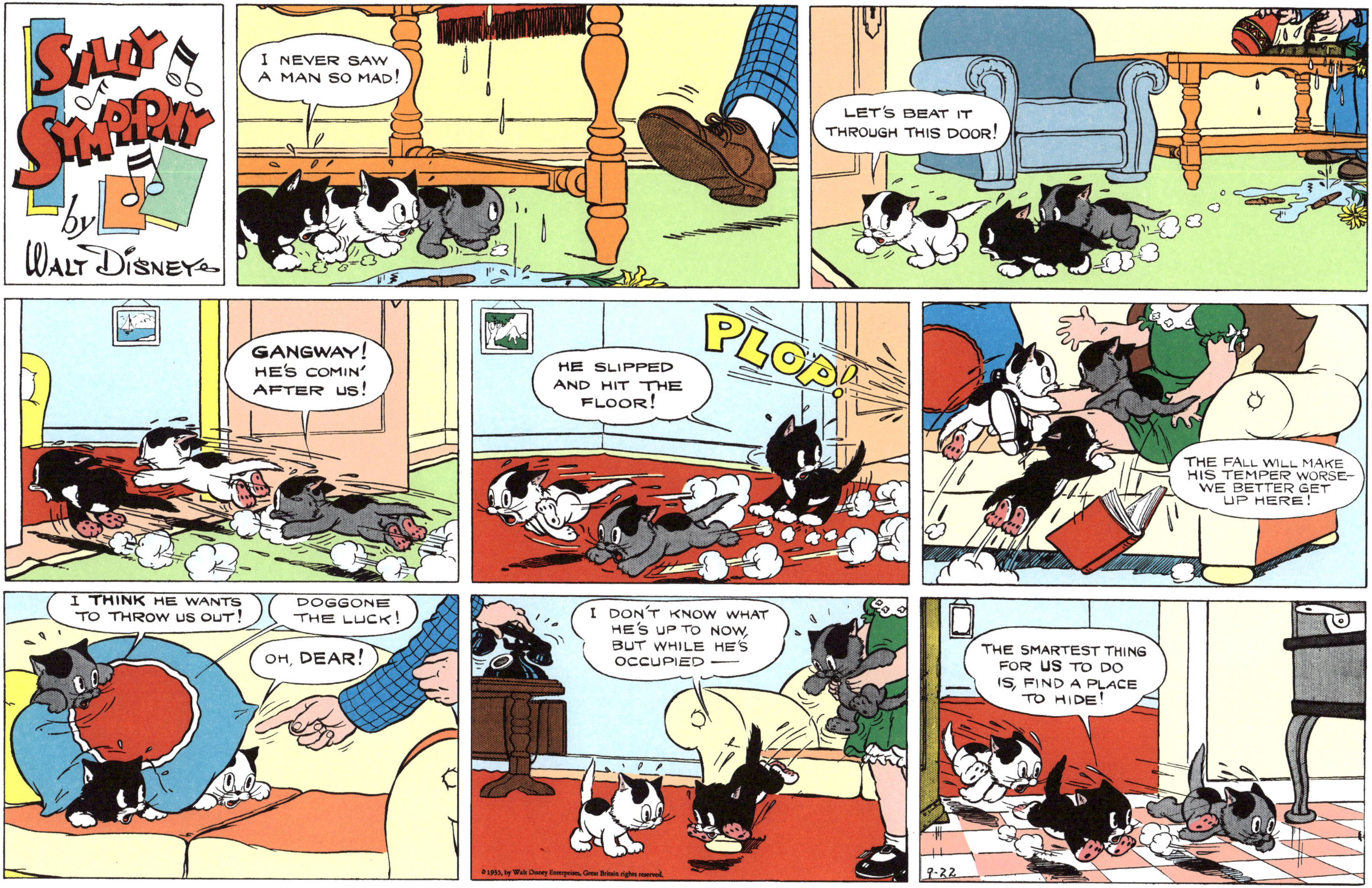
SILLY SYMPHONY
by WALT DISNEY
I NEVER SAW A MAN SO MAD!
LET'S BEAT IT THROUGH THIS DOOR!
GANGWAY! HE'S COMIN' AFTER US!
PLOP!
HE SLIPPED AND HIT THE FLOOR!
THE FALL WILL MAKE HIS TEMPER WORSE— WE BETTER GET UP HERE!
I THINK HE WANTS TO THROW US OUT!
DOGGONE THE LUCK!
OH, DEAR!
I DON'T KNOW WHAT HE'S UP TO NOW, BUT WHILE HE'S OCCUPIED —
© 1935, by Walt Disney Enterprises, Great Britain rights reserved.
THE SMARTEST THING FOR US TO DO IS, FIND A PLACE TO HIDE!
9-22

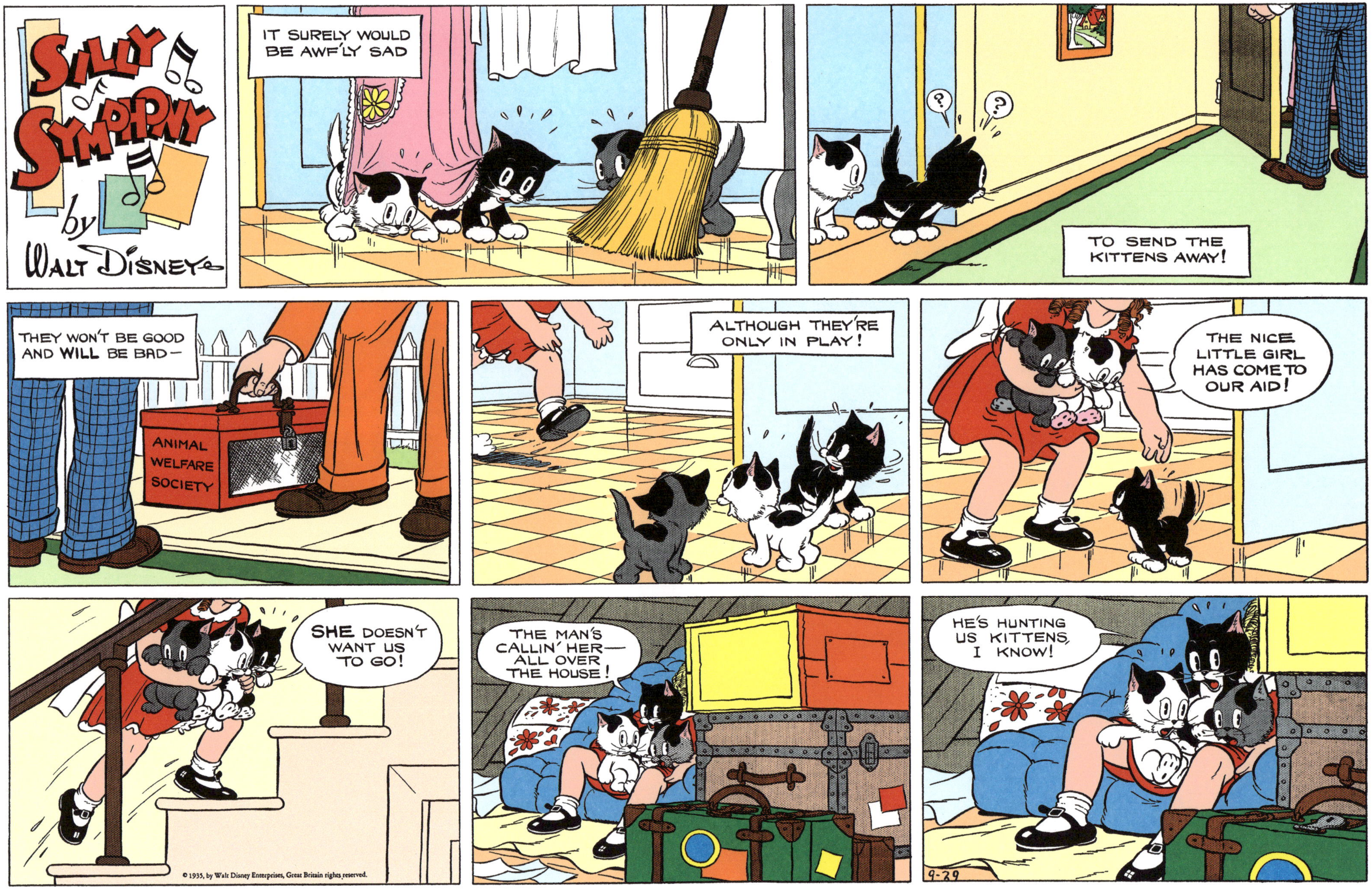
SILLY SYMPHONY
by WALT DISNEY
IT SURELY WOULD BE AWF'LY SAD
TO SEND THE KITTENS AWAY!
THEY WON'T BE GOOD AND WILL BE BAD—
ANIMAL WELFARE SOCIETY
ALTHOUGH THEY'RE ONLY IN PLAY!
THE NICE LITTLE GIRL HAS COME TO OUR AID!
SHE DOESN'T WANT US TO GO!
© 1935, by Walt Disney Enterprises, Great Britain rights reserved.
THE MAN'S CALLIN' HER— ALL OVER THE HOUSE!
HE'S HUNTING US KITTENS, I KNOW!
9-29

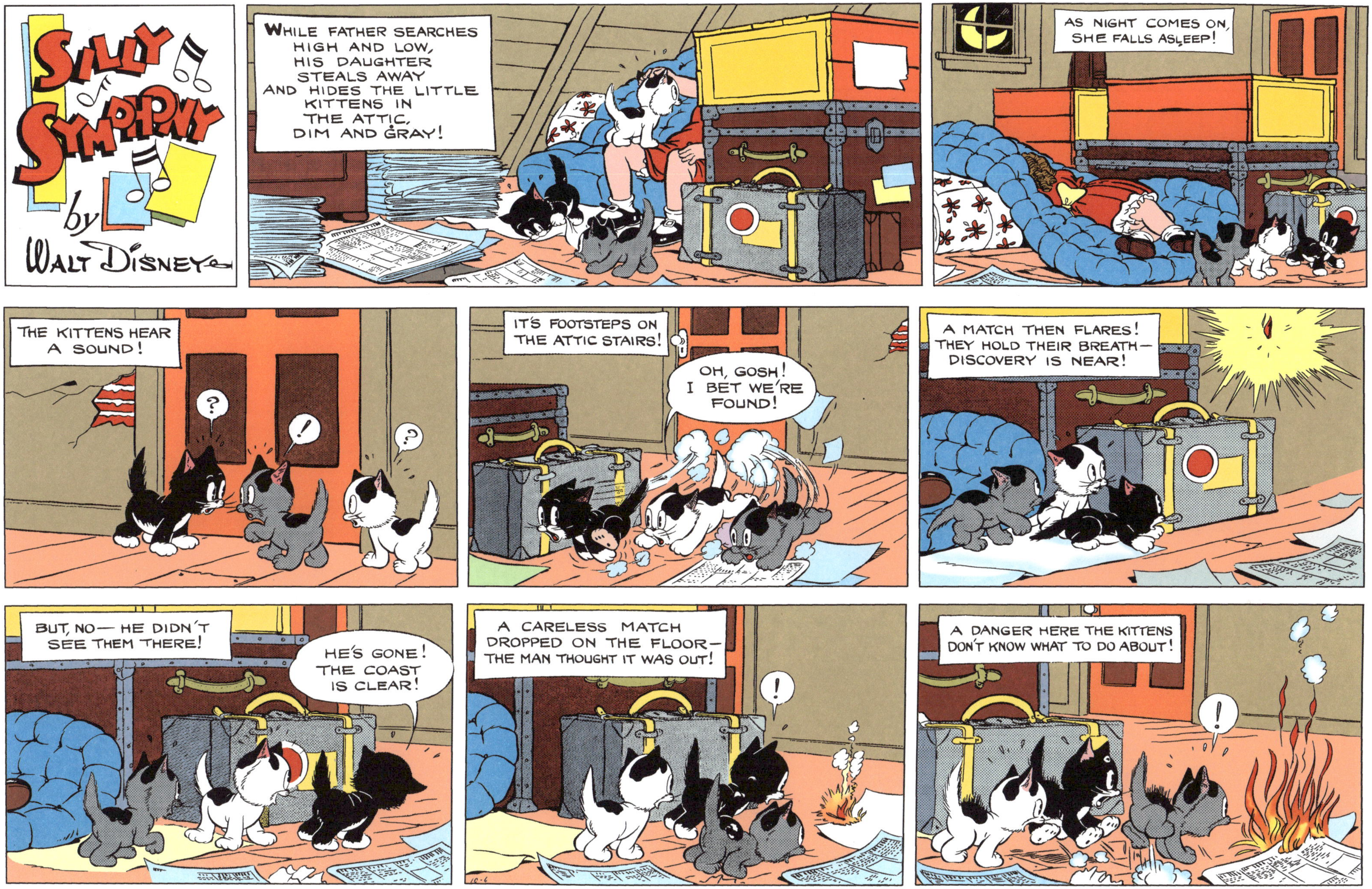
SILLY SYMPHONY
by WALT DISNEY
WHILE FATHER SEARCHES HIGH AND LOW, HIS DAUGHTER STEALS AWAY AND HIDES THE LITTLE KITTENS IN THE ATTIC, DIM AND GRAY!
AS NIGHT COMES ON, SHE FALLS ASLEEP!
THE KITTENS HEAR A SOUND!
?
!
?
IT'S FOOTSTEPS ON THE ATTIC STAIRS!
OH, GOSH! I BET WE'RE FOUND!
A MATCH THEN FLARES! THEY HOLD THEIR BREATH— DISCOVERY IS NEAR!
BUT, NO— HE DIDN'T SEE THEM THERE!
HE'S GONE! THE COAST IS CLEAR!
A CARELESS MATCH DROPPED ON THE FLOOR— THE MAN THOUGHT IT WAS OUT!
!
A DANGER HERE THE KITTENS DON'T KNOW WHAT TO DO ABOUT!
!

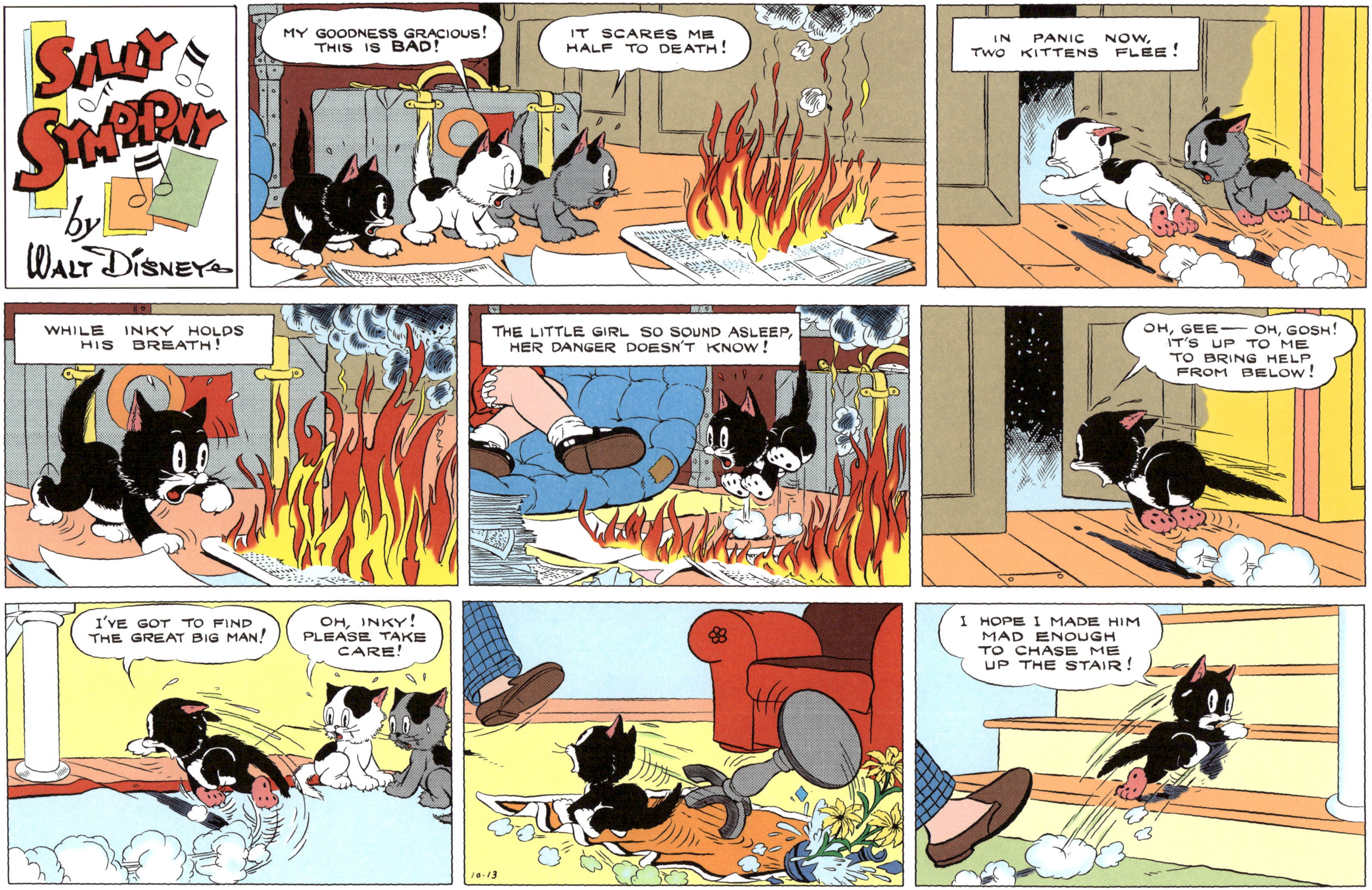
SILLY SYMPHONY
by WALT DISNEY
MY GOODNESS GRACIOUS! THIS IS BAD!
IT SCARES ME HALF TO DEATH!
IN PANIC NOW, TWO KITTENS FLEE!
WHILE INKY HOLDS HIS BREATH!
THE LITTLE GIRL SO SOUND ASLEEP, HER DANGER DOESN'T KNOW!
OH, GEE— OH, GOSH! IT'S UP TO ME TO BRING HELP FROM BELOW!
I'VE GOT TO FIND THE GREAT BIG MAN!
OH, INKY! PLEASE TAKE CARE!
10-13
I HOPE I MADE HIM MAD ENOUGH TO CHASE ME UP THE STAIR!

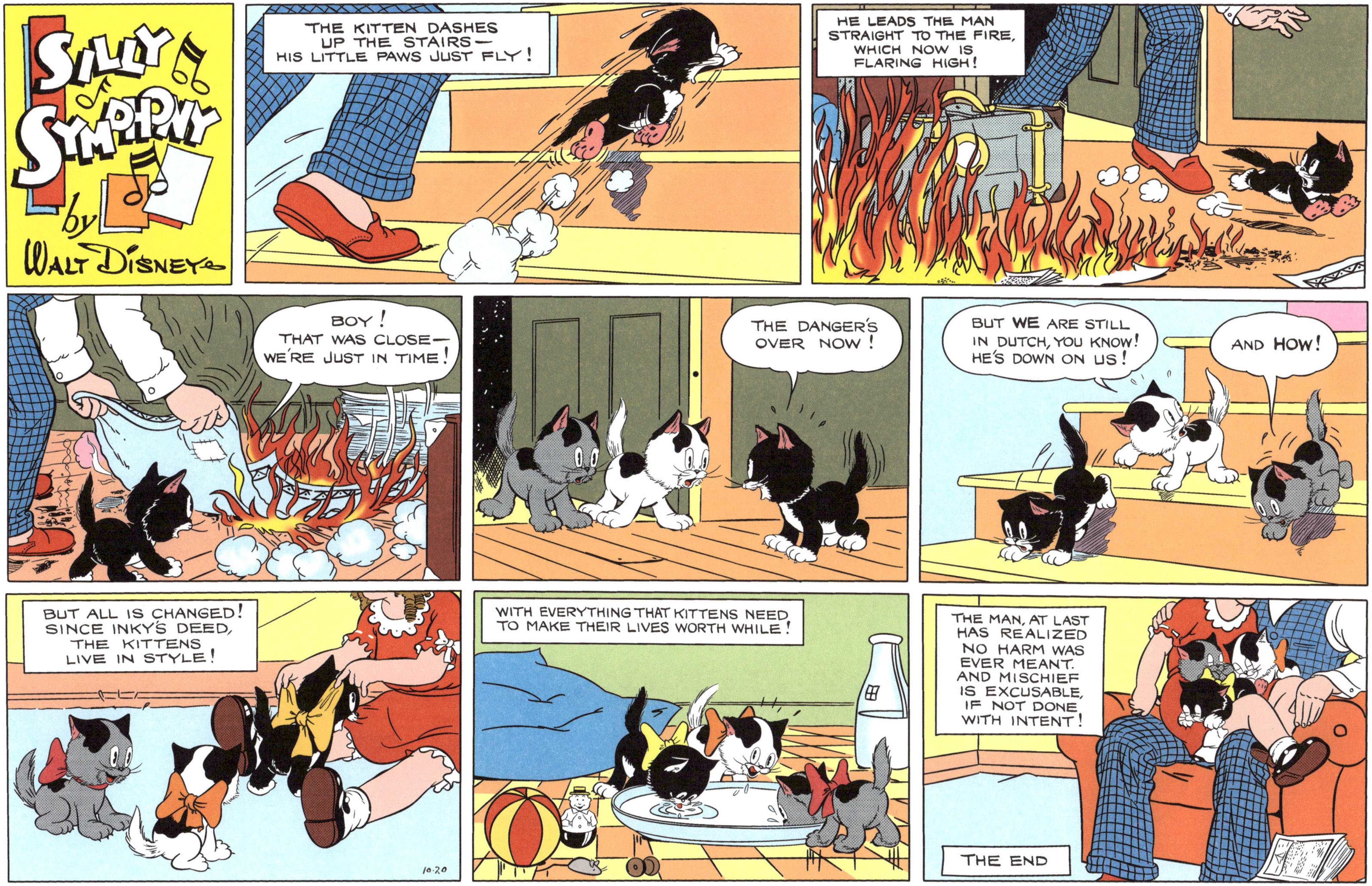
SILLY SYMPHONY
by
WALT DISNEY
THE KITTEN DASHES UP THE STAIRS— HIS LITTLE PAWS JUST FLY!
HE LEADS THE MAN STRAIGHT TO THE FIRE, WHICH NOW IS FLARING HIGH!
BOY! THAT WAS CLOSE— WE'RE JUST IN TIME!
THE DANGER'S OVER NOW!
BUT WE ARE STILL IN DUTCH, YOU KNOW! HE'S DOWN ON US!
AND HOW!
BUT ALL IS CHANGED! SINCE INKY'S DEED, THE KITTENS LIVE IN STYLE!
10-20
WITH EVERYTHING THAT KITTENS NEED TO MAKE THEIR LIVES WORTH WHILE!
THE MAN, AT LAST HAS REALIZED NO HARM WAS EVER MEANT. AND MISCHIEF IS EXCUSABLE, IF NOT DONE WITH INTENT!
THE END

THE LIFE AND ADVENTURES OF ELMER ELEPHANT

October 27, 1935 - January 12, 1936
Written by Ted Osborne, drawn by Al Taliaferro

In the spring of 1936 the Disney studio released *Elmer Elephant*, the story of a little pachyderm who is ridiculed by other jungle children because of his ungainly trunk. In the end, Elmer not only learns self-acceptance but becomes a hero by using that trunk as a fire hose, putting out a fire and saving his sweetheart, Tillie Tiger.

This comic continuity, appearing in newspapers several months before the film's release, introduces Elmer, Tillie, and the bullying kids, but takes their story in a different direction. Here the issue is not Elmer's "funny nose," but his bravery or lack of it. Of course Elmer's true character is never in doubt, but he must prove himself. This time his heroics do not involve putting out fires, but have to do with an original plot device involving some new characters that are never seen in the film.

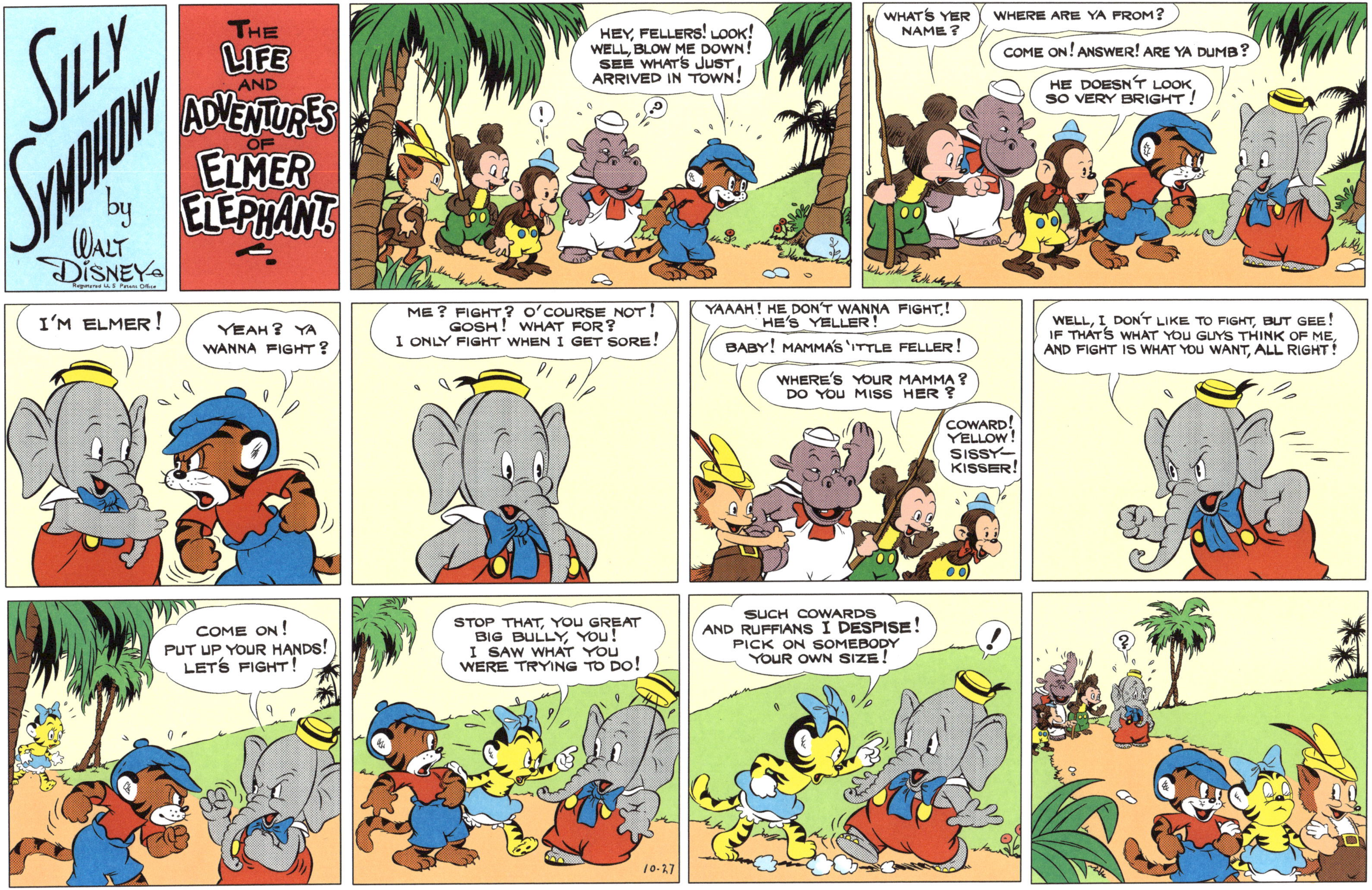
SILLY SYMPHONY
by
WALT DISNEY
Registered U.S. Patent Office
THE LIFE AND ADVENTURES OF ELMER ELEPHANT
HEY, FELLERS! LOOK! WELL, BLOW ME DOWN! SEE WHAT'S JUST ARRIVED IN TOWN!
WHAT'S YER NAME?
WHERE ARE YA FROM?
COME ON! ANSWER! ARE YA DUMB?
HE DOESN'T LOOK SO VERY BRIGHT!
I'M ELMER!
YEAH? YA WANNA FIGHT?
ME? FIGHT? O'COURSE NOT! GOSH! WHAT FOR? I ONLY FIGHT WHEN I GET SORE!
YAAAH! HE DON'T WANNA FIGHT! HE'S YELLER!
BABY! MAMMA'S 'ITTLE FELLER!
WHERE'S YOUR MAMMA? DO YOU MISS HER?
COWARD! YELLOW! SISSY-KISSER!
WELL, I DON'T LIKE TO FIGHT, BUT GEE! IF THAT'S WHAT YOU GUYS THINK OF ME, AND FIGHT IS WHAT YOU WANT, ALL RIGHT!
COME ON! PUT UP YOUR HANDS! LET'S FIGHT!
STOP THAT, YOU GREAT BIG BULLY, YOU! I SAW WHAT YOU WERE TRYING TO DO!
10-27
SUCH COWARDS AND RUFFIANS I DESPISE! PICK ON SOMEBODY YOUR OWN SIZE!

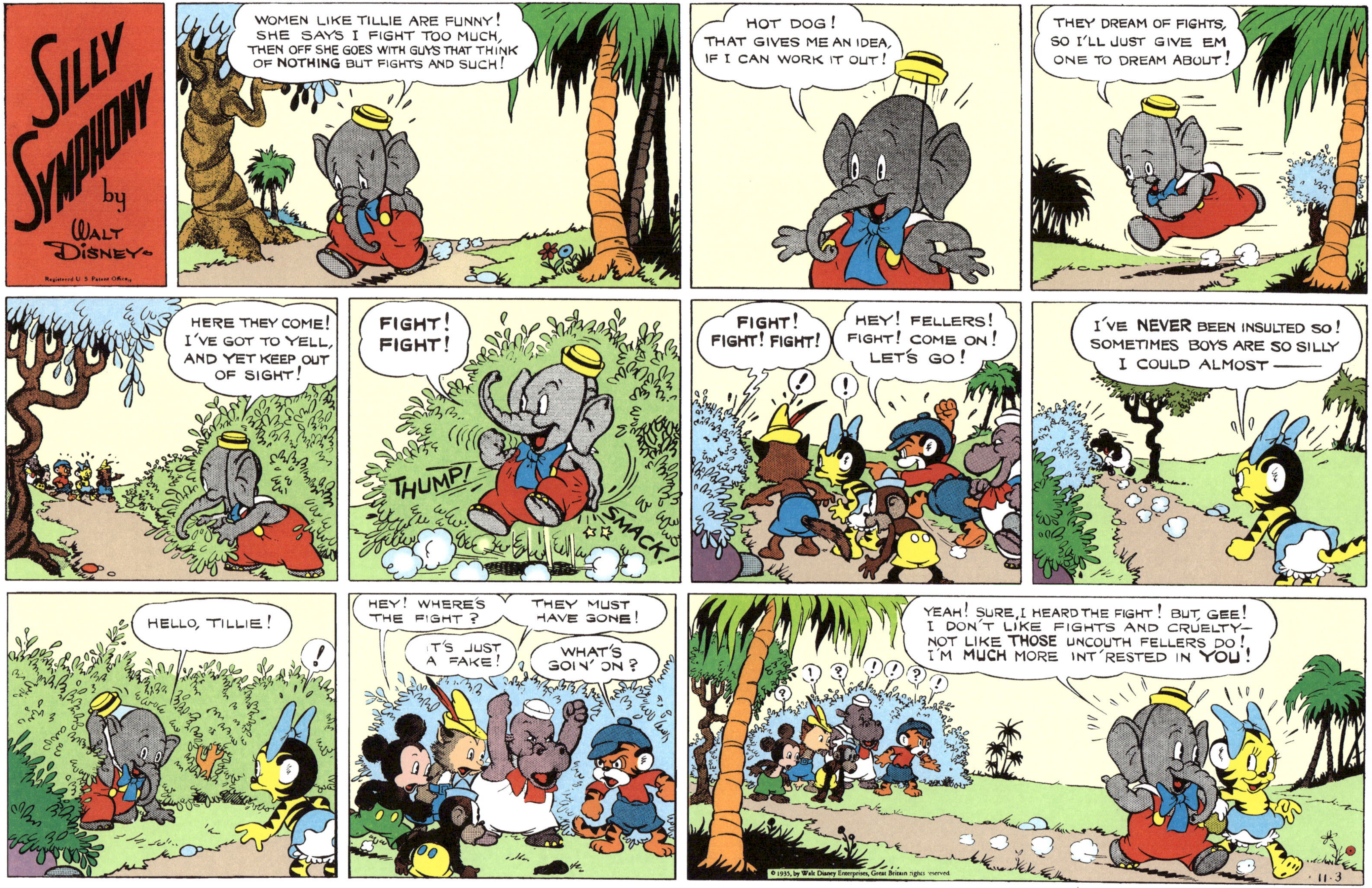
SILLY SYMPHONY
by
WALT DISNEY
Registered U. S. Patent Office
WOMEN LIKE TILLIE ARE FUNNY! SHE SAYS I FIGHT TOO MUCH, THEN OFF SHE GOES WITH GUYS THAT THINK OF NOTHING BUT FIGHTS AND SUCH!
HOT DOG! THAT GIVES ME AN IDEA, IF I CAN WORK IT OUT!
THEY DREAM OF FIGHTS, SO I'LL JUST GIVE EM ONE TO DREAM ABOUT!
HERE THEY COME! I'VE GOT TO YELL, AND YET KEEP OUT OF SIGHT!
FIGHT! FIGHT!
THUMP!
SMACK!
FIGHT! FIGHT! FIGHT!
HEY! FELLERS! FIGHT! COME ON! LET'S GO!
I'VE NEVER BEEN INSULTED SO! SOMETIMES BOYS ARE SO SILLY I COULD ALMOST ——
HELLO, TILLIE!
HEY! WHERE'S THE FIGHT?
THEY MUST HAVE GONE!
IT'S JUST A FAKE!
WHAT'S GOIN' ON?
YEAH! SURE, I HEARD THE FIGHT! BUT, GEE! I DON'T LIKE FIGHTS AND CRUELTY— NOT LIKE THOSE UNCOUTH FELLERS DO! I'M MUCH MORE INT'RESTED IN YOU!
© 1935, by Walt Disney Enterprises, Great Britain rights reserved
11-3

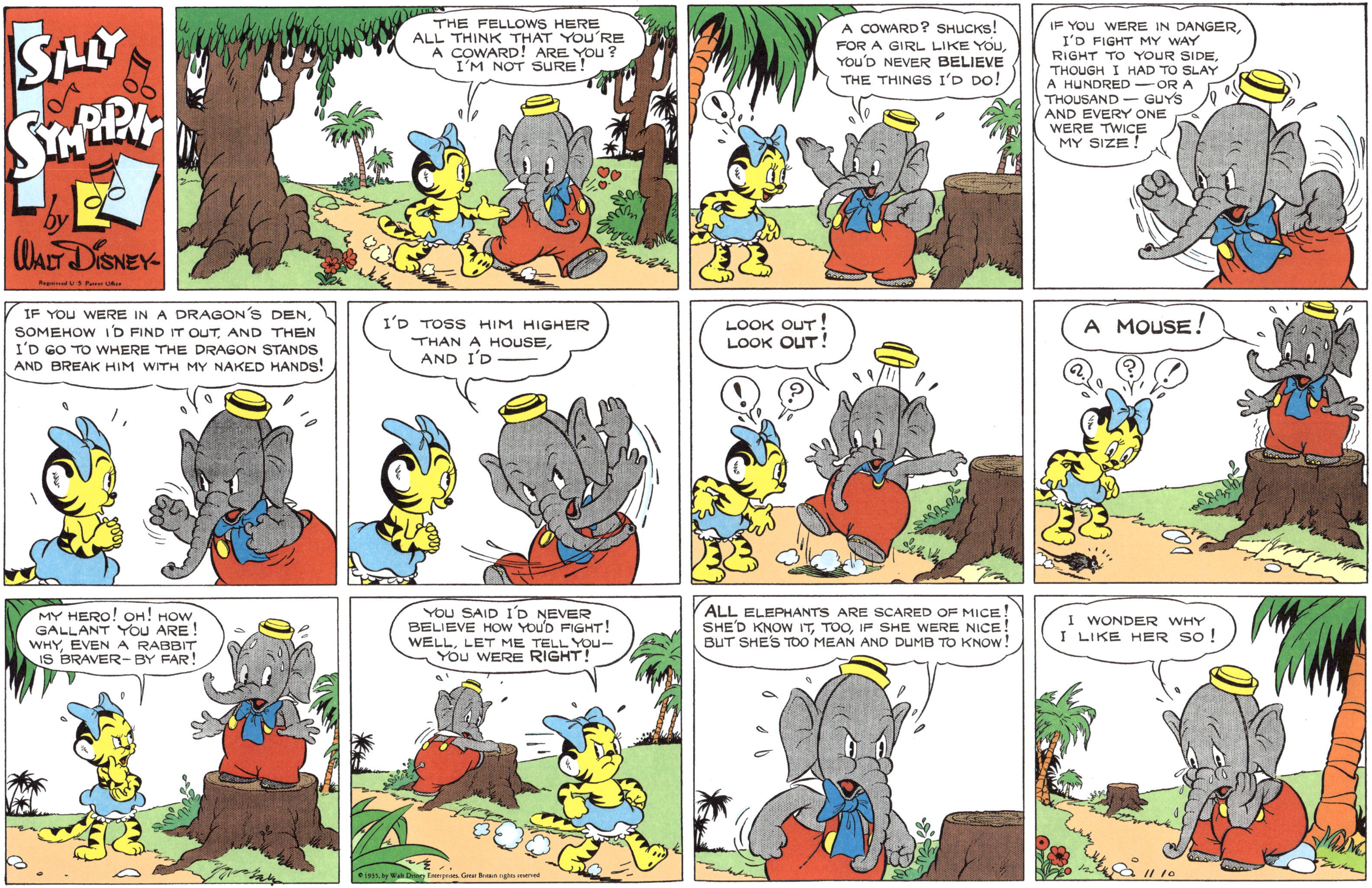
SILLY SYMPHONY
by WALT DISNEY
Registered U.S. Patent Office
THE FELLOWS HERE ALL THINK THAT YOU'RE A COWARD! ARE YOU? I'M NOT SURE!
A COWARD? SHUCKS! FOR A GIRL LIKE YOU, YOU'D NEVER BELIEVE THE THINGS I'D DO!
IF YOU WERE IN DANGER, I'D FIGHT MY WAY RIGHT TO YOUR SIDE, THOUGH I HAD TO SLAY A HUNDRED — OR A THOUSAND — GUYS AND EVERY ONE WERE TWICE MY SIZE!
IF YOU WERE IN A DRAGON'S DEN, SOMEHOW I'D FIND IT OUT, AND THEN I'D GO TO WHERE THE DRAGON STANDS AND BREAK HIM WITH MY NAKED HANDS!
I'D TOSS HIM HIGHER THAN A HOUSE, AND I'D ——
LOOK OUT! LOOK OUT!
A MOUSE!
MY HERO! OH! HOW GALLANT YOU ARE! WHY, EVEN A RABBIT IS BRAVER– BY FAR!
YOU SAID I'D NEVER BELIEVE HOW YOU'D FIGHT! WELL, LET ME TELL YOU– YOU WERE RIGHT!
© 1935, by Walt Disney Enterprises. Great Britain rights reserved
ALL ELEPHANTS ARE SCARED OF MICE! SHE'D KNOW IT, TOO, IF SHE WERE NICE! BUT SHE'S TOO MEAN AND DUMB TO KNOW!
I WONDER WHY I LIKE HER SO!
11 10

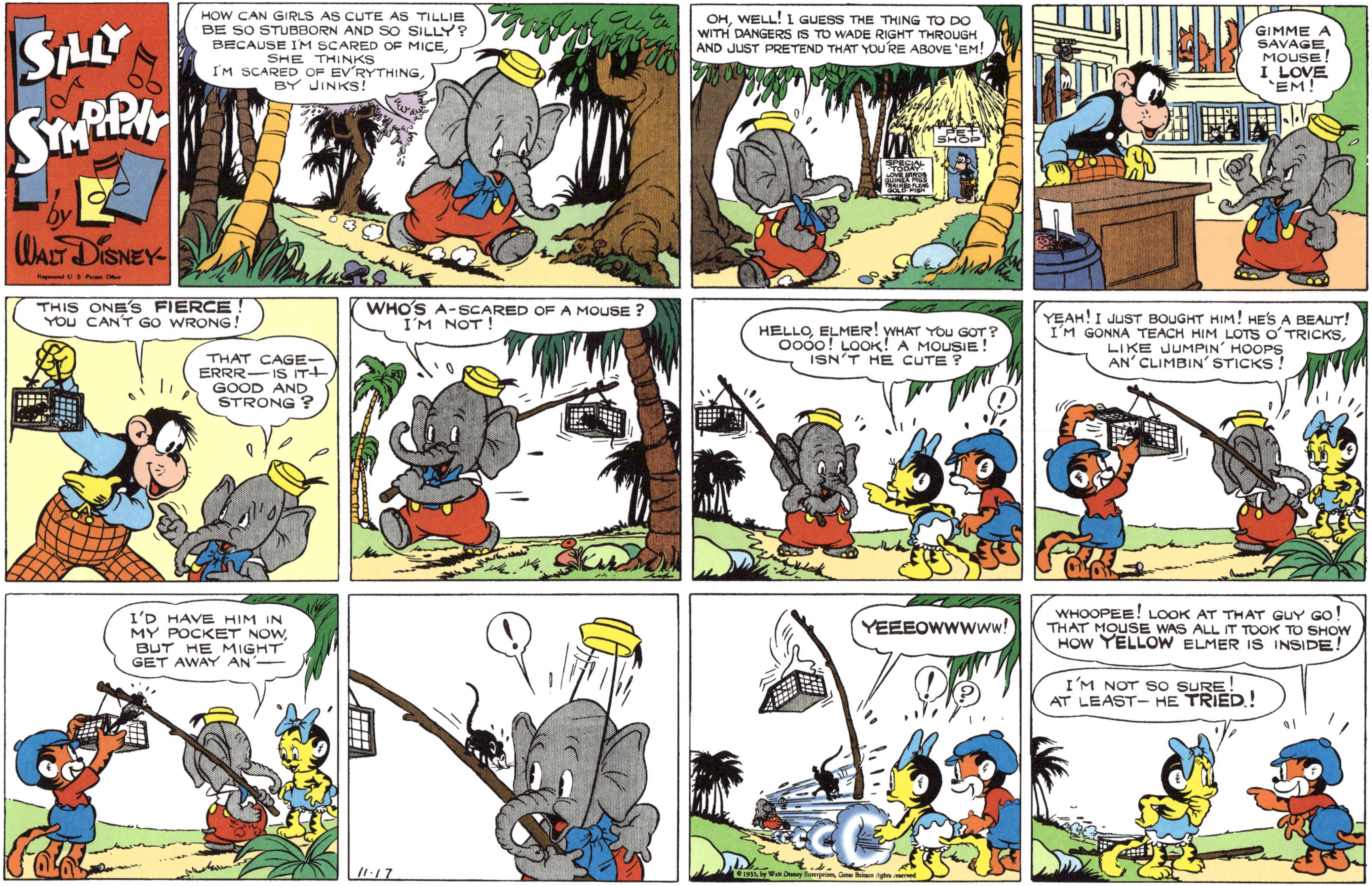
Silly Symphony
by Walt Disney
Registered U.S. Patent Office
HOW CAN GIRLS AS CUTE AS TILLIE BE SO STUBBORN AND SO SILLY? BECAUSE I'M SCARED OF MICE, SHE THINKS I'M SCARED OF EV'RYTHING, BY JINKS!
OH, WELL! I GUESS THE THING TO DO WITH DANGERS IS TO WADE RIGHT THROUGH AND JUST PRETEND THAT YOU'RE ABOVE 'EM!
PET SHOP
SPECIAL -TODAY- LOVE BIRDS GUINEA PIGS TRAINED FLEAS GOLD FISH
GIMME A SAVAGE MOUSE! I LOVE 'EM!
THIS ONE'S FIERCE! YOU CAN'T GO WRONG!
THAT CAGE— ERRR—IS IT— GOOD AND STRONG?
WHO'S A-SCARED OF A MOUSE? I'M NOT!
HELLO, ELMER! WHAT YOU GOT? OOOO! LOOK! A MOUSIE! ISN'T HE CUTE?
YEAH! I JUST BOUGHT HIM! HE'S A BEAUT! I'M GONNA TEACH HIM LOTS O' TRICKS, LIKE JUMPIN' HOOPS AN' CLIMBIN' STICKS!
I'D HAVE HIM IN MY POCKET NOW, BUT HE MIGHT GET AWAY AN'—
11-17
YEEEOWWWWW!
© 1935, by Walt Disney Enterprises, Great Britain rights reserved
WHOOPEE! LOOK AT THAT GUY GO! THAT MOUSE WAS ALL IT TOOK TO SHOW HOW YELLOW ELMER IS INSIDE!
I'M NOT SO SURE! AT LEAST— HE TRIED.!

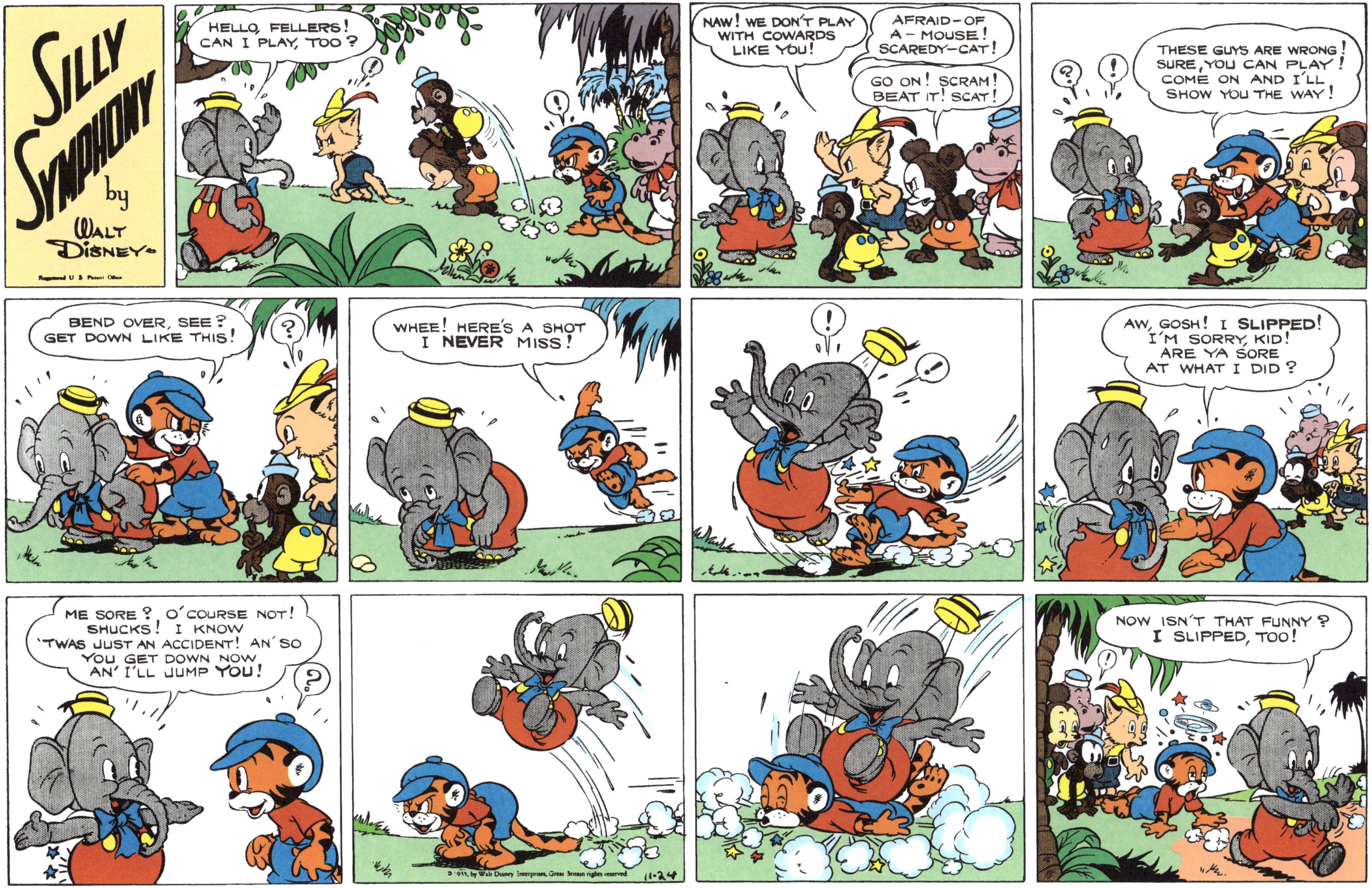
SILLY SYMPHONY
by WALT DISNEY
Registered U.S. Patent Office
HELLO, FELLERS! CAN I PLAY, TOO?
!
!
NAW! WE DON'T PLAY WITH COWARDS LIKE YOU!
AFRAID-OF A-MOUSE! SCAREDY-CAT!
GO ON! SCRAM! BEAT IT! SCAT!
?
!
THESE GUYS ARE WRONG! SURE, YOU CAN PLAY! COME ON AND I'LL SHOW YOU THE WAY!
BEND OVER, SEE? GET DOWN LIKE THIS!
?
WHEE! HERE'S A SHOT I NEVER MISS!
!
!
AW, GOSH! I SLIPPED! I'M SORRY, KID! ARE YA SORE AT WHAT I DID?
ME SORE? O'COURSE NOT! SHUCKS! I KNOW 'TWAS JUST AN ACCIDENT! AN' SO YOU GET DOWN NOW AN' I'LL JUMP YOU!
?
© 1935, by Walt Disney Enterprises, Great Britain rights reserved
11-24
!
NOW ISN'T THAT FUNNY? I SLIPPED, TOO!

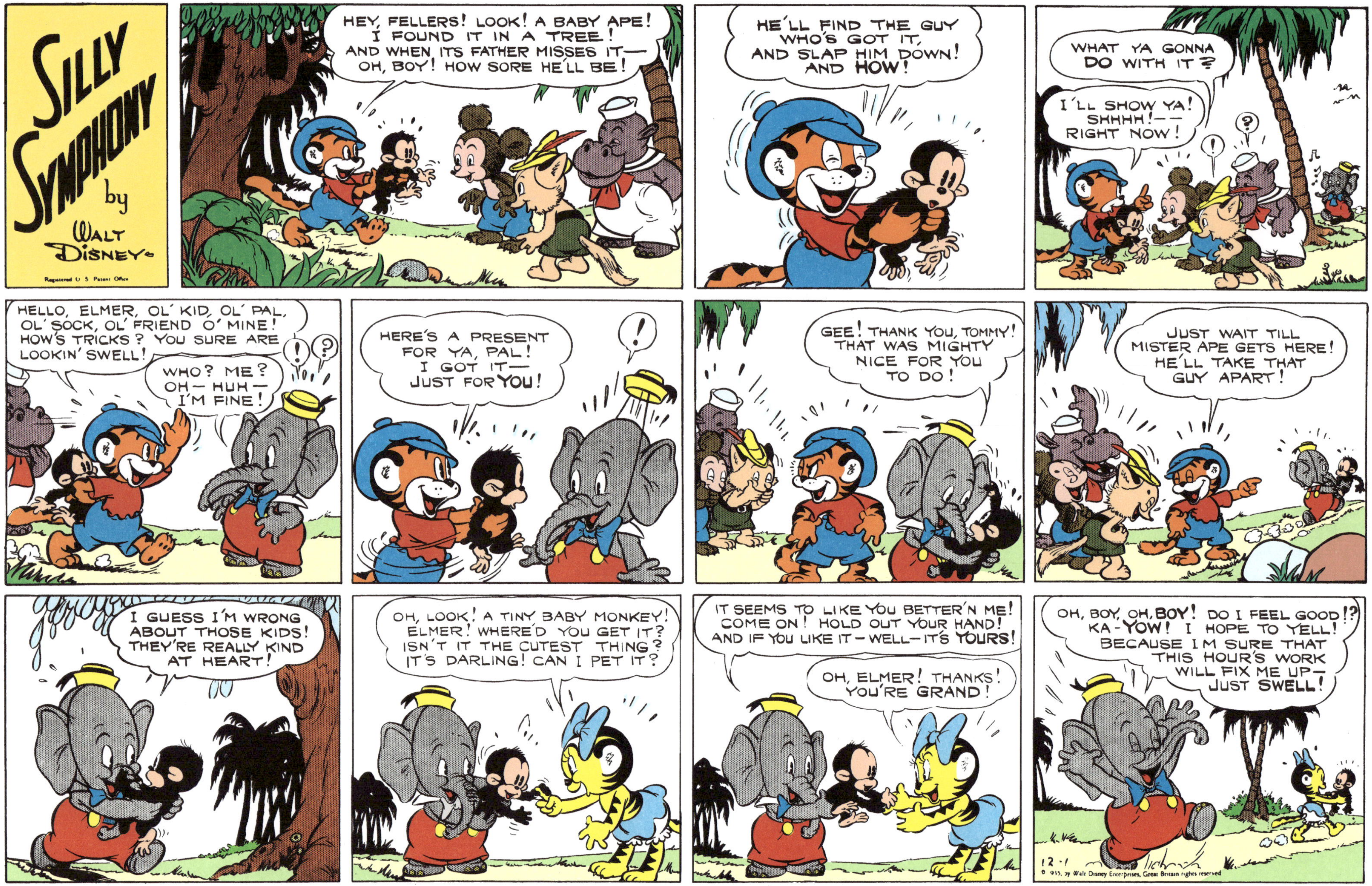
SILLY SYMPHONY by WALT DISNEY
Registered U S Patent Office
HEY, FELLERS! LOOK! A BABY APE! I FOUND IT IN A TREE! AND WHEN ITS FATHER MISSES IT— OH, BOY! HOW SORE HE'LL BE!
HE'LL FIND THE GUY WHO'S GOT IT, AND SLAP HIM DOWN! AND HOW!
WHAT YA GONNA DO WITH IT?
I'LL SHOW YA! SHHHH!—— RIGHT NOW!
HELLO, ELMER, OL' KID, OL' PAL, OL' SOCK, OL' FRIEND O' MINE! HOW'S TRICKS? YOU SURE ARE LOOKIN' SWELL!
WHO? ME? OH — HUH — I'M FINE!
HERE'S A PRESENT FOR YA, PAL! I GOT IT— JUST FOR YOU!
GEE! THANK YOU, TOMMY! THAT WAS MIGHTY NICE FOR YOU TO DO!
JUST WAIT TILL MISTER APE GETS HERE! HE'LL TAKE THAT GUY APART!
I GUESS I'M WRONG ABOUT THOSE KIDS! THEY'RE REALLY KIND AT HEART!
OH, LOOK! A TINY BABY MONKEY! ELMER! WHERE'D YOU GET IT? ISN'T IT THE CUTEST THING? IT'S DARLING! CAN I PET IT?
IT SEEMS TO LIKE YOU BETTER'N ME! COME ON! HOLD OUT YOUR HAND! AND IF YOU LIKE IT – WELL – IT'S YOURS!
OH, ELMER! THANKS! YOU'RE GRAND!
OH, BOY, OH, BOY! DO I FEEL GOOD!? KA-YOW! I HOPE TO YELL! BECAUSE I'M SURE THAT THIS HOUR'S WORK WILL FIX ME UP— JUST SWELL!
12-1
© 1935, by Walt Disney Enterprises, Great Britain rights reserved

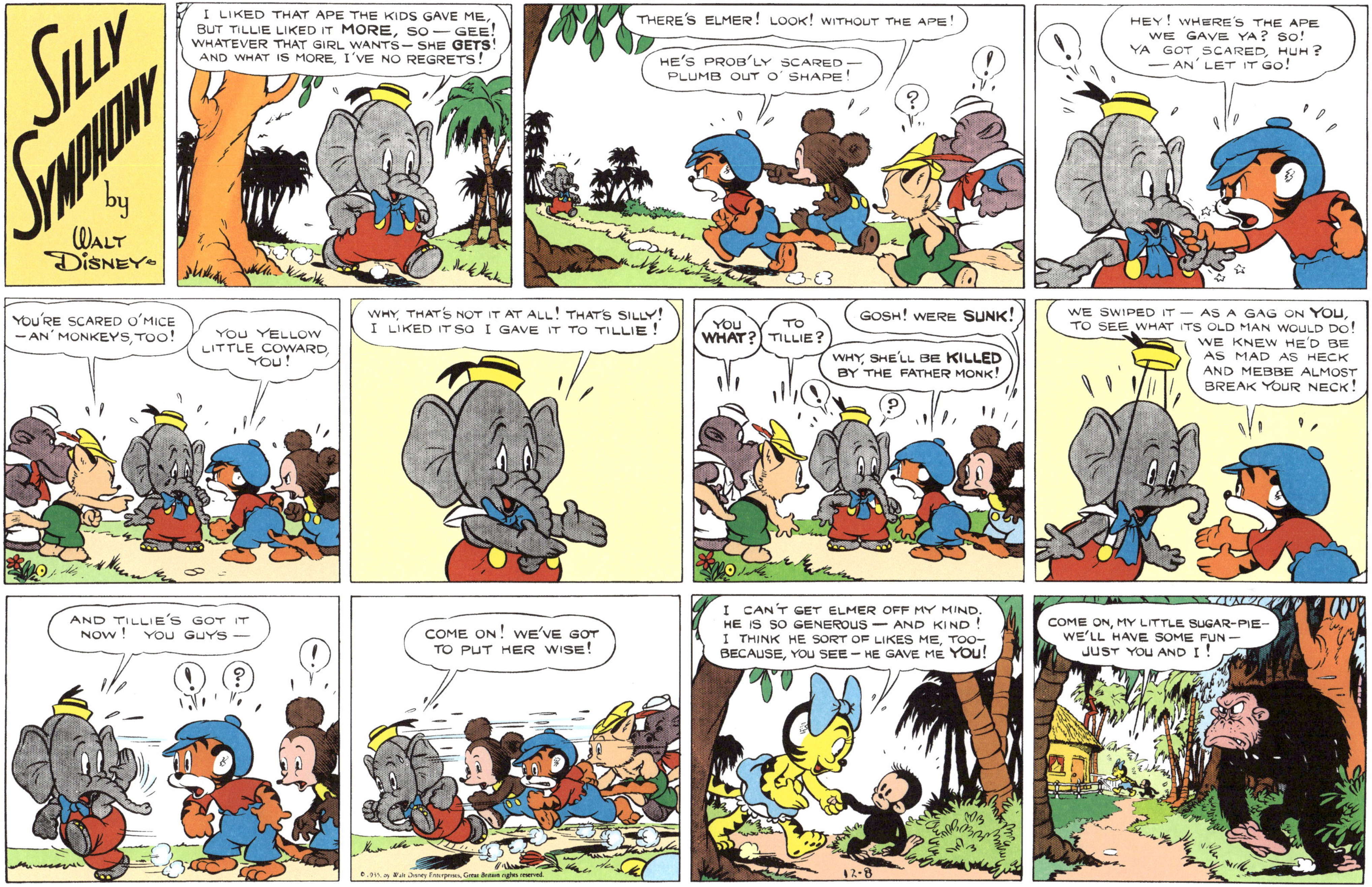
SILLY SYMPHONY by WALT DISNEY
I LIKED THAT APE THE KIDS GAVE ME, BUT TILLIE LIKED IT MORE, SO — GEE! WHATEVER THAT GIRL WANTS — SHE GETS! AND WHAT IS MORE, I'VE NO REGRETS!
THERE'S ELMER! LOOK! WITHOUT THE APE!
HE'S PROB'LY SCARED — PLUMB OUT O' SHAPE!
HEY! WHERE'S THE APE WE GAVE YA? SO! YA GOT SCARED, HUH? — AN' LET IT GO!
YOU'RE SCARED O' MICE — AN' MONKEYS, TOO!
YOU YELLOW LITTLE COWARD, YOU!
WHY, THAT'S NOT IT AT ALL! THAT'S SILLY! I LIKED IT SO I GAVE IT TO TILLIE!
YOU WHAT?
TO TILLIE?
GOSH! WERE SUNK!
WHY, SHE'LL BE KILLED BY THE FATHER MONK!
WE SWIPED IT — AS A GAG ON YOU, TO SEE WHAT ITS OLD MAN WOULD DO! WE KNEW HE'D BE AS MAD AS HECK AND MEBBE ALMOST BREAK YOUR NECK!
AND TILLIE'S GOT IT NOW! YOU GUYS —
COME ON! WE'VE GOT TO PUT HER WISE!
© 1935, by Walt Disney Enterprises, Great Britain rights reserved.
I CAN'T GET ELMER OFF MY MIND. HE IS SO GENEROUS — AND KIND! I THINK HE SORT OF LIKES ME, TOO — BECAUSE, YOU SEE — HE GAVE ME YOU!
12-8
COME ON, MY LITTLE SUGAR-PIE — WE'LL HAVE SOME FUN — JUST YOU AND I!

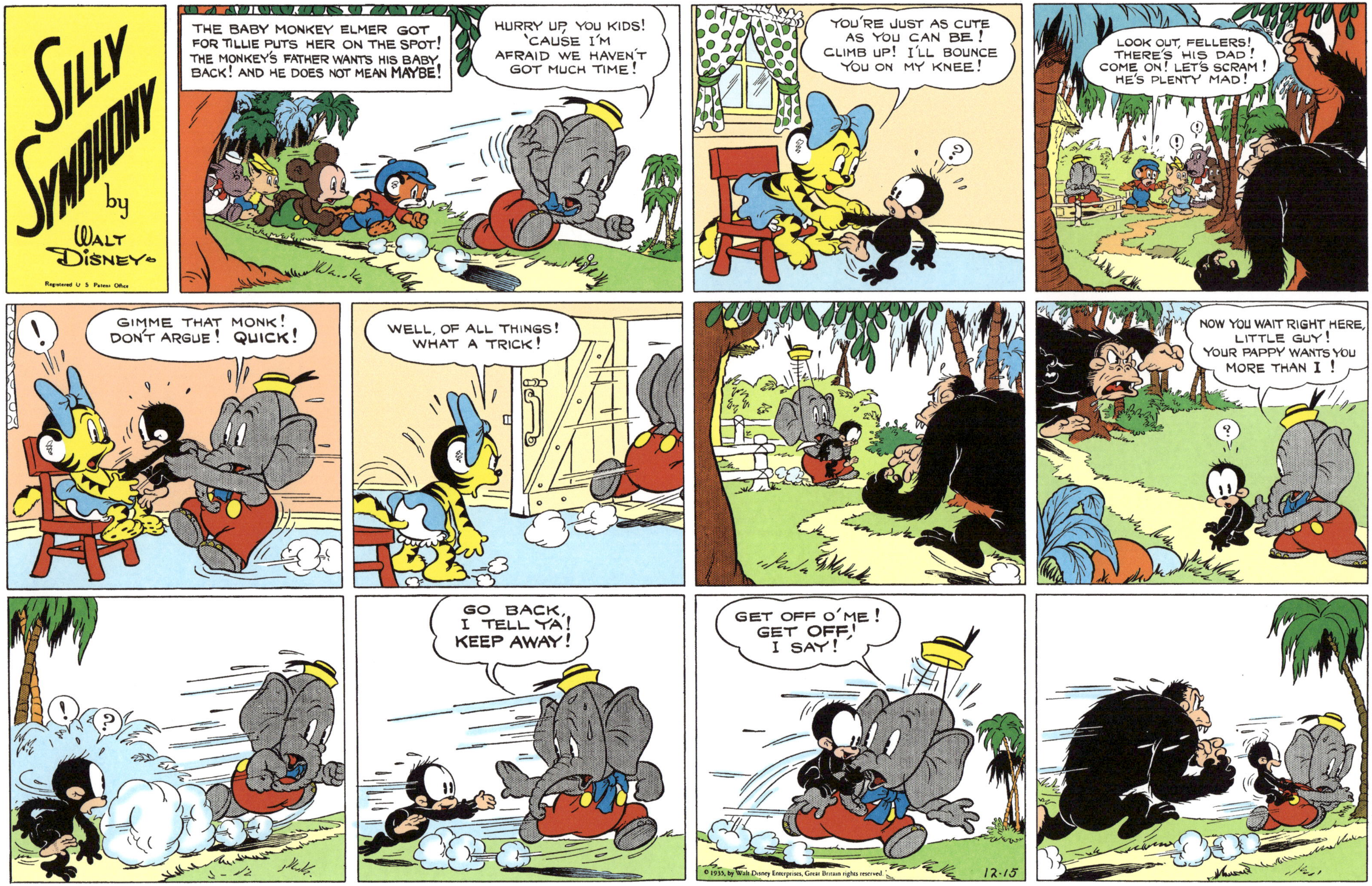
SILLY SYMPHONY
by
WALT DISNEY
Registered U S Patent Office
THE BABY MONKEY ELMER GOT FOR TILLIE PUTS HER ON THE SPOT! THE MONKEY'S FATHER WANTS HIS BABY BACK! AND HE DOES NOT MEAN MAYBE!
HURRY UP, YOU KIDS! 'CAUSE I'M AFRAID WE HAVEN'T GOT MUCH TIME!
YOU'RE JUST AS CUTE AS YOU CAN BE! CLIMB UP! I'LL BOUNCE YOU ON MY KNEE!
?
LOOK OUT, FELLERS! THERE'S HIS DAD! COME ON! LET'S SCRAM! HE'S PLENTY MAD!
!
!
!
GIMME THAT MONK! DON'T ARGUE! QUICK!
WELL, OF ALL THINGS! WHAT A TRICK!
NOW YOU WAIT RIGHT HERE, LITTLE GUY! YOUR PAPPY WANTS YOU MORE THAN I!
?
!
?
GO BACK, I TELL YA! KEEP AWAY!
GET OFF O'ME! GET OFF! I SAY!
© 1935, by Walt Disney Enterprises, Great Britain rights reserved.
12-15

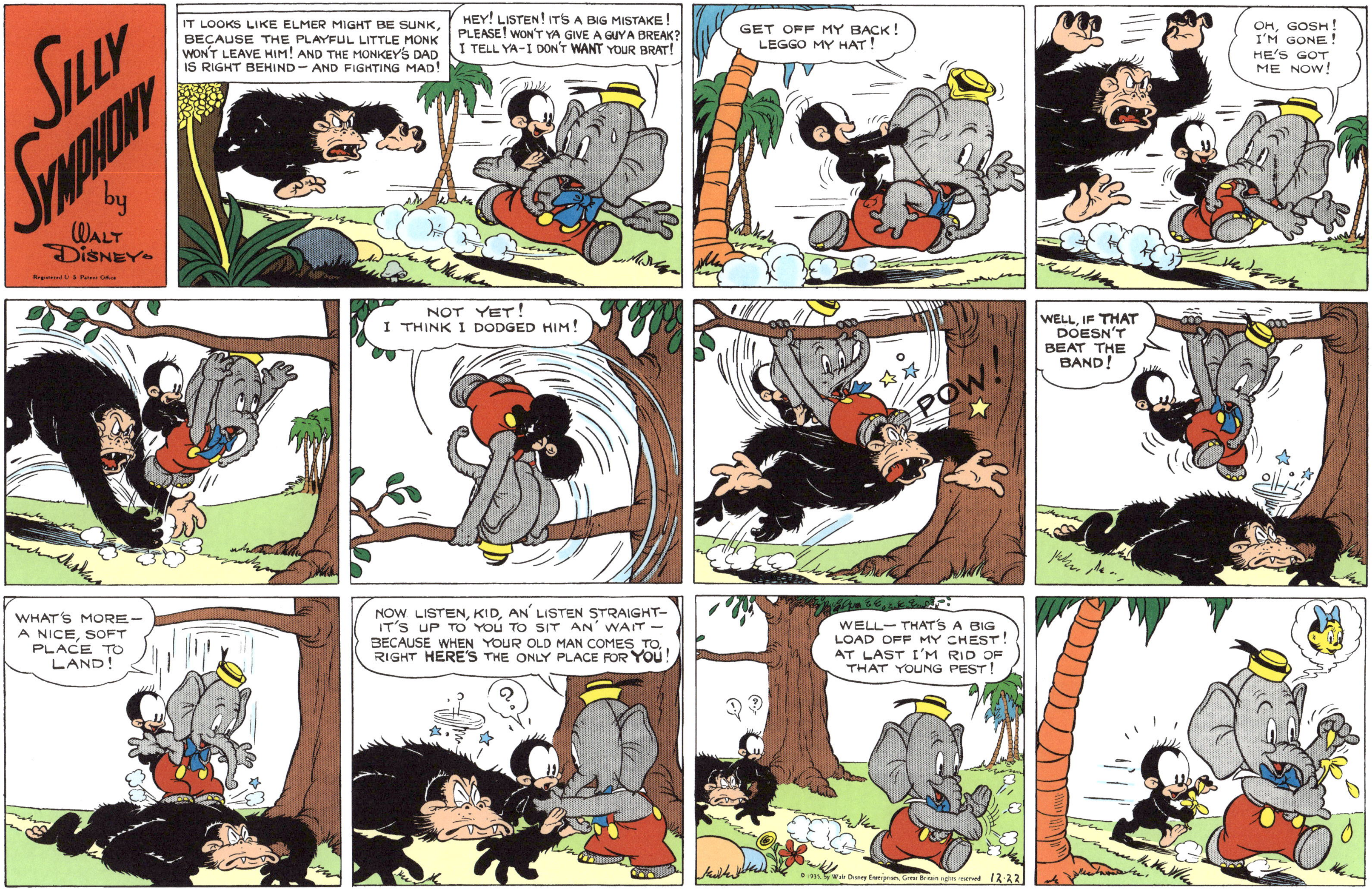
SILLY SYMPHONY
by
WALT DISNEY
Registered U S Patent Office
IT LOOKS LIKE ELMER MIGHT BE SUNK, BECAUSE THE PLAYFUL LITTLE MONK WON'T LEAVE HIM! AND THE MONKEY'S DAD IS RIGHT BEHIND — AND FIGHTING MAD!
HEY! LISTEN! IT'S A BIG MISTAKE! PLEASE! WON'T YA GIVE A GUY A BREAK? I TELL YA — I DON'T WANT YOUR BRAT!
GET OFF MY BACK! LEGGO MY HAT!
OH, GOSH! I'M GONE! HE'S GOT ME NOW!
NOT YET! I THINK I DODGED HIM!
POW!
WELL, IF THAT DOESN'T BEAT THE BAND!
WHAT'S MORE — A NICE, SOFT PLACE TO LAND!
NOW LISTEN, KID, AN' LISTEN STRAIGHT — IT'S UP TO YOU TO SIT AN' WAIT — BECAUSE WHEN YOUR OLD MAN COMES TO, RIGHT HERE'S THE ONLY PLACE FOR YOU!
?
WELL — THAT'S A BIG LOAD OFF MY CHEST! AT LAST I'M RID OF THAT YOUNG PEST!
! ?
© 1935, by Walt Disney Enterprises, Great Britain rights reserved
12-22

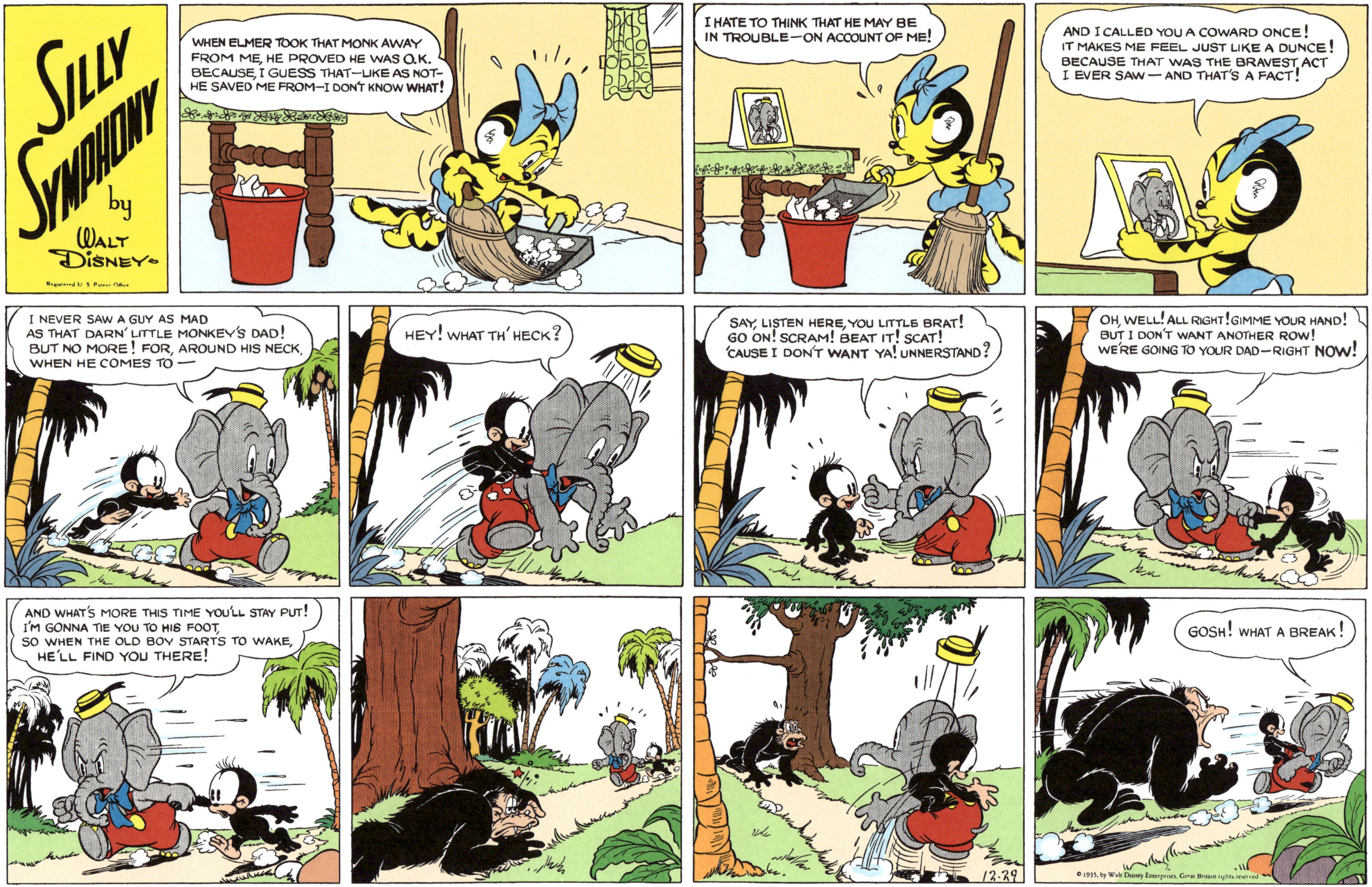
SILLY SYMPHONY
by
WALT DISNEY
Registered U. S. Patent Office
WHEN ELMER TOOK THAT MONK AWAY FROM ME, HE PROVED HE WAS O.K. BECAUSE, I GUESS THAT—LIKE AS NOT—HE SAVED ME FROM—I DON'T KNOW WHAT!
I HATE TO THINK THAT HE MAY BE IN TROUBLE—ON ACCOUNT OF ME!
AND I CALLED YOU A COWARD ONCE! IT MAKES ME FEEL JUST LIKE A DUNCE! BECAUSE THAT WAS THE BRAVEST ACT I EVER SAW — AND THAT'S A FACT!
I NEVER SAW A GUY AS MAD AS THAT DARN' LITTLE MONKEY'S DAD! BUT NO MORE! FOR, AROUND HIS NECK, WHEN HE COMES TO —
HEY! WHAT TH' HECK?
SAY, LISTEN HERE, YOU LITTLE BRAT! GO ON! SCRAM! BEAT IT! SCAT! 'CAUSE I DON'T WANT YA! UNNERSTAND?
OH, WELL! ALL RIGHT! GIMME YOUR HAND! BUT I DON'T WANT ANOTHER ROW! WE'RE GOING TO YOUR DAD—RIGHT NOW!
AND WHAT'S MORE THIS TIME YOU'LL STAY PUT! I'M GONNA TIE YOU TO HIS FOOT, SO WHEN THE OLD BOY STARTS TO WAKE, HE'LL FIND YOU THERE!
12-29
GOSH! WHAT A BREAK!
© 1935, by Walt Disney Enterprises, Great Britain rights reserved

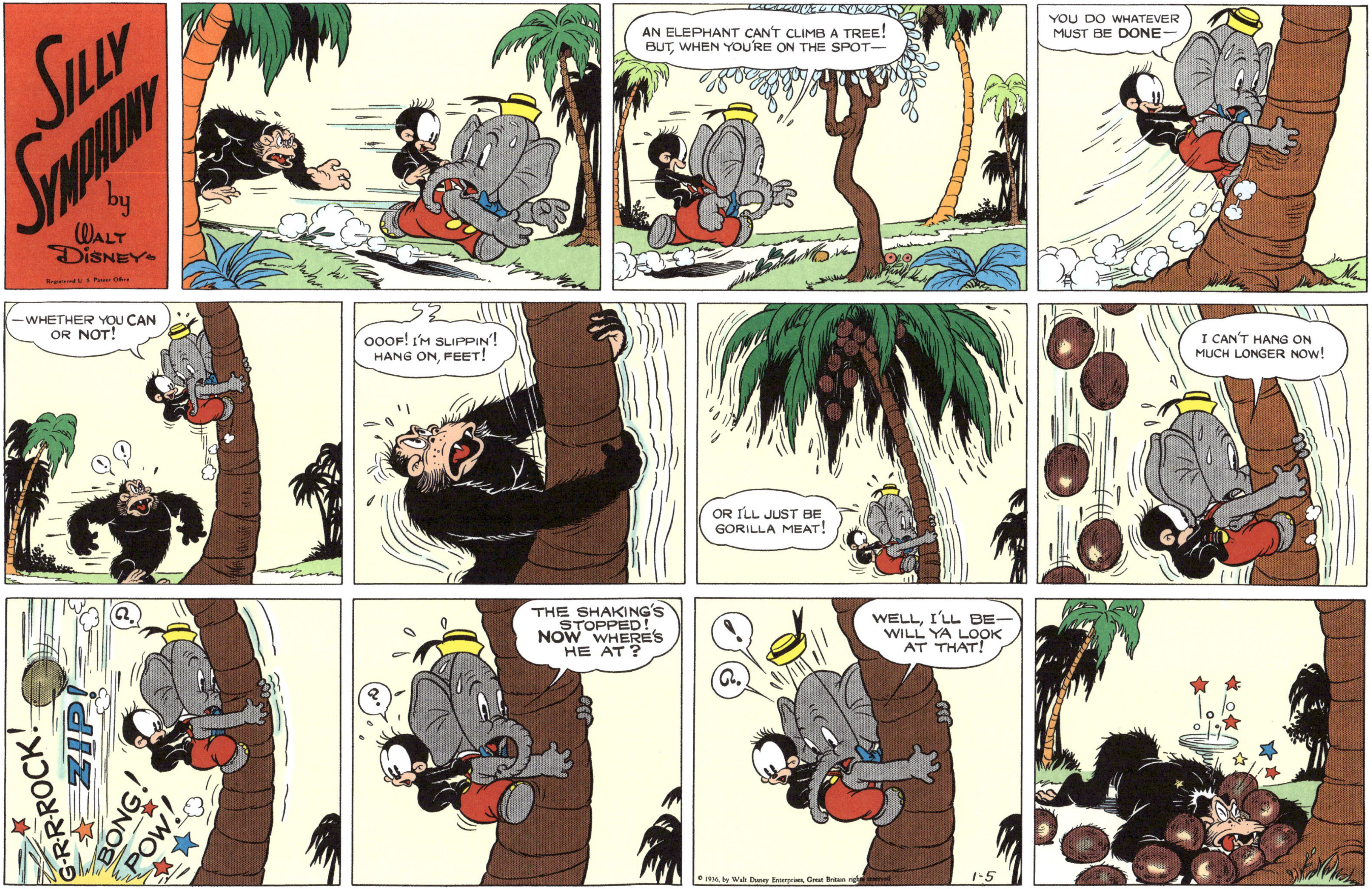
SILLY SYMPHONY
by
WALT DISNEY
Registered U. S. Patent Office
AN ELEPHANT CAN'T CLIMB A TREE! BUT, WHEN YOU'RE ON THE SPOT—
YOU DO WHATEVER MUST BE DONE—
—WHETHER YOU CAN OR NOT!
OOOF! I'M SLIPPIN'! HANG ON, FEET!
OR I'LL JUST BE GORILLA MEAT!
I CAN'T HANG ON MUCH LONGER NOW!
G-R-R-ROCK! ZIP! BONG! POW!
THE SHAKING'S STOPPED! NOW WHERE'S HE AT?
WELL, I'LL BE— WILL YA LOOK AT THAT!
© 1936, by Walt Disney Enterprises, Great Britain rights reserved
1-5

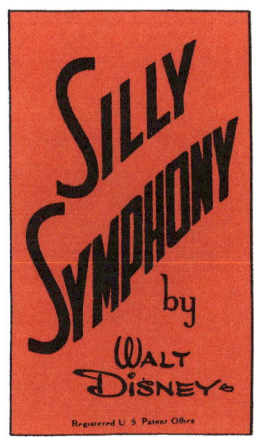

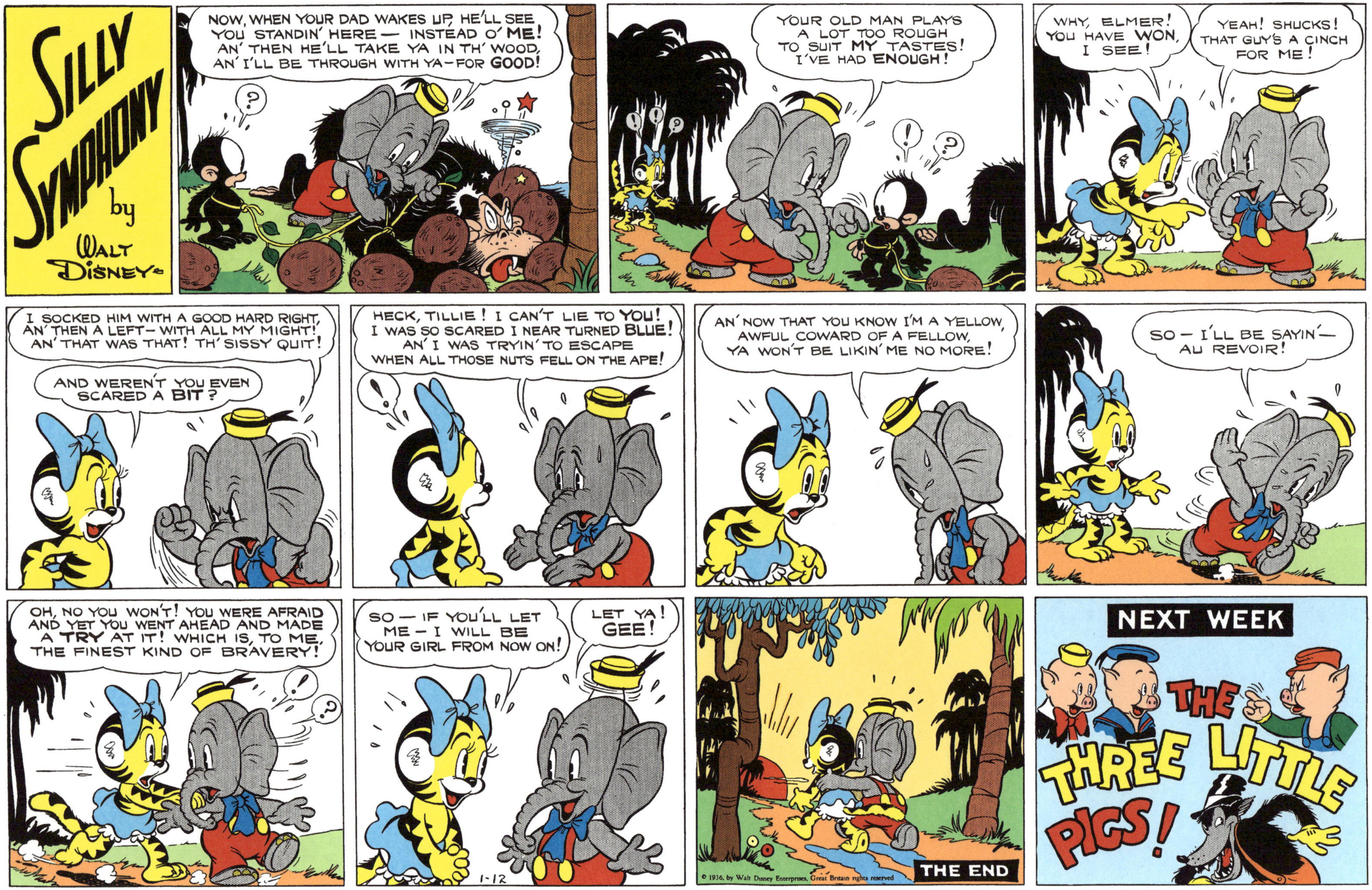

SILLY SYMPHONY
by
WALT DISNEY
NOW, WHEN YOUR DAD WAKES UP, HE'LL SEE YOU STANDIN' HERE — INSTEAD O' ME! AN' THEN HE'LL TAKE YA IN TH' WOOD, AN' I'LL BE THROUGH WITH YA — FOR GOOD!
?
YOUR OLD MAN PLAYS A LOT TOO ROUGH TO SUIT MY TASTES! I'VE HAD ENOUGH!
! ! ?
! ?
WHY, ELMER! YOU HAVE WON, I SEE!
YEAH! SHUCKS! THAT GUY'S A CINCH FOR ME!
I SOCKED HIM WITH A GOOD HARD RIGHT, AN' THEN A LEFT — WITH ALL MY MIGHT! AN' THAT WAS THAT! TH' SISSY QUIT!
AND WEREN'T YOU EVEN SCARED A BIT?
HECK, TILLIE! I CAN'T LIE TO YOU! I WAS SO SCARED I NEAR TURNED BLUE! AN' I WAS TRYIN' TO ESCAPE WHEN ALL THOSE NUTS FELL ON THE APE!
!
AN' NOW THAT YOU KNOW I'M A YELLOW, AWFUL COWARD OF A FELLOW, YA WON'T BE LIKIN' ME NO MORE!
SO — I'LL BE SAYIN' — AU REVOIR!
OH, NO YOU WON'T! YOU WERE AFRAID AND YET YOU WENT AHEAD AND MADE A TRY AT IT! WHICH IS, TO ME, THE FINEST KIND OF BRAVERY!
! ?
SO — IF YOU'LL LET ME — I WILL BE YOUR GIRL FROM NOW ON!
LET YA! GEE!
1-12
© 1936, by Walt Disney Enterprises, Great Britain rights reserved
THE END
NEXT WEEK
THE THREE LITTLE PIGS!

Silly Symphonies

THE FURTHER ADVENTURES OF THE THREE LITTLE PIGS

January 19 - August 23, 1936
Written by Ted Osborne, drawn by Al Taliaferro

The unexpected worldwide success of *Three Little Pigs* in 1933 elevated the Pigs and the Big Bad Wolf to a level of popularity that rivaled that of Mickey Mouse and his gang. Inevitably, the Disney studio brought them back to the screen in sequels to the original film. The first sequel, *The Big Bad Wolf*, was released in April 1934. Two years later, the *Silly Symphony* comic page heralded the second sequel, *Three Little Wolves*, which introduced three nasty little lupine offspring and was released to theaters roughly halfway through this continuity's run in newspapers.

The resulting comic tale is a delightful concoction that blends gags and visuals from *Three Little Wolves*, and sidelong glances at the first two films, with new story material that appears in none of the films. Disney aficionados can enjoy combing these strips for images drawn from the films—perhaps most obviously the exterior of the Wolf's house at the base of a tree, pictured as it appears in *Three Little Wolves*.

Equally delightful is the original material. *Three Little Wolves* is perhaps the wittiest of the Pig films, featuring the Wolf's disguise as Little Bo Peep (!) and climaxing with the Wolf Pacifier, an elaborate machine invented by Practical Pig. These devices are nowhere to be seen in the comic version, but in their place we get other wildly improbable schemes by the Wolf, including more outlandish disguises. Writer Ted Osborne endows Practical Pig with some subtly droll touches of character development: compelled to drop everything to once again go rescue his brothers from the Wolf, he's not frightened or concerned, merely annoyed at the inconvenience. Even when he himself is trapped and tied up, Practical Pig maintains his cool, criticizing the Wolf for his shoddy workmanship.

In other details, too, Osborne shows his hand. Note the passage in which the Wolf impersonates a Boy Scout leader. The Boy Scouts of America were at the height of their popularity in the 1930s and the organization's influence was reflected in the movies and elsewhere in pop culture. Here the Wolf's recruiting station features the Scout motto, "Be Prepared;" he correctly demonstrates knot-tying and other woodcraft, and even includes a reference to Ernest Thompson Seton (one of the founders of the Scouts). Similarly, when the Wolf turns sculptor and crafts a couple of Pig decoys, he invokes the names of Rodin and Phidias. The combination of this subtle wit with a healthy dose of slapstick makes this continuity a worthy counterpart to *Three Little Wolves*, as well as a gem of comic art in its own right.

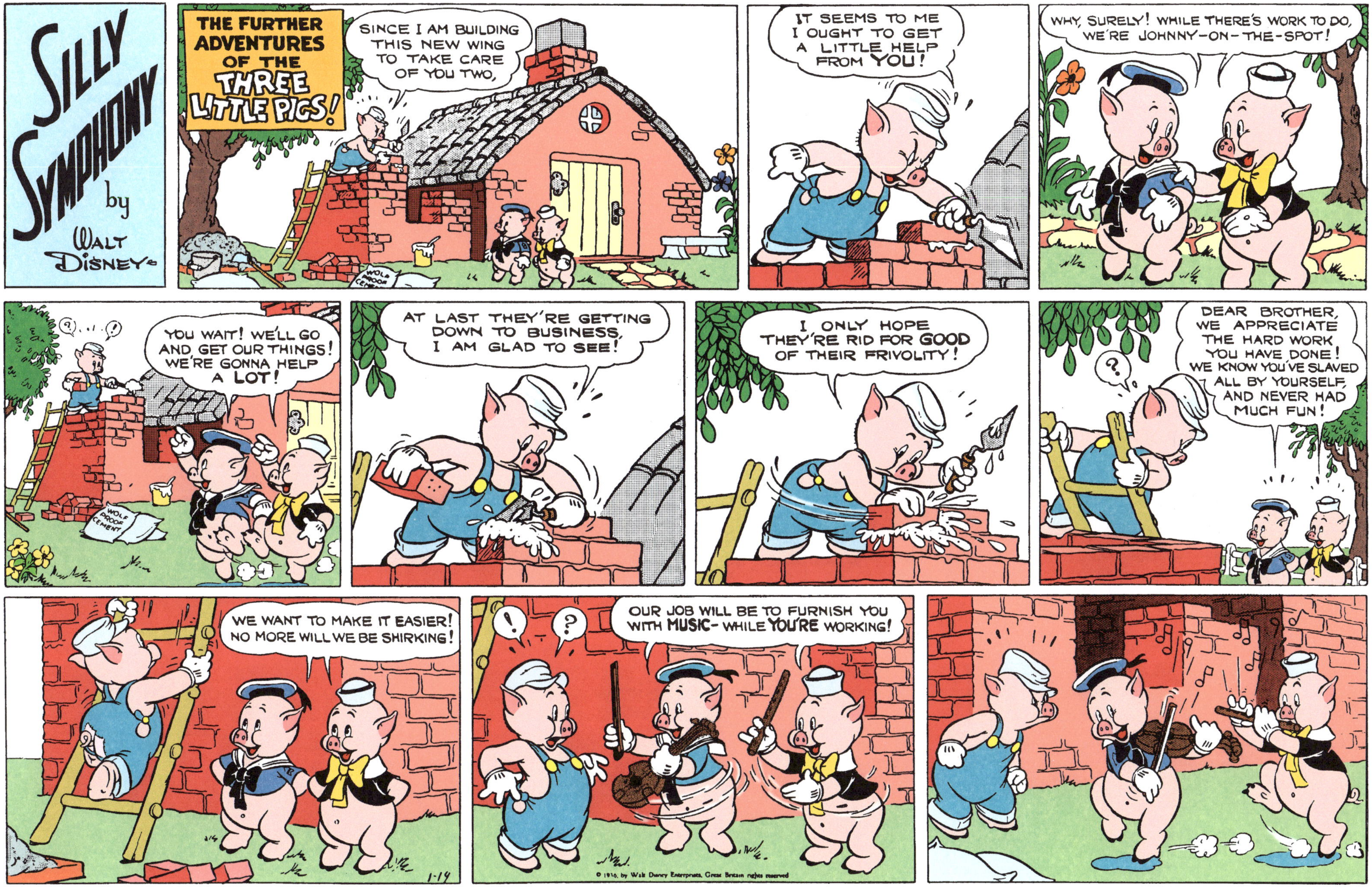
SILLY SYMPHONY
by
WALT DISNEY
THE FURTHER ADVENTURES OF THE THREE LITTLE PIGS!
SINCE I AM BUILDING THIS NEW WING TO TAKE CARE OF YOU TWO,
IT SEEMS TO ME I OUGHT TO GET A LITTLE HELP FROM YOU!
WHY, SURELY! WHILE THERE'S WORK TO DO, WE'RE JOHNNY-ON-THE-SPOT!
YOU WAIT! WE'LL GO AND GET OUR THINGS! WE'RE GONNA HELP A LOT!
WOLF PROOF CEMENT
AT LAST THEY'RE GETTING DOWN TO BUSINESS, I AM GLAD TO SEE!
I ONLY HOPE THEY'RE RID FOR GOOD OF THEIR FRIVOLITY!
DEAR BROTHER, WE APPRECIATE THE HARD WORK YOU HAVE DONE! WE KNOW YOU'VE SLAVED ALL BY YOURSELF, AND NEVER HAD MUCH FUN!
WE WANT TO MAKE IT EASIER! NO MORE WILL WE BE SHIRKING!
OUR JOB WILL BE TO FURNISH YOU WITH MUSIC- WHILE YOU'RE WORKING!
© 1936, by Walt Disney Enterprises. Great Britain rights reserved

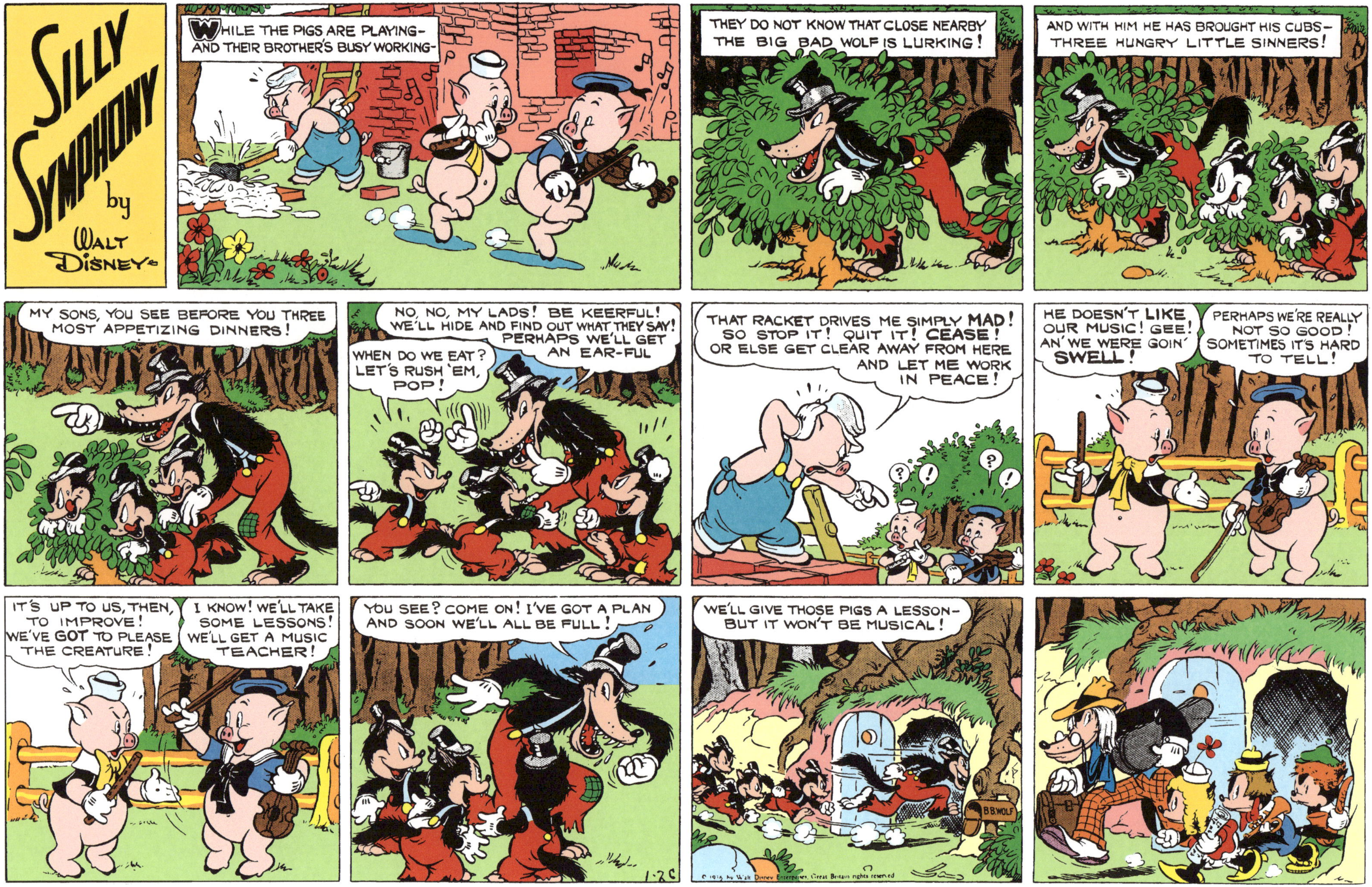

SILLY SYMPHONY
by WALT DISNEY
WHILE THE PIGS ARE PLAYING- AND THEIR BROTHER'S BUSY WORKING-
THEY DO NOT KNOW THAT CLOSE NEARBY THE BIG BAD WOLF IS LURKING!
AND WITH HIM HE HAS BROUGHT HIS CUBS- THREE HUNGRY LITTLE SINNERS!
MY SONS, YOU SEE BEFORE YOU THREE MOST APPETIZING DINNERS!
WHEN DO WE EAT? LET'S RUSH 'EM, POP!
NO, NO, MY LADS! BE KEERFUL! WE'LL HIDE AND FIND OUT WHAT THEY SAY! PERHAPS WE'LL GET AN EAR-FUL
THAT RACKET DRIVES ME SIMPLY MAD! SO STOP IT! QUIT IT! CEASE! OR ELSE GET CLEAR AWAY FROM HERE AND LET ME WORK IN PEACE!
HE DOESN'T LIKE OUR MUSIC! GEE! AN' WE WERE GOIN' SWELL!
PERHAPS WE'RE REALLY NOT SO GOOD! SOMETIMES IT'S HARD TO TELL!
IT'S UP TO US, THEN, TO IMPROVE! WE'VE GOT TO PLEASE THE CREATURE!
I KNOW! WE'LL TAKE SOME LESSONS! WE'LL GET A MUSIC TEACHER!
YOU SEE? COME ON! I'VE GOT A PLAN AND SOON WE'LL ALL BE FULL!
1-26
WE'LL GIVE THOSE PIGS A LESSON- BUT IT WON'T BE MUSICAL!
B.B.WOLF

SILLY SYMPHONY by WALT DISNEY
HERE IS THE PLACE TO TRAP THE PIGS! I'M SURE THAT IT IS EMPTY, FOR MY FRIEND, THE LATE LAMENTED OWNER, DOESN'T LIVE HERE ANY MORE!
WE ASKED HIM OVER TO OUR DEN FOR DINNER! AND HE CAME—THE SAP! I'M SURE YOU LADS REMEMBER HIM! HE WAS A MOST DELICIOUS CHAP!
NOW—YOU GO IN AND WAIT FOR ME, AND EACH ONE FIND A KNIFE AND FORK! I'M GOING DOWN TO BAIT OUR TRAP! TONIGHT, MY SONS, WE'RE EATING PORK!
MR. SCHUBERT MUZIC TEACHER
SPECIALIST ON FIDDLE AND TIN FLUTE FOR ADVANCED PUPILS
© 1936, by Walt Disney Enterprises Great Britain rights reserved
OUR BROTHER DOESN'T LIKE OUR PLAYING! I HOPE HE DOESN'T MAKE US MOVE!
?
HE WON'T—BECAUSE RIGHT THERE'S TH' ANSWER! WE'LL TAKE LESSONS—AND IMPROVE!
HERE THEY COME! GET STARTED! QUICK!
SQUEAK! SQUAWK! TOODLEDY-OOO!
MR. SCHUBERT? WE WOULD LIKE TO TAKE LESSONS, PLEASE, FROM YOU!
A LESSON? TO BE SURE! OH, YES! JUST COME RIGHT IN, MY FRIENDS! YOU BET! I GUARANTEE YOU'LL GET A LESSON THAT YOU NEVER WILL FORGET!
R.R

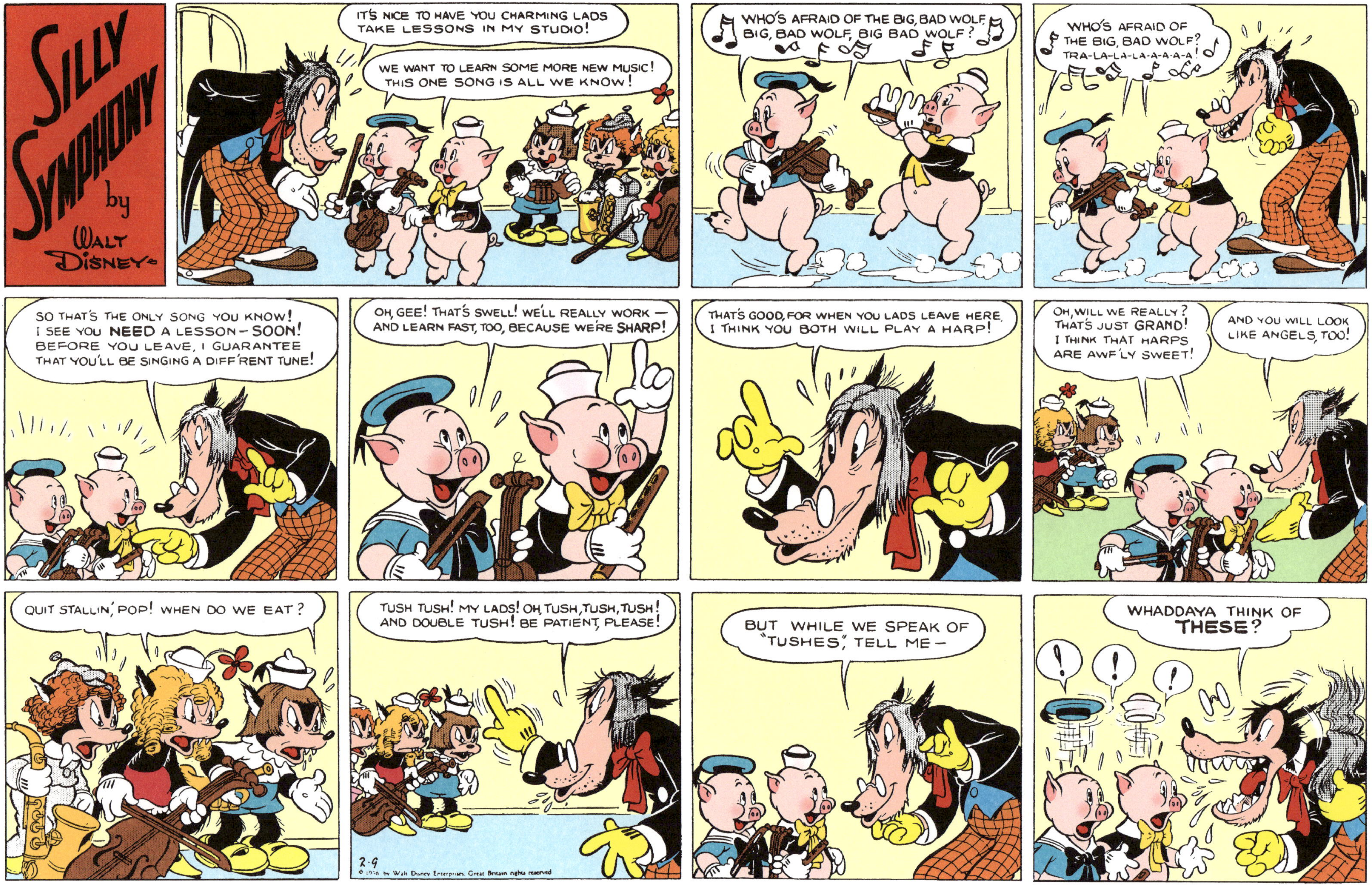
SILLY SYMPHONY
by WALT DISNEY
IT'S NICE TO HAVE YOU CHARMING LADS TAKE LESSONS IN MY STUDIO!
WE WANT TO LEARN SOME MORE NEW MUSIC! THIS ONE SONG IS ALL WE KNOW!
WHO'S AFRAID OF THE BIG, BAD WOLF, BIG, BAD WOLF, BIG BAD WOLF?
WHO'S AFRAID OF THE BIG, BAD WOLF? TRA-LA-LA-LA-A-A-A-A!
SO THAT'S THE ONLY SONG YOU KNOW! I SEE YOU NEED A LESSON–SOON! BEFORE YOU LEAVE, I GUARANTEE THAT YOU'LL BE SINGING A DIFF'RENT TUNE!
OH, GEE! THAT'S SWELL! WE'LL REALLY WORK — AND LEARN FAST, TOO, BECAUSE WE'RE SHARP!
THAT'S GOOD, FOR WHEN YOU LADS LEAVE HERE, I THINK YOU BOTH WILL PLAY A HARP!
OH, WILL WE REALLY? THAT'S JUST GRAND! I THINK THAT HARPS ARE AWF'LY SWEET!
AND YOU WILL LOOK LIKE ANGELS, TOO!
QUIT STALLIN', POP! WHEN DO WE EAT?
TUSH TUSH! MY LADS! OH, TUSH, TUSH, TUSH! AND DOUBLE TUSH! BE PATIENT, PLEASE!
2-9
© 1936 by Walt Disney Enterprises, Great Britain rights reserved
BUT WHILE WE SPEAK OF "TUSHES," TELL ME—
WHADDAYA THINK OF THESE?
!
!
!

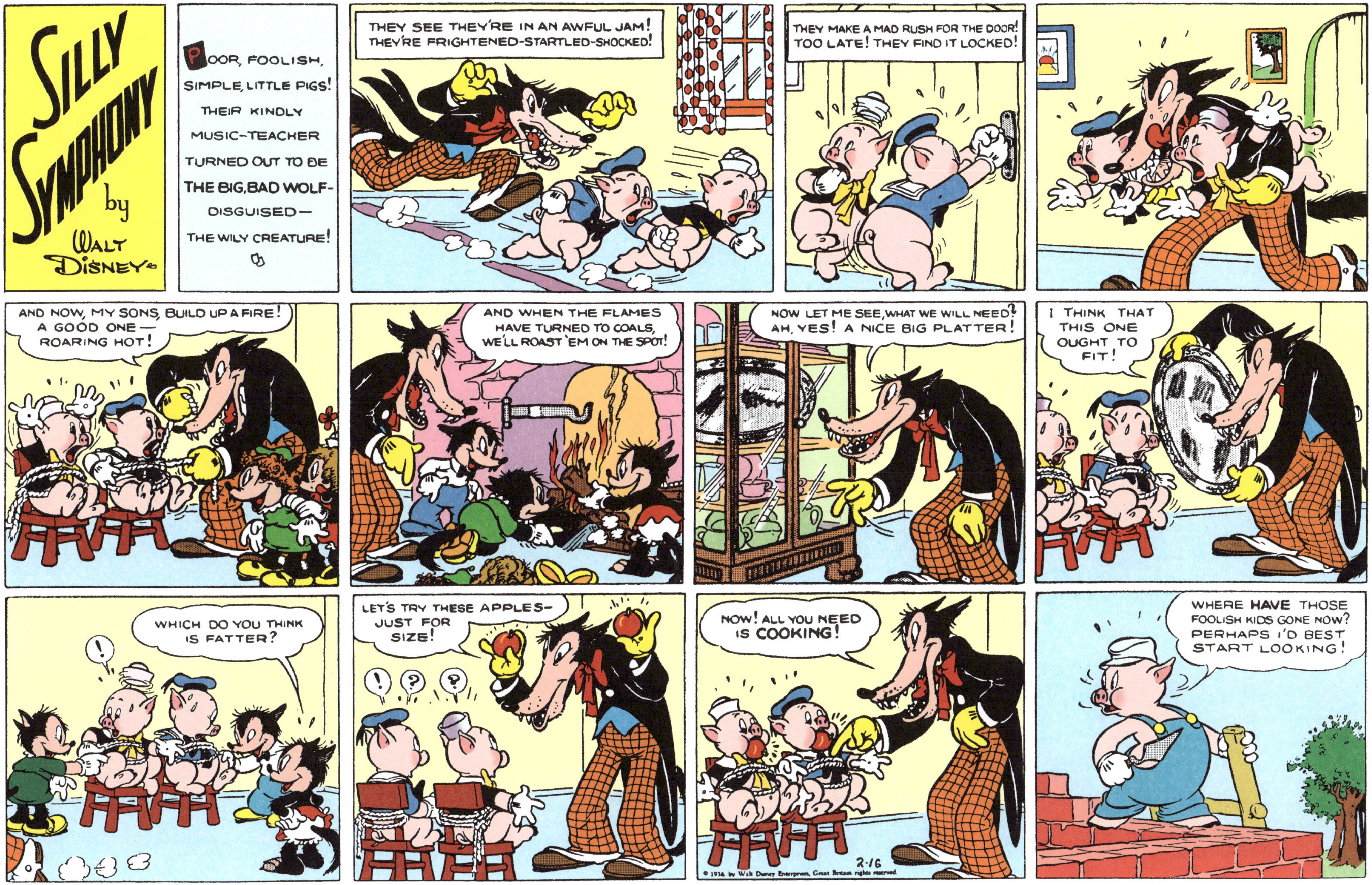
SILLY SYMPHONY by WALT DISNEY
POOR, FOOLISH, SIMPLE, LITTLE PIGS! THEIR KINDLY MUSIC-TEACHER TURNED OUT TO BE THE BIG, BAD WOLF- DISGUISED- THE WILY CREATURE!
THEY SEE THEY'RE IN AN AWFUL JAM! THEY'RE FRIGHTENED-STARTLED-SHOCKED!
THEY MAKE A MAD RUSH FOR THE DOOR! TOO LATE! THEY FIND IT LOCKED!
AND NOW, MY SONS, BUILD UP A FIRE! A GOOD ONE— ROARING HOT!
AND WHEN THE FLAMES HAVE TURNED TO COALS, WE'LL ROAST 'EM ON THE SPOT!
NOW LET ME SEE, WHAT WE WILL NEED? AH, YES! A NICE BIG PLATTER!
I THINK THAT THIS ONE OUGHT TO FIT!
WHICH DO YOU THINK IS FATTER?
LET'S TRY THESE APPLES- JUST FOR SIZE!
NOW! ALL YOU NEED IS COOKING!
2-16
© 1936 by Walt Disney Enterprises, Great Britain rights reserved
WHERE HAVE THOSE FOOLISH KIDS GONE NOW? PERHAPS I'D BEST START LOOKING!

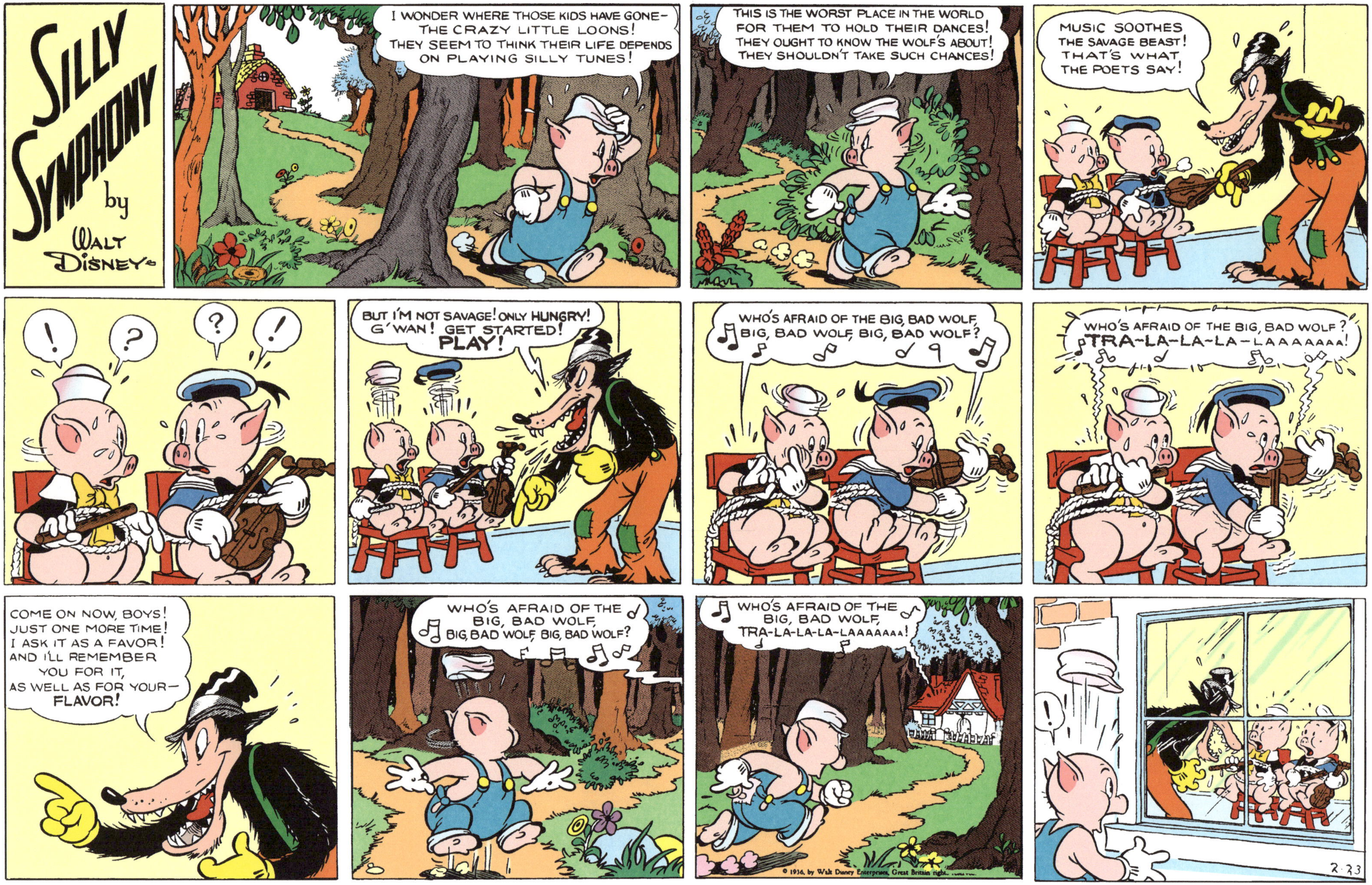

SILLY SYMPHONY
by
WALT DISNEY
I WONDER WHERE THOSE KIDS HAVE GONE– THE CRAZY LITTLE LOONS! THEY SEEM TO THINK THEIR LIFE DEPENDS ON PLAYING SILLY TUNES!
THIS IS THE WORST PLACE IN THE WORLD FOR THEM TO HOLD THEIR DANCES! THEY OUGHT TO KNOW THE WOLF'S ABOUT! THEY SHOULDN'T TAKE SUCH CHANCES!
MUSIC SOOTHES THE SAVAGE BEAST! THAT'S WHAT THE POETS SAY!
! ? ? !
BUT I'M NOT SAVAGE! ONLY HUNGRY! G'WAN! GET STARTED! PLAY!
WHO'S AFRAID OF THE BIG, BAD WOLF, BIG, BAD WOLF, BIG, BAD WOLF?
WHO'S AFRAID OF THE BIG, BAD WOLF? TRA-LA-LA-LA-LAAAAAAA!
COME ON NOW, BOYS! JUST ONE MORE TIME! I ASK IT AS A FAVOR! AND I'LL REMEMBER YOU FOR IT, AS WELL AS FOR YOUR– FLAVOR!
WHO'S AFRAID OF THE BIG, BAD WOLF, BIG, BAD WOLF, BIG, BAD WOLF?
WHO'S AFRAID OF THE BIG, BAD WOLF, TRA-LA-LA-LA-LAAAAAAA!
© 1936, by Walt Disney Enterprises, Great Britain
!
2-23

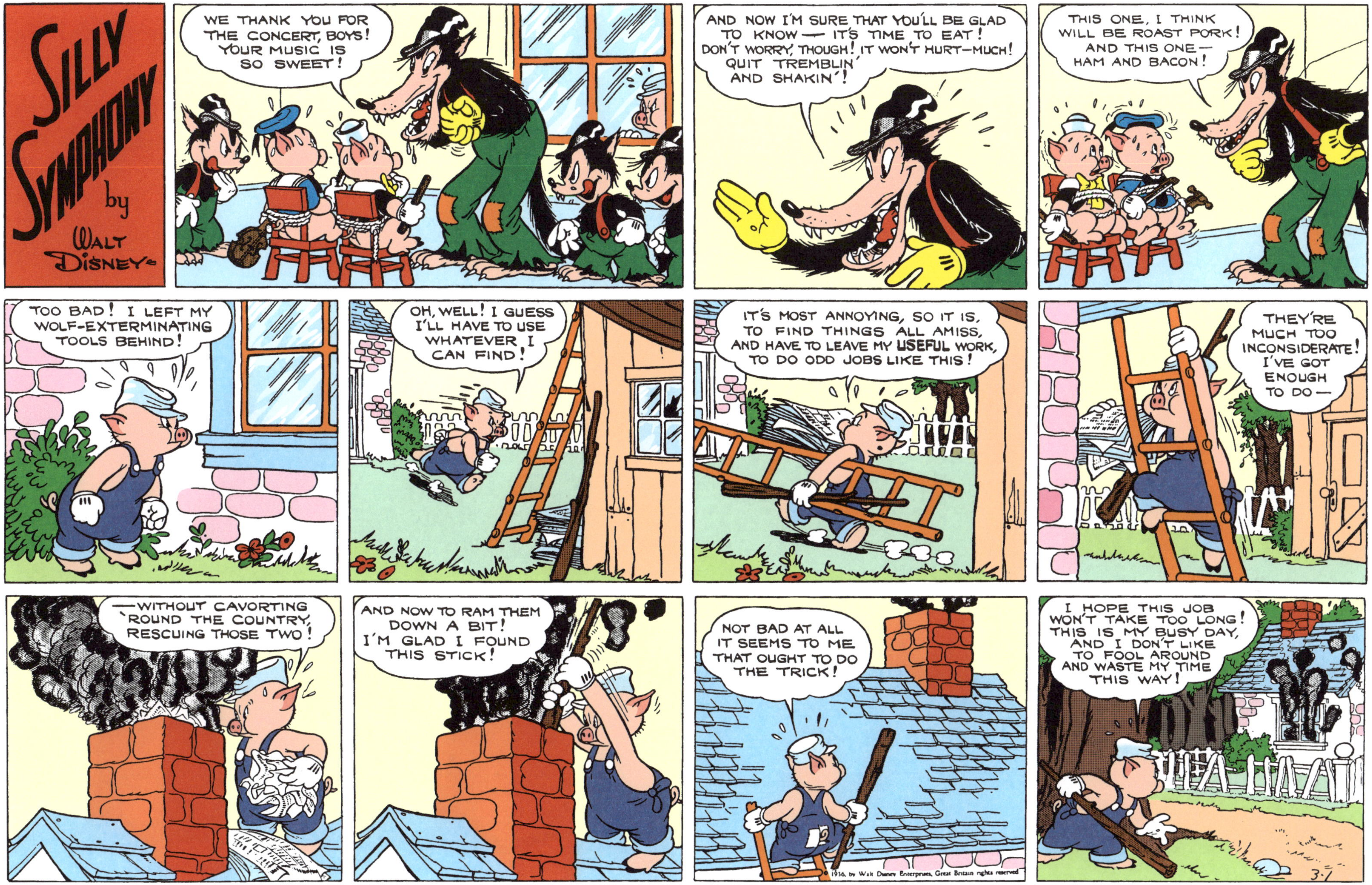
SILLY SYMPHONY
by
WALT DISNEY
WE THANK YOU FOR THE CONCERT, BOYS! YOUR MUSIC IS SO SWEET!
AND NOW I'M SURE THAT YOU'LL BE GLAD TO KNOW — IT'S TIME TO EAT! DON'T WORRY, THOUGH! IT WON'T HURT—MUCH! QUIT TREMBLIN' AND SHAKIN'!
THIS ONE, I THINK WILL BE ROAST PORK! AND THIS ONE— HAM AND BACON!
TOO BAD! I LEFT MY WOLF-EXTERMINATING TOOLS BEHIND!
OH, WELL! I GUESS I'LL HAVE TO USE WHATEVER I CAN FIND!
IT'S MOST ANNOYING, SO IT IS, TO FIND THINGS ALL AMISS, AND HAVE TO LEAVE MY USEFUL WORK, TO DO ODD JOBS LIKE THIS!
THEY'RE MUCH TOO INCONSIDERATE! I'VE GOT ENOUGH TO DO —
—WITHOUT CAVORTING 'ROUND THE COUNTRY, RESCUING THOSE TWO!
AND NOW TO RAM THEM DOWN A BIT! I'M GLAD I FOUND THIS STICK!
NOT BAD AT ALL IT SEEMS TO ME THAT OUGHT TO DO THE TRICK!
© 1936, by Walt Disney Enterprises, Great Britain rights reserved
I HOPE THIS JOB WON'T TAKE TOO LONG! THIS IS MY BUSY DAY, AND I DON'T LIKE TO FOOL AROUND AND WASTE MY TIME THIS WAY!
3-1

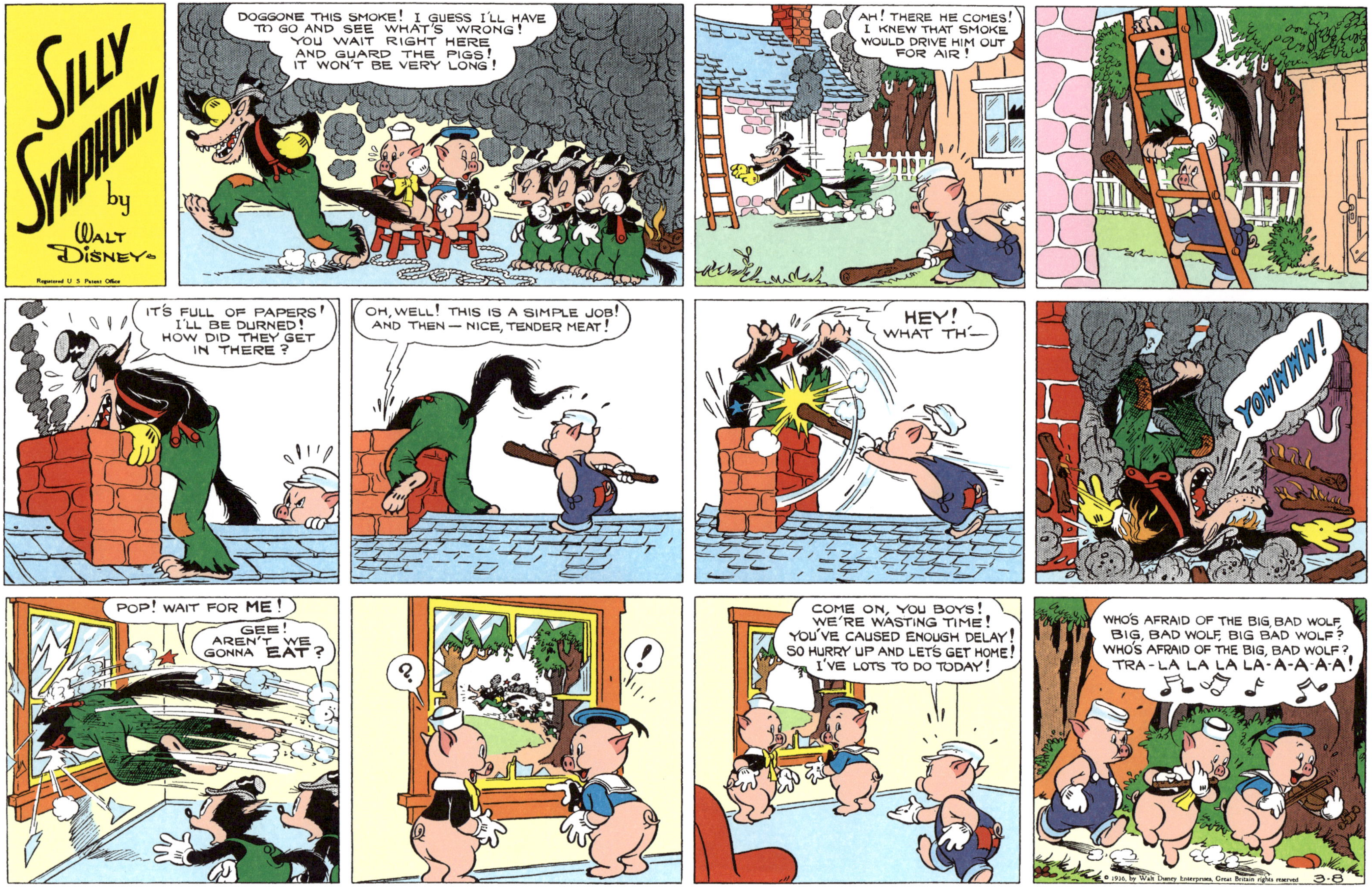
SILLY SYMPHONY
by
WALT DISNEY
Registered U S Patent Office
DOGGONE THIS SMOKE! I GUESS I'LL HAVE TO GO AND SEE WHAT'S WRONG! YOU WAIT RIGHT HERE AND GUARD THE PIGS! IT WON'T BE VERY LONG!
AH! THERE HE COMES! I KNEW THAT SMOKE WOULD DRIVE HIM OUT FOR AIR!
IT'S FULL OF PAPERS! I'LL BE DURNED! HOW DID THEY GET IN THERE?
OH, WELL! THIS IS A SIMPLE JOB! AND THEN — NICE, TENDER MEAT!
HEY! WHAT TH'—
YOWWWW!
POP! WAIT FOR ME!
GEE! AREN'T WE GONNA EAT?
?
!
COME ON, YOU BOYS! WE'RE WASTING TIME! YOU'VE CAUSED ENOUGH DELAY! SO HURRY UP AND LET'S GET HOME! I'VE LOTS TO DO TODAY!
WHO'S AFRAID OF THE BIG, BAD WOLF, BIG, BAD WOLF, BIG BAD WOLF? WHO'S AFRAID OF THE BIG, BAD WOLF? TRA-LA LA LA LA-A-A-A-A!
© 1936, by Walt Disney Enterprises, Great Britain rights reserved 3-8

SILLY SYMPHONY
by
WALT DISNEY
OUR BROTHER WORKS SO VERY HARD, I AM SURPRISED HE DOESN'T TIRE! PERHAPS WE OUGHT TO HELP HIM SOME!
O.K.! I WILL! I'LL LIGHT THE FIRE!
IN ALL THE TIME YOU'VE LIVED WITH ME, NOT ONE GOOD LICK OF WORK YOU'VE DONE! YOU'VE LOLLED AROUND, AND LOAFED AND SNOOZED! YET, IF YOU KNEW IT, WORK IS FUN!
THIS WORLD WAS MADE FOR WORKERS! NOT FOR THOSE WHO ONLY DANCE AND PLAY! SO START RIGHT NOW! MAKE UP YOUR MINDS TO DO ONE USEFUL DEED EACH DAY!
OUR BROTHER'S RIGHT! WE SHOULD REFORM! NO MORE WILL WE BE LAZY LOUTS!
WE'LL DO A GOOD TURN EV'RY DAY! HOORAY! WE'LL JOIN THE BOY SCOUTS!
THEY DO NOT KNOW THE BIG BAD WOLF HAS OVERHEARD THEIR LAST REMARK!
THEY'VE GIVEN HIM SOME IDEAS, TOO! AND HE IS HAPPY AS A LARK!
© 1936 by Walt Disney Enterprises Great Britain rights reserved
TO DO GOOD TURNS AND TIE NEW KNOTS! THOSE ARE THE THINGS THEY WANT TO LEARN!
DISGUISES
UNIFORMS
SNARES TRAPS
PIG LURES
O.K.—I'LL TIE 'EM UP IN KNOTS! AND THEN—I'LL DO 'EM TO A TURN!
B.B. WOLF
3-15

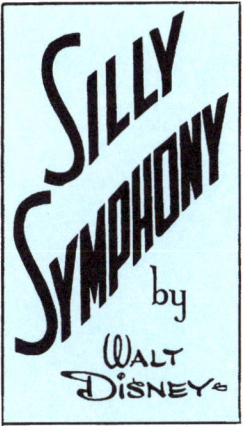

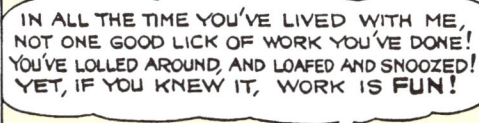

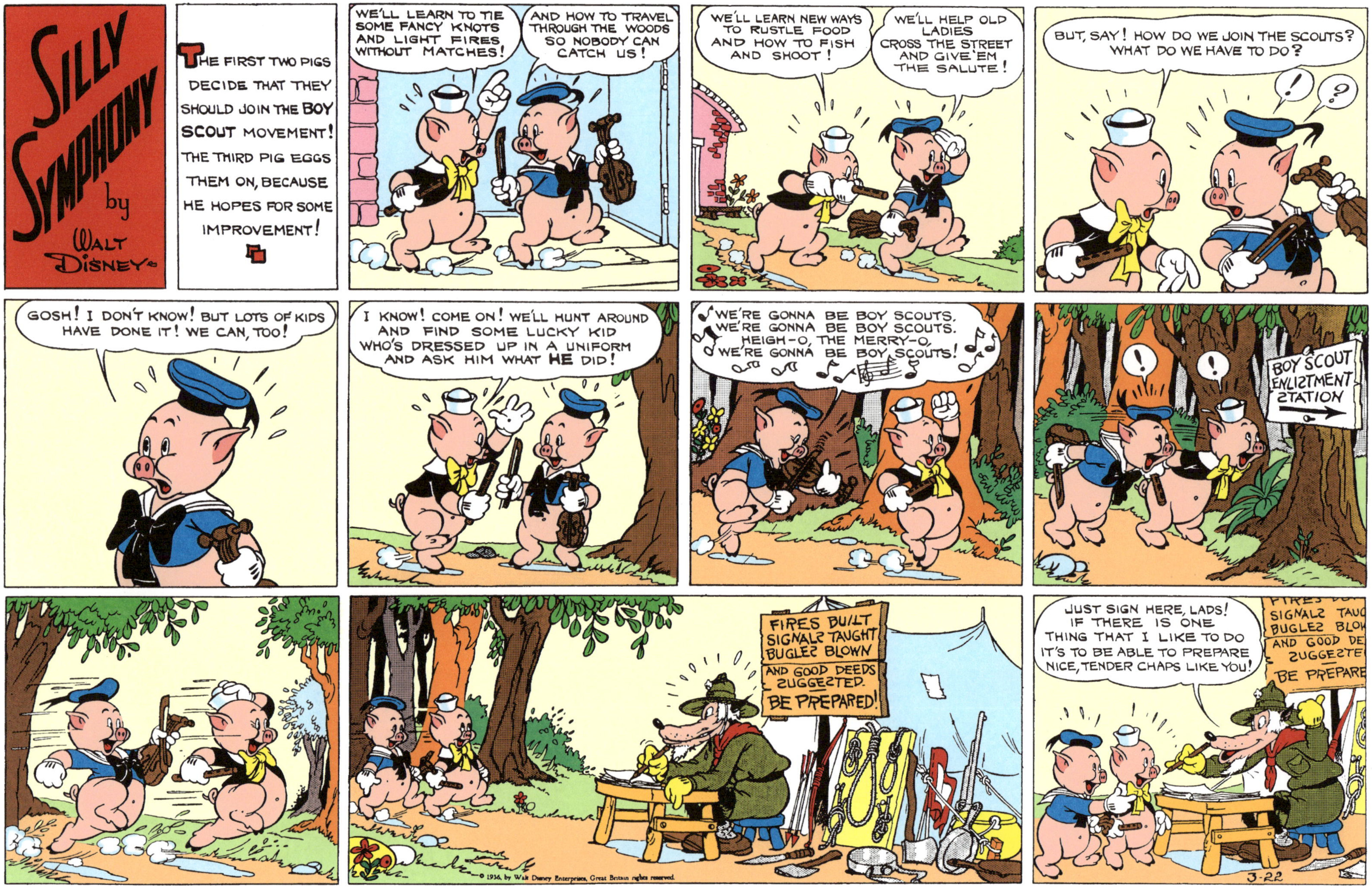
SILLY SYMPHONY
by
WALT DISNEY
THE FIRST TWO PIGS DECIDE THAT THEY SHOULD JOIN THE BOY SCOUT MOVEMENT! THE THIRD PIG EGGS THEM ON, BECAUSE HE HOPES FOR SOME IMPROVEMENT!
WE'LL LEARN TO TIE SOME FANCY KNOTS AND LIGHT FIRES WITHOUT MATCHES!
AND HOW TO TRAVEL THROUGH THE WOODS SO NOBODY CAN CATCH US!
WE'LL LEARN NEW WAYS TO RUSTLE FOOD AND HOW TO FISH AND SHOOT!
WE'LL HELP OLD LADIES CROSS THE STREET AND GIVE 'EM THE SALUTE!
BUT, SAY! HOW DO WE JOIN THE SCOUTS? WHAT DO WE HAVE TO DO?
GOSH! I DON'T KNOW! BUT LOTS OF KIDS HAVE DONE IT! WE CAN, TOO!
I KNOW! COME ON! WE'LL HUNT AROUND AND FIND SOME LUCKY KID WHO'S DRESSED UP IN A UNIFORM AND ASK HIM WHAT HE DID!
WE'RE GONNA BE BOY SCOUTS. WE'RE GONNA BE BOY SCOUTS. HEIGH-O, THE MERRY-O, WE'RE GONNA BE BOY SCOUTS!
BOY SCOUT ENLISTMENT STATION
FIRES BUILT SIGNALS TAUGHT BUGLES BLOWN
AND GOOD DEEDS SUGGESTED
BE PREPARED!
© 1936, by Walt Disney Enterprises, Great Britain rights reserved.
JUST SIGN HERE, LADS! IF THERE IS ONE THING THAT I LIKE TO DO IT'S TO BE ABLE TO PREPARE NICE, TENDER CHAPS LIKE YOU!
3-22

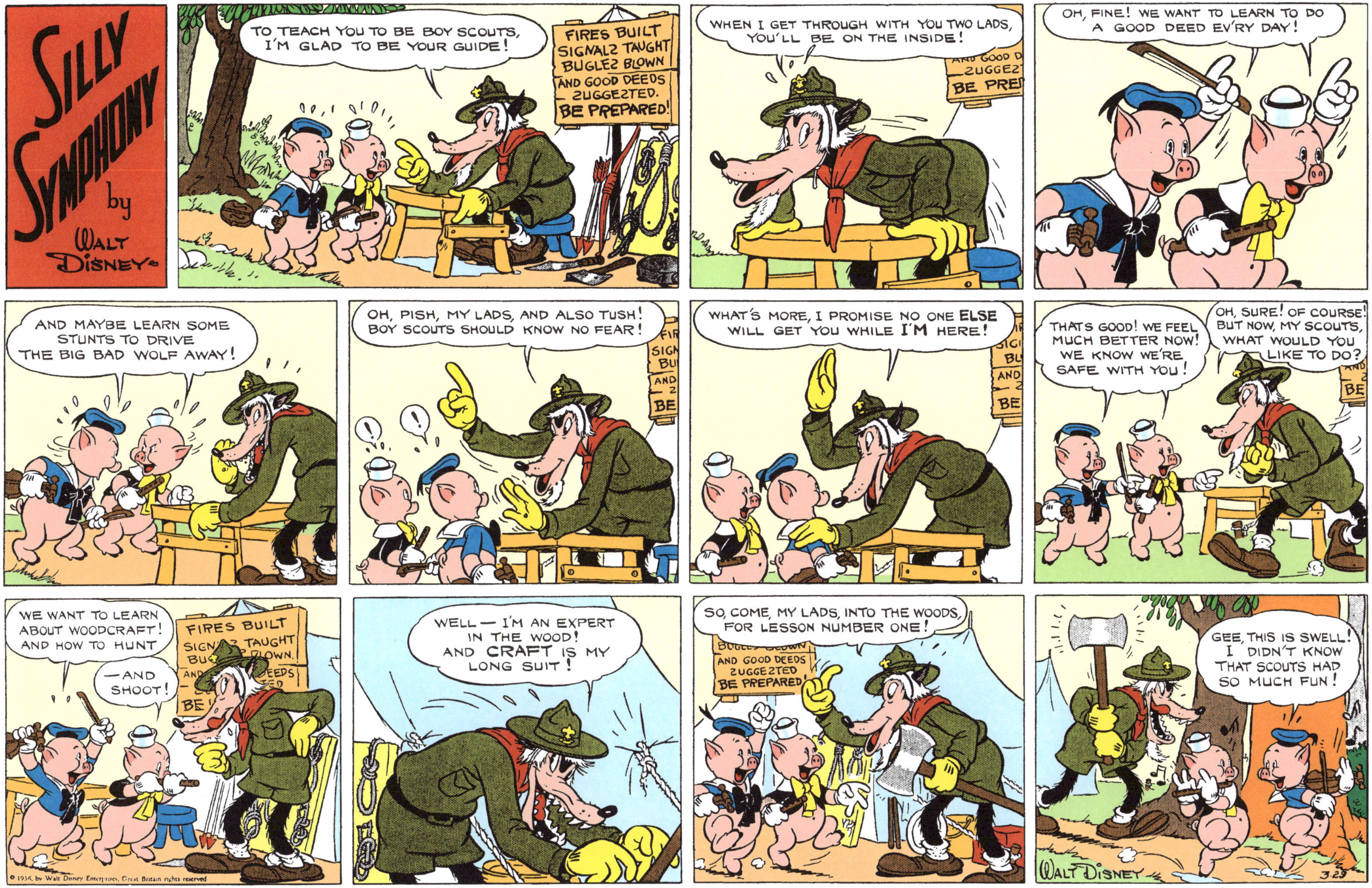
SILLY SYMPHONY
by WALT DISNEY
TO TEACH YOU TO BE BOY SCOUTS, I'M GLAD TO BE YOUR GUIDE!
FIRES BUILT SIGNALZ TAUGHT BUGLEZ BLOWN AND GOOD DEEDS ZUGGEZTED. BE PREPARED!
WHEN I GET THROUGH WITH YOU TWO LADS, YOU'LL BE ON THE INSIDE!
OH, FINE! WE WANT TO LEARN TO DO A GOOD DEED EV'RY DAY!
AND MAYBE LEARN SOME STUNTS TO DRIVE THE BIG BAD WOLF AWAY!
OH, PISH, MY LADS, AND ALSO TUSH! BOY SCOUTS SHOULD KNOW NO FEAR!
WHAT'S MORE, I PROMISE NO ONE ELSE WILL GET YOU WHILE I'M HERE!
THAT'S GOOD! WE FEEL MUCH BETTER NOW! WE KNOW WE'RE SAFE WITH YOU!
OH, SURE! OF COURSE! BUT NOW, MY SCOUTS, WHAT WOULD YOU LIKE TO DO?
WE WANT TO LEARN ABOUT WOODCRAFT! AND HOW TO HUNT
—AND SHOOT!
© 1936, by Walt Disney Enterprises, Great Britain rights reserved
WELL — I'M AN EXPERT IN THE WOOD! AND CRAFT IS MY LONG SUIT!
SO, COME, MY LADS, INTO THE WOODS, FOR LESSON NUMBER ONE!
AND GOOD DEEDS ZUGGEZTED BE PREPARED!
GEE, THIS IS SWELL! I DIDN'T KNOW THAT SCOUTS HAD SO MUCH FUN!
WALT DISNEY
3-29

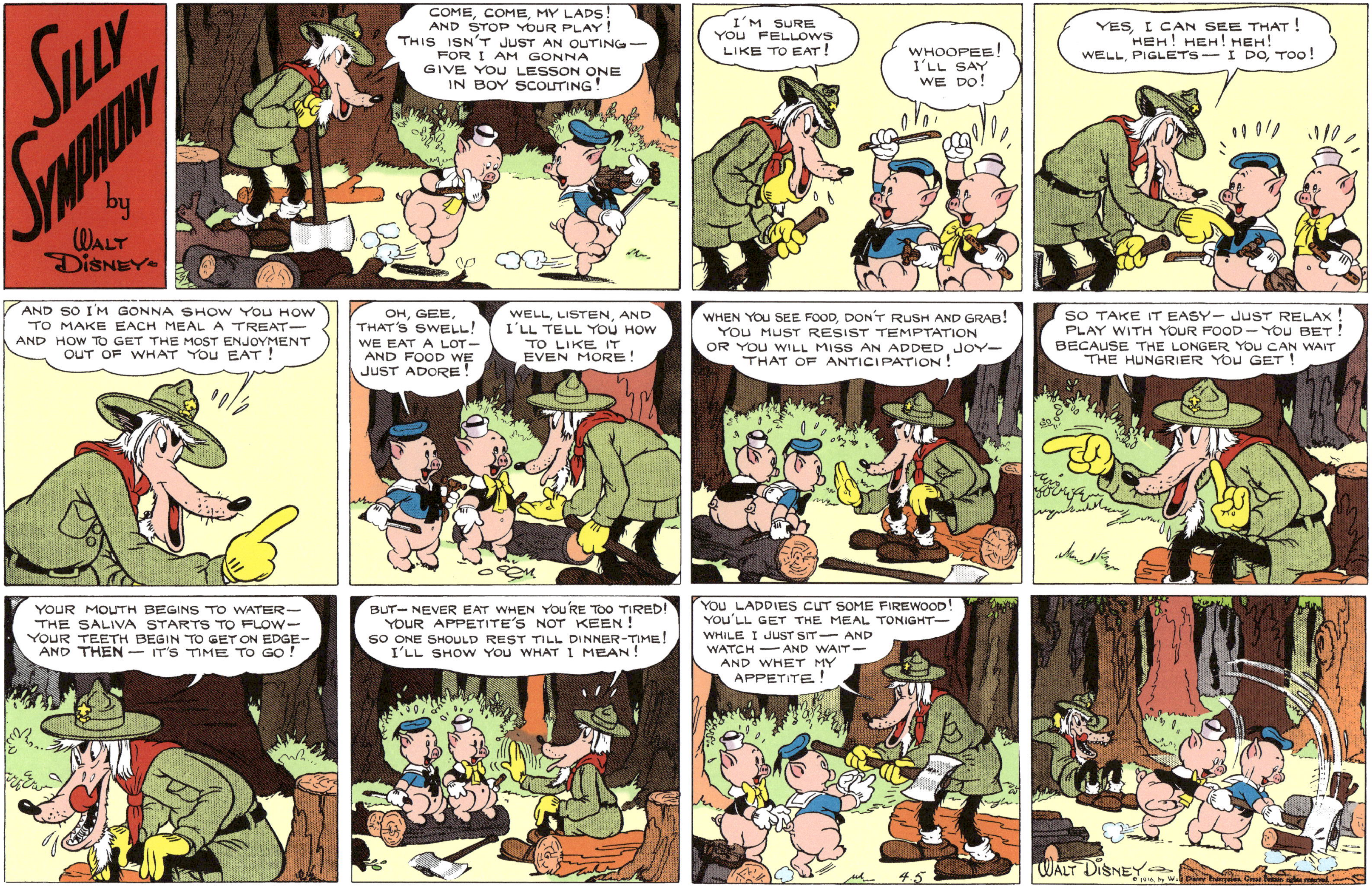
SILLY SYMPHONY
by
WALT DISNEY
COME, COME, MY LADS! AND STOP YOUR PLAY! THIS ISN'T JUST AN OUTING— FOR I AM GONNA GIVE YOU LESSON ONE IN BOY SCOUTING!
I'M SURE YOU FELLOWS LIKE TO EAT!
WHOOPEE! I'LL SAY WE DO!
YES, I CAN SEE THAT! HEH! HEH! HEH! WELL, PIGLETS— I DO, TOO!
AND SO I'M GONNA SHOW YOU HOW TO MAKE EACH MEAL A TREAT— AND HOW TO GET THE MOST ENJOYMENT OUT OF WHAT YOU EAT!
OH, GEE, THAT'S SWELL! WE EAT A LOT— AND FOOD WE JUST ADORE!
WELL, LISTEN, AND I'LL TELL YOU HOW TO LIKE IT EVEN MORE!
WHEN YOU SEE FOOD, DON'T RUSH AND GRAB! YOU MUST RESIST TEMPTATION OR YOU WILL MISS AN ADDED JOY— THAT OF ANTICIPATION!
SO TAKE IT EASY— JUST RELAX! PLAY WITH YOUR FOOD—YOU BET! BECAUSE THE LONGER YOU CAN WAIT THE HUNGRIER YOU GET!
YOUR MOUTH BEGINS TO WATER— THE SALIVA STARTS TO FLOW— YOUR TEETH BEGIN TO GET ON EDGE— AND THEN— IT'S TIME TO GO!
BUT— NEVER EAT WHEN YOU'RE TOO TIRED! YOUR APPETITE'S NOT KEEN! SO ONE SHOULD REST TILL DINNER-TIME! I'LL SHOW YOU WHAT I MEAN!
YOU LADDIES CUT SOME FIREWOOD! YOU'LL GET THE MEAL TONIGHT— WHILE I JUST SIT— AND WATCH —AND WAIT— AND WHET MY APPETITE!
4-5
WALT DISNEY

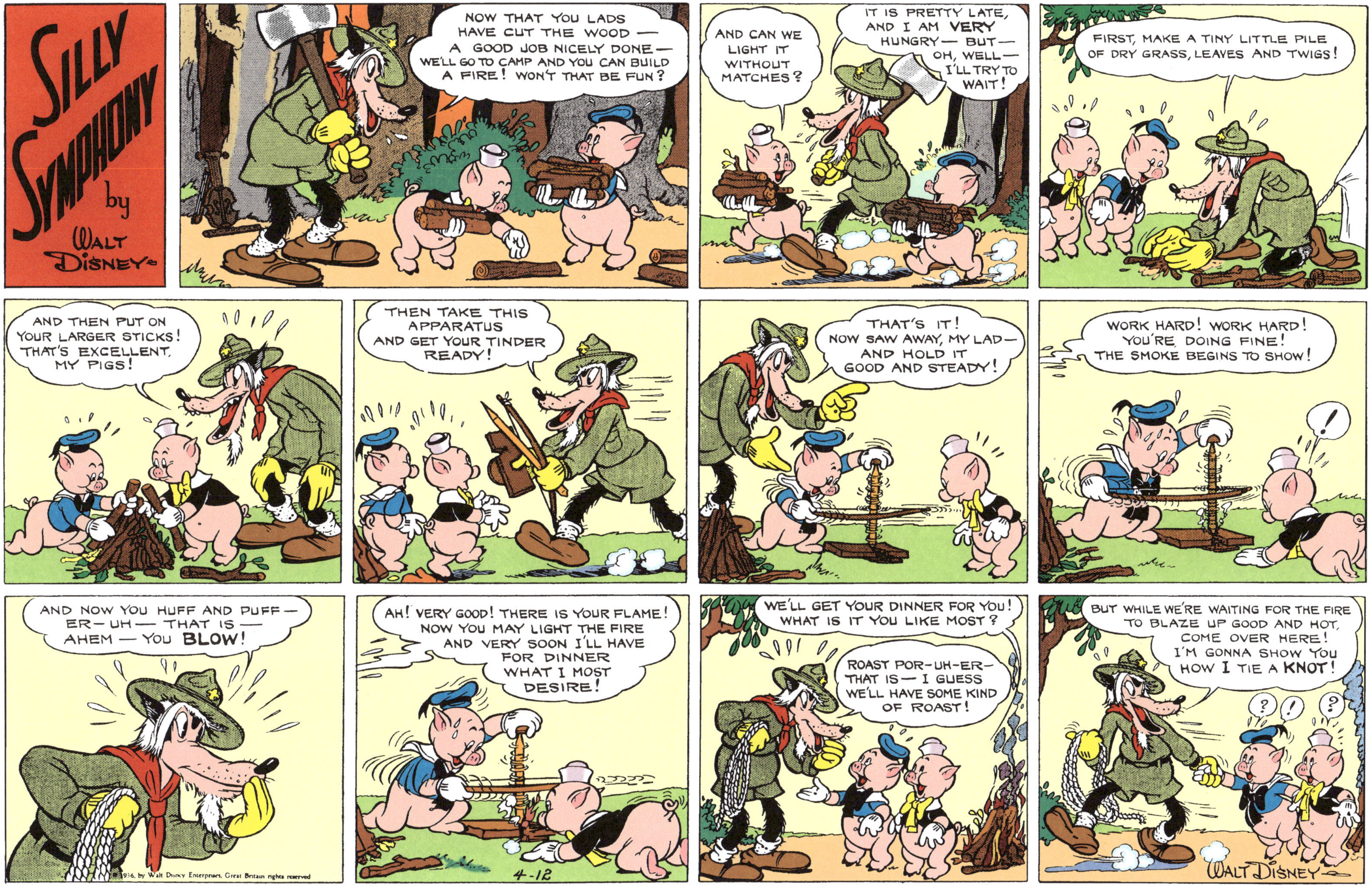
SILLY SYMPHONY by WALT DISNEY
NOW THAT YOU LADS HAVE CUT THE WOOD — A GOOD JOB NICELY DONE — WE'LL GO TO CAMP AND YOU CAN BUILD A FIRE! WON'T THAT BE FUN?
AND CAN WE LIGHT IT WITHOUT MATCHES?
IT IS PRETTY LATE, AND I AM VERY HUNGRY — BUT — OH, WELL — I'LL TRY TO WAIT!
FIRST, MAKE A TINY LITTLE PILE OF DRY GRASS, LEAVES AND TWIGS!
AND THEN PUT ON YOUR LARGER STICKS! THAT'S EXCELLENT, MY PIGS!
THEN TAKE THIS APPARATUS AND GET YOUR TINDER READY!
THAT'S IT! NOW SAW AWAY, MY LAD — AND HOLD IT GOOD AND STEADY!
WORK HARD! WORK HARD! YOU'RE DOING FINE! THE SMOKE BEGINS TO SHOW!
!
AND NOW YOU HUFF AND PUFF — ER — UH — THAT IS — AHEM — YOU BLOW!
© 1936, by Walt Disney Enterprises, Great Britain rights reserved
AH! VERY GOOD! THERE IS YOUR FLAME! NOW YOU MAY LIGHT THE FIRE AND VERY SOON I'LL HAVE FOR DINNER WHAT I MOST DESIRE!
4-12
WE'LL GET YOUR DINNER FOR YOU! WHAT IS IT YOU LIKE MOST?
ROAST POR-UH-ER — THAT IS — I GUESS WE'LL HAVE SOME KIND OF ROAST!
BUT WHILE WE'RE WAITING FOR THE FIRE TO BLAZE UP GOOD AND HOT, COME OVER HERE! I'M GONNA SHOW YOU HOW I TIE A KNOT!
?! ?
WALT DISNEY

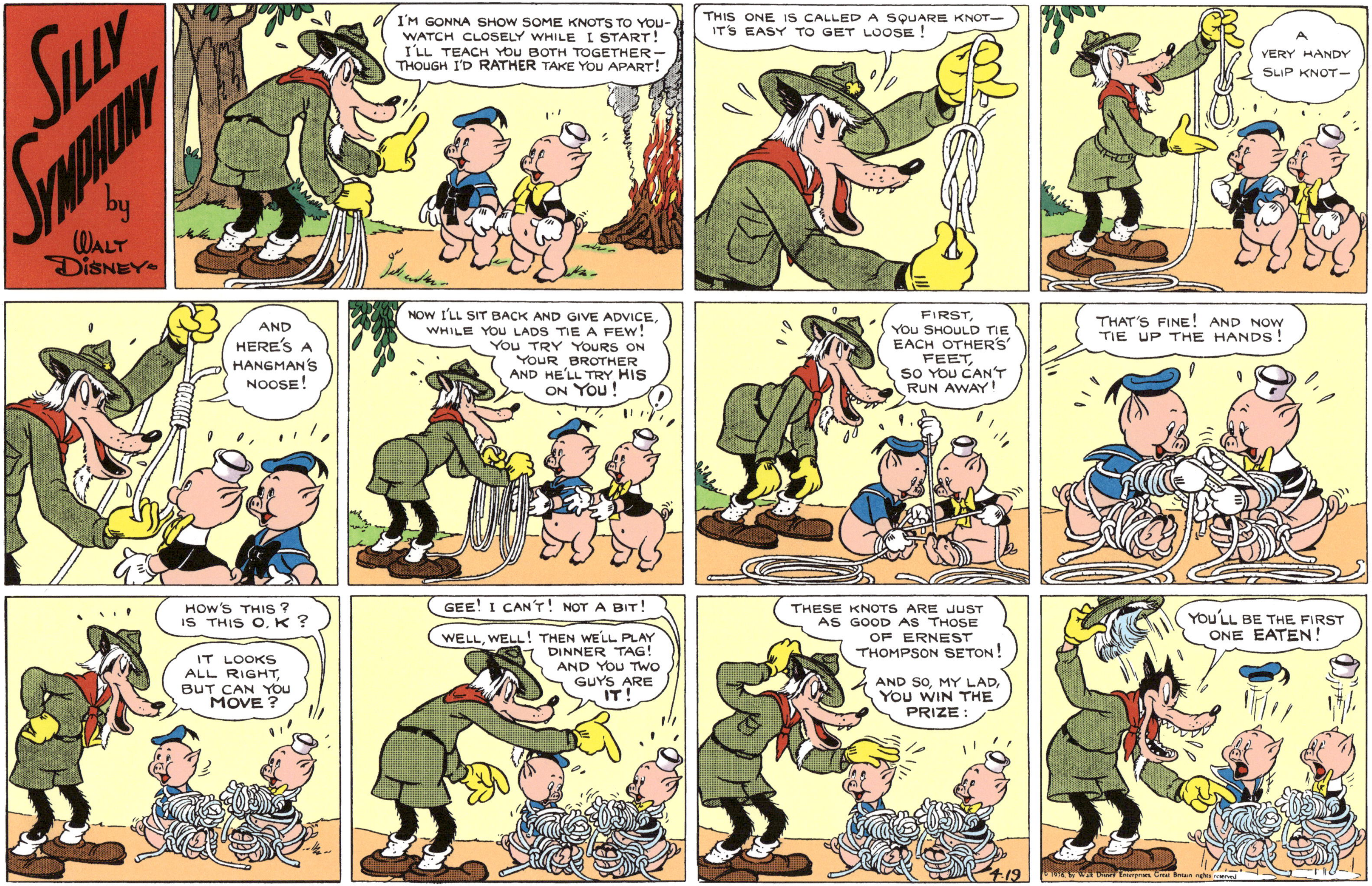
SILLY SYMPHONY
by
WALT DISNEY
I'M GONNA SHOW SOME KNOTS TO YOU— WATCH CLOSELY WHILE I START! I'LL TEACH YOU BOTH TOGETHER— THOUGH I'D RATHER TAKE YOU APART!
THIS ONE IS CALLED A SQUARE KNOT— IT'S EASY TO GET LOOSE!
A VERY HANDY SLIP KNOT—
AND HERE'S A HANGMAN'S NOOSE!
NOW I'LL SIT BACK AND GIVE ADVICE, WHILE YOU LADS TIE A FEW! YOU TRY YOURS ON YOUR BROTHER AND HE'LL TRY HIS ON YOU!
!
FIRST, YOU SHOULD TIE EACH OTHER'S FEET, SO YOU CAN'T RUN AWAY!
THAT'S FINE! AND NOW TIE UP THE HANDS!
HOW'S THIS? IS THIS O.K?
IT LOOKS ALL RIGHT, BUT CAN YOU MOVE?
GEE! I CAN'T! NOT A BIT!
WELL, WELL! THEN WE'LL PLAY DINNER TAG! AND YOU TWO GUYS ARE IT!
THESE KNOTS ARE JUST AS GOOD AS THOSE OF ERNEST THOMPSON SETON!
AND SO, MY LAD, YOU WIN THE PRIZE:
4-19
YOU'LL BE THE FIRST ONE EATEN!
© 1936, by Walt Disney Enterprises, Great Britain rights reserved

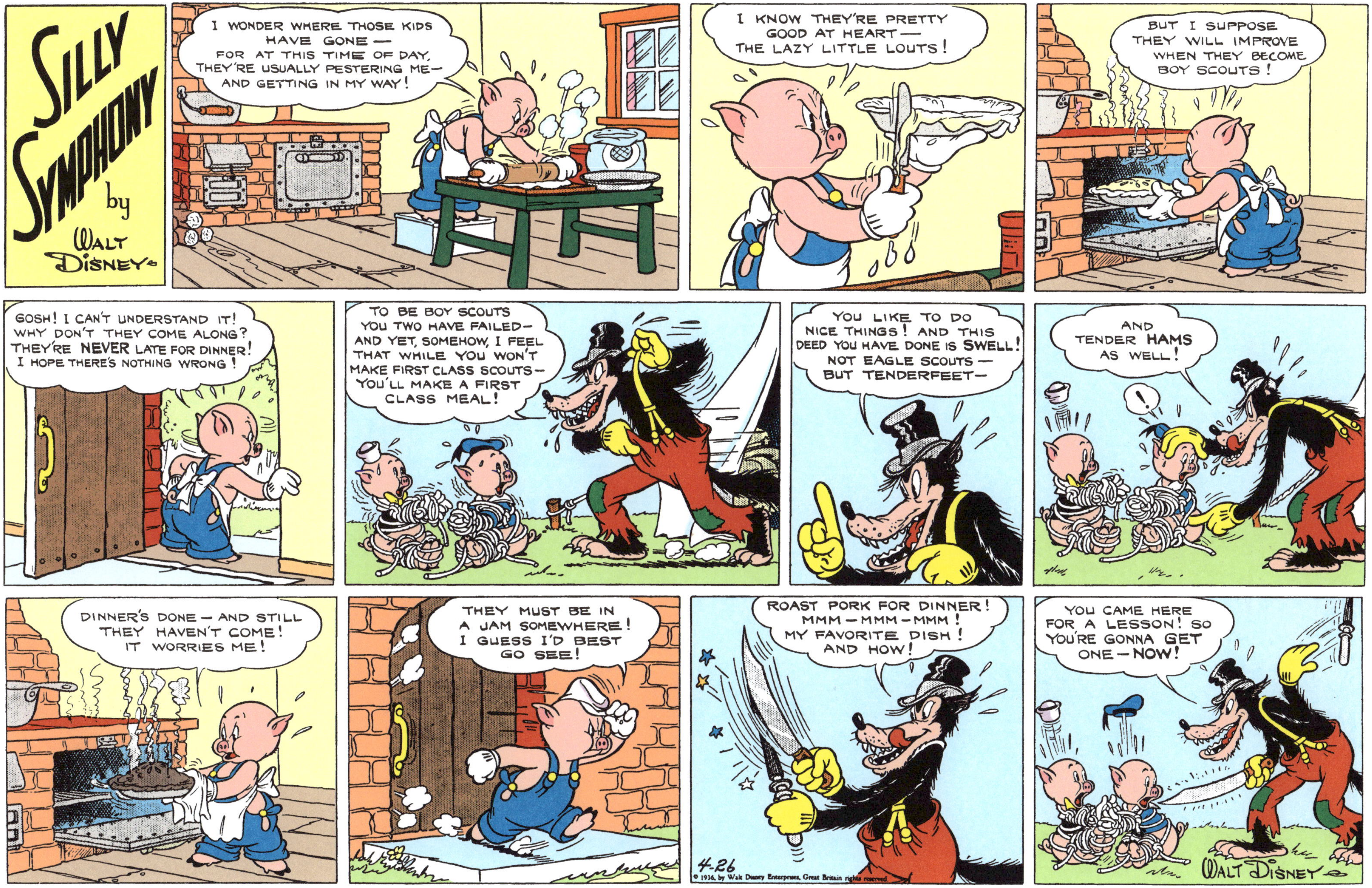
SILLY SYMPHONY by WALT DISNEY
I WONDER WHERE THOSE KIDS HAVE GONE — FOR AT THIS TIME OF DAY, THEY'RE USUALLY PESTERING ME — AND GETTING IN MY WAY!
I KNOW THEY'RE PRETTY GOOD AT HEART — THE LAZY LITTLE LOUTS!
BUT I SUPPOSE THEY WILL IMPROVE WHEN THEY BECOME BOY SCOUTS!
GOSH! I CAN'T UNDERSTAND IT! WHY DON'T THEY COME ALONG? THEY'RE NEVER LATE FOR DINNER! I HOPE THERE'S NOTHING WRONG!
TO BE BOY SCOUTS YOU TWO HAVE FAILED — AND YET, SOMEHOW, I FEEL THAT WHILE YOU WON'T MAKE FIRST CLASS SCOUTS — YOU'LL MAKE A FIRST CLASS MEAL!
YOU LIKE TO DO NICE THINGS! AND THIS DEED YOU HAVE DONE IS SWELL! NOT EAGLE SCOUTS — BUT TENDERFEET —
AND TENDER HAMS AS WELL!
!
DINNER'S DONE — AND STILL THEY HAVEN'T COME! IT WORRIES ME!
THEY MUST BE IN A JAM SOMEWHERE! I GUESS I'D BEST GO SEE!
ROAST PORK FOR DINNER! MMM — MMM — MMM! MY FAVORITE DISH! AND HOW!
4-26
© 1936, by Walt Disney Enterprises, Great Britain rights reserved.
YOU CAME HERE FOR A LESSON! SO YOU'RE GONNA GET ONE — NOW!
WALT DISNEY

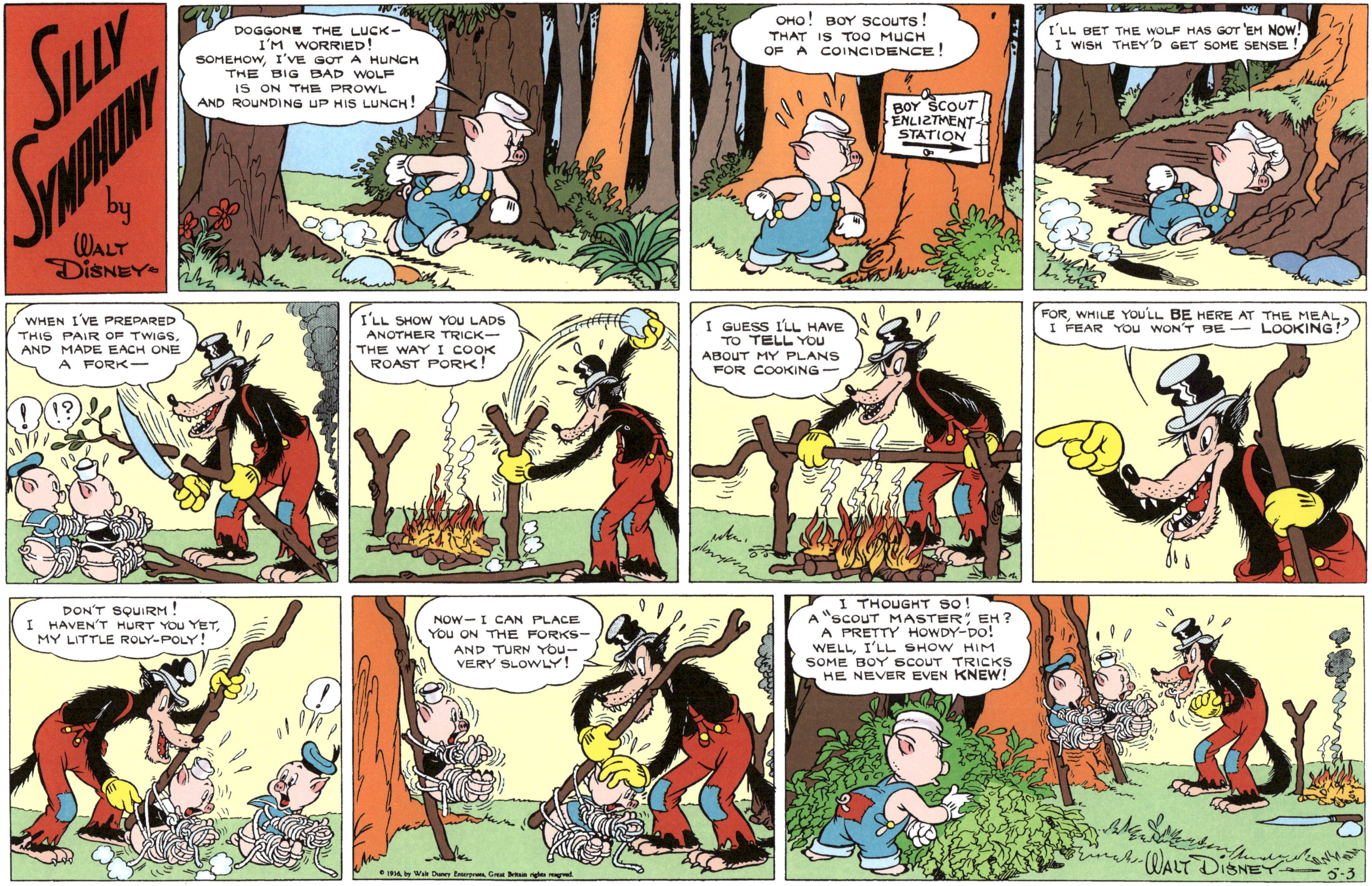

Silly Symphony by Walt Disney
DOGGONE THE LUCK— I'M WORRIED! SOMEHOW, I'VE GOT A HUNCH THE BIG BAD WOLF IS ON THE PROWL AND ROUNDING UP HIS LUNCH!
OHO! BOY SCOUTS! THAT IS TOO MUCH OF A COINCIDENCE!
BOY SCOUT ENLIZTMENT STATION
I'LL BET THE WOLF HAS GOT 'EM NOW! I WISH THEY'D GET SOME SENSE!
WHEN I'VE PREPARED THIS PAIR OF TWIGS, AND MADE EACH ONE A FORK—
!
!?
I'LL SHOW YOU LADS ANOTHER TRICK— THE WAY I COOK ROAST PORK!
I GUESS I'LL HAVE TO TELL YOU ABOUT MY PLANS FOR COOKING—
FOR, WHILE YOU'LL BE HERE AT THE MEAL, I FEAR YOU WON'T BE — LOOKING!
DON'T SQUIRM! I HAVEN'T HURT YOU YET, MY LITTLE ROLY-POLY!
!
NOW— I CAN PLACE YOU ON THE FORKS— AND TURN YOU— VERY SLOWLY!
© 1936, by Walt Disney Enterprises, Great Britain rights reserved.
I THOUGHT SO! A "SCOUT MASTER," EH? A PRETTY HOWDY-DO! WELL, I'LL SHOW HIM SOME BOY SCOUT TRICKS HE NEVER EVEN KNEW!
WALT DISNEY
5-3

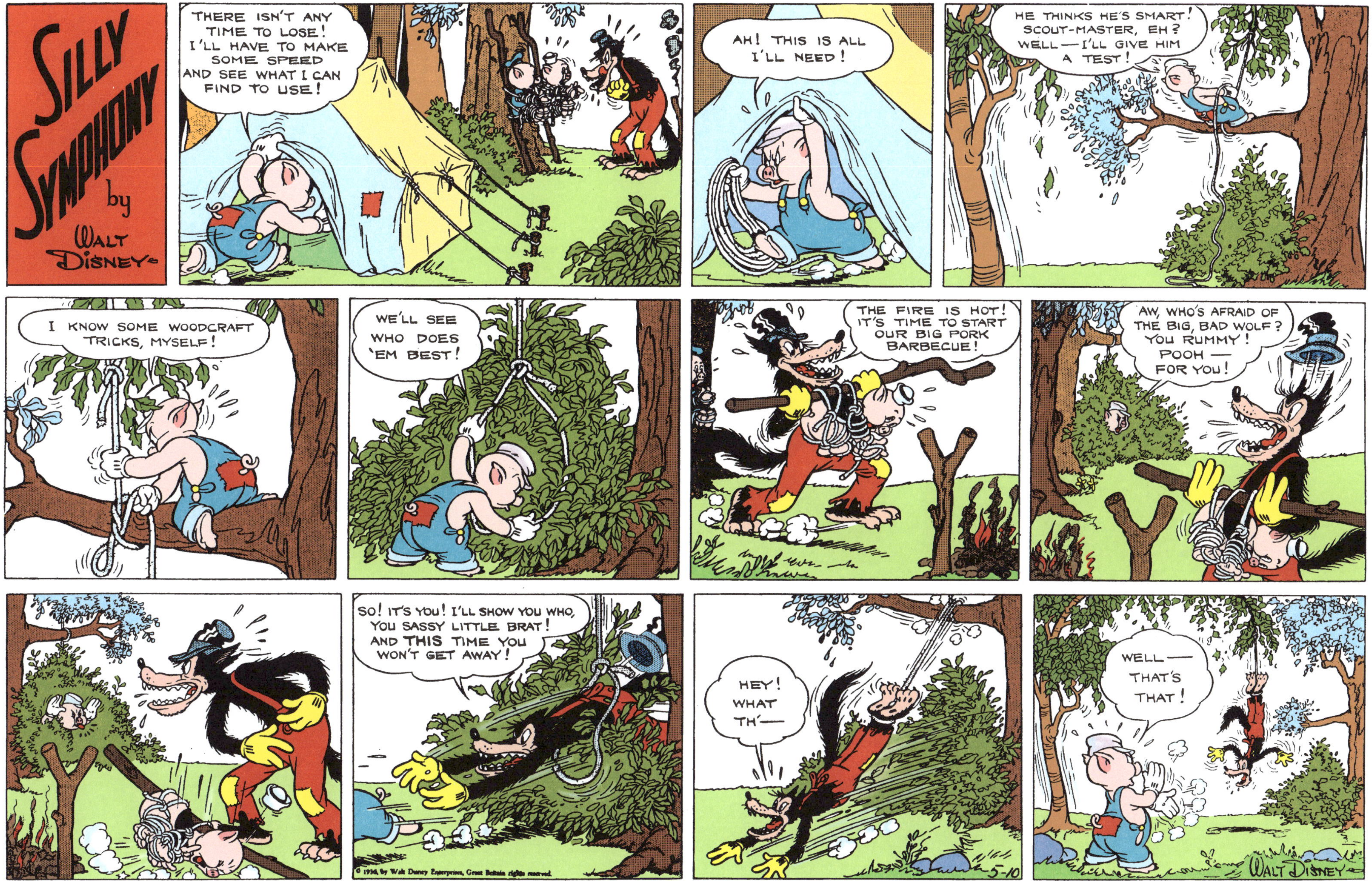
SILLY SYMPHONY by WALT DISNEY
THERE ISN'T ANY TIME TO LOSE! I'LL HAVE TO MAKE SOME SPEED AND SEE WHAT I CAN FIND TO USE!
AH! THIS IS ALL I'LL NEED!
HE THINKS HE'S SMART! SCOUT-MASTER, EH? WELL—I'LL GIVE HIM A TEST!
I KNOW SOME WOODCRAFT TRICKS, MYSELF!
WE'LL SEE WHO DOES 'EM BEST!
THE FIRE IS HOT! IT'S TIME TO START OUR BIG PORK BARBECUE!
AW, WHO'S AFRAID OF THE BIG, BAD WOLF? YOU RUMMY! POOH — FOR YOU!
SO! IT'S YOU! I'LL SHOW YOU WHO, YOU SASSY LITTLE BRAT! AND THIS TIME YOU WON'T GET AWAY!
HEY! WHAT TH'—
WELL— THAT'S THAT!
5-10
WALT DISNEY

SILLY SYMPHONY
by
WALT DISNEY
YOU CRAZY KIDS! YOU SEEM TO THINK THAT ALL I HAVE TO DO—
—IS GO AROUND THE WHOLE DAY LONG, JUST RESCUING YOU TWO!
AND YOU, "SCOUT-MASTER," YOU ARE LUCKY THAT I'M TENDER-HEARTED—AND ALSO THAT YOU DIDN'T FINISH DOING WHAT YOU STARTED!
I KNOW—YOU DIDN'T HARM THEM MUCH! BUT IF YOU HAD—YOU RAT—I'LL SHOW YOU WHAT I WOULD HAVE DONE!
THIS—
AND THIS—
AND THAT!
YOU SEE? THAT'S WHAT I WOULD HAVE DONE, BUT I WON'T DO IT! NO! I WOULDN'T EVEN THINK OF IT! SO QUIT YOUR HOWLING SO!
YOU'LL HAVE NO TROUBLE GETTING DOWN—SO DON'T GIVE UP YOUR HOPES! YOU SAY YOU'RE A SCOUT-MASTER—SO I'M SURE YOU KNOW THE ROPES!
WE'LL LEAVE HIM HANGING WHERE HE IS—A NICE REPENTANT SINNER! AND HURRY HOME, WHERE YOU TWO KIDS CAN EAT—NOT BE—A DINNER!
WHO'S AFRAID OF THE BIG, BAD WOLF? BIG, BAD WOLF, BIG BAD WOLF? WHO'S AFRAID OF THE BIG, BAD WOLF? TRA-LA-LA-LA-LA-A-A-A!
© 1936, by Walt Disney Enterprises. Great Britain rights reserved.
5-17
WALT DISNEY

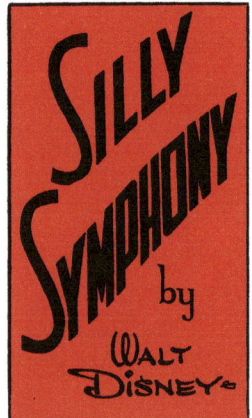

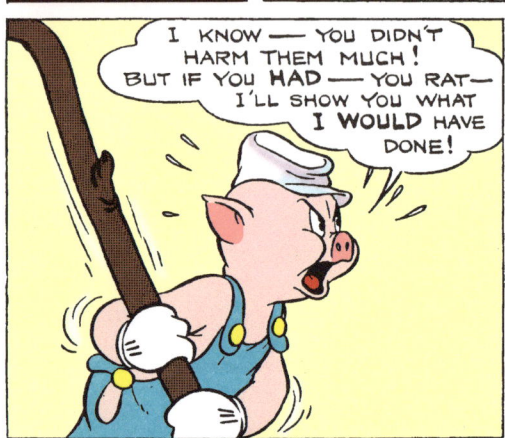

SILLY SYMPHONY
by WALT DISNEY
YOU KIDS HAVE BEEN TOO LUCKY! FOR YEARS, YOU'VE BEEN IN SCRAPES, AND MANAGED TO GET OUT OF THEM BY NARROWEST ESCAPES!
?
?
YOU WOULDN'T BE HERE NOW, EXCEPT FOR LUCKY BREAKS — AND ME! AND IF YOUR LUCK SHOULD TURN SOME DAY, WHERE DO YOU THINK YOU'D BE?
WE'VE GOT TO HAVE A SIGNAL YOU CAN USE WHEN DANGER'S NEAR!
YOU'VE BEEN TOO LUCKY FOR TOO LONG — AND IT CAN'T LAST, I FEAR!
I'M MAKING YOU THIS WHISTLE! WHEN THE WOLF COMES INTO VIEW, YOU SIMPLY BLOW — AND I WILL HEAR, AND COME AND RESCUE YOU!
THERE NOW! IT'S FINISHED! AND I SAY THAT IT LOOKS PRETTY NEAT!
BUT ARE YOU SURE THAT IT WILL BLOW?
HUH! YOU JUST LISTEN!
FWEEEET!
WELL, HERE YOU ARE! AND GUARD IT WELL!
YOU BET WE WILL! AND HOW! 'CAUSE IT PROTECTS US FROM THE WOLF! HE'LL NEVER CATCH US NOW!
WHO'S AFRAID OF THE BIG, BAD WOLF, BIG, BAD WOLF, BIG BAD WOLF? WHO'S AFRAID OF THE BIG, BAD WOLF?
© 1936, by Walt Disney Enterprises, Great Britain rights reserved
FWEET FWEET FWEET FWEET FWEEEEEEEET!
WALT DISNEY 5-24

SILLY SYMPHONY
by
WALT DISNEY
I'VE GOT TO GO OUT, AND I WANT YOU TWO TO STAY, RIGHT HERE, FOR IN THE HOUSE I'LL KNOW YOU'RE SAFE! THERE'S NOT A THING TO FEAR!
UNCLE OTTO
BUT IF THE BIG BAD WOLF COMES 'ROUND, YOU BOTH KNOW WHAT TO DO — JUST BLOW THAT WHISTLE! I WILL HEAR AND COME AND RESCUE YOU!
OH, SHUCKS! DON'T WORRY ABOUT US! WE'RE ALWAYS ON OUR GUARD! BUT IF HE COMES, WE'LL WHISTLE!
AND WHAT'S MORE, WE'LL WHISTLE HARD!
REMEMBER MY INSTRUCTIONS, THEN— AND DON'T YOU DARE FORGET 'EM! AND KEEP YOUR HEADS! FOR IF YOU DON'T, THE WOLF IS APT TO GET 'EM!
THOSE CRAZY KIDS! THEY SEE THE WOLF— AND ALMOST DIE OF FRIGHT! BUT YET THEY'RE VERY, VERY BRAVE— WHEN HE IS OUT OF SIGHT!
I THINK THE WISEST THING TO DO IS SEE IF I CAN SNEAK BACK HOME AND GIVE THE BOYS A TEST!
A WOLF DRILL, SO TO SPEAK!
OPEN THE DOOR AND LET ME IN!
HMMM! NOT A SOUND! THAT'S QUEER! I WONDER IF THEY POSSIBLY HAVE OVERCOME THEIR FEAR!
© 1936, by Walt Disney Enterprises, World rights reserved
THEY DIDN'T SIGNAL ME AT ALL! PERHAPS— AT LAST— THEY'RE MEN! I'LL GO INSIDE AND TELL THEM THAT—
NOPE! GUESS I'M WRONG AGAIN!
WALT DISNEY
5-31

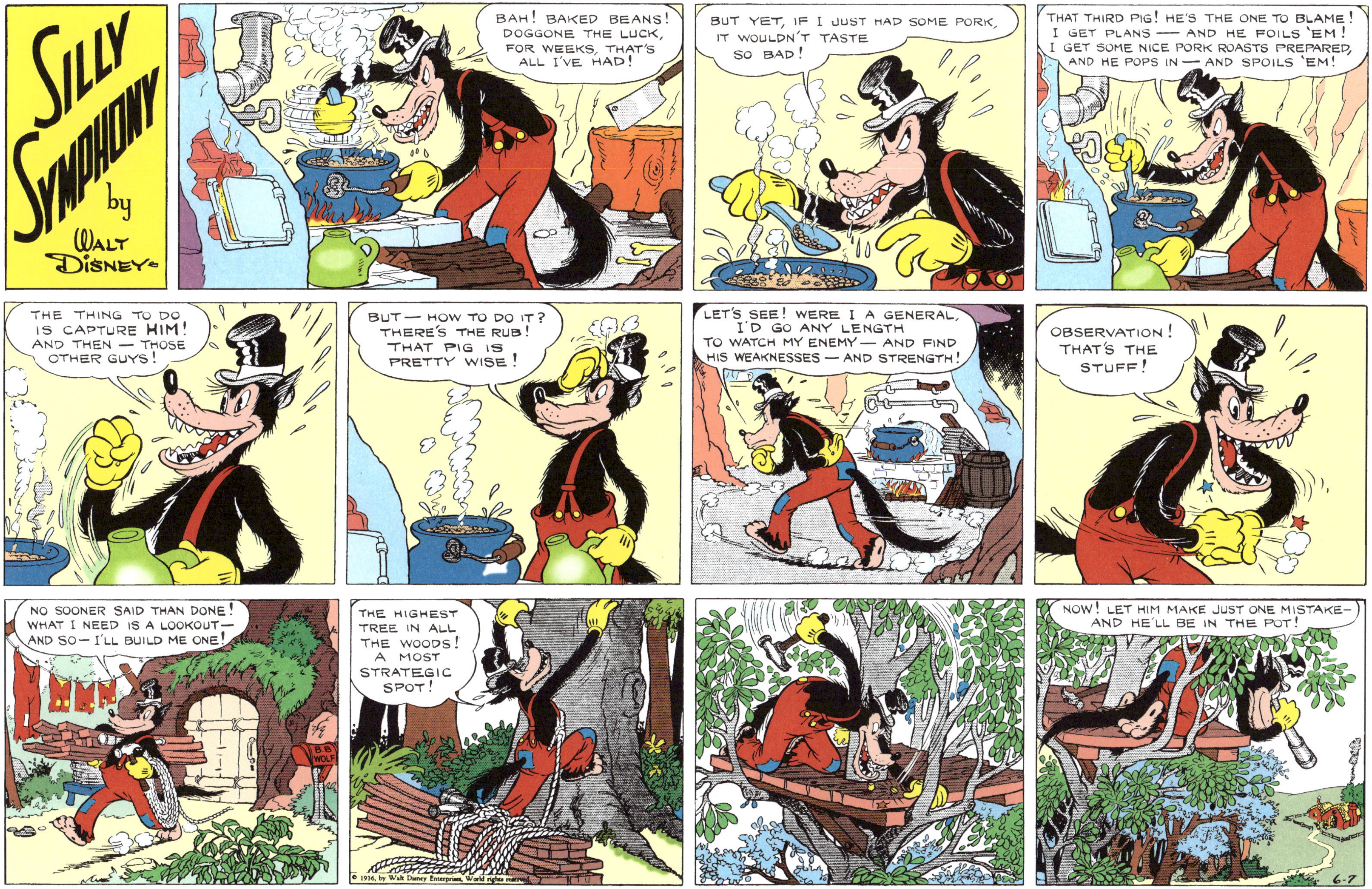
SILLY SYMPHONY
by
WALT DISNEY
BAH! BAKED BEANS! DOGGONE THE LUCK, FOR WEEKS, THAT'S ALL I'VE HAD!
BUT YET, IF I JUST HAD SOME PORK, IT WOULDN'T TASTE SO BAD!
THAT THIRD PIG! HE'S THE ONE TO BLAME! I GET PLANS — AND HE FOILS 'EM! I GET SOME NICE PORK ROASTS PREPARED, AND HE POPS IN — AND SPOILS 'EM!
THE THING TO DO IS CAPTURE HIM! AND THEN — THOSE OTHER GUYS!
BUT — HOW TO DO IT? THERE'S THE RUB! THAT PIG IS PRETTY WISE!
LET'S SEE! WERE I A GENERAL, I'D GO ANY LENGTH TO WATCH MY ENEMY — AND FIND HIS WEAKNESSES — AND STRENGTH!
OBSERVATION! THAT'S THE STUFF!
NO SOONER SAID THAN DONE! WHAT I NEED IS A LOOKOUT — AND SO — I'LL BUILD ME ONE!
B.B. WOLF
THE HIGHEST TREE IN ALL THE WOODS! A MOST STRATEGIC SPOT!
© 1936, by Walt Disney Enterprises, World rights reserved
NOW! LET HIM MAKE JUST ONE MISTAKE — AND HE'LL BE IN THE POT!
6-7

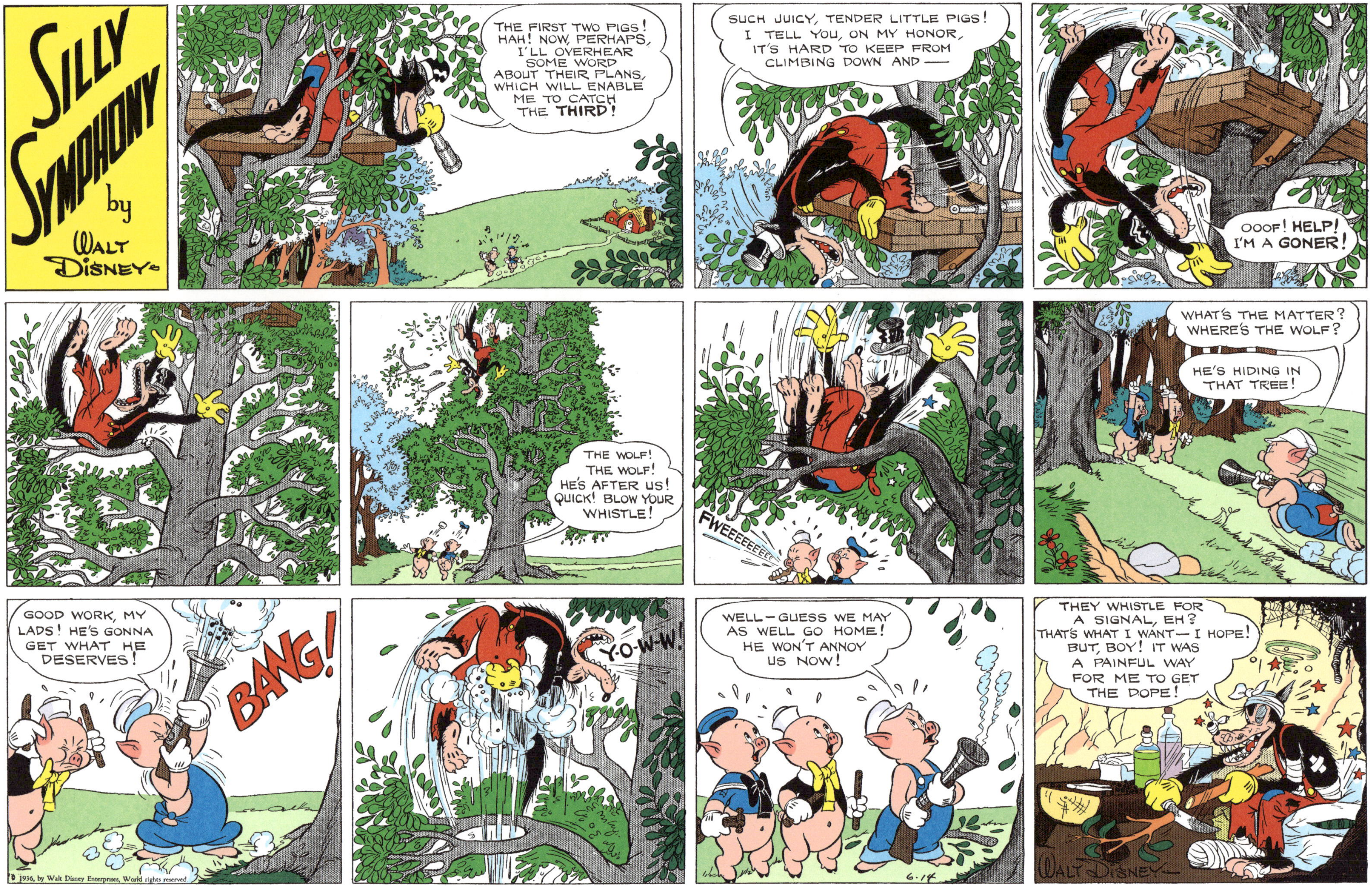

SILLY SYMPHONY
by
WALT DISNEY
THE FIRST TWO PIGS! HAH! NOW, PERHAPS, I'LL OVERHEAR SOME WORD ABOUT THEIR PLANS, WHICH WILL ENABLE ME TO CATCH THE THIRD!
SUCH JUICY, TENDER LITTLE PIGS! I TELL YOU, ON MY HONOR, IT'S HARD TO KEEP FROM CLIMBING DOWN AND —
OOOF! HELP! I'M A GONER!
THE WOLF! THE WOLF! HE'S AFTER US! QUICK! BLOW YOUR WHISTLE!
FWEEEEEEEE!
WHAT'S THE MATTER? WHERE'S THE WOLF?
HE'S HIDING IN THAT TREE!
GOOD WORK, MY LADS! HE'S GONNA GET WHAT HE DESERVES!
BANG!
© 1936, by Walt Disney Enterprises, World rights reserved
Y-O-W-W!
WELL — GUESS WE MAY AS WELL GO HOME! HE WON'T ANNOY US NOW!
6-14
THEY WHISTLE FOR A SIGNAL, EH? THAT'S WHAT I WANT — I HOPE! BUT, BOY! IT WAS A PAINFUL WAY FOR ME TO GET THE DOPE!
WALT DISNEY

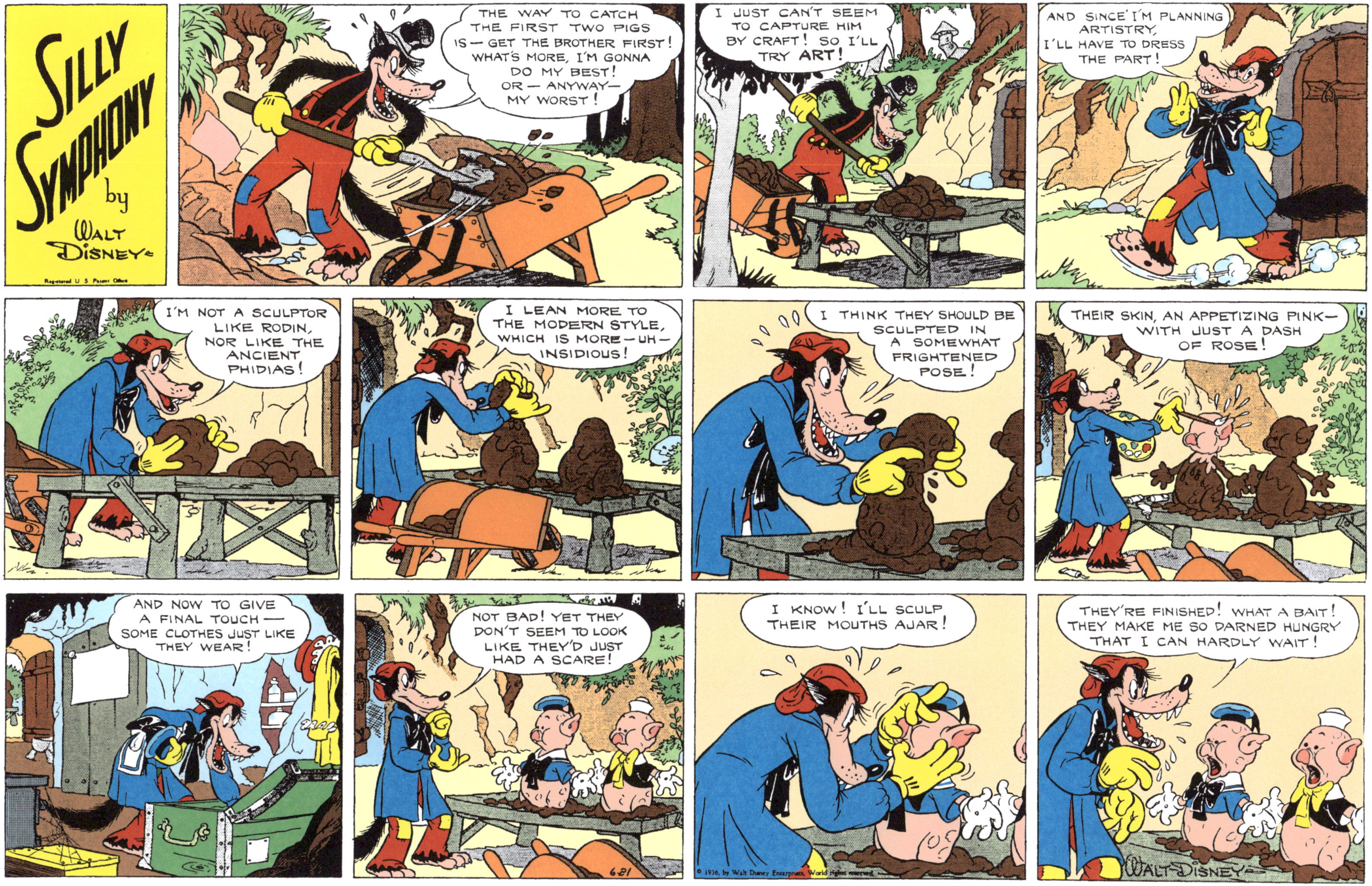
SILLY SYMPHONY by WALT DISNEY
Registered U.S. Patent Office
THE WAY TO CATCH THE FIRST TWO PIGS IS — GET THE BROTHER FIRST! WHAT'S MORE, I'M GONNA DO MY BEST! OR — ANYWAY — MY WORST!
I JUST CAN'T SEEM TO CAPTURE HIM BY CRAFT! SO I'LL TRY ART!
AND SINCE I'M PLANNING ARTISTRY, I'LL HAVE TO DRESS THE PART!
I'M NOT A SCULPTOR LIKE RODIN, NOR LIKE THE ANCIENT PHIDIAS!
I LEAN MORE TO THE MODERN STYLE, WHICH IS MORE — UH — INSIDIOUS!
I THINK THEY SHOULD BE SCULPTED IN A SOMEWHAT FRIGHTENED POSE!
THEIR SKIN, AN APPETIZING PINK — WITH JUST A DASH OF ROSE!
AND NOW TO GIVE A FINAL TOUCH — SOME CLOTHES JUST LIKE THEY WEAR!
NOT BAD! YET THEY DON'T SEEM TO LOOK LIKE THEY'D JUST HAD A SCARE!
6-21
I KNOW! I'LL SCULP THEIR MOUTHS AJAR!
© 1936, by Walt Disney Enterprises. World rights reserved.
THEY'RE FINISHED! WHAT A BAIT! THEY MAKE ME SO DARNED HUNGRY THAT I CAN HARDLY WAIT!
WALT DISNEY

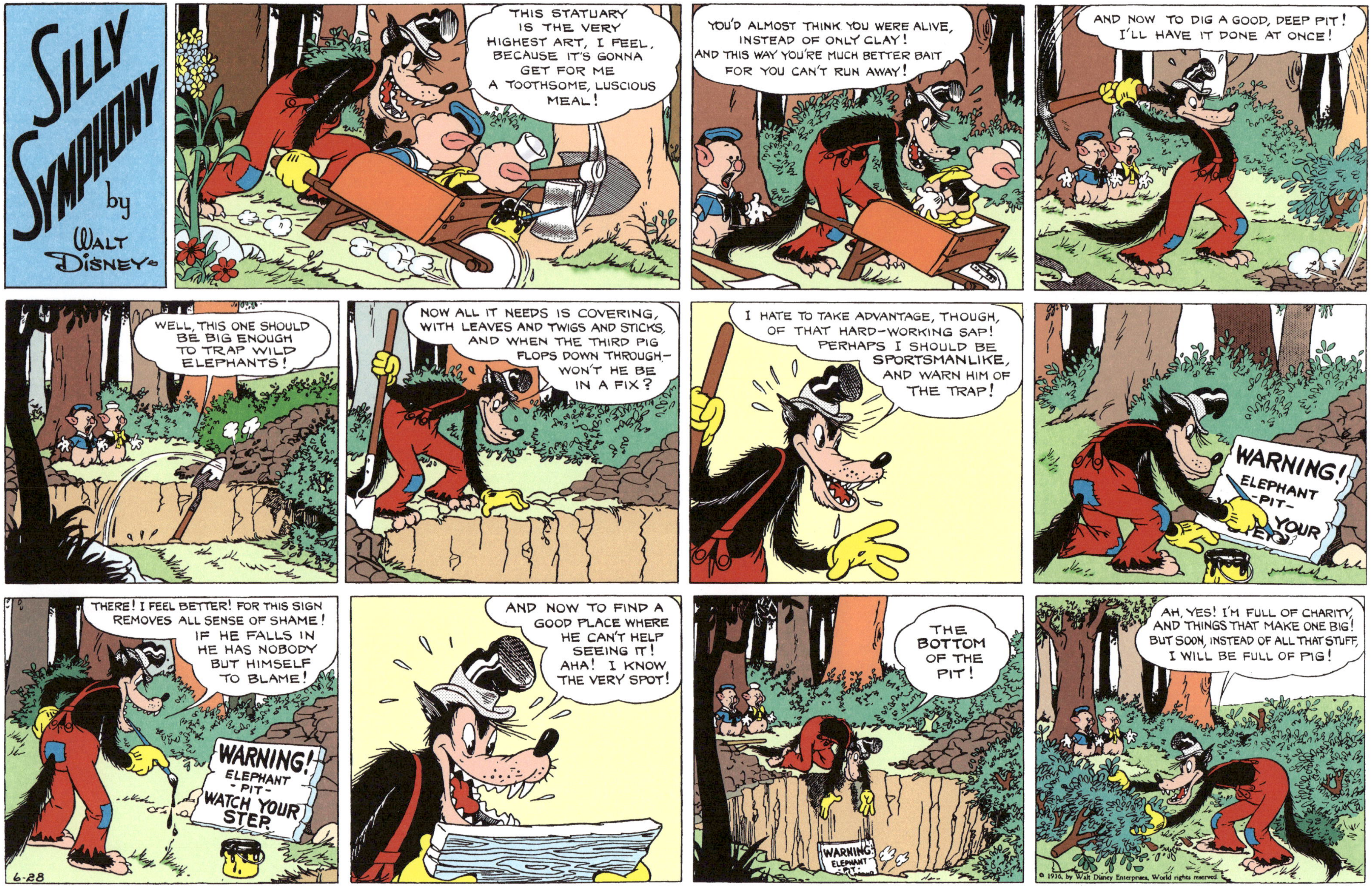
SILLY SYMPHONY by WALT DISNEY
THIS STATUARY IS THE VERY HIGHEST ART, I FEEL, BECAUSE IT'S GONNA GET FOR ME A TOOTHSOME, LUSCIOUS MEAL!
YOU'D ALMOST THINK YOU WERE ALIVE, INSTEAD OF ONLY CLAY! AND THIS WAY YOU'RE MUCH BETTER BAIT FOR YOU CAN'T RUN AWAY!
AND NOW TO DIG A GOOD, DEEP PIT! I'LL HAVE IT DONE AT ONCE!
WELL, THIS ONE SHOULD BE BIG ENOUGH TO TRAP WILD ELEPHANTS!
NOW ALL IT NEEDS IS COVERING, WITH LEAVES AND TWIGS AND STICKS, AND WHEN THE THIRD PIG FLOPS DOWN THROUGH— WON'T HE BE IN A FIX?
I HATE TO TAKE ADVANTAGE, THOUGH, OF THAT HARD-WORKING SAP! PERHAPS I SHOULD BE SPORTSMANLIKE, AND WARN HIM OF THE TRAP!
WARNING! ELEPHANT -PIT- YOUR
THERE! I FEEL BETTER! FOR THIS SIGN REMOVES ALL SENSE OF SHAME! IF HE FALLS IN HE HAS NOBODY BUT HIMSELF TO BLAME!
WARNING! ELEPHANT -PIT- WATCH YOUR STEP
6-28
AND NOW TO FIND A GOOD PLACE WHERE HE CAN'T HELP SEEING IT! AHA! I KNOW THE VERY SPOT!
THE BOTTOM OF THE PIT!
WARNING! ELEPHANT
AH, YES! I'M FULL OF CHARITY, AND THINGS THAT MAKE ONE BIG! BUT SOON, INSTEAD OF ALL THAT STUFF, I WILL BE FULL OF PIG!
© 1936, by Walt Disney Enterprises, World rights reserved

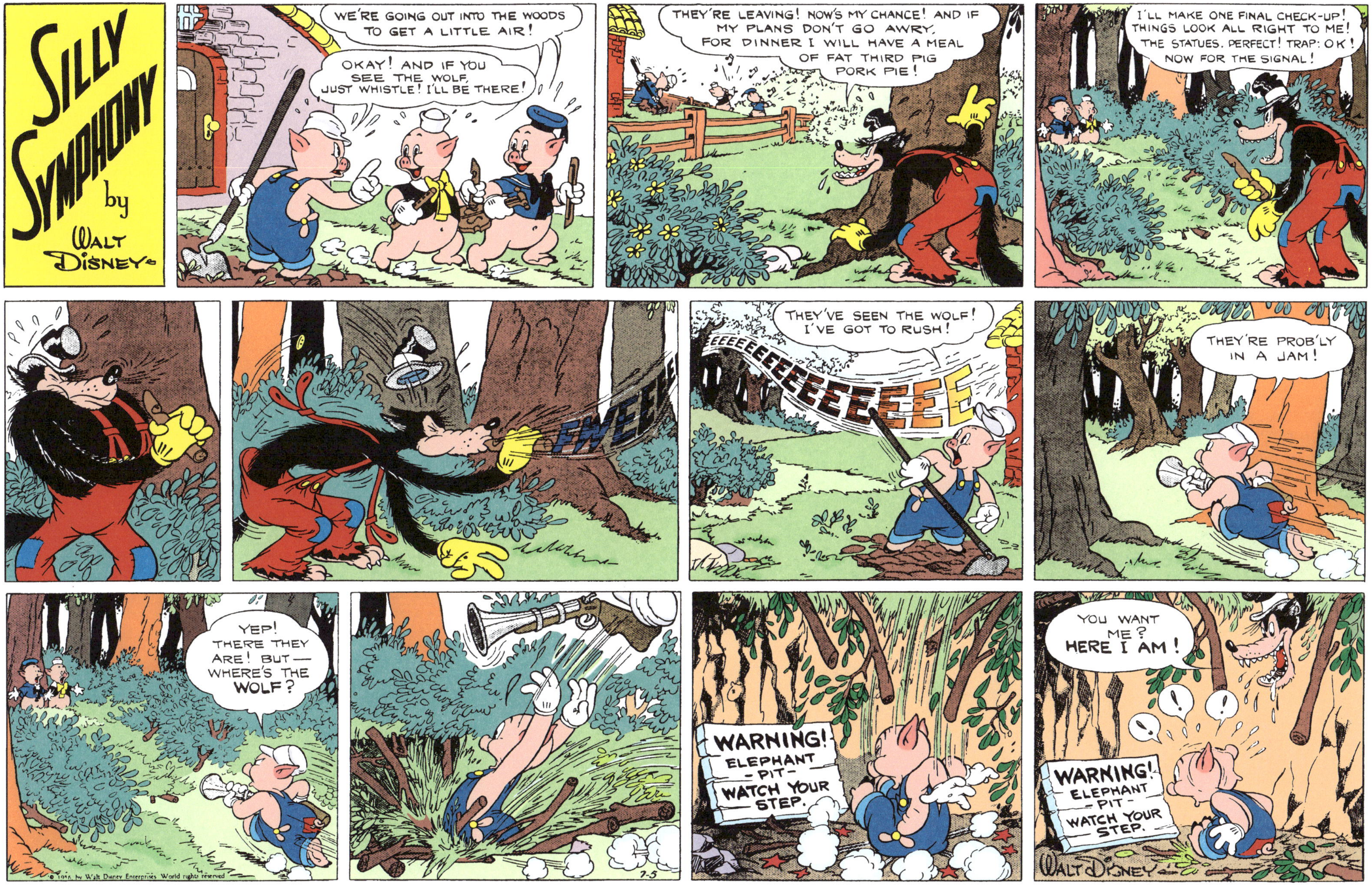
SILLY SYMPHONY
by
WALT DISNEY
WE'RE GOING OUT INTO THE WOODS TO GET A LITTLE AIR!
OKAY! AND IF YOU SEE THE WOLF, JUST WHISTLE! I'LL BE THERE!
THEY'RE LEAVING! NOW'S MY CHANCE! AND IF MY PLANS DON'T GO AWRY, FOR DINNER I WILL HAVE A MEAL OF FAT THIRD PIG PORK PIE!
I'LL MAKE ONE FINAL CHECK-UP! THINGS LOOK ALL RIGHT TO ME! THE STATUES, PERFECT! TRAP: OK! NOW FOR THE SIGNAL!
FWEEEE
THEY'VE SEEN THE WOLF! I'VE GOT TO RUSH!
EEEEEEEEEEEEEEEEEE
THEY'RE PROB'LY IN A JAM!
YEP! THERE THEY ARE! BUT— WHERE'S THE WOLF?
by Walt Disney Enterprises World rights reserved
7-5
WARNING! ELEPHANT —PIT— WATCH YOUR STEP.
YOU WANT ME? HERE I AM!
WARNING! ELEPHANT —PIT— WATCH YOUR STEP.
WALT DISNEY

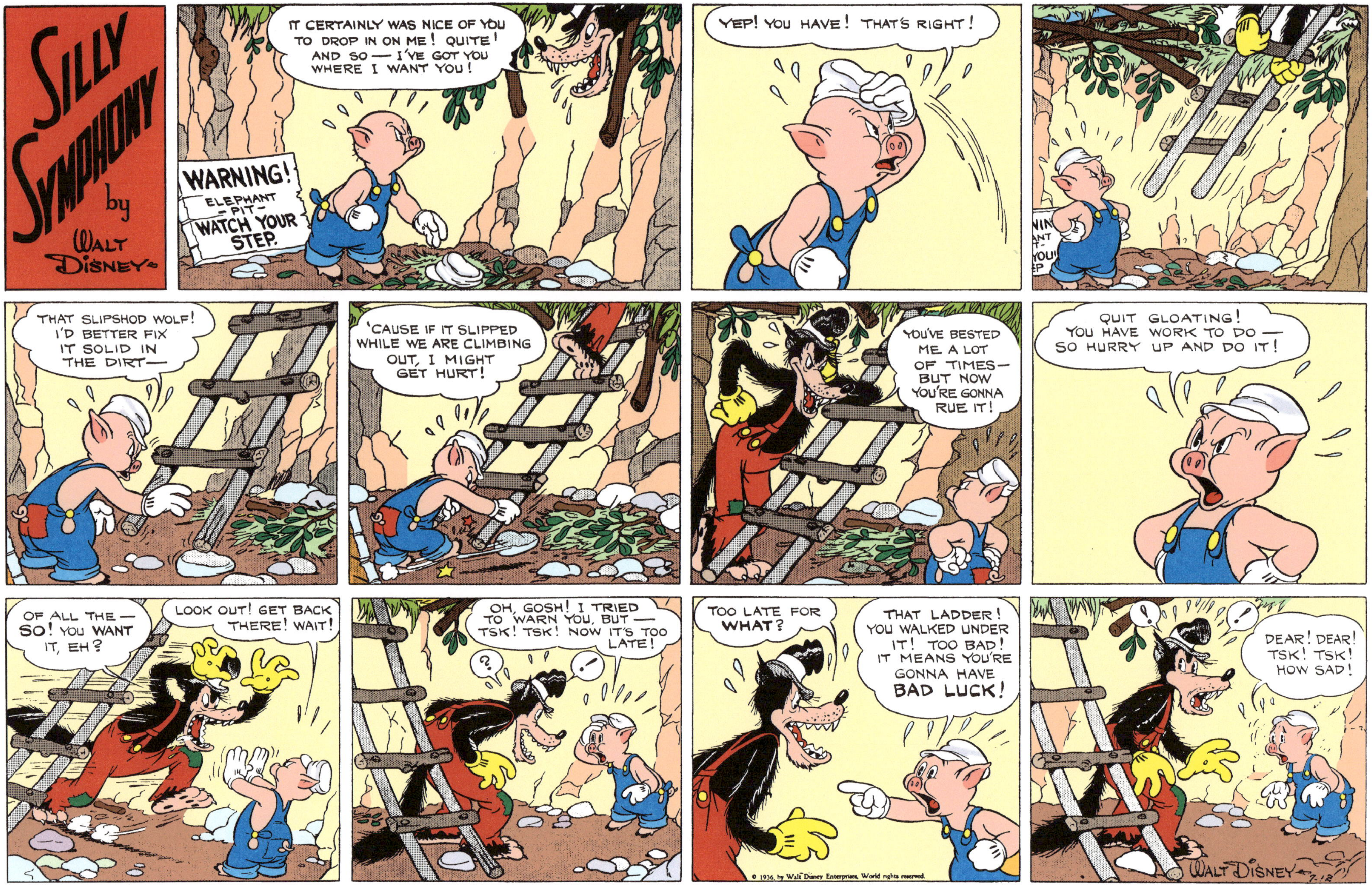
SILLY SYMPHONY by WALT DISNEY
IT CERTAINLY WAS NICE OF YOU TO DROP IN ON ME! QUITE! AND SO — I'VE GOT YOU WHERE I WANT YOU!
WARNING! ELEPHANT -PIT- WATCH YOUR STEP.
YEP! YOU HAVE! THAT'S RIGHT!
THAT SLIPSHOD WOLF! I'D BETTER FIX IT SOLID IN THE DIRT—
'CAUSE IF IT SLIPPED WHILE WE ARE CLIMBING OUT, I MIGHT GET HURT!
YOU'VE BESTED ME A LOT OF TIMES— BUT NOW YOU'RE GONNA RUE IT!
QUIT GLOATING! YOU HAVE WORK TO DO — SO HURRY UP AND DO IT!
OF ALL THE — SO! YOU WANT IT, EH?
LOOK OUT! GET BACK THERE! WAIT!
OH, GOSH! I TRIED TO WARN YOU, BUT — TSK! TSK! NOW IT'S TOO LATE!
TOO LATE FOR WHAT?
THAT LADDER! YOU WALKED UNDER IT! TOO BAD! IT MEANS YOU'RE GONNA HAVE BAD LUCK!
DEAR! DEAR! TSK! TSK! HOW SAD!
© 1936, by Walt Disney Enterprises. World rights reserved.
WALT DISNEY 7-12

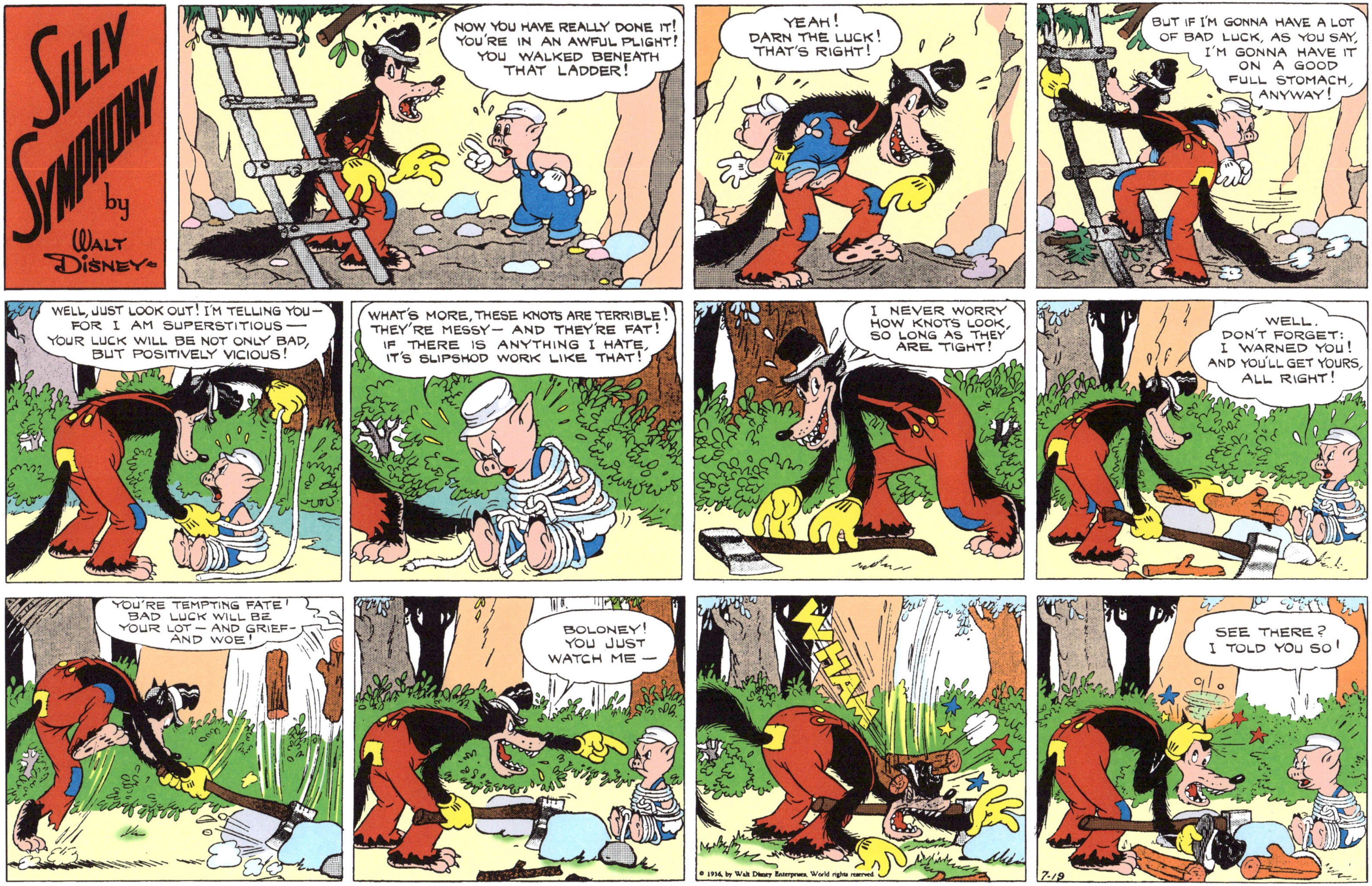
SILLY SYMPHONY
by
WALT DISNEY
NOW YOU HAVE REALLY DONE IT! YOU'RE IN AN AWFUL PLIGHT! YOU WALKED BENEATH THAT LADDER!
YEAH! DARN THE LUCK! THAT'S RIGHT!
BUT IF I'M GONNA HAVE A LOT OF BAD LUCK, AS YOU SAY, I'M GONNA HAVE IT ON A GOOD FULL STOMACH, ANYWAY!
WELL, JUST LOOK OUT! I'M TELLING YOU— FOR I AM SUPERSTITIOUS— YOUR LUCK WILL BE NOT ONLY BAD, BUT POSITIVELY VICIOUS!
WHAT'S MORE, THESE KNOTS ARE TERRIBLE! THEY'RE MESSY— AND THEY'RE FAT! IF THERE IS ANYTHING I HATE, IT'S SLIPSHOD WORK LIKE THAT!
I NEVER WORRY HOW KNOTS LOOK, SO LONG AS THEY ARE TIGHT!
WELL, DON'T FORGET: I WARNED YOU! AND YOU'LL GET YOURS, ALL RIGHT!
YOU'RE TEMPTING FATE! BAD LUCK WILL BE YOUR LOT — AND GRIEF— AND WOE!
BOLONEY! YOU JUST WATCH ME —
WHAM
© 1936, by Walt Disney Enterprises, World rights reserved
SEE THERE? I TOLD YOU SO!
7-19

SILLY SYMPHONY by WALT DISNEY
I'M GOING OUT TO GET MORE WOOD! AND THEN — OUR FIRE WILL BURN AND WE'LL HAVE DINNER, YOU AN I, AS SOON AS I RETURN!
HEY! LOOK! TWO LITTLE PIGS AND THEY'RE — THEY'RE JUST LIKE YOU AND ME!
WHAT'S MORE, THERE IS OUR BROTHER TIED AS TIGHT AS TIGHT CAN BE!
HE'S RESCUED US A DOZEN TIMES! LET'S TRY TO HELP HIM NOW!
AND I DON'T SEE THE BIG BAD WOLF AROUND HERE, ANYHOW!
GOOD WORK, MY LADS UNTIE THESE ROPES, AND BRING ONE STATUE - QUICKLY!
THAT'S IT! NOW I'LL TRADE CLOTHES WITH HIM! MY GOSH — BUT HE LOOKS SICKLY
YOU'RE IN MY CLOTHES - BUT YET, SOMEHOW, YOU DON'T LOOK LIKE I DO! THE TROUBLE IS, YOU LOOK TOO SCARED!
I'LL DO SOME SCULPING, TOO!
THAT'S BETTER! YEP! IT'S QUITE OKAY!
NOW — YOU GO HIDE, YOU GUYS! AND WHEN THE WOLF GETS BACK, I'M GONNA GIVE HIM A SURPRISE!
?
!
!
© 1936, by Walt Disney Enterprises, World rights reserved.
7-26

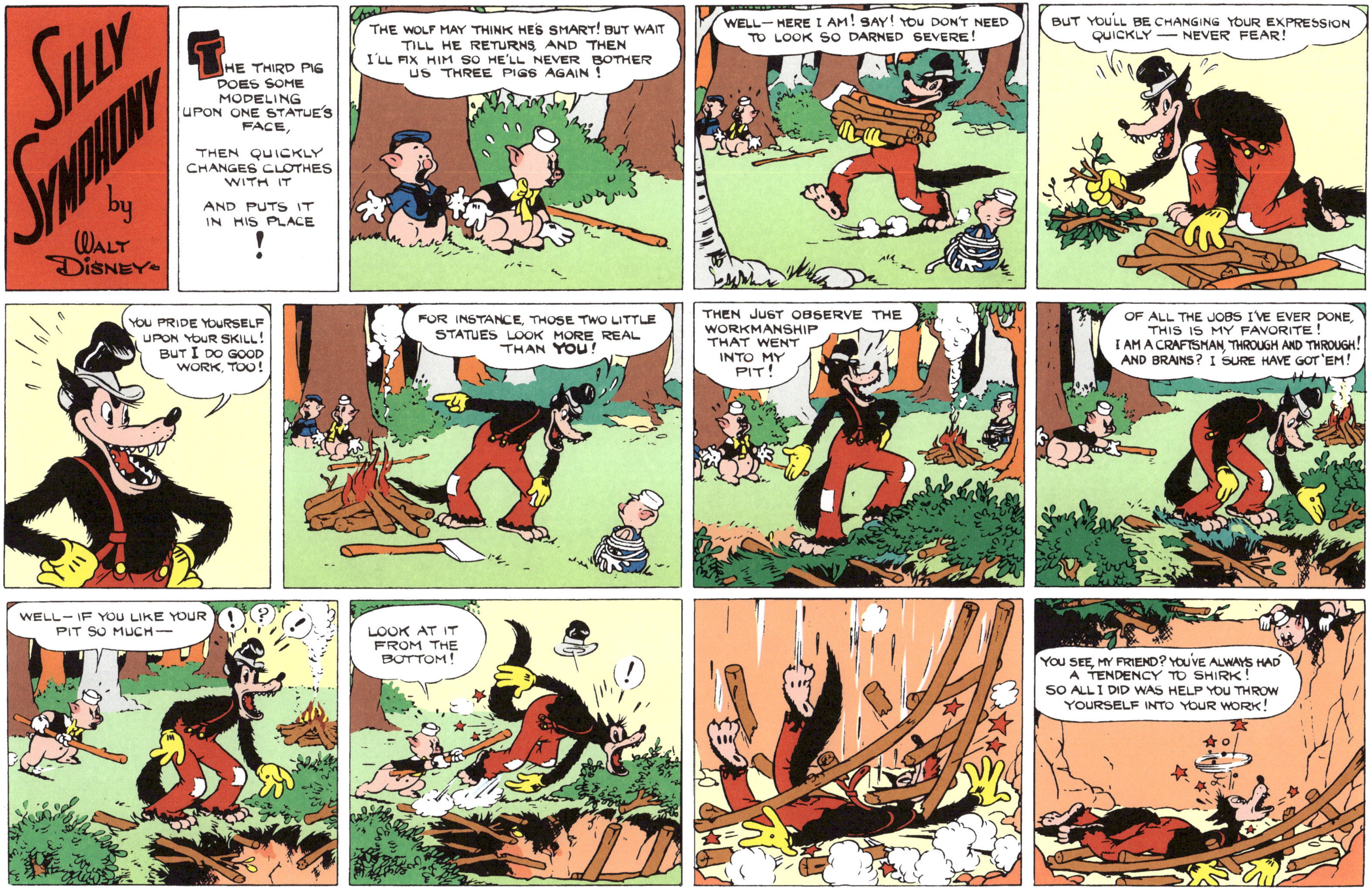
SILLY SYMPHONY
by
WALT DISNEY
THE THIRD PIG DOES SOME MODELING UPON ONE STATUE'S FACE,
THEN QUICKLY CHANGES CLOTHES WITH IT
AND PUTS IT IN HIS PLACE
!
THE WOLF MAY THINK HE'S SMART! BUT WAIT TILL HE RETURNS, AND THEN I'LL FIX HIM SO HE'LL NEVER BOTHER US THREE PIGS AGAIN!
WELL— HERE I AM! SAY! YOU DON'T NEED TO LOOK SO DARNED SEVERE!
BUT YOU'LL BE CHANGING YOUR EXPRESSION QUICKLY — NEVER FEAR!
YOU PRIDE YOURSELF UPON YOUR SKILL! BUT I DO GOOD WORK, TOO!
FOR INSTANCE, THOSE TWO LITTLE STATUES LOOK MORE REAL THAN YOU!
THEN JUST OBSERVE THE WORKMANSHIP THAT WENT INTO MY PIT!
OF ALL THE JOBS I'VE EVER DONE, THIS IS MY FAVORITE! I AM A CRAFTSMAN, THROUGH AND THROUGH! AND BRAINS? I SURE HAVE GOT 'EM!
WELL— IF YOU LIKE YOUR PIT SO MUCH—
! ? !
LOOK AT IT FROM THE BOTTOM!
!
YOU SEE, MY FRIEND? YOU'VE ALWAYS HAD A TENDENCY TO SHIRK! SO ALL I DID WAS HELP YOU THROW YOURSELF INTO YOUR WORK!

SILLY SYMPHONY
by
WALT DISNEY
I'LL BET THE BIG BAD WOLF'S SO MAD HE'S SIMPLY FURIOUS — FOR, ONCE AGAIN, WE CAUGHT HIM IN A TRAP HE MADE FOR US!
HE'S GOT TO LEARN THAT WHEN HE FOOLS AROUND WITH ME, THERE'S TROUBLE! WHAT'S MORE, HE'S GONNA HAVE SOME NOW!
YE GODS! I'M SEEING DOUBLE!
I WARNED YOU THAT YOU'D HAVE BAD LUCK! BUT, NO! YOU WOULDN'T LISTEN! AND NOW THAT DINNER-TIME IS HERE, ANOTHER MEAL YOU'RE MISSIN'!
!
!
LET'S GIVE HIM BACK HIS STATUES! WE DON'T NEED 'EM ANY MORE!
JUST FIRE AWAY! IT'S WHAT HE GETS FOR MAKING US GUYS SORE!
?
!
?
!
SOMEHOW, I THINK WE'D BETTER GO! PERHAPS WE'LL SEE YOU SOON! GOOD-BYE! AND THANK YOU FOR A VERY PLEASANT AFTERNOON!
!
8-9
I'M GONNA GET THOSE BRATS—OR BUST! BUT NOT FOR DINNER! BOSH! I'M HUNGRY NOW FOR JUST ONE THING—AND THAT'S REVENGE, BY GOSH!
B.B. WOLF
DYNAMITE
WALT DISNEY
© 1936, by Walt Disney Enterprises
World rights reserved

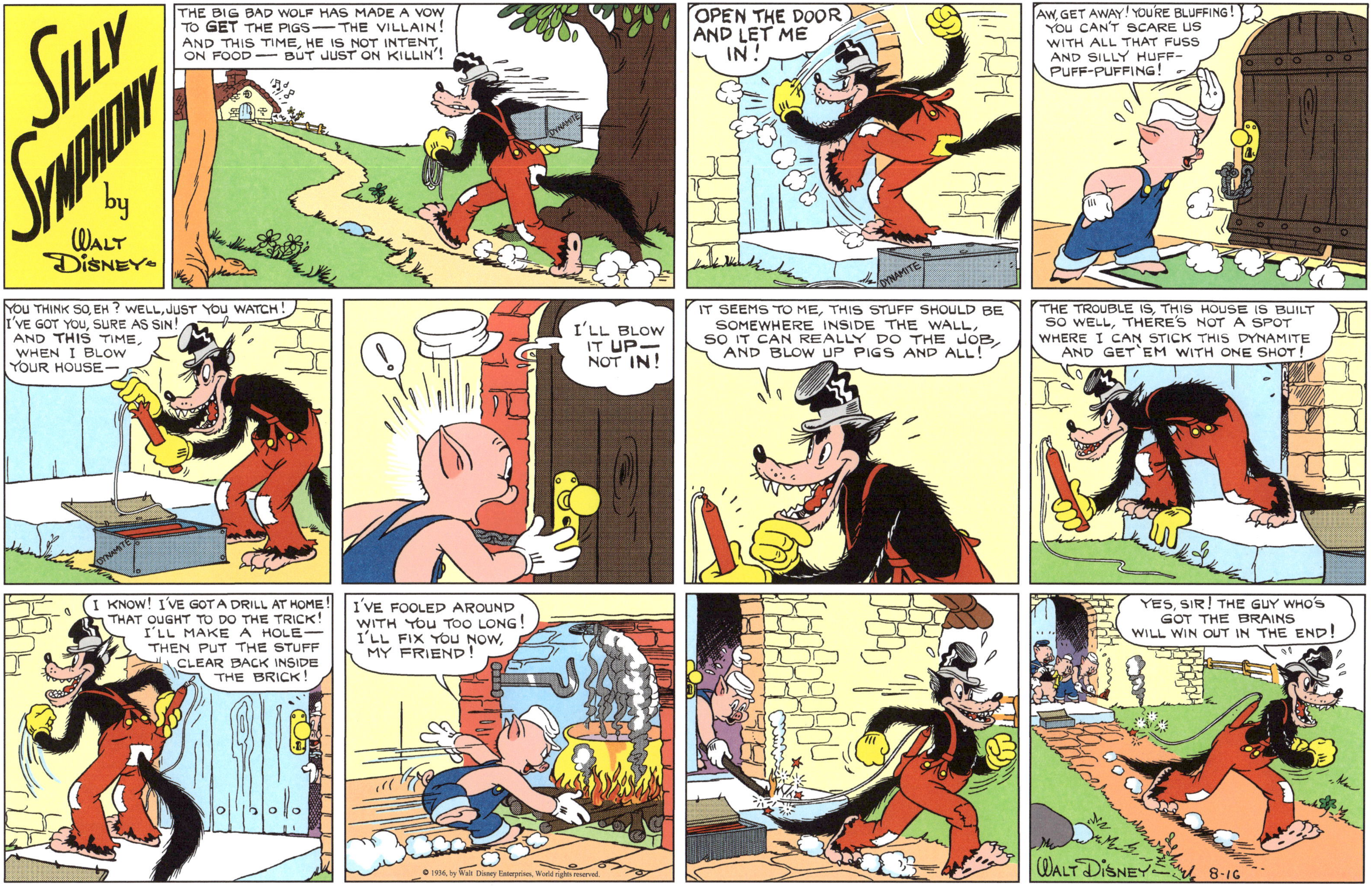
SILLY SYMPHONY by WALT DISNEY
THE BIG BAD WOLF HAS MADE A VOW TO GET THE PIGS — THE VILLAIN! AND THIS TIME, HE IS NOT INTENT ON FOOD — BUT JUST ON KILLIN'!
DYNAMITE
OPEN THE DOOR AND LET ME IN!
DYNAMITE
AW, GET AWAY! YOU'RE BLUFFING! YOU CAN'T SCARE US WITH ALL THAT FUSS AND SILLY HUFF-PUFF-PUFFING!
YOU THINK SO, EH? WELL, JUST YOU WATCH! I'VE GOT YOU, SURE AS SIN! AND THIS TIME, WHEN I BLOW YOUR HOUSE—
DYNAMITE
!
I'LL BLOW IT UP— NOT IN!
IT SEEMS TO ME, THIS STUFF SHOULD BE SOMEWHERE INSIDE THE WALL, SO IT CAN REALLY DO THE JOB, AND BLOW UP PIGS AND ALL!
THE TROUBLE IS, THIS HOUSE IS BUILT SO WELL, THERE'S NOT A SPOT WHERE I CAN STICK THIS DYNAMITE AND GET 'EM WITH ONE SHOT!
I KNOW! I'VE GOT A DRILL AT HOME! THAT OUGHT TO DO THE TRICK! I'LL MAKE A HOLE— THEN PUT THE STUFF CLEAR BACK INSIDE THE BRICK!
I'VE FOOLED AROUND WITH YOU TOO LONG! I'LL FIX YOU NOW, MY FRIEND!
© 1936, by Walt Disney Enterprises, World rights reserved.
YES, SIR! THE GUY WHO'S GOT THE BRAINS WILL WIN OUT IN THE END!
WALT DISNEY 8-16

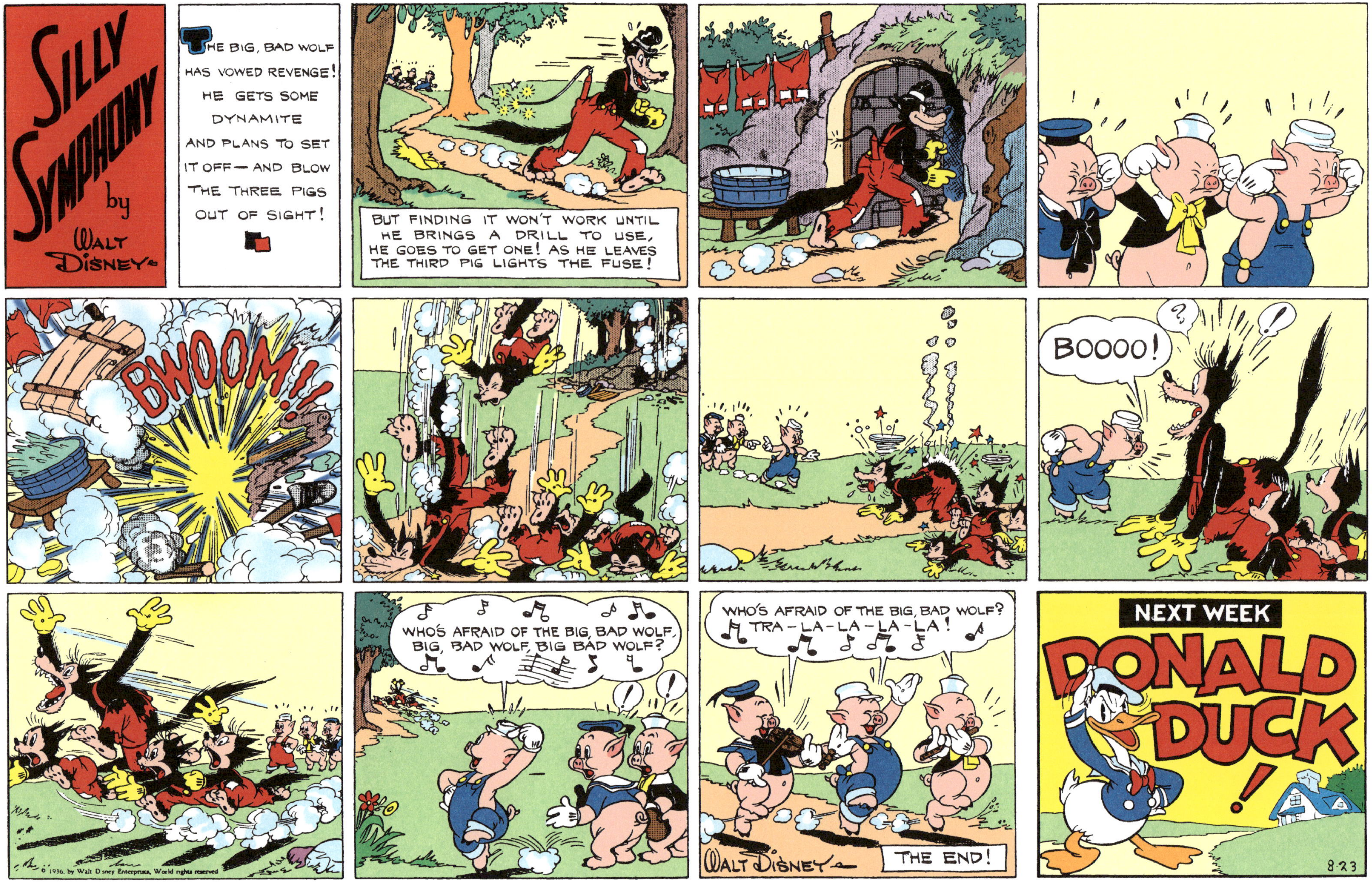
SILLY SYMPHONY by WALT DISNEY
THE BIG, BAD WOLF HAS VOWED REVENGE! HE GETS SOME DYNAMITE AND PLANS TO SET IT OFF—AND BLOW THE THREE PIGS OUT OF SIGHT!
BUT FINDING IT WON'T WORK UNTIL HE BRINGS A DRILL TO USE, HE GOES TO GET ONE! AS HE LEAVES THE THIRD PIG LIGHTS THE FUSE!
BWOOM!!
BOOOO!
© 1936, by Walt Disney Enterprises, World rights reserved
WHO'S AFRAID OF THE BIG, BAD WOLF, BIG, BAD WOLF, BIG BAD WOLF?
WHO'S AFRAID OF THE BIG, BAD WOLF? TRA-LA-LA-LA-LA!
WALT DISNEY
THE END!
NEXT WEEK
DONALD DUCK!
8-23

SILLY SYMPHONIES

DONALD DUCK

August 30, 1936 - December 5, 1937
Written by Ted Osborne, drawn by Al Taliaferro

A significant slice of Disney history is captured in these pages. The fifteen months of this run marked a critical phase in Donald Duck's rise to superstardom. Originally a one-shot performer, then a regular in Mickey Mouse's circle of friends, Donald had always been seen as a supporting character, his irritable nature a refreshingly comic change of pace. But one can't keep an angry duck down, and the more disagreeable Donald became, the more audiences wanted to see him in the spotlight. Early in the autumn of 1936, as this comic continuity was getting underway, the studio released *Donald and Pluto*—a short in which, as the title implied, Donald shared top billing with Pluto the pup, and Mickey Mouse was never seen at all. Clearly the Duck was being groomed for top stardom and the Sunday comics would play a key role in his campaign.

Seen through this historical lens, the Duck series becomes doubly fascinating. The attentive Disney fan will notice that Donald's graphic design, both on the screen and in the comics, had undergone a marked change since his introduction in 1934. By August 1936 his evolution was still not quite complete, and as the strips continue one can observe subtle changes in his appearance. In other ways, too, the comics reflect the movies. In one September 1936 page Donald is chased by an angry bull, one who unmistakably resembles the same bull that had menaced Mickey and Minnie on the screen in *Mickey's Rival*. In the 1935 short *On Ice* Donald had been seen singing "Hi-Le, Hi-Lo," a traditional novelty waltz; in the latter months of 1936 the comic page makes a concerted attempt to turn this into a theme song for him. Other movie references, too, crop up throughout the run of this series. As late as the closing weeks of the continuity in 1937, we can see the little burro who had appeared earlier in the year in *Don Donald*, the Duck's first official starring film.

Equally interesting is Donald's character development. In the early months, building on his irascible nature, Osborne and Taliaferro present a Duck who is not only misanthropic but downright sociopathic. Later he begins to curb his temperament. In the summer of 1937 there's even a fascinating subseries in which Donald tries to reform, restraining his violent impulses and attempting good deeds. Of course this effort doesn't last long, but while it does, readers are treated to a glimpse of his psychology. This in turn leads the strip in new and unpredictable directions—including a minor feud between Donald and Clarabelle Cow, an unlikely development that never occurs in the movies.

For many Disney enthusiasts, the big news in this Sunday series is the introduction of Donald's nephews, Huey, Dewey, and Louie, in October 1937. The three little hellions made such a hit with newspaper readers that they were introduced into the animated cartoons as well. Their first screen vehicle, *Donald's Nephews* (1938), was a loose adaptation of the October-November 1937 comic pages, and a new trio of Disney stars was born.

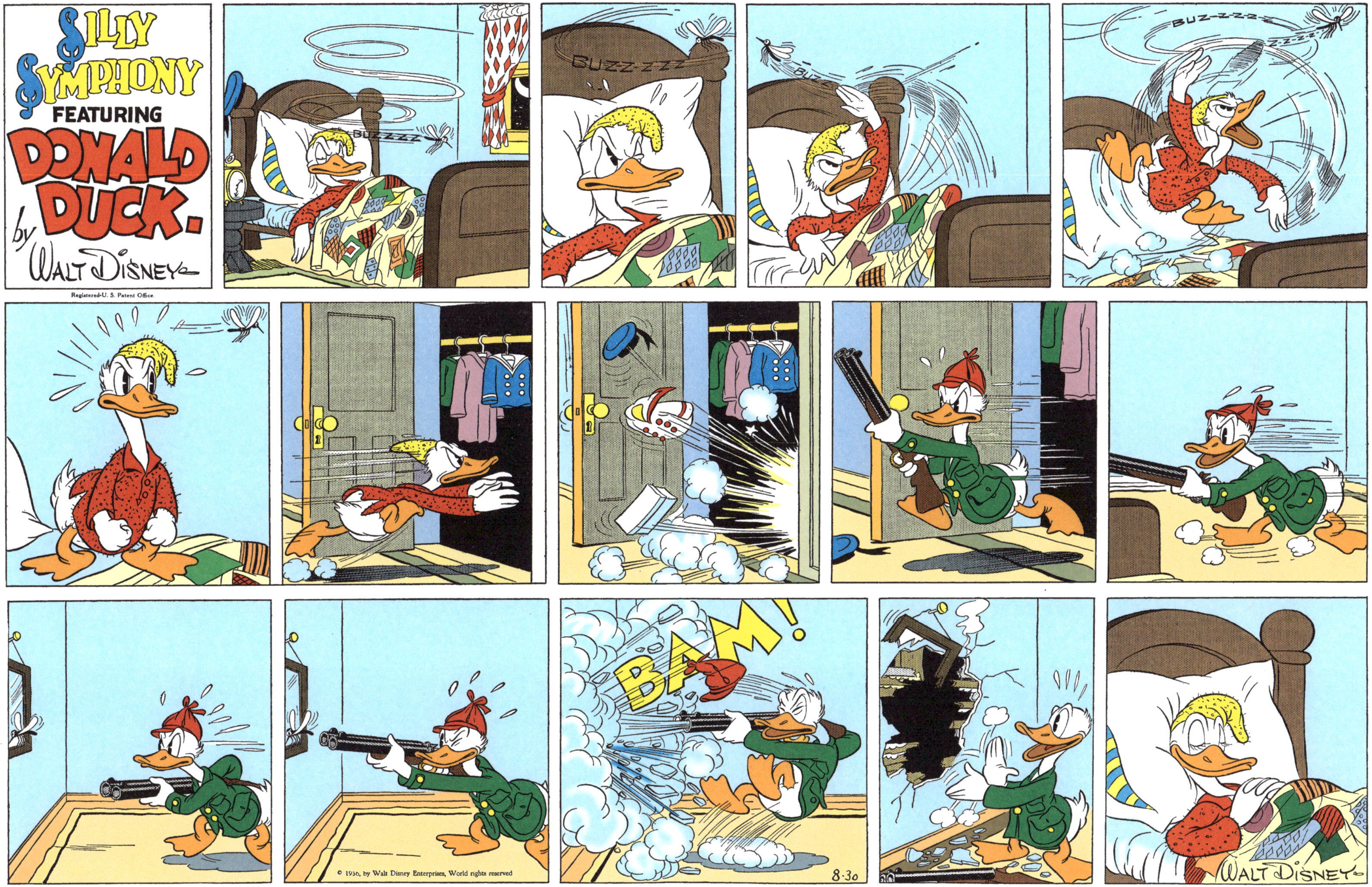
SILLY SYMPHONY
FEATURING
DONALD DUCK.
by WALT DISNEY
Registered-U. S. Patent Office
BUZZ-Z-Z-Z
BAM!
© 1936, by Walt Disney Enterprises, World rights reserved
8-30
WALT DISNEY

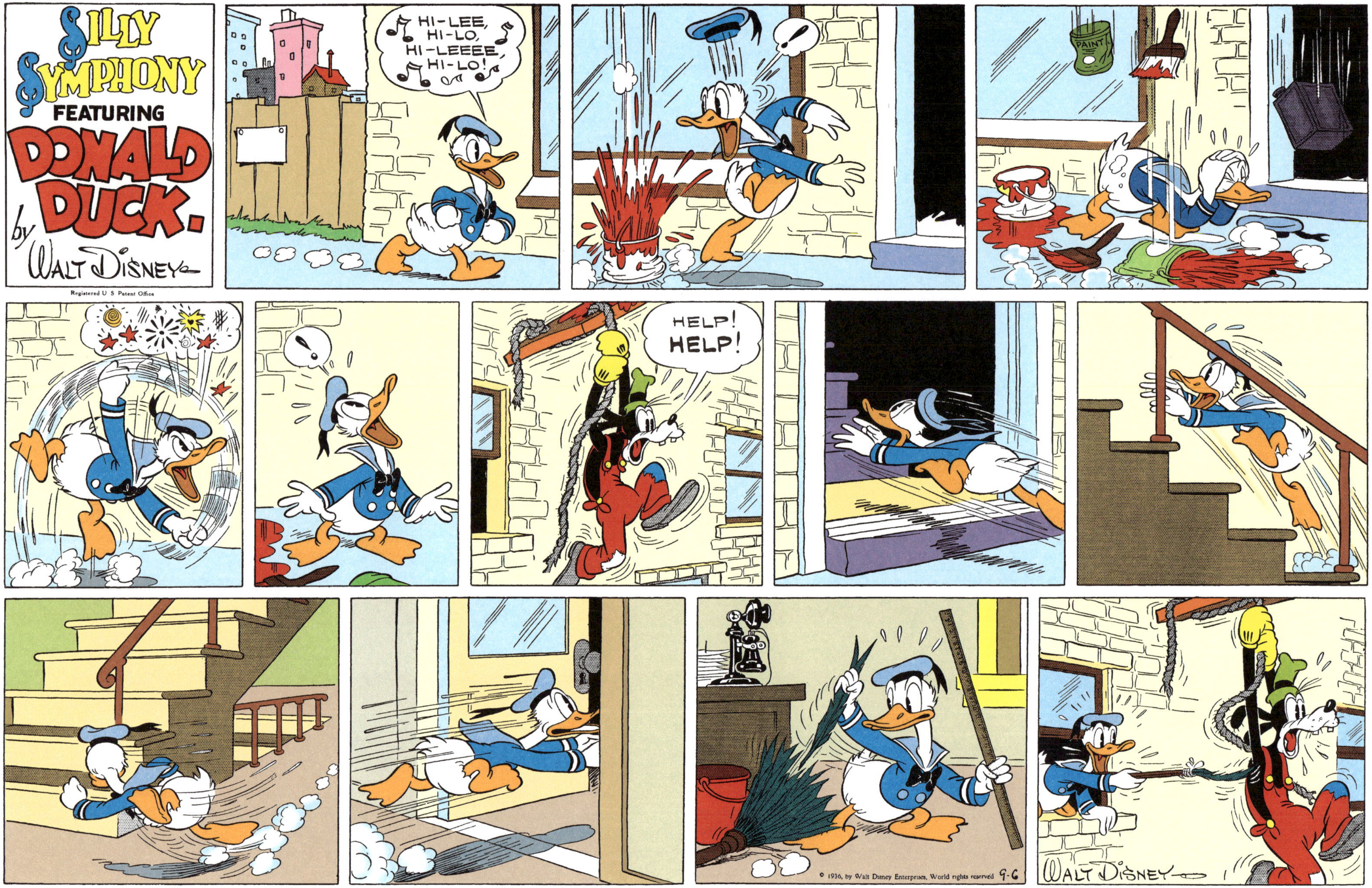

SILLY SYMPHONY
FEATURING
DONALD DUCK.
by WALT DISNEY
Registered U S Patent Office
HI-LEE, HI-LO, HI-LEEEE, HI-LO!
PAINT
HELP! HELP!
© 1936, by Walt Disney Enterprises, World rights reserved 9-6
WALT DISNEY

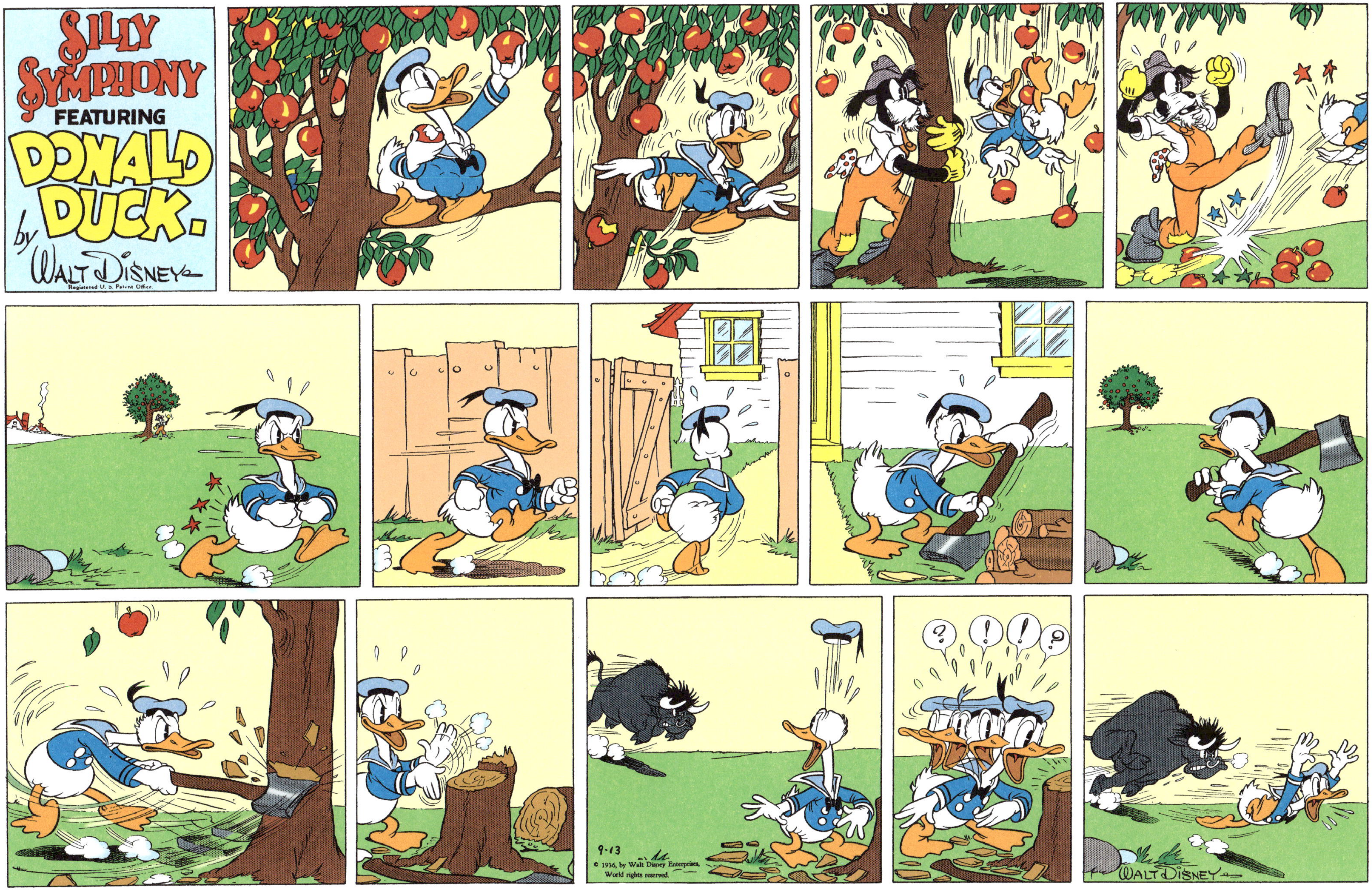
SILLY SYMPHONY
FEATURING
DONALD DUCK.
by WALT DISNEY
Registered U. S. Patent Office.
9-13
© 1936, by Walt Disney Enterprises, World rights reserved.
?
!
!
?
WALT DISNEY

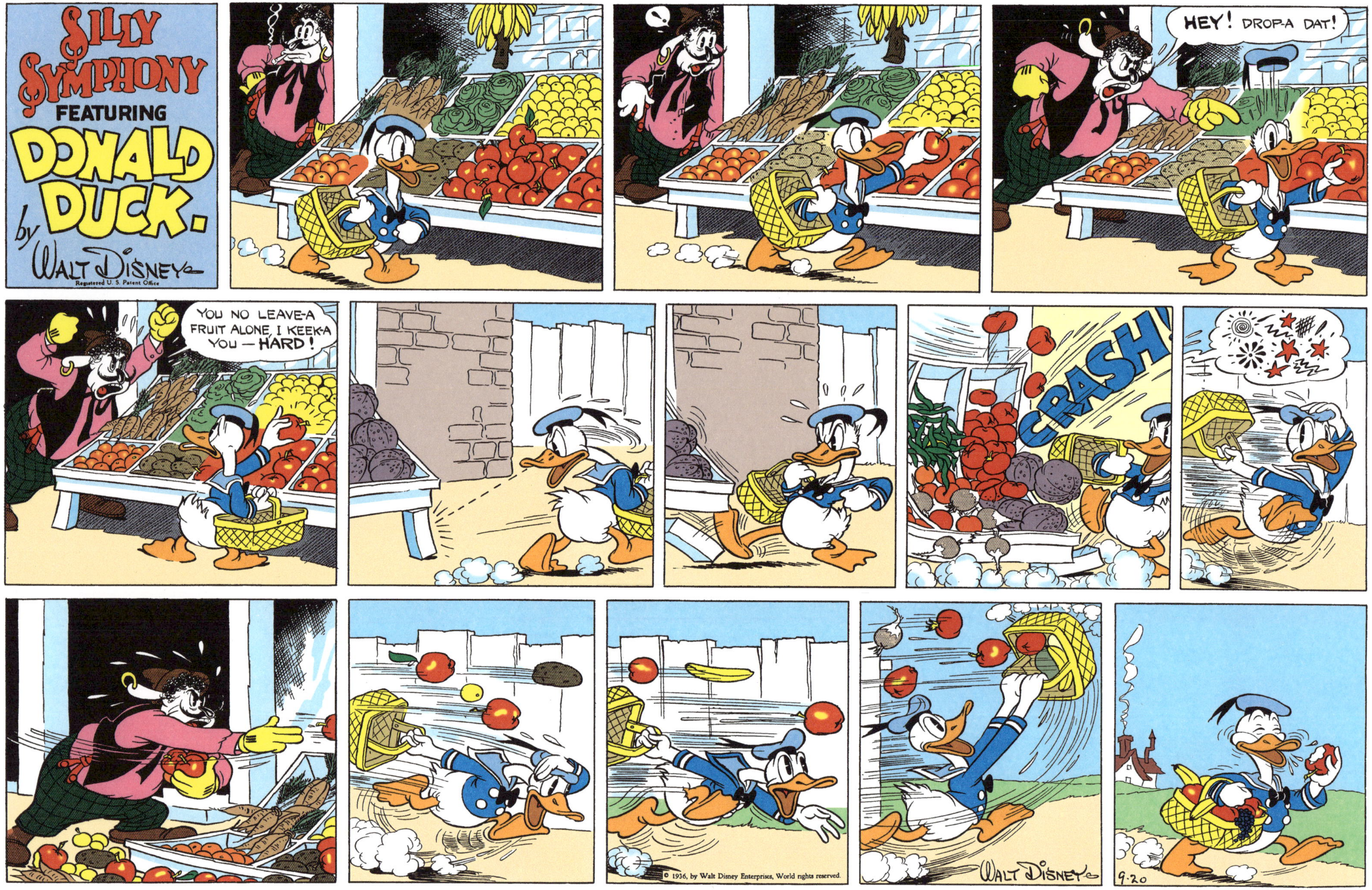
SILLY SYMPHONY
FEATURING
DONALD DUCK.
by WALT DISNEY
Registered U. S. Patent Office
HEY! DROP-A DAT!
YOU NO LEAVE-A FRUIT ALONE, I KEEK-A YOU — HARD!
CRASH!
© 1936, by Walt Disney Enterprises, World rights reserved.
WALT DISNEY
9·20

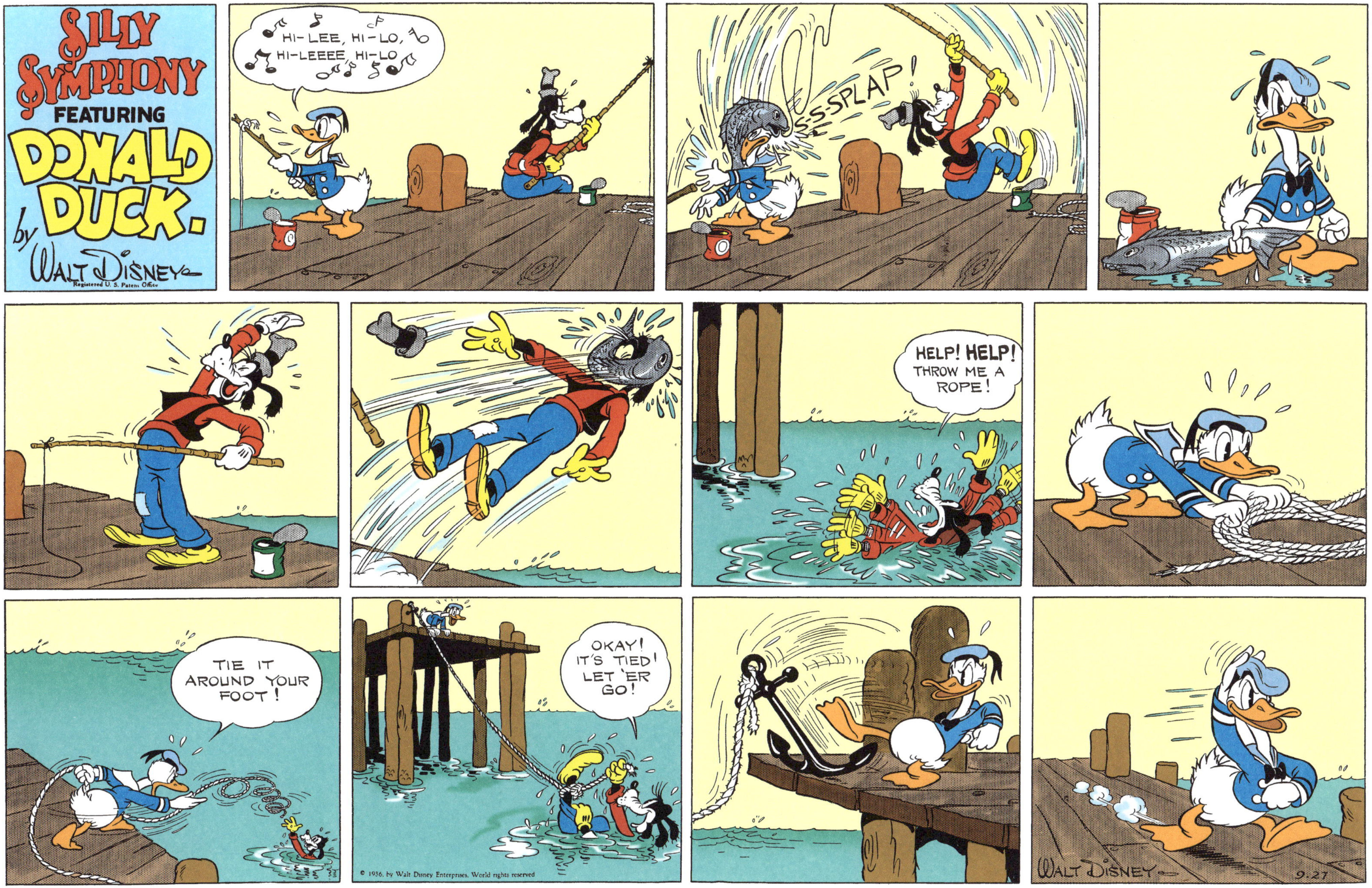
SILLY SYMPHONY
FEATURING
DONALD DUCK.
by WALT DISNEY
Registered U. S. Patent Office
HI-LEE, HI-LO, HI-LEEEE, HI-LO
S-S-SPLAP!
HELP! HELP! THROW ME A ROPE!
TIE IT AROUND YOUR FOOT!
OKAY! IT'S TIED! LET 'ER GO!
© 1936, by Walt Disney Enterprises. World rights reserved
WALT DISNEY
9-27

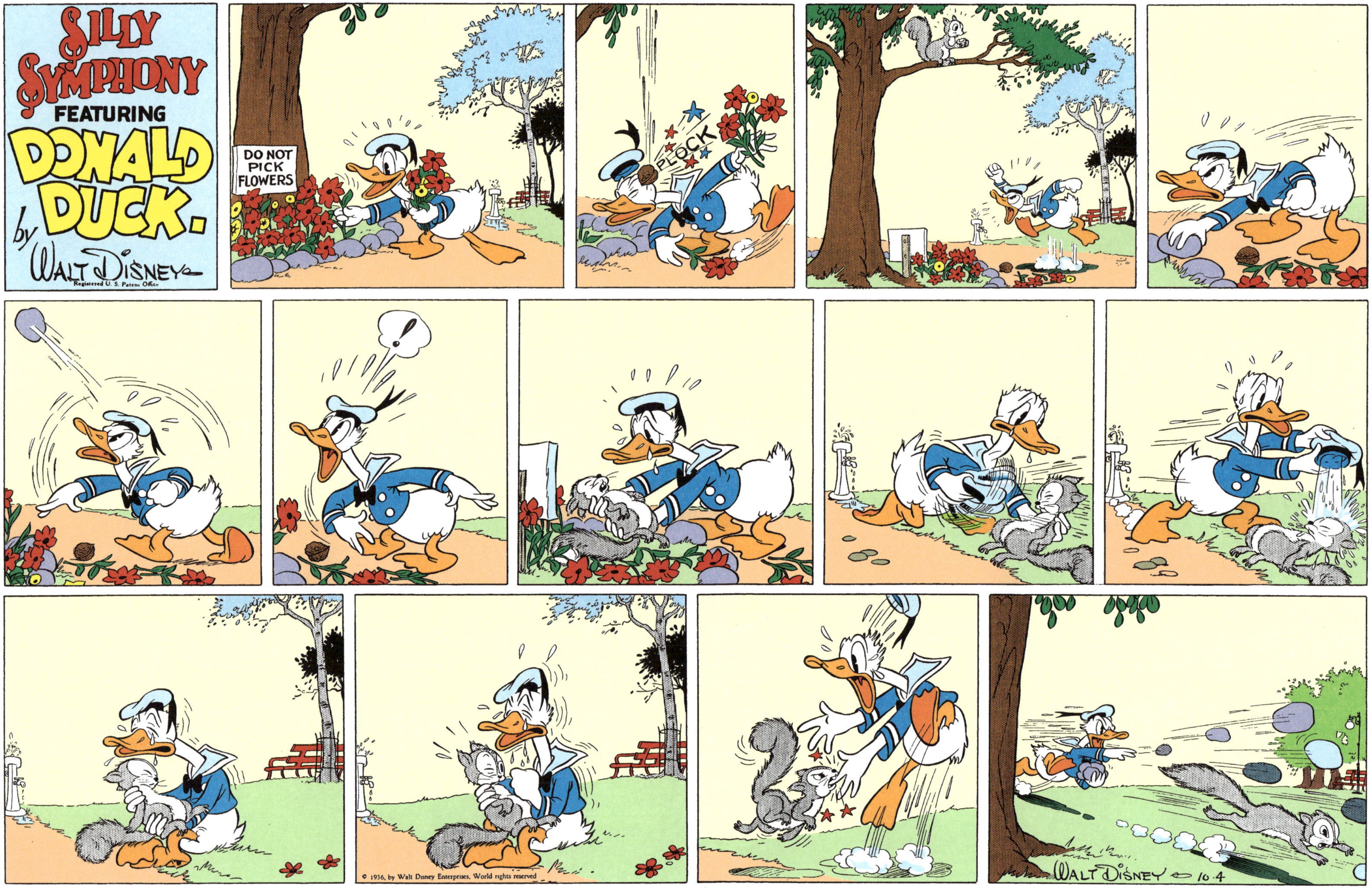
SILLY SYMPHONY
FEATURING
DONALD DUCK.
by WALT DISNEY
Registered U. S. Patent Office
DO NOT PICK FLOWERS
PLOCK
!
© 1936, by Walt Disney Enterprises, World rights reserved
WALT DISNEY 10.4

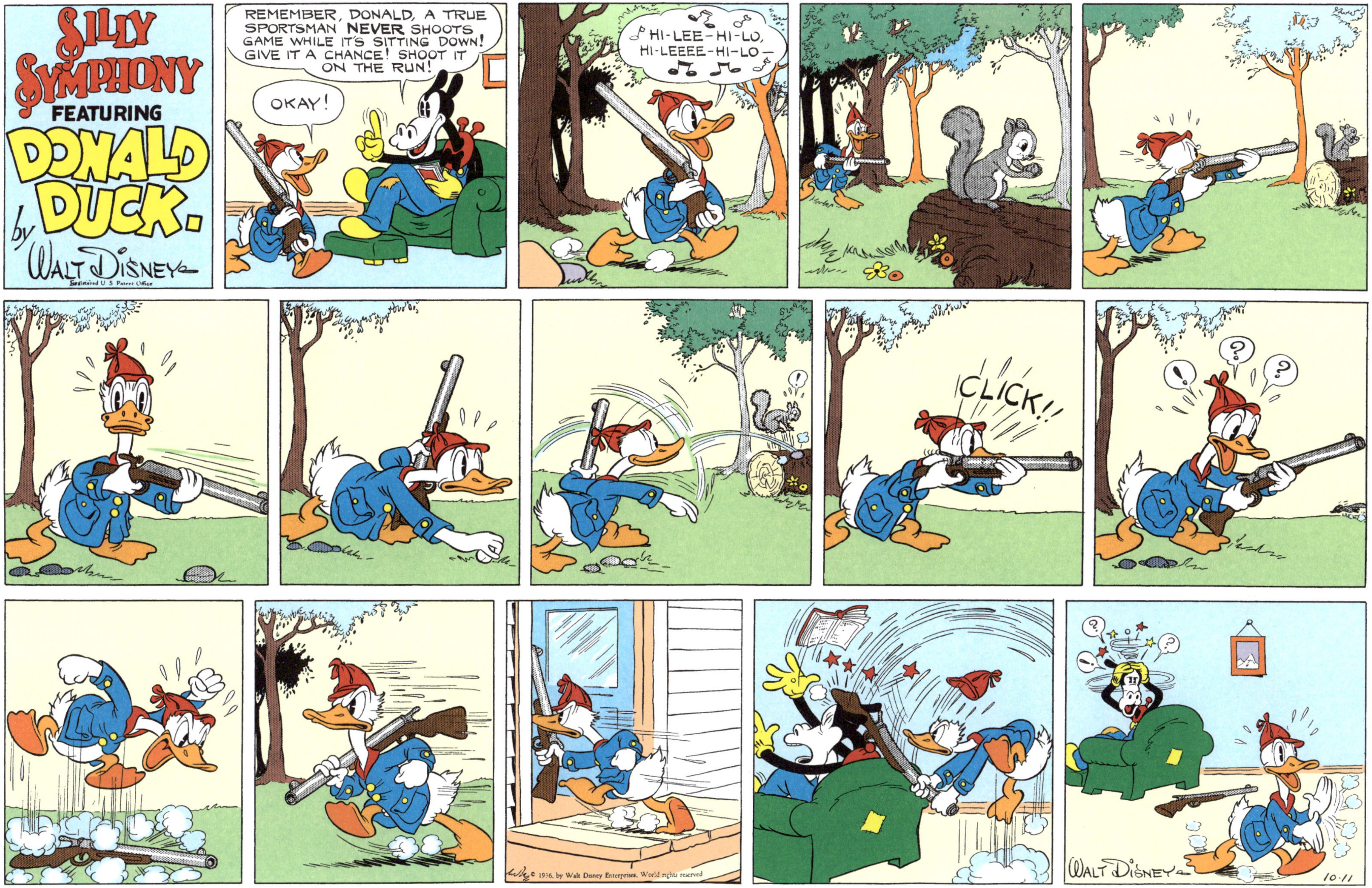
SILLY SYMPHONY
FEATURING
DONALD DUCK.
by WALT DISNEY
Registered U S Patent Office
REMEMBER, DONALD, A TRUE SPORTSMAN NEVER SHOOTS GAME WHILE IT'S SITTING DOWN! GIVE IT A CHANCE! SHOOT IT ON THE RUN!
OKAY!
HI-LEE-HI-LO, HI-LEEEE-HI-LO—
!
CLICK!!
!
?
?
© 1936, by Walt Disney Enterprises, World rights reserved
?
!
?
WALT DISNEY
10-11

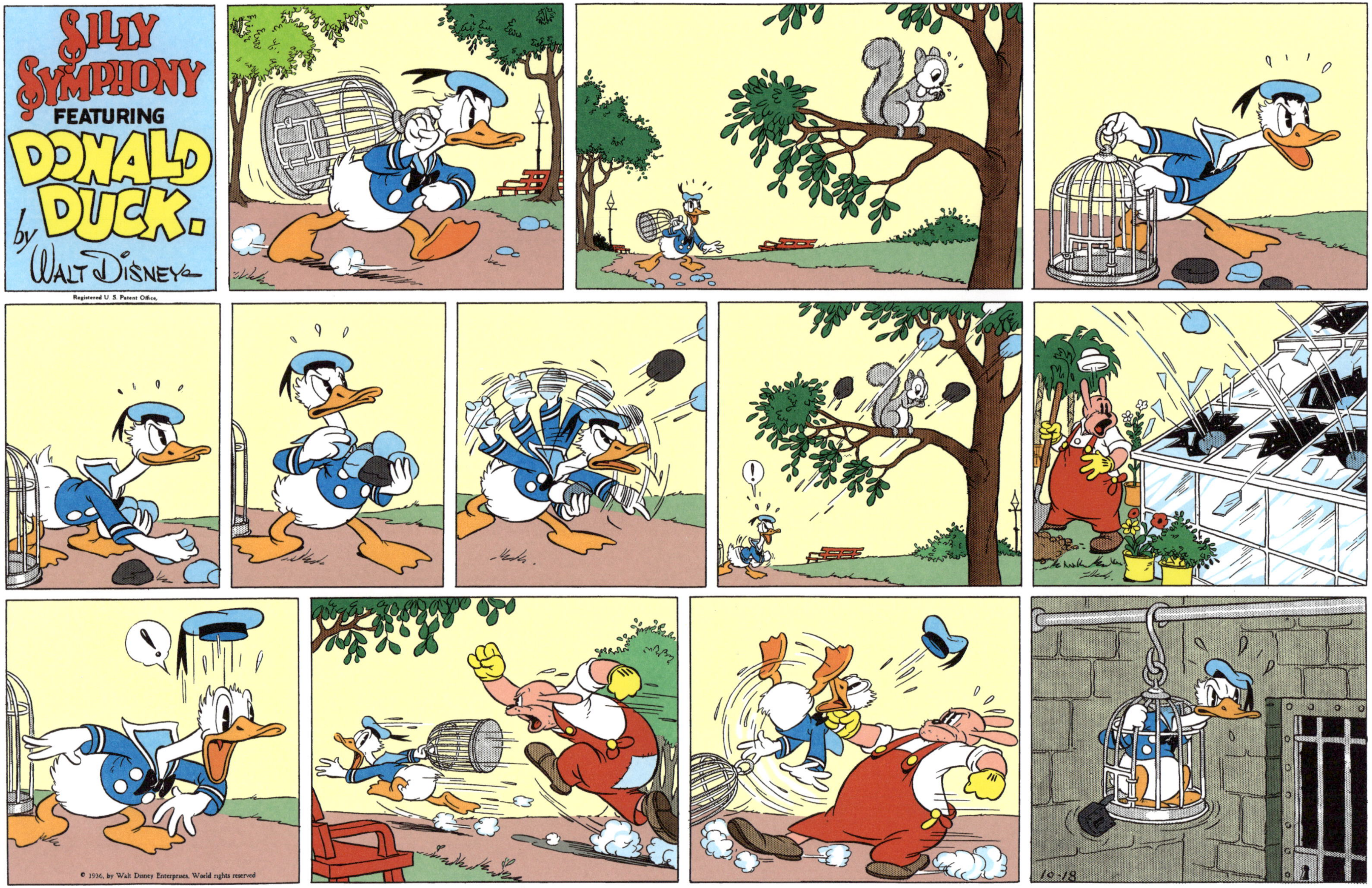

Silly Symphony featuring Donald Duck.
by Walt Disney
Registered U. S. Patent Office.
!
!
© 1936, by Walt Disney Enterprises, World rights reserved
10-18

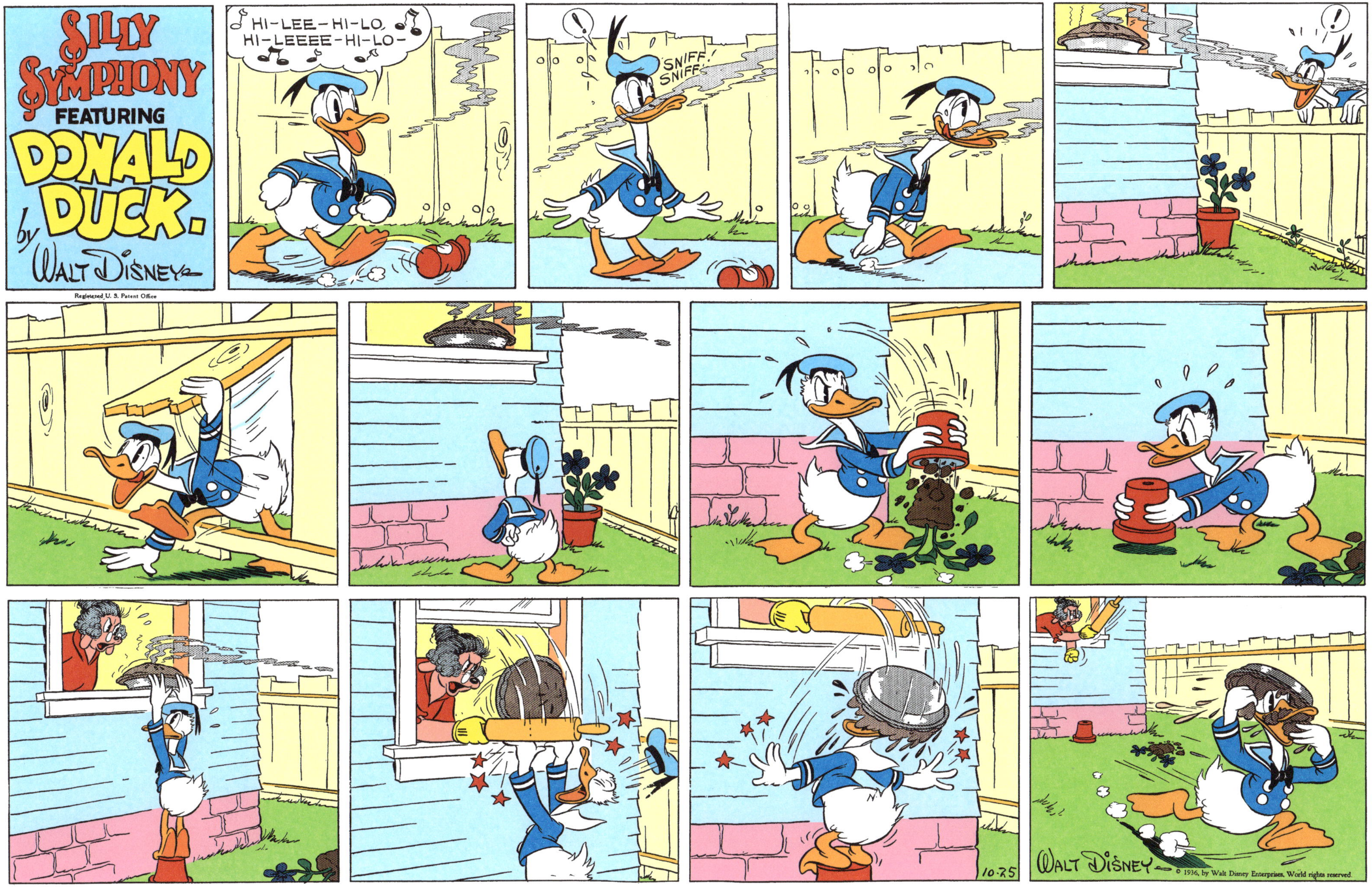
SILLY SYMPHONY
FEATURING
DONALD DUCK.
by WALT DISNEY
Registered U. S. Patent Office
HI-LEE-HI-LO, HI-LEEEE-HI-LO-
!
SNIFF! SNIFF!
!
10-25
WALT DISNEY
© 1936, by Walt Disney Enterprises, World rights reserved.

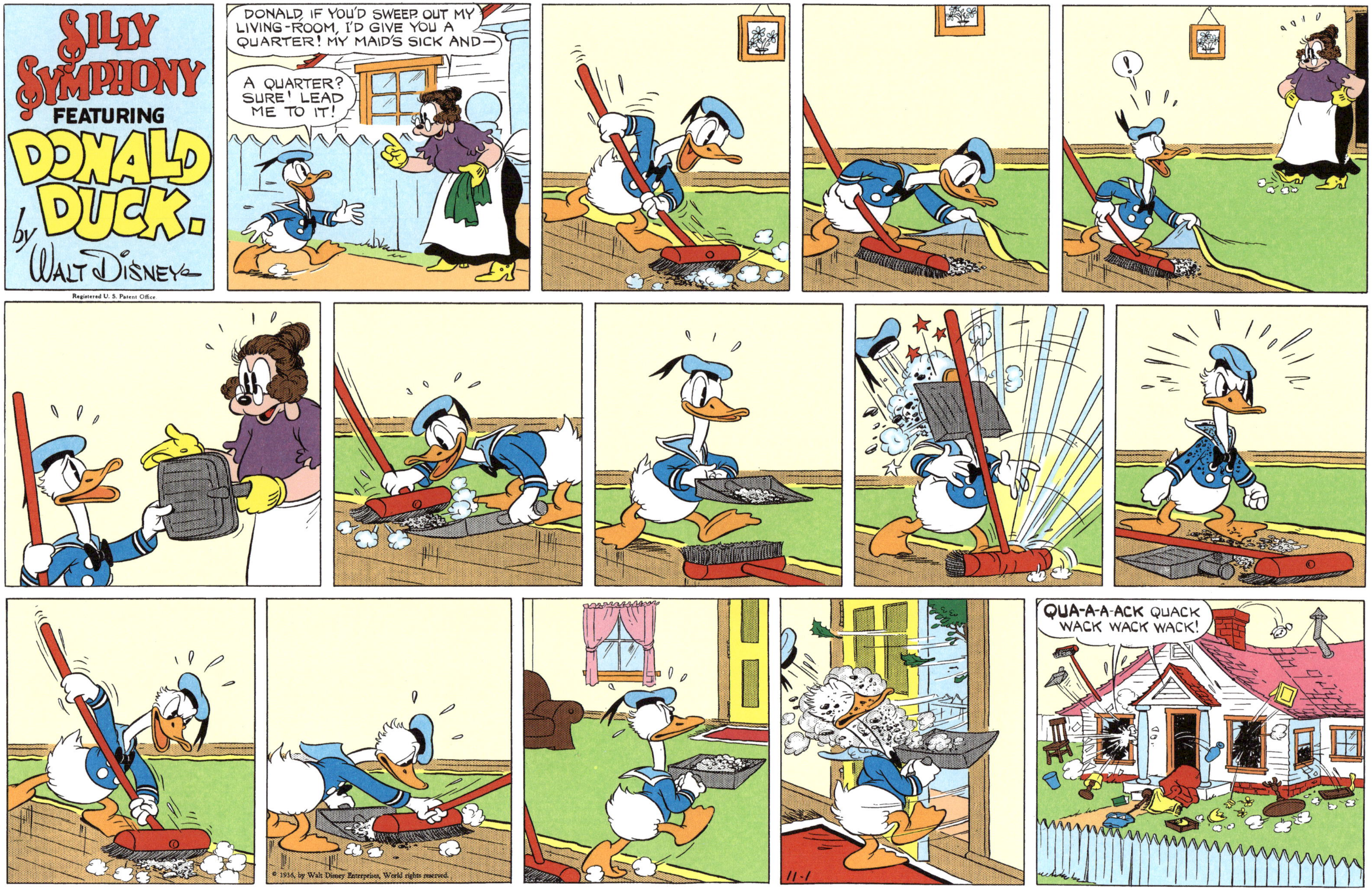
SILLY SYMPHONY
FEATURING
DONALD DUCK.
by
WALT DISNEY
Registered U. S. Patent Office
DONALD, IF YOU'D SWEEP OUT MY LIVING-ROOM, I'D GIVE YOU A QUARTER! MY MAID'S SICK AND—
A QUARTER? SURE! LEAD ME TO IT!
!
© 1936, by Walt Disney Enterprises, World rights reserved.
11-1
QUA-A-A-ACK QUACK WACK WACK WACK!

SILLY SYMPHONY
FEATURING
DONALD DUCK.
by WALT DISNEY
Registered U S Patent Office
HONK!
HEY, M——
BIJOU THEATRE
DRUGS
CANDY
CAND
© 1936, by Walt Disney Enterprises, World rights reserved
11·8
WALT DISNEY

SILLY SYMPHONY
FEATURING
DONALD DUCK.
by WALT DISNEY
Registered U. S. Patent Office.
HI-LEE HI-LO
HI-LEEEE HI-LO!
POSITIVELY
ABSOLUTELY
NO FISHING
OF ANY FORM,
SHAPE OR SIZE
!
POSITIVELY
ABSOLUTELY
NO FISHING
OF ANY FORM,
SHAPE OR SIZE
!
HEY!
AW, FOOEY—
BLAAAAAA—
!
GRR-R!
GR-R-R-R
11-15
© 1936, by Walt Disney Enterprises, World rights reserved
WALT DISNEY

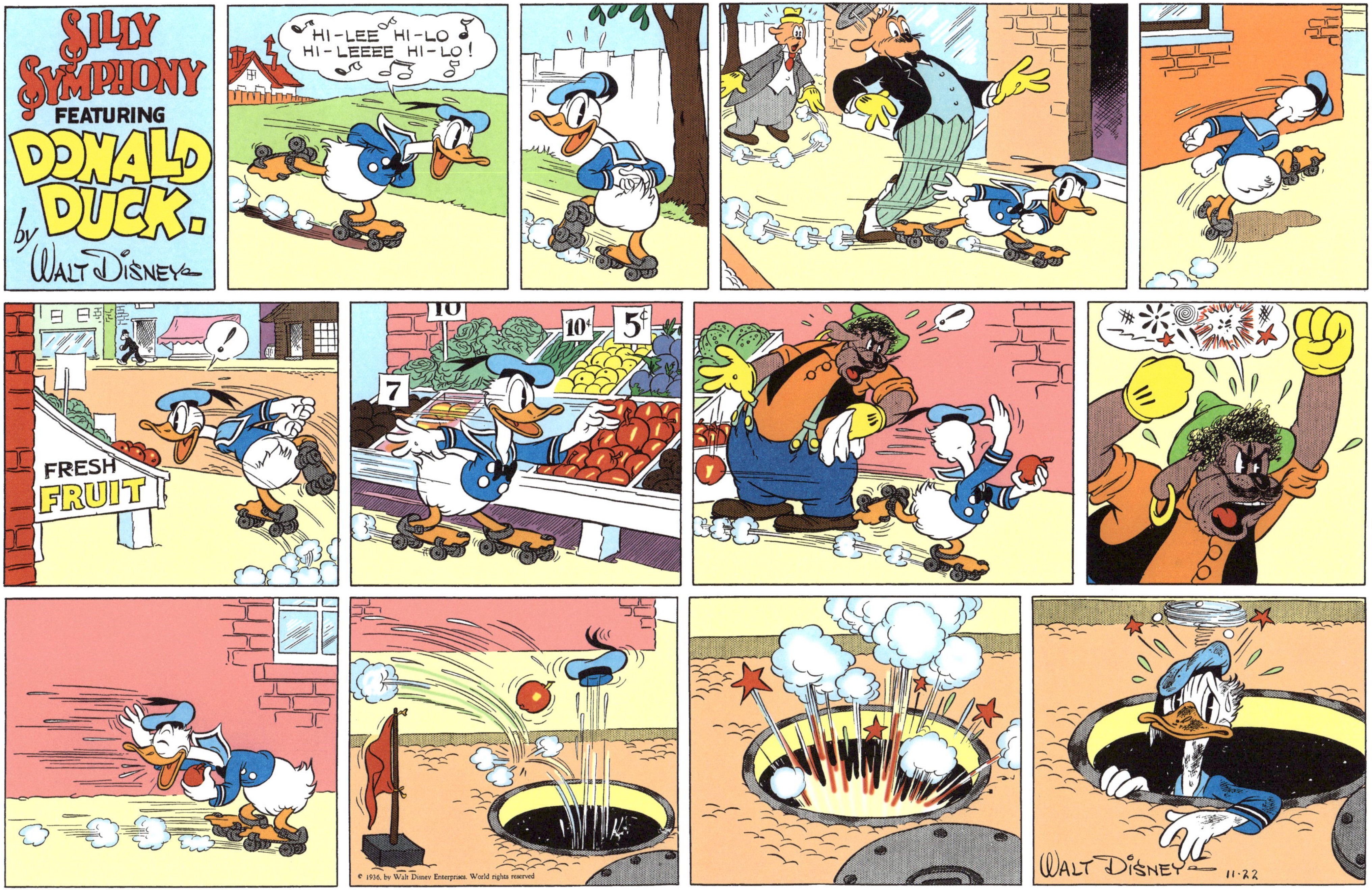
SILLY SYMPHONY
FEATURING
DONALD DUCK.
by WALT DISNEY
HI-LEE HI-LO HI-LEEEE HI-LO!
10
10¢
5¢
7
FRESH
FRUIT
!
© 1936, by Walt Disney Enterprises. World rights reserved
WALT DISNEY 11-22

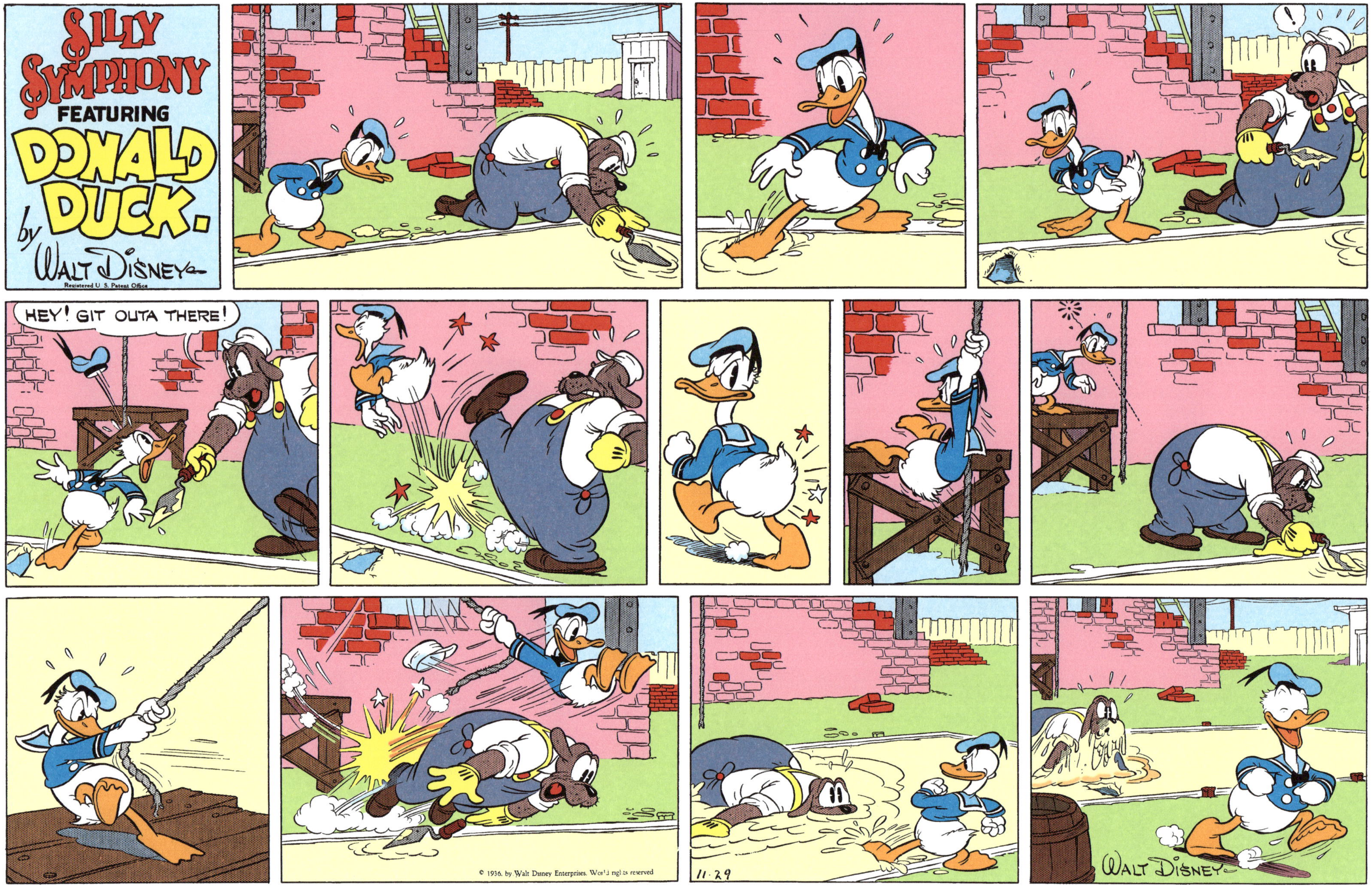
SILLY SYMPHONY
FEATURING
DONALD DUCK.
by WALT DISNEY
Registered U. S. Patent Office
HEY! GIT OUTA THERE!
© 1936, by Walt Disney Enterprises. World rights reserved
11-29
WALT DISNEY

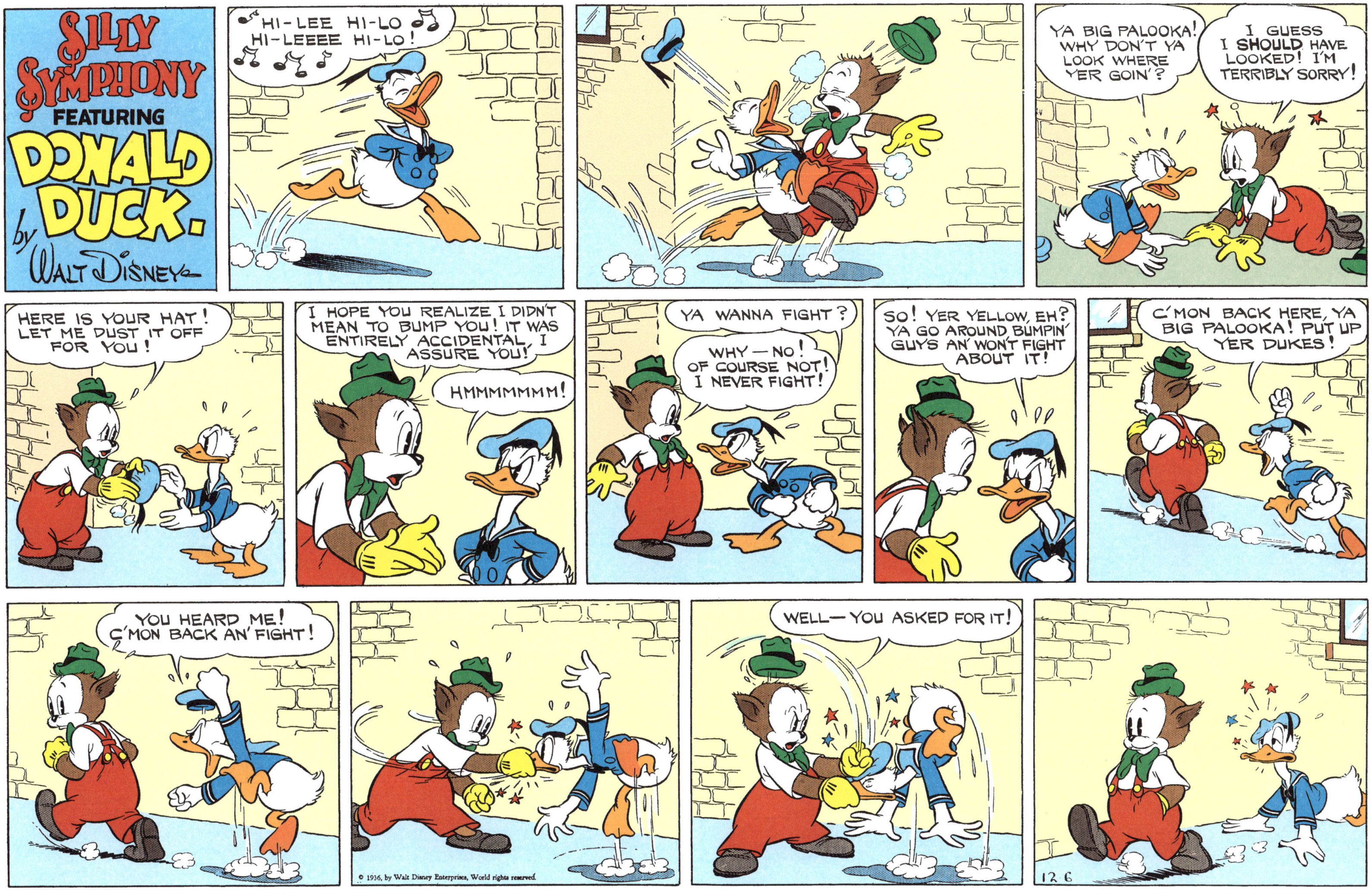
SILLY SYMPHONY
FEATURING
DONALD DUCK.
by WALT DISNEY
HI-LEE HI-LO HI-LEEEE HI-LO!
YA BIG PALOOKA! WHY DON'T YA LOOK WHERE YER GOIN'?
I GUESS I SHOULD HAVE LOOKED! I'M TERRIBLY SORRY!
HERE IS YOUR HAT! LET ME DUST IT OFF FOR YOU!
I HOPE YOU REALIZE I DIDN'T MEAN TO BUMP YOU! IT WAS ENTIRELY ACCIDENTAL, I ASSURE YOU!
HMMMMMMM!
YA WANNA FIGHT?
WHY—NO! OF COURSE NOT! I NEVER FIGHT!
SO! YER YELLOW, EH? YA GO AROUND BUMPIN' GUYS AN' WON'T FIGHT ABOUT IT!
C'MON BACK HERE, YA BIG PALOOKA! PUT UP YER DUKES!
YOU HEARD ME! C'MON BACK AN' FIGHT!
© 1936, by Walt Disney Enterprises, World rights reserved.
WELL—YOU ASKED FOR IT!
12 6

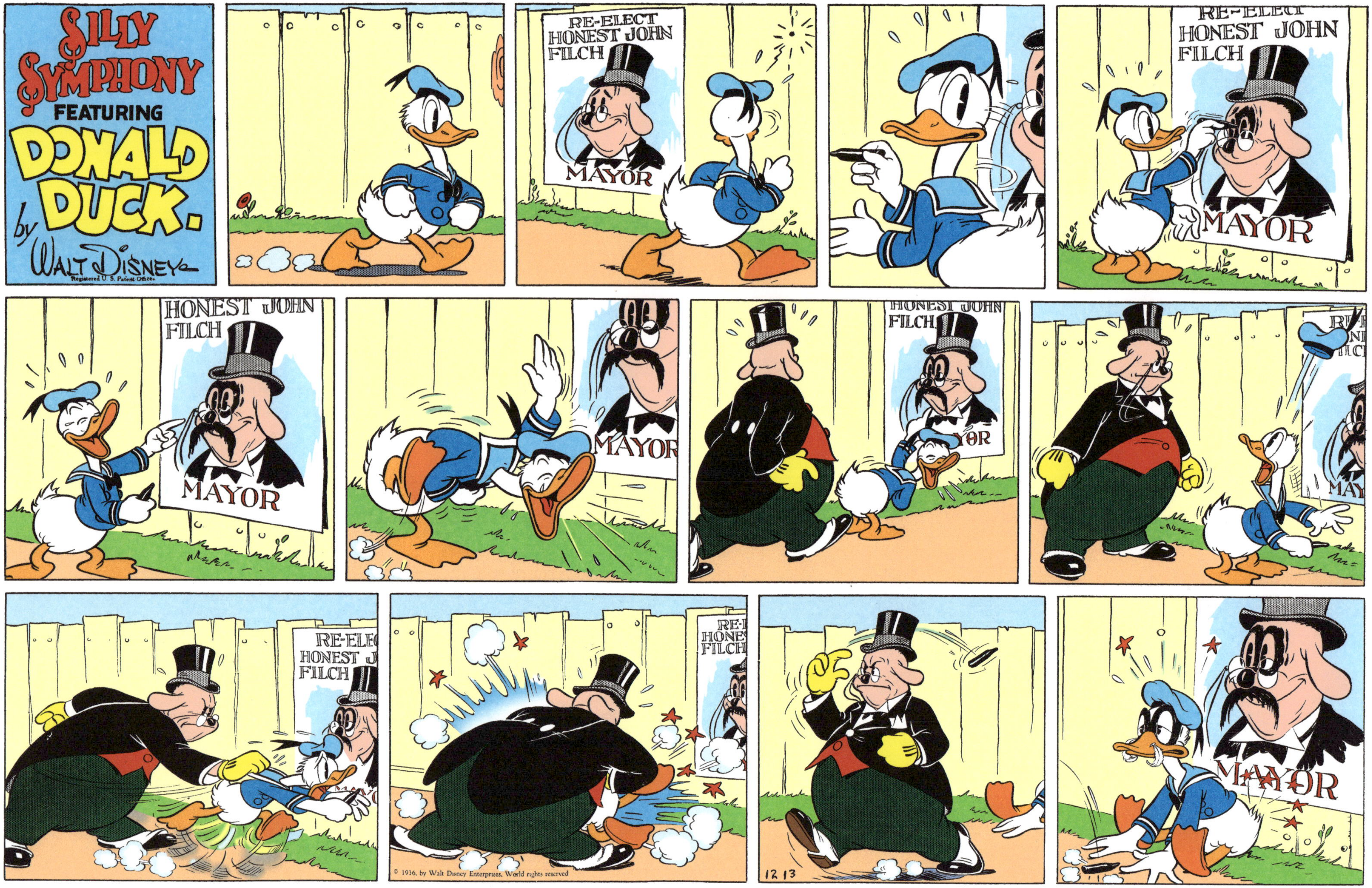
SILLY SYMPHONY
FEATURING
DONALD DUCK.
by
WALT DISNEY
Registered U.S. Patent Office
RE-ELECT
HONEST JOHN
FILCH
MAYOR
© 1936, by Walt Disney Enterprises, World rights reserved
12 13

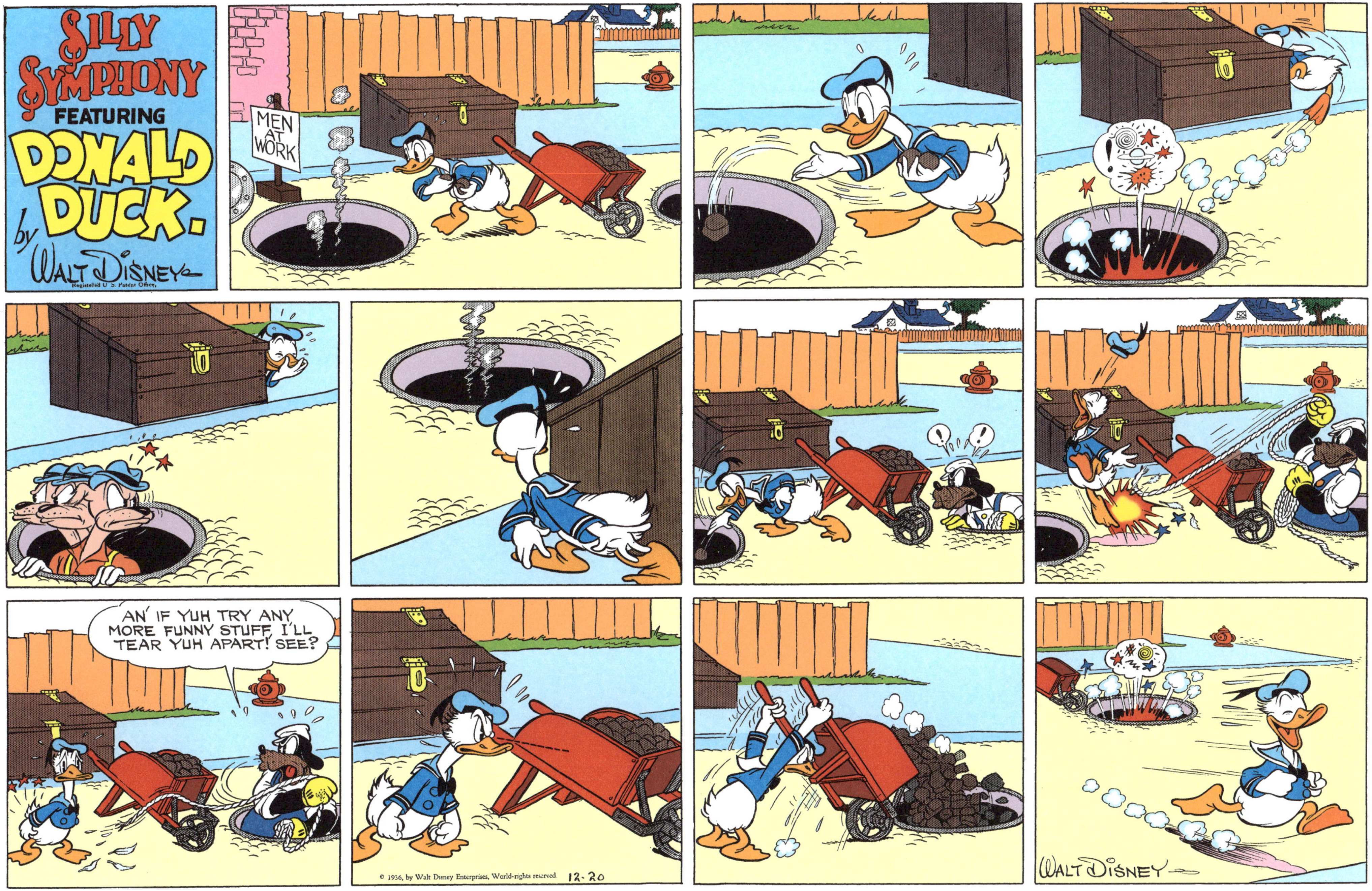
SILLY SYMPHONY
FEATURING
DONALD DUCK.
by WALT DISNEY
Registered U.S. Patent Office.
MEN AT WORK
AN' IF YUH TRY ANY MORE FUNNY STUFF, I'LL TEAR YUH APART! SEE?
© 1936, by Walt Disney Enterprises, World-rights reserved. 12-20
WALT DISNEY

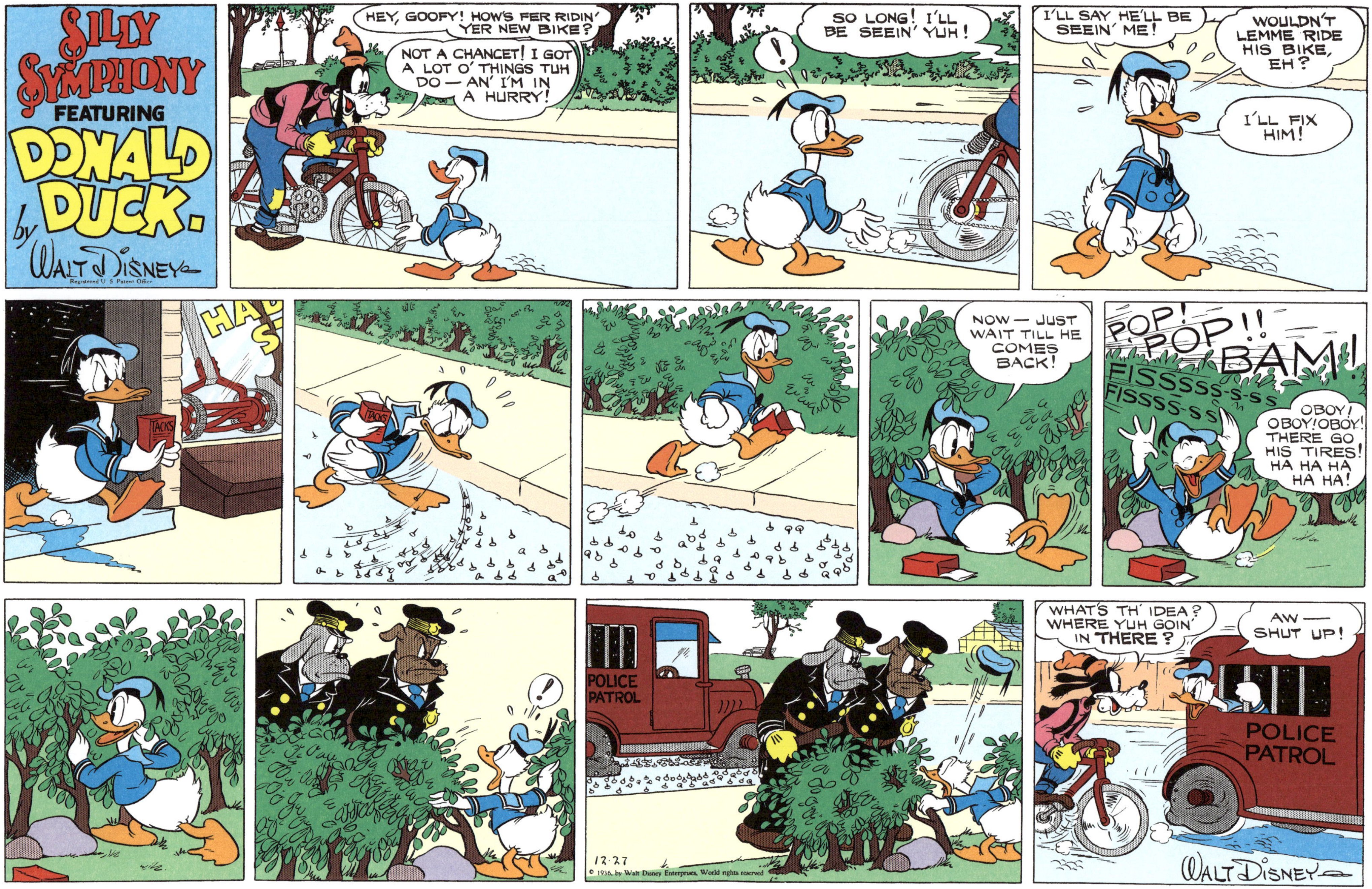
SILLY SYMPHONY
FEATURING
DONALD DUCK.
by WALT DISNEY
Registered U S Patent Office
HEY, GOOFY! HOW'S FER RIDIN' YER NEW BIKE?
NOT A CHANCET! I GOT A LOT O' THINGS TUH DO — AN' I'M IN A HURRY!
SO LONG! I'LL BE SEEIN' YUH!
!
I'LL SAY HE'LL BE SEEIN' ME!
WOULDN'T LEMME RIDE HIS BIKE, EH?
I'LL FIX HIM!
TACKS
TACKS
NOW — JUST WAIT TILL HE COMES BACK!
POP! POP!! BAM!
FISSSSS-S-SS
FISSSS-SS
OBOY! OBOY! OBOY! THERE GO HIS TIRES! HA HA HA HA HA!
!
POLICE PATROL
12-27
© 1936, by Walt Disney Enterprises, World rights reserved
WHAT'S TH' IDEA? WHERE YUH GOIN' IN THERE?
AW — SHUT UP!
POLICE PATROL
WALT DISNEY

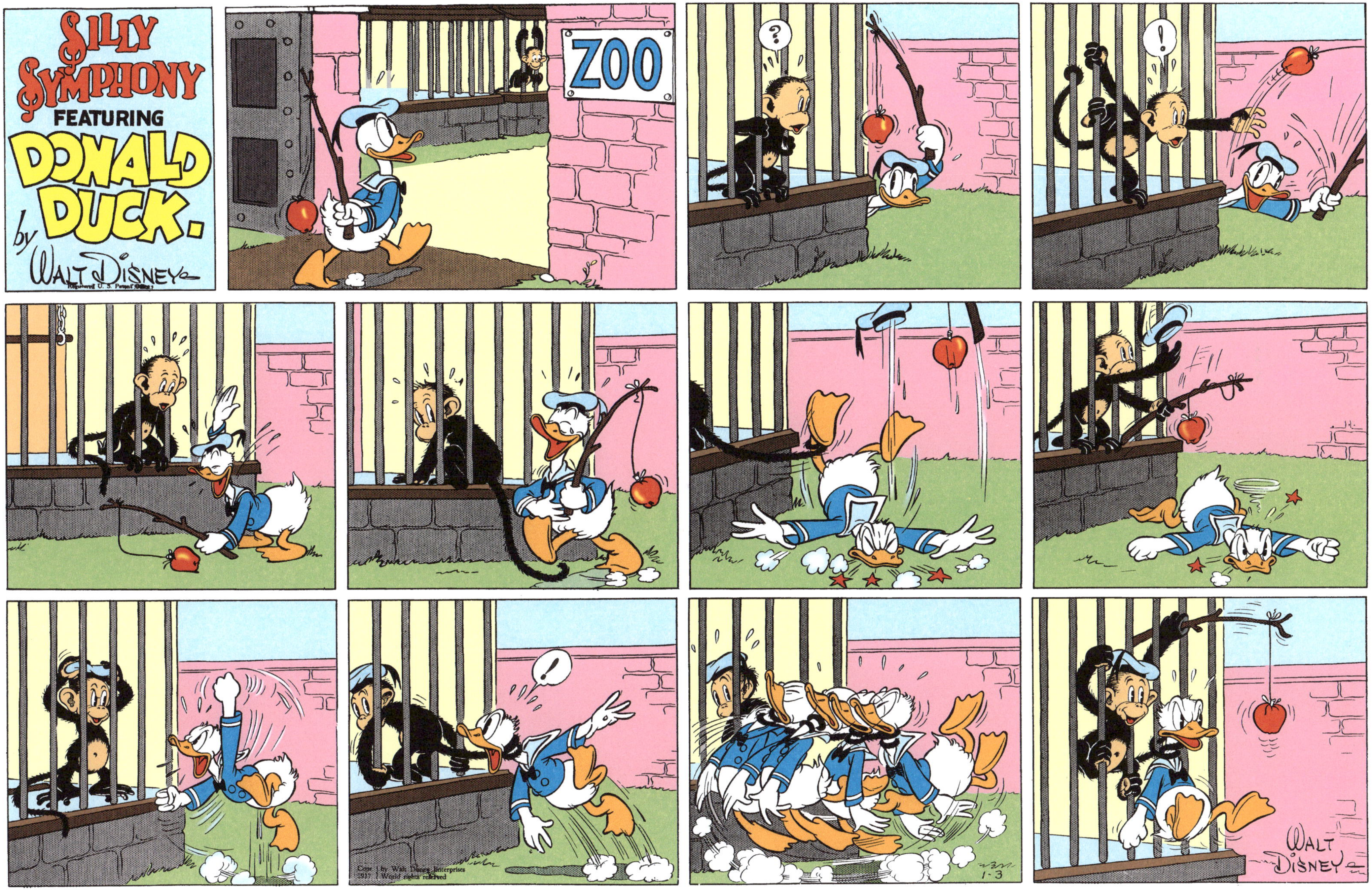
SILLY SYMPHONY
FEATURING
DONALD DUCK.
by WALT DISNEY
Registered U. S. Patent Office
ZOO
?
!
!
Copr. 1937 by Walt Disney Enterprises
World rights reserved
1-3
WALT DISNEY

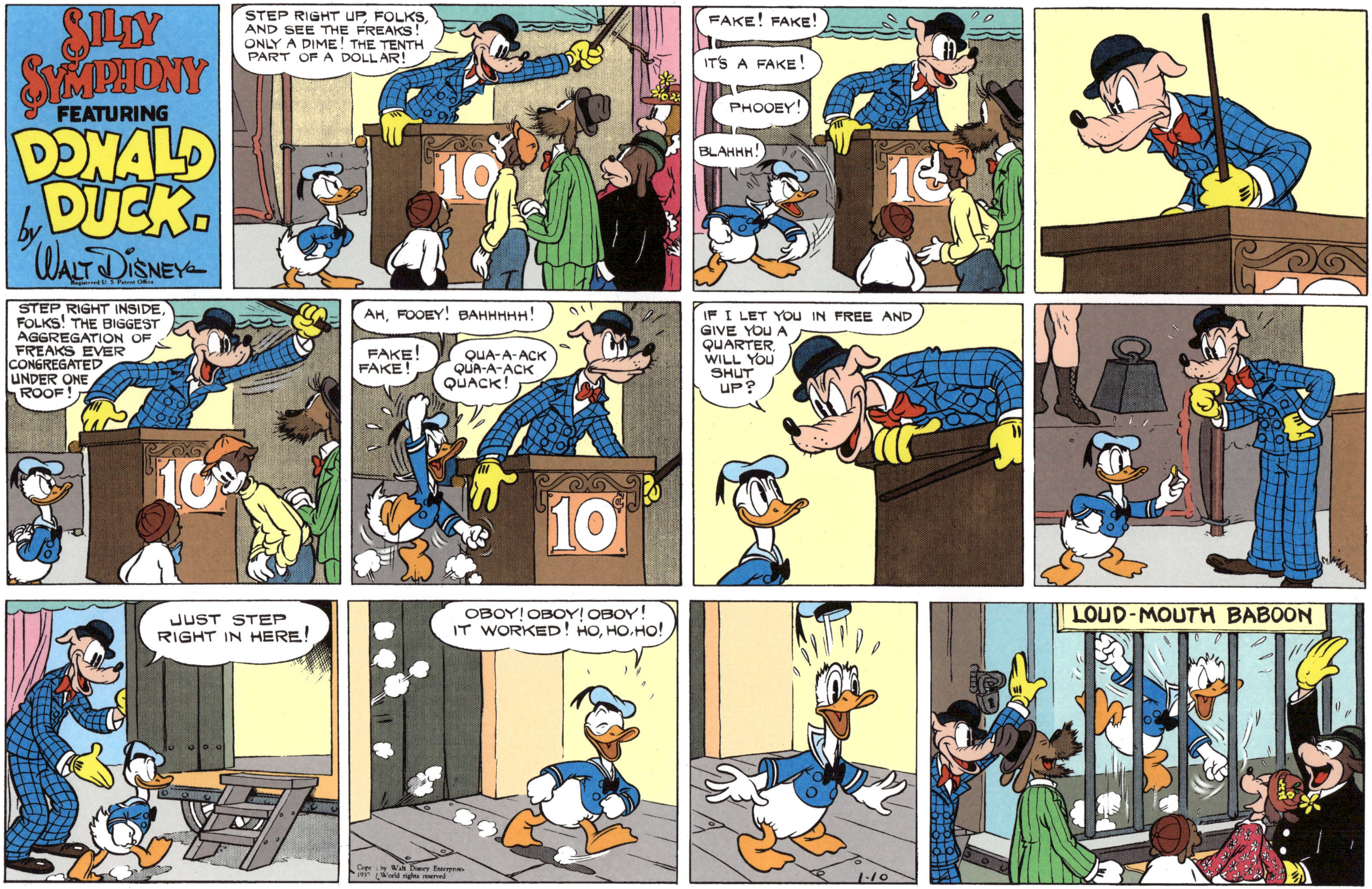
SILLY SYMPHONY
FEATURING
DONALD DUCK.
by WALT DISNEY
Registered U.S. Patent Office
STEP RIGHT UP, FOLKS, AND SEE THE FREAKS! ONLY A DIME! THE TENTH PART OF A DOLLAR!
10
FAKE! FAKE!
IT'S A FAKE!
PHOOEY!
BLAHHH!
STEP RIGHT INSIDE, FOLKS! THE BIGGEST AGGREGATION OF FREAKS EVER CONGREGATED UNDER ONE ROOF!
AH, FOOEY! BAHHHHH!
FAKE! FAKE!
QUA-A-ACK QUA-A-ACK QUACK!
IF I LET YOU IN FREE AND GIVE YOU A QUARTER, WILL YOU SHUT UP?
JUST STEP RIGHT IN HERE!
OBOY! OBOY! OBOY! IT WORKED! HO, HO, HO!
Copr. 1937 by Walt Disney Enterprises World rights reserved
1-10
LOUD-MOUTH BABOON

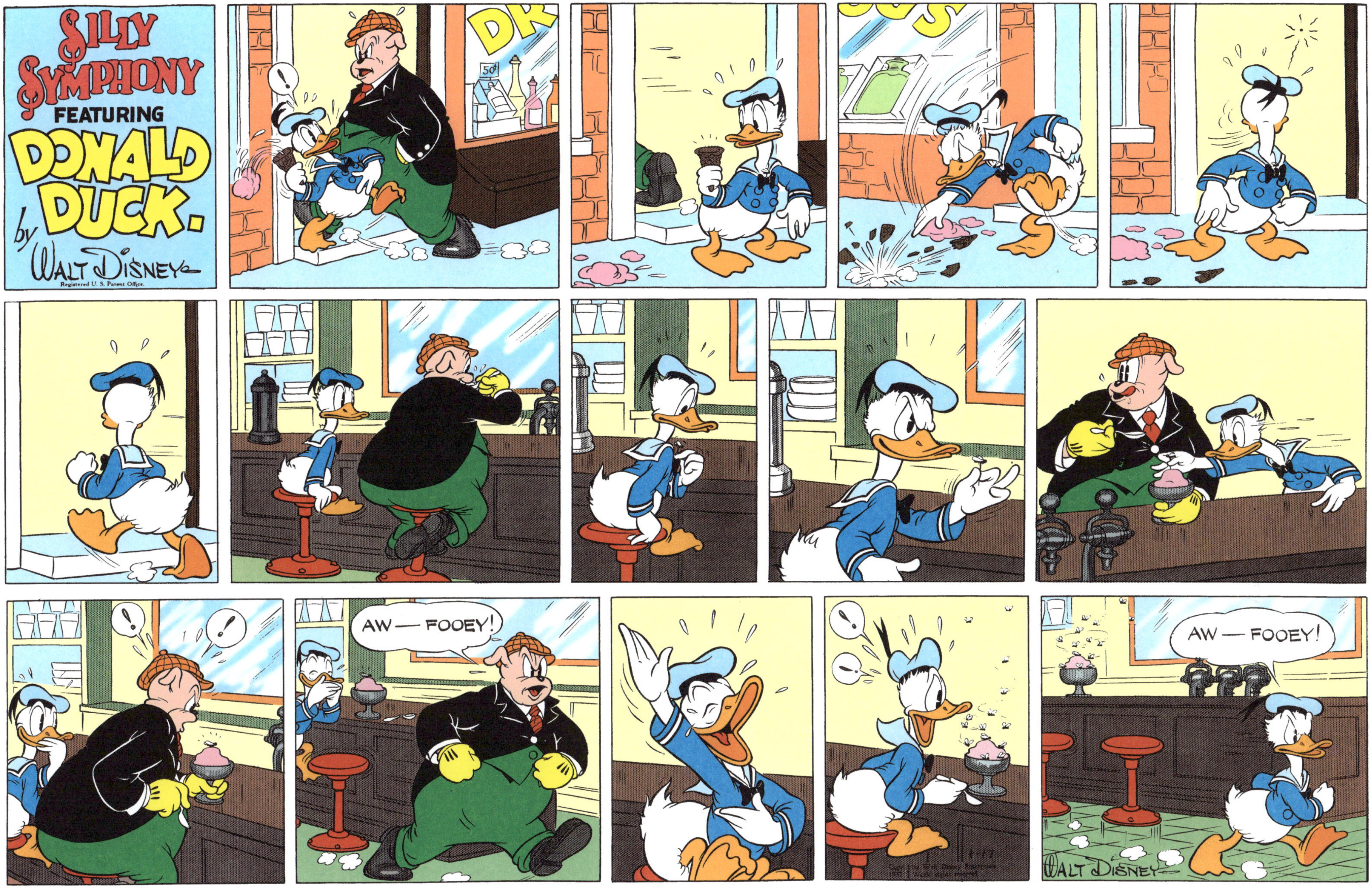
SILLY SYMPHONY
FEATURING
DONALD DUCK.
by WALT DISNEY
Registered U. S. Patent Office.
AW — FOOEY!
AW — FOOEY!
WALT DISNEY

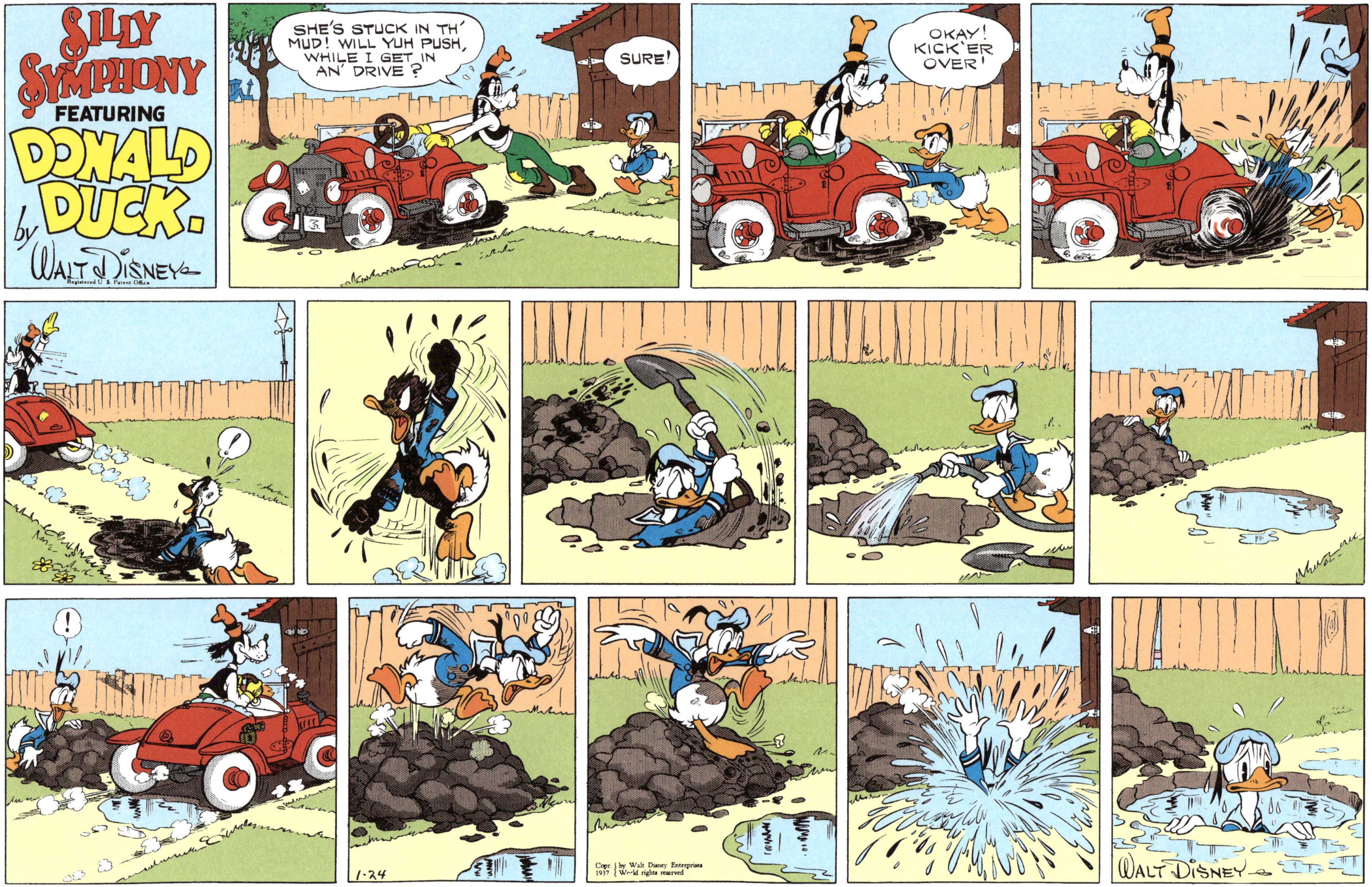
SILLY SYMPHONY
FEATURING
DONALD DUCK.
by WALT DISNEY
Registered U. S. Patent Office
SHE'S STUCK IN TH' MUD! WILL YUH PUSH, WHILE I GET IN AN' DRIVE ?
SURE!
OKAY! KICK 'ER OVER!
!
!
1-24
Copr. 1937 by Walt Disney Enterprises World rights reserved
WALT DISNEY

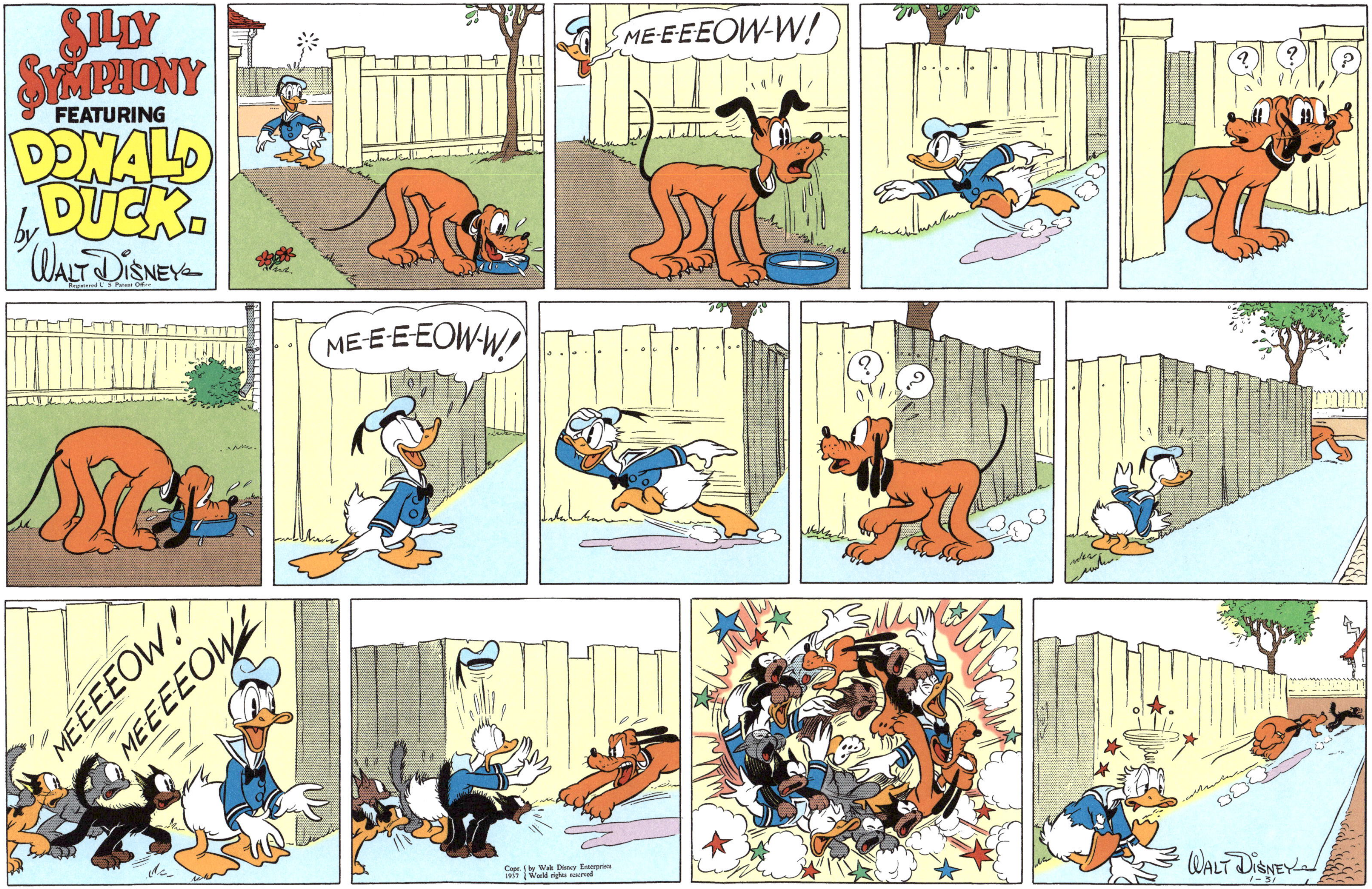
SILLY SYMPHONY
FEATURING
DONALD DUCK.
by WALT DISNEY
Registered U. S. Patent Office
ME-E-E-EOW-W!
?
?
?
ME-E-E-EOW-W!
?
?
ME-E-E-EOW!
ME-E-E-EOW!
Copr. 1937 by Walt Disney Enterprises World rights reserved
WALT DISNEY
1-31

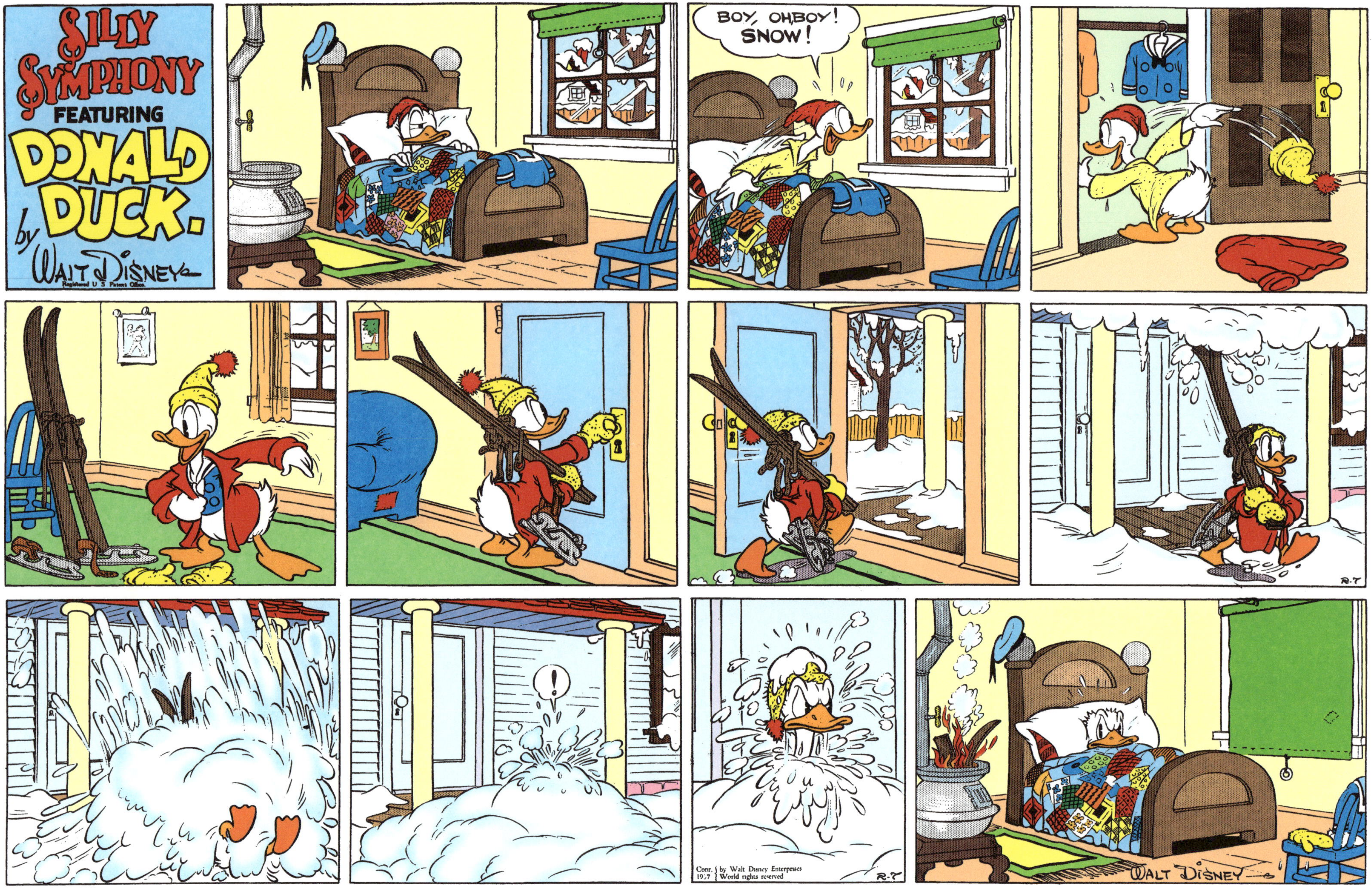
SILLY SYMPHONY
FEATURING
DONALD DUCK.
by WALT DISNEY
Registered U S Patent Office
BOY, OHBOY! SNOW!
!
Copr. by Walt Disney Enterprises
1937 World rights reserved
WALT DISNEY

SILLY SYMPHONY
FEATURING
DONALD DUCK.
by WALT DISNEY
Registered U. S. Patent Office.
LOOK, MISTER! I CLEANED OFF YOUR SIDEWALK FOR YOU! IS IT WORTH ANYTHING TO YOU?
WELL, BLESS MY SOUL! SO YOU DID!
OF COURSE, IT'S WORTH SOMETHING TO ME! HERE'S FIFTY CENTS!
BOY! WHAT A SLICK WAY TO MAKE MONEY! AN' IF HIS WAS WORTH FIFTY CENTS, THIS ONE OUGHT TO BE WORTH TWO DOLLARS!
2-14
Copr. 1937 by Walt Disney Enterprises World rights reserved
FOR RENT
WALT DISNEY

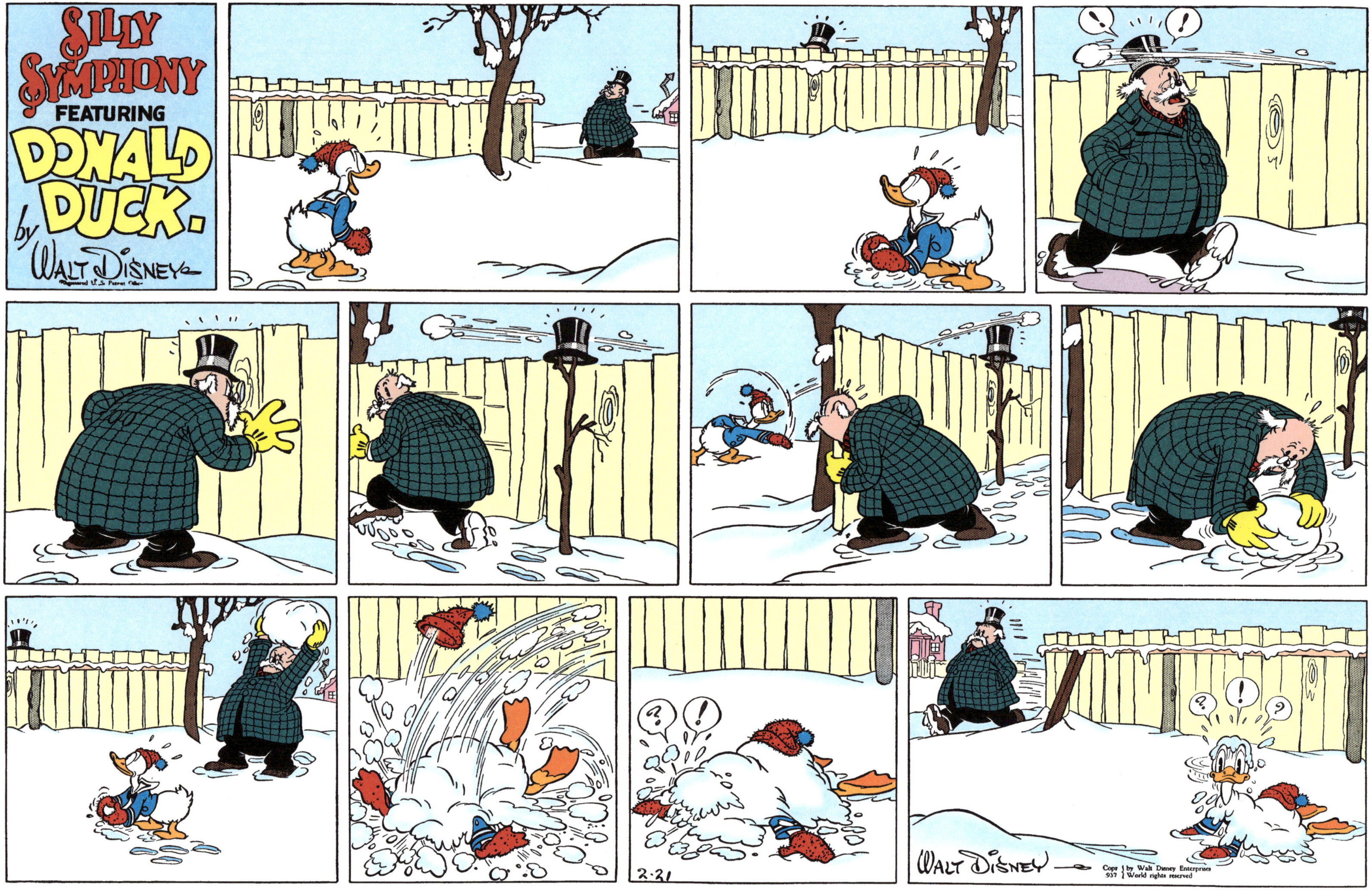
SILLY SYMPHONY
FEATURING
DONALD DUCK.
by
WALT DISNEY
2·21
WALT DISNEY
Copr 1937 by Walt Disney Enterprises
World rights reserved

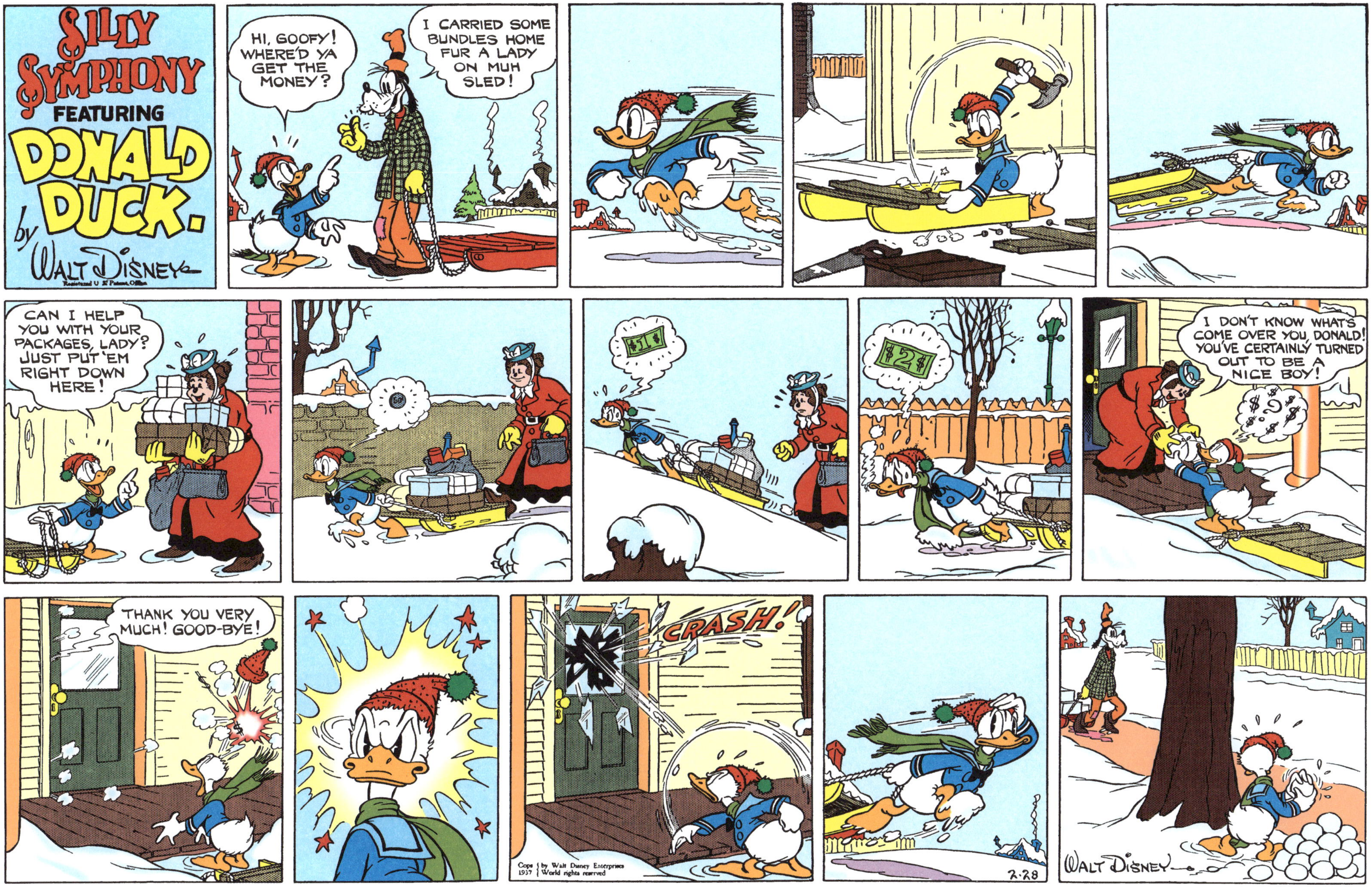
SILLY SYMPHONY
FEATURING
DONALD DUCK.
by WALT DISNEY
HI, GOOFY! WHERE'D YA GET THE MONEY?
I CARRIED SOME BUNDLES HOME FUR A LADY ON MUH SLED!
CAN I HELP YOU WITH YOUR PACKAGES, LADY? JUST PUT 'EM RIGHT DOWN HERE!
$1
$2
I DON'T KNOW WHAT'S COME OVER YOU, DONALD! YOU'VE CERTAINLY TURNED OUT TO BE A NICE BOY!
THANK YOU VERY MUCH! GOOD-BYE!
CRASH!
Copr 1937 by Walt Disney Enterprises World rights reserved
2-28
WALT DISNEY

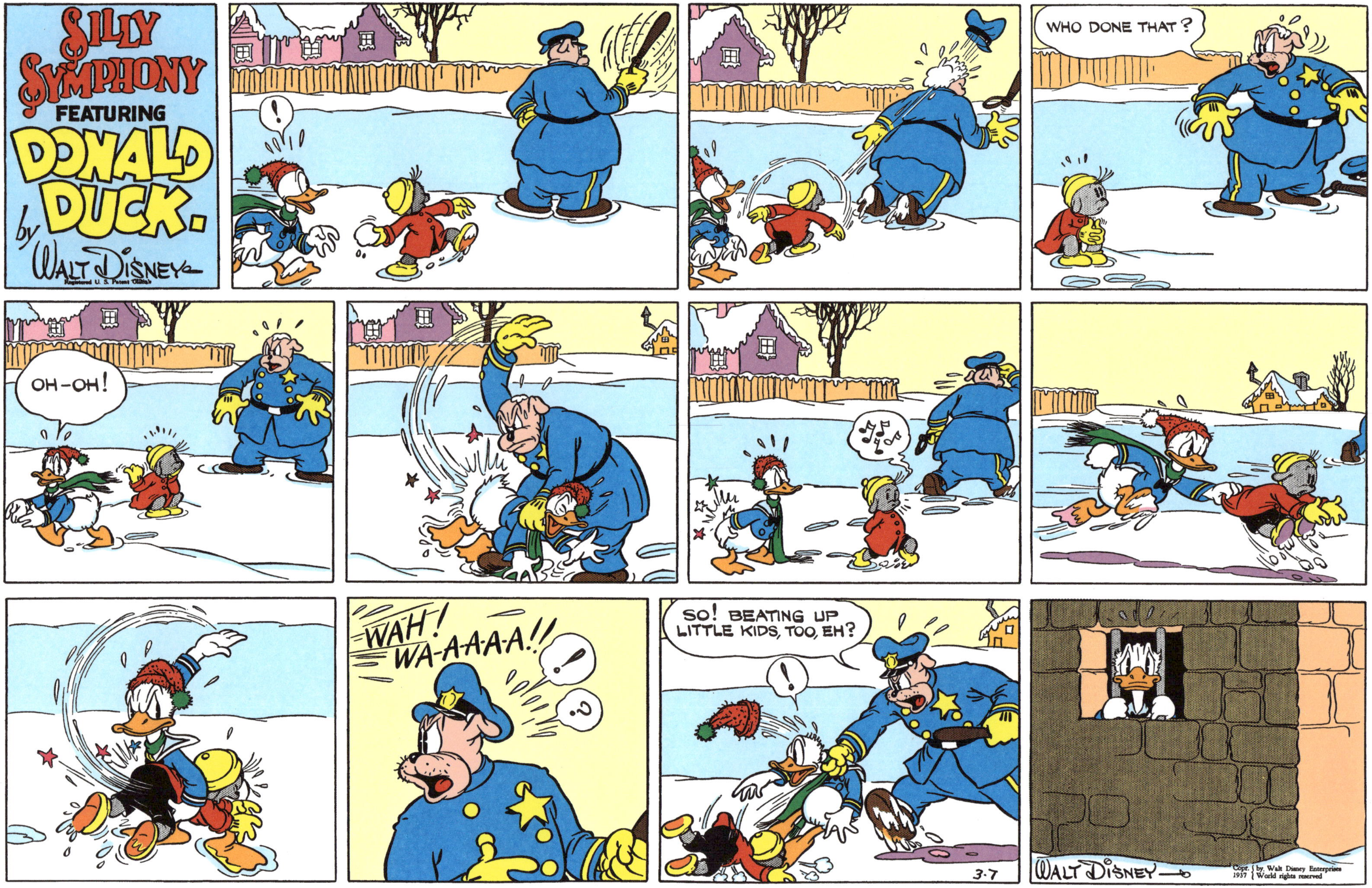
SILLY SYMPHONY
FEATURING
DONALD DUCK.
by WALT DISNEY
Registered U. S. Patent Office
!
WHO DONE THAT?
OH-OH!
WAH! WA-A-A-A-A!!
!
?
SO! BEATING UP LITTLE KIDS, TOO, EH?
!
3-7
WALT DISNEY
Copr. 1937 by Walt Disney Enterprises World rights reserved

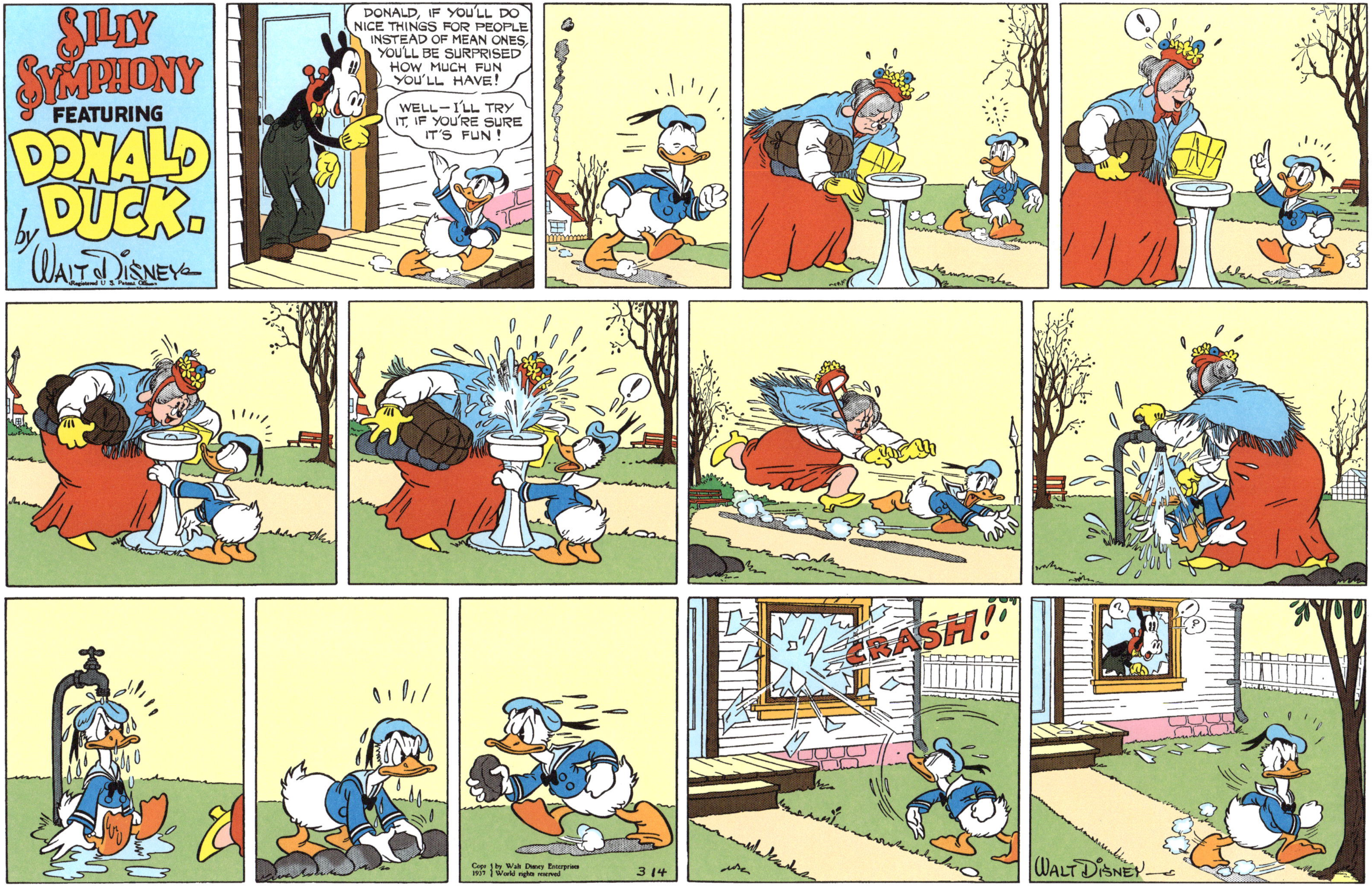
SILLY SYMPHONY
FEATURING
DONALD DUCK.
by WALT DISNEY
Registered U. S. Patent Office
DONALD, IF YOU'LL DO NICE THINGS FOR PEOPLE INSTEAD OF MEAN ONES, YOU'LL BE SURPRISED HOW MUCH FUN YOU'LL HAVE!
WELL—I'LL TRY IT, IF YOU'RE SURE IT'S FUN!
!
!
Copr. 1937 by Walt Disney Enterprises World rights reserved
3 14
CRASH!
WALT DISNEY

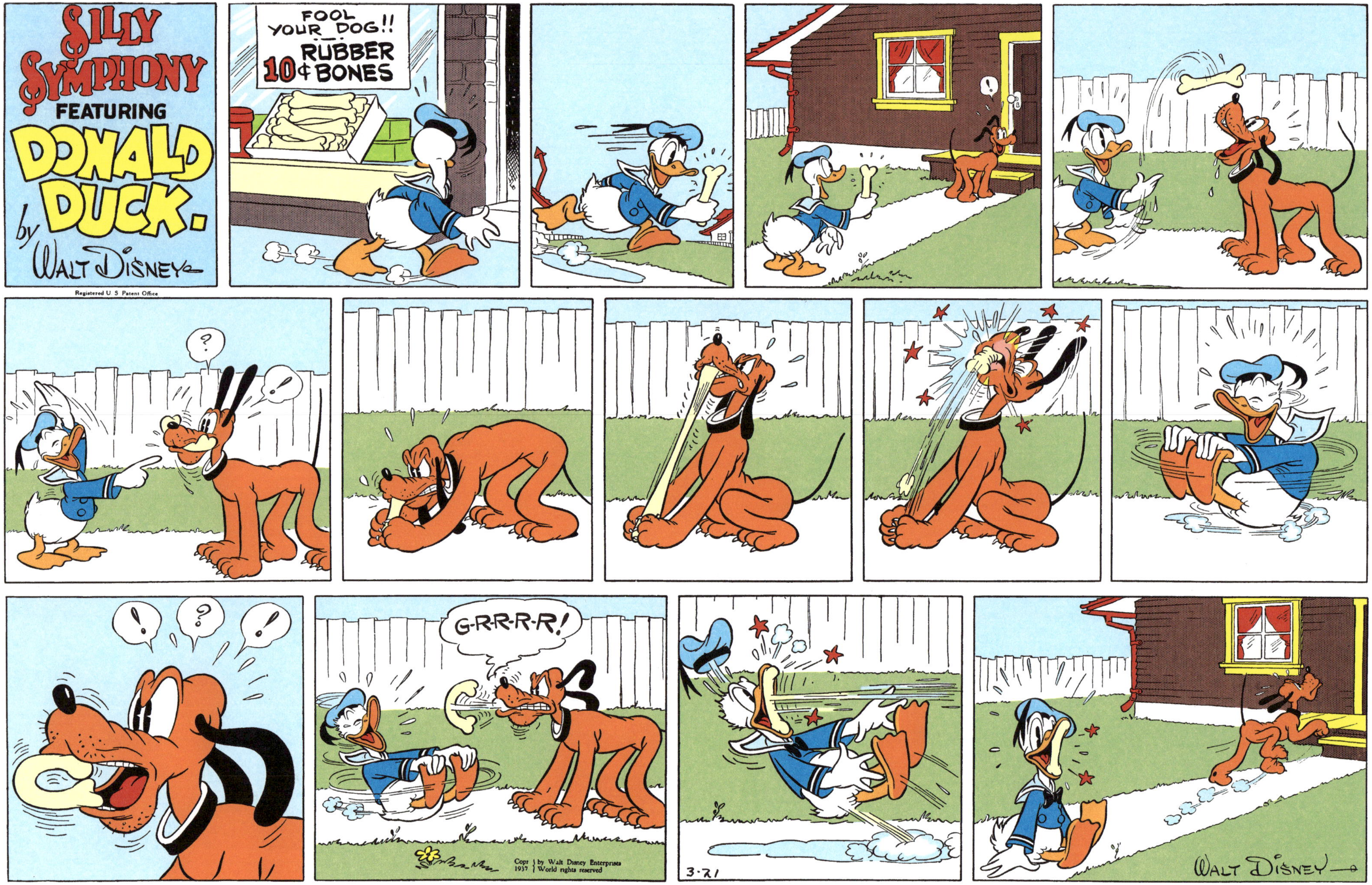
SILLY SYMPHONY
FEATURING
DONALD DUCK.
by WALT DISNEY
Registered U.S. Patent Office
FOOL YOUR DOG!!
RUBBER 10¢ BONES
!
?
!
!
?
!
G-R-R-R-R!
Copr. 1937 by Walt Disney Enterprises World rights reserved
3-21
WALT DISNEY

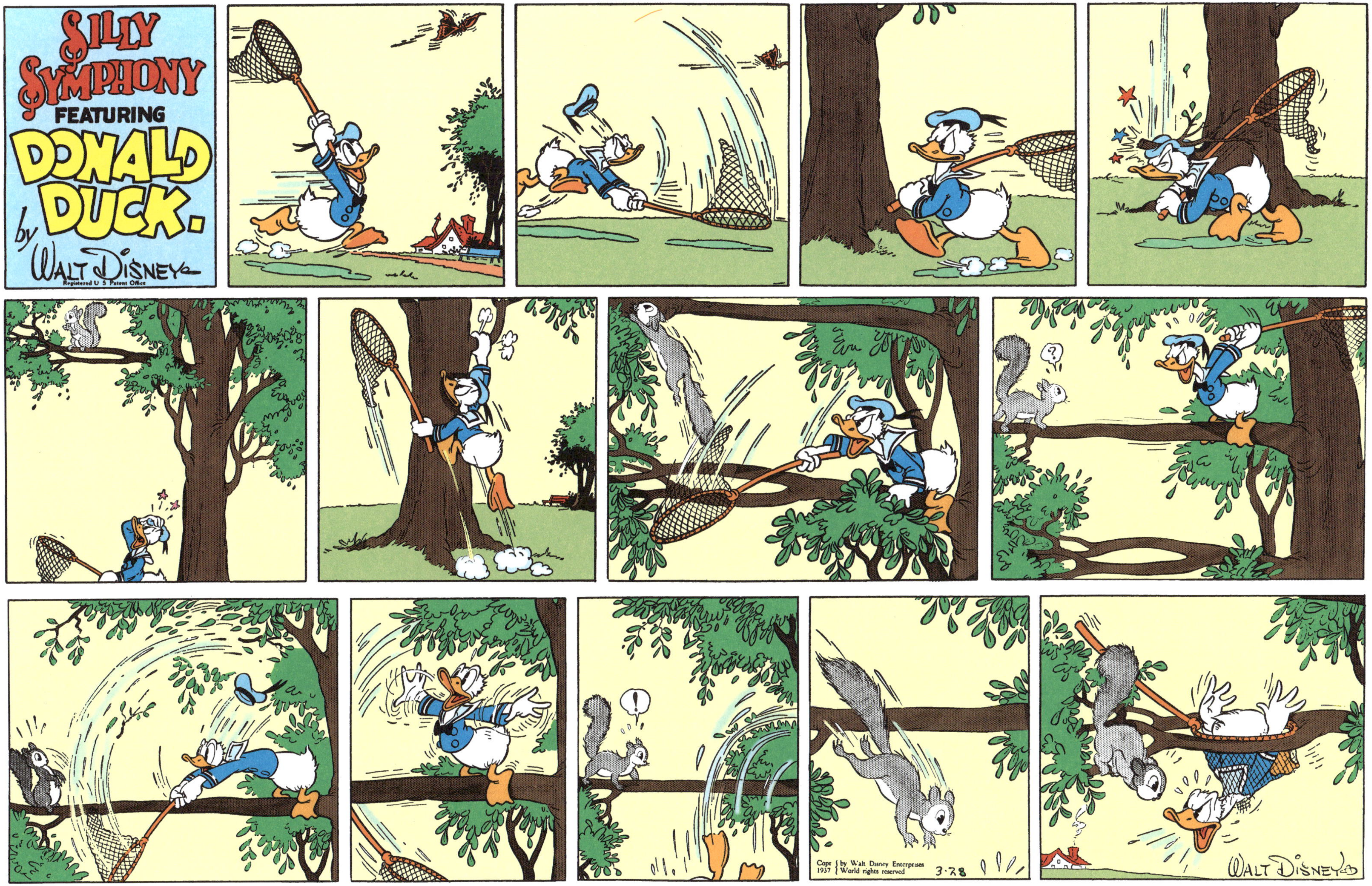
SILLY SYMPHONY
FEATURING
DONALD DUCK.
by
WALT DISNEY
Registered U S Patent Office
?
!
Copr by Walt Disney Enterprises
1937 World rights reserved
3-28
WALT DISNEY

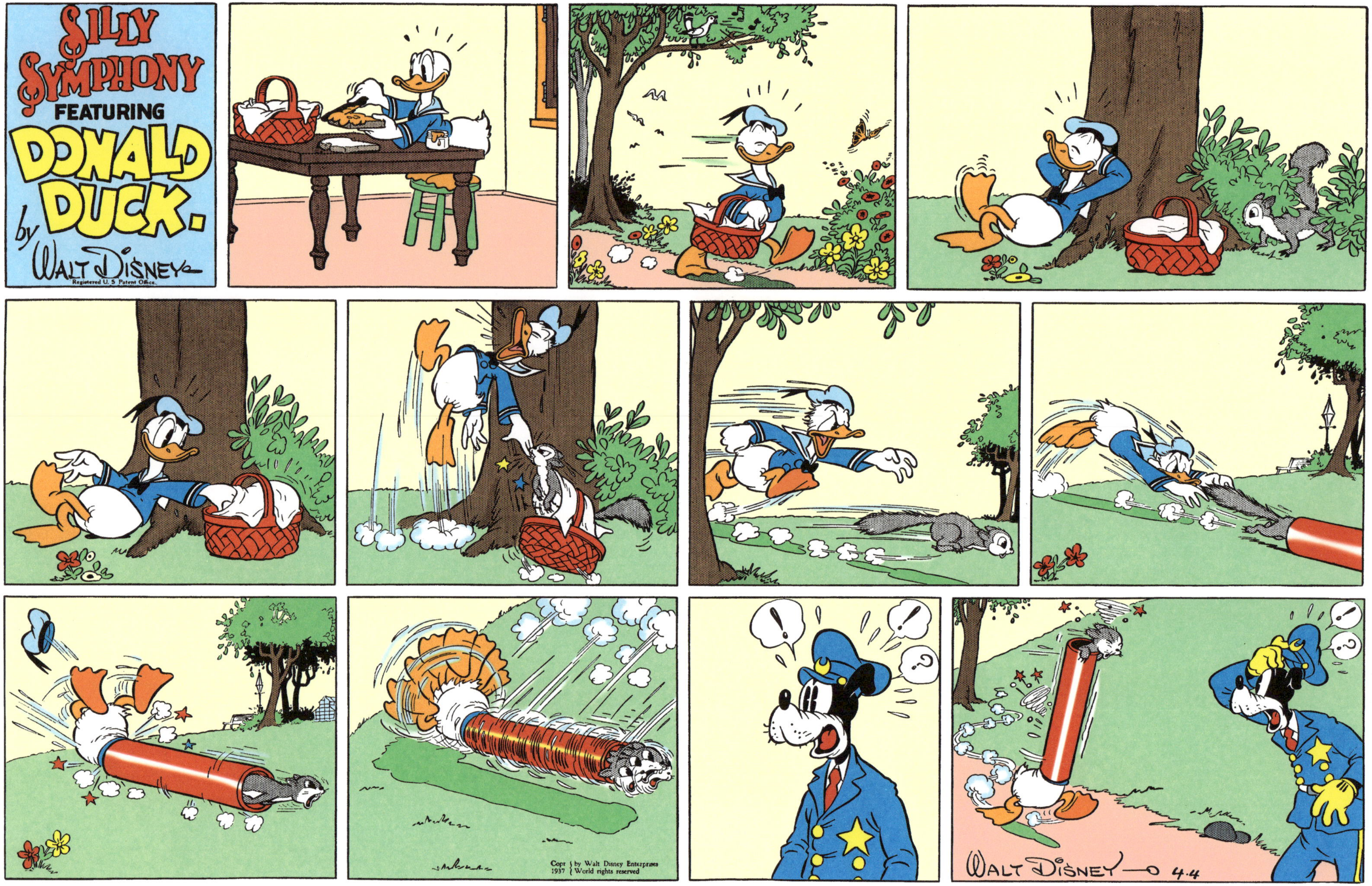
SILLY SYMPHONY
FEATURING
DONALD DUCK.
by WALT DISNEY
Registered U.S. Patent Office.
Copr. 1937 by Walt Disney Enterprises World rights reserved
!
!
?
!
?
WALT DISNEY 4.4

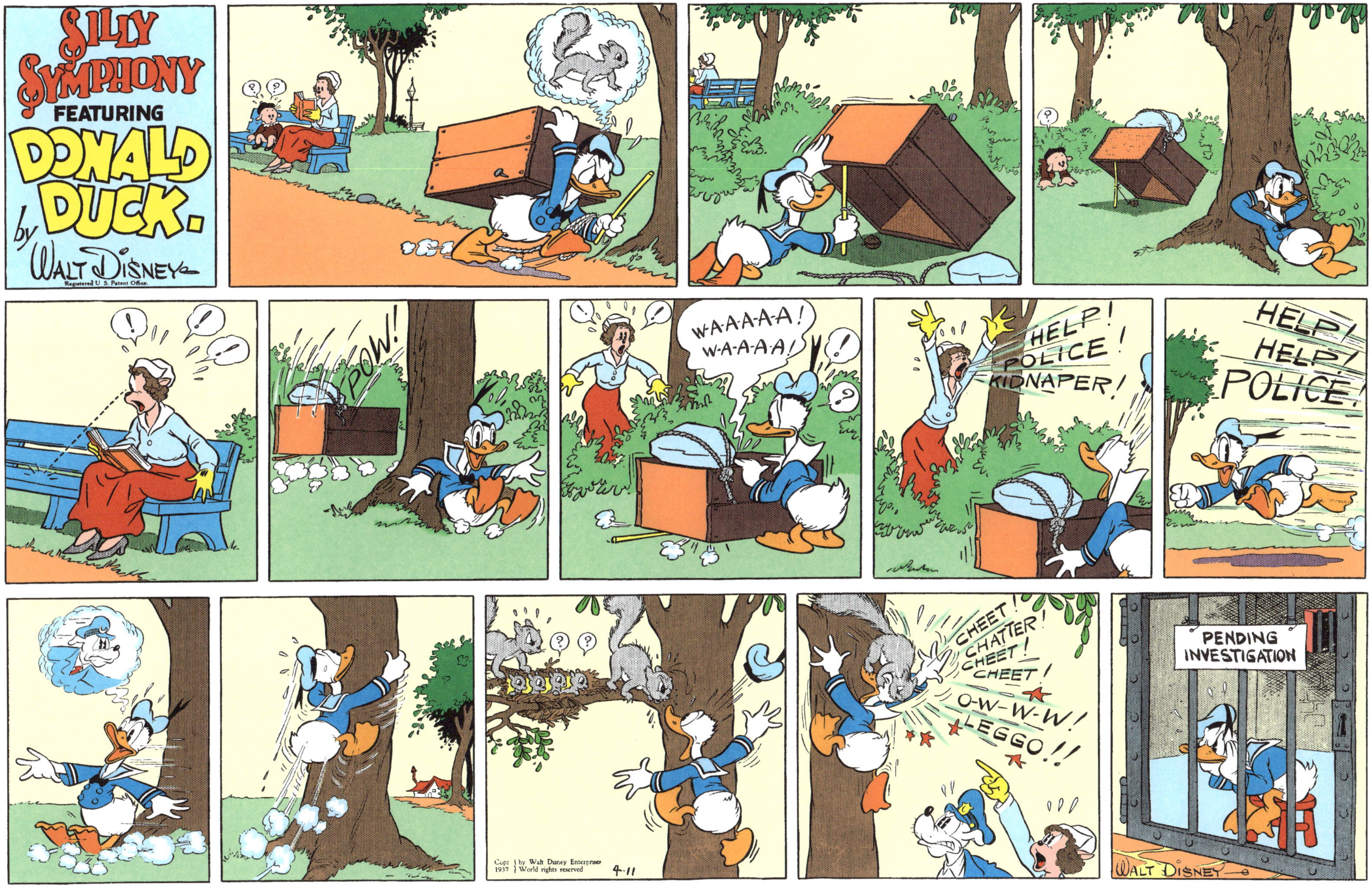
Silly Symphony
featuring
Donald Duck.
by Walt Disney
Registered U. S. Patent Office.
?
?
!
!
!
POW!
!
!
W-A-A-A-A-A!
W-A-A-A-A!
!
?
HELP!
POLICE!
KIDNAPER!
HELP!
HELP!
POLICE!
?
?
Copr. 1937 by Walt Disney Enterprises World rights reserved
4-11
CHEET!
CHATTER!
CHEET!
CHEET!
O-W-W-W!
LEGGO!!
PENDING INVESTIGATION
WALT DISNEY

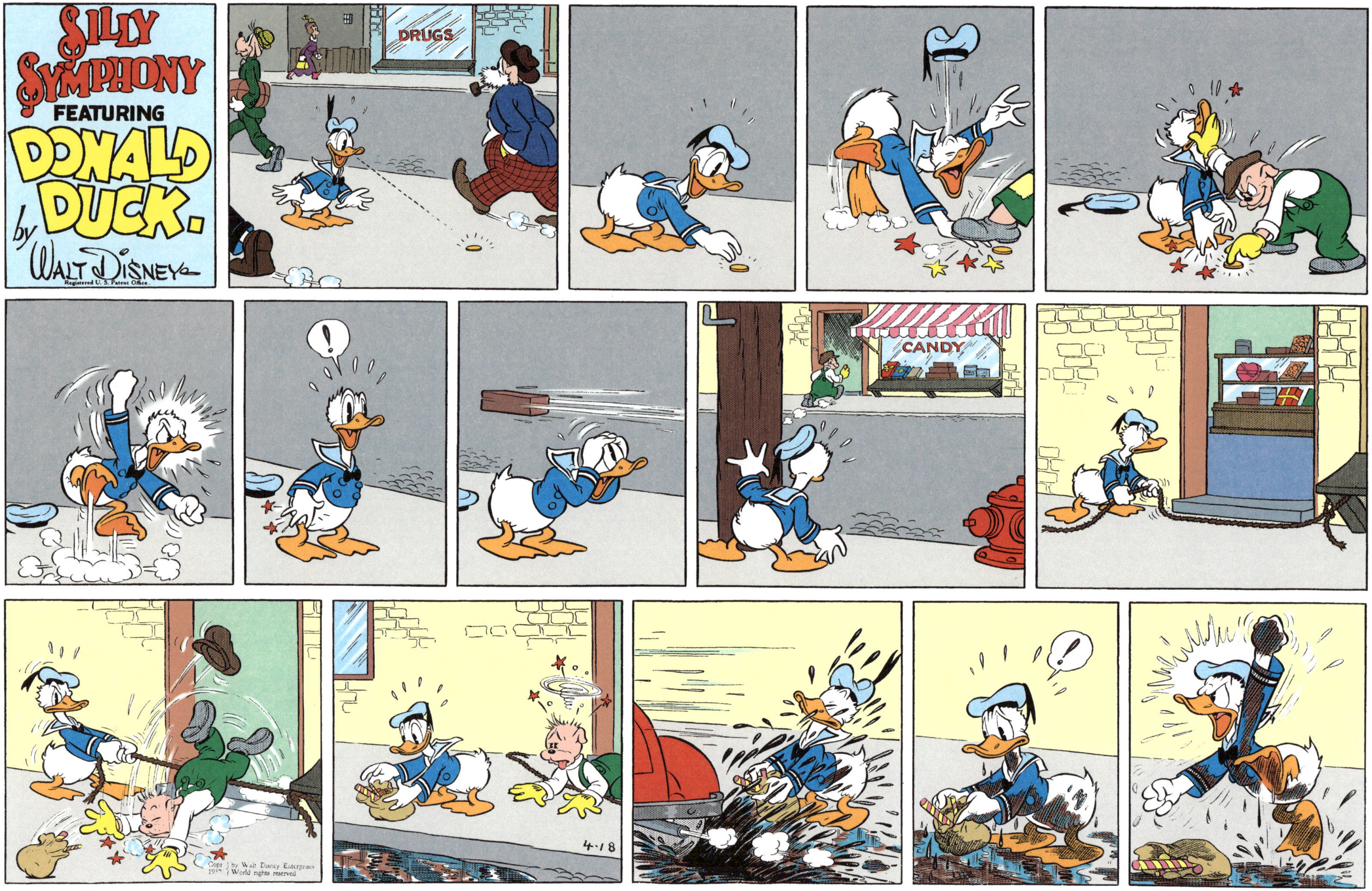
SILLY SYMPHONY
FEATURING
DONALD DUCK.
by WALT DISNEY
Registered U. S. Patent Office.
DRUGS
!
CANDY
Copr. by Walt Disney Enterprises
1937 World rights reserved
4·18
!

109 • April 25, 1937

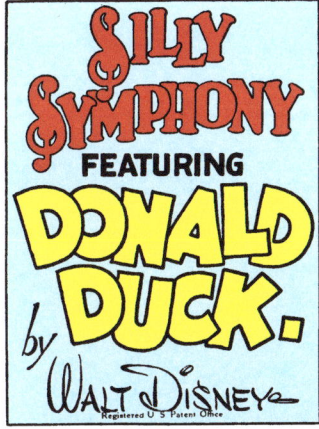

SILLY SYMPHONY
FEATURING
DONALD DUCK.
by WALT DISNEY
Registered U S Patent Office
?
!
?
!
Copr 1937 by Walt Disney Enterprises World rights reserved
? ?
!
HOODUNIT MAGICIAN
WALT DISNEY
5.2

SILLY SYMPHONY
FEATURING
DONALD DUCK.
by WALT DISNEY
Registered U. S. Patent Office.
I HAVE TO RUN OVER TO THE NEIGHBOR'S! DON'T LET MY CARROTS BURN, WILL YOU?
OKAY! LEAVE IT TO ME!
COOKIES
HEY! CUT THAT OUT!
!
COOKIE
!
5-9
!
Copr 1937 by Walt Disney Enterprises World rights reserved
!
?

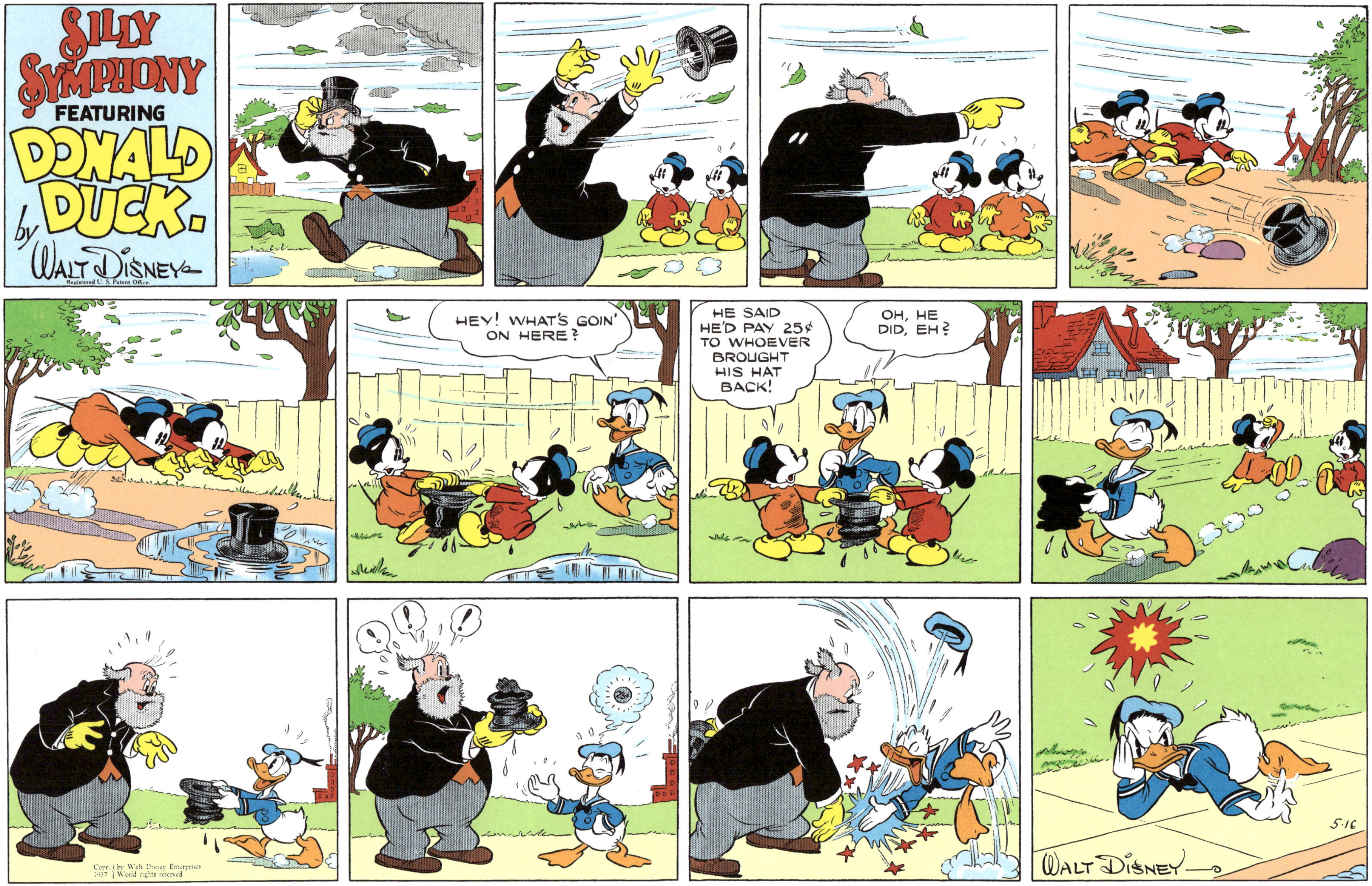
SILLY SYMPHONY
FEATURING
DONALD DUCK.
by WALT DISNEY
Registered U. S. Patent Office.
HEY! WHAT'S GOIN' ON HERE?
HE SAID HE'D PAY 25¢ TO WHOEVER BROUGHT HIS HAT BACK!
OH, HE DID, EH?
Copr. 1937 by Walt Disney Enterprises World rights reserved
!
!
!
5·16
WALT DISNEY

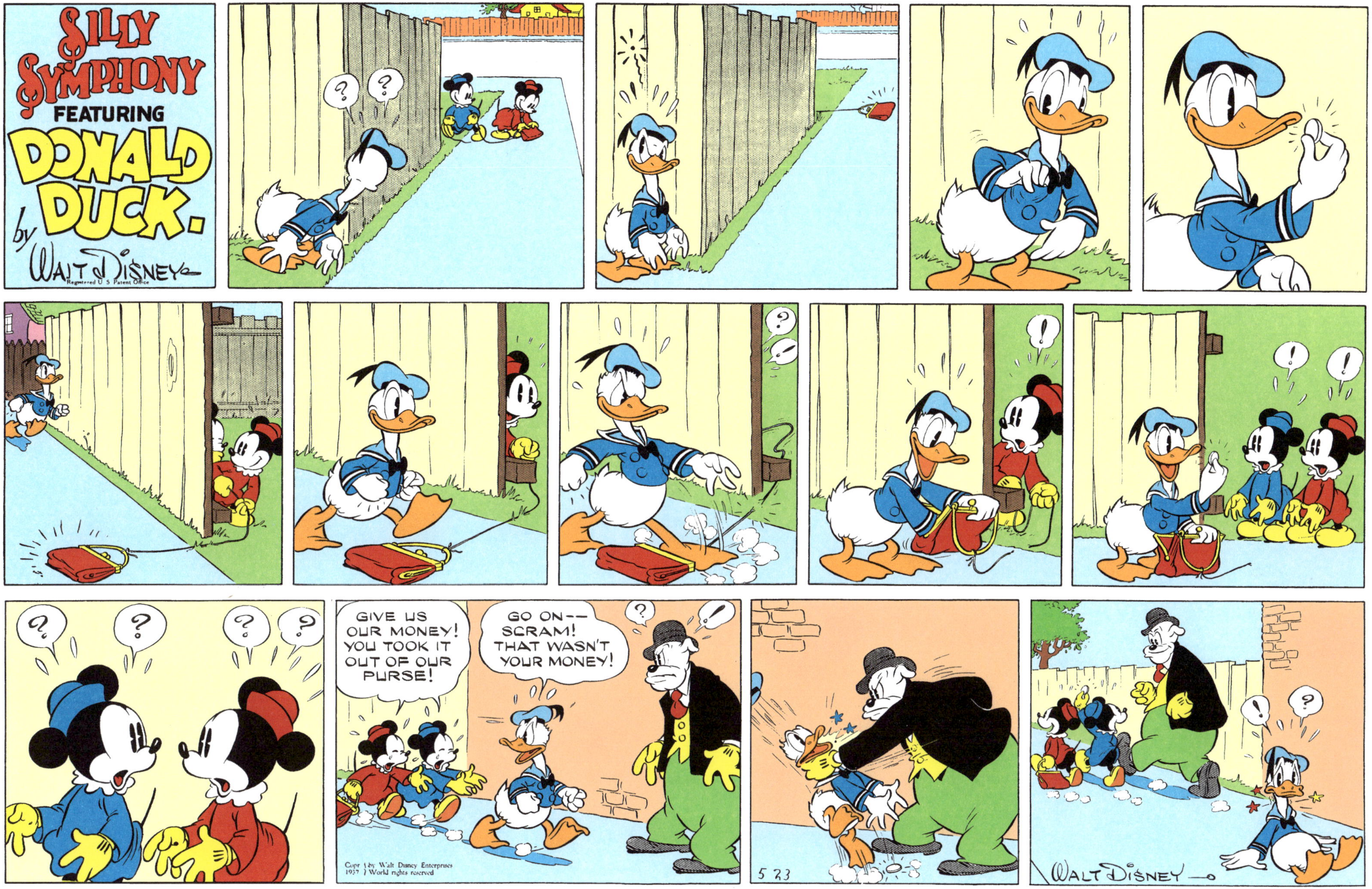

SILLY SYMPHONY
FEATURING
DONALD DUCK.
by WALT DISNEY
Registered U S Patent Office
GIVE US OUR MONEY! YOU TOOK IT OUT OF OUR PURSE!
GO ON-- SCRAM! THAT WASN'T YOUR MONEY!
Copr. by Walt Disney Enterprises
1937 World rights reserved
5 23
WALT DISNEY

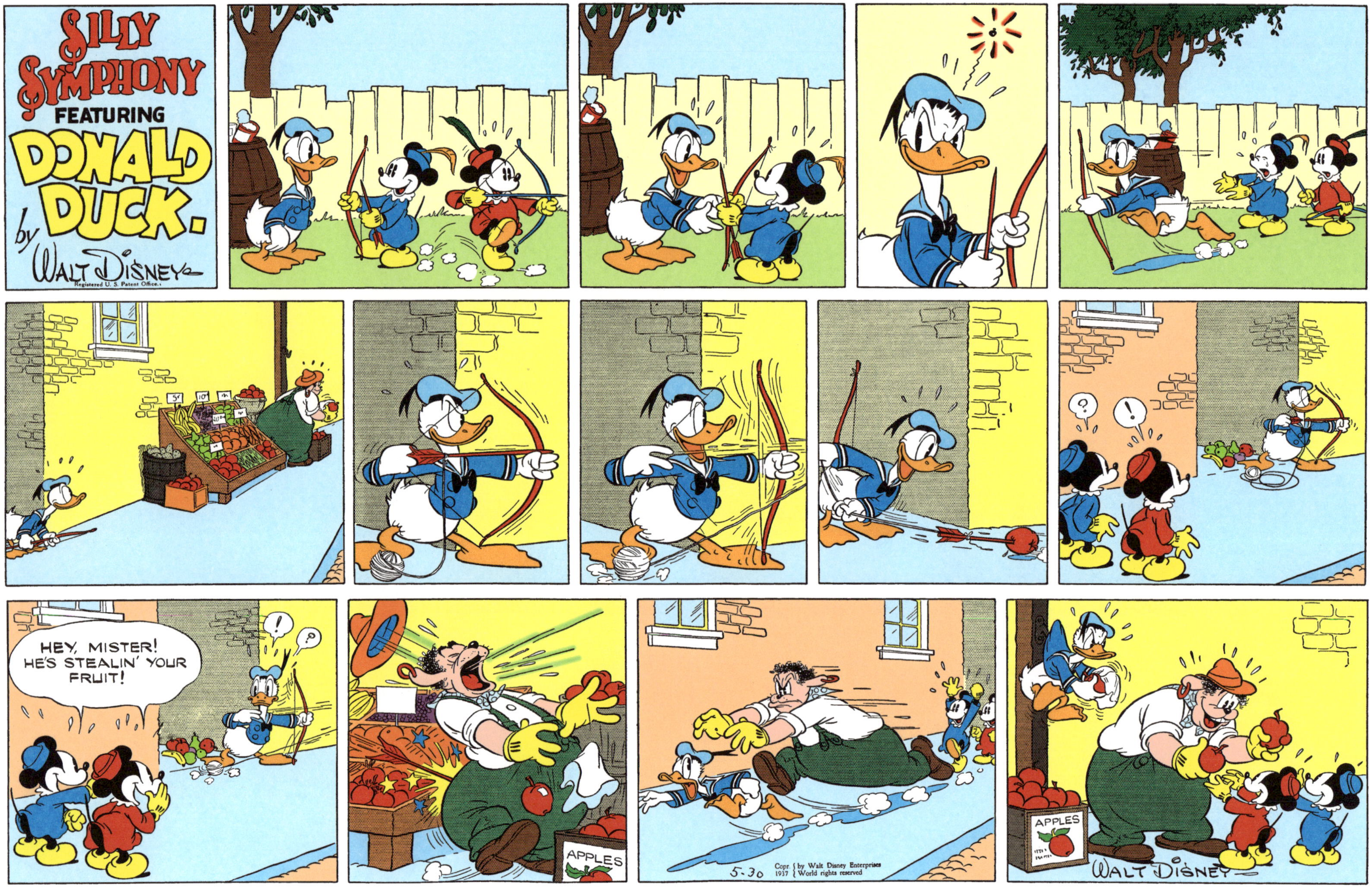
SILLY SYMPHONY
FEATURING
DONALD DUCK.
by WALT DISNEY
Registered U. S. Patent Office.
HEY, MISTER! HE'S STEALIN' YOUR FRUIT!
APPLES
5-30
Copr. 1937 by Walt Disney Enterprises World rights reserved
APPLES
WALT DISNEY

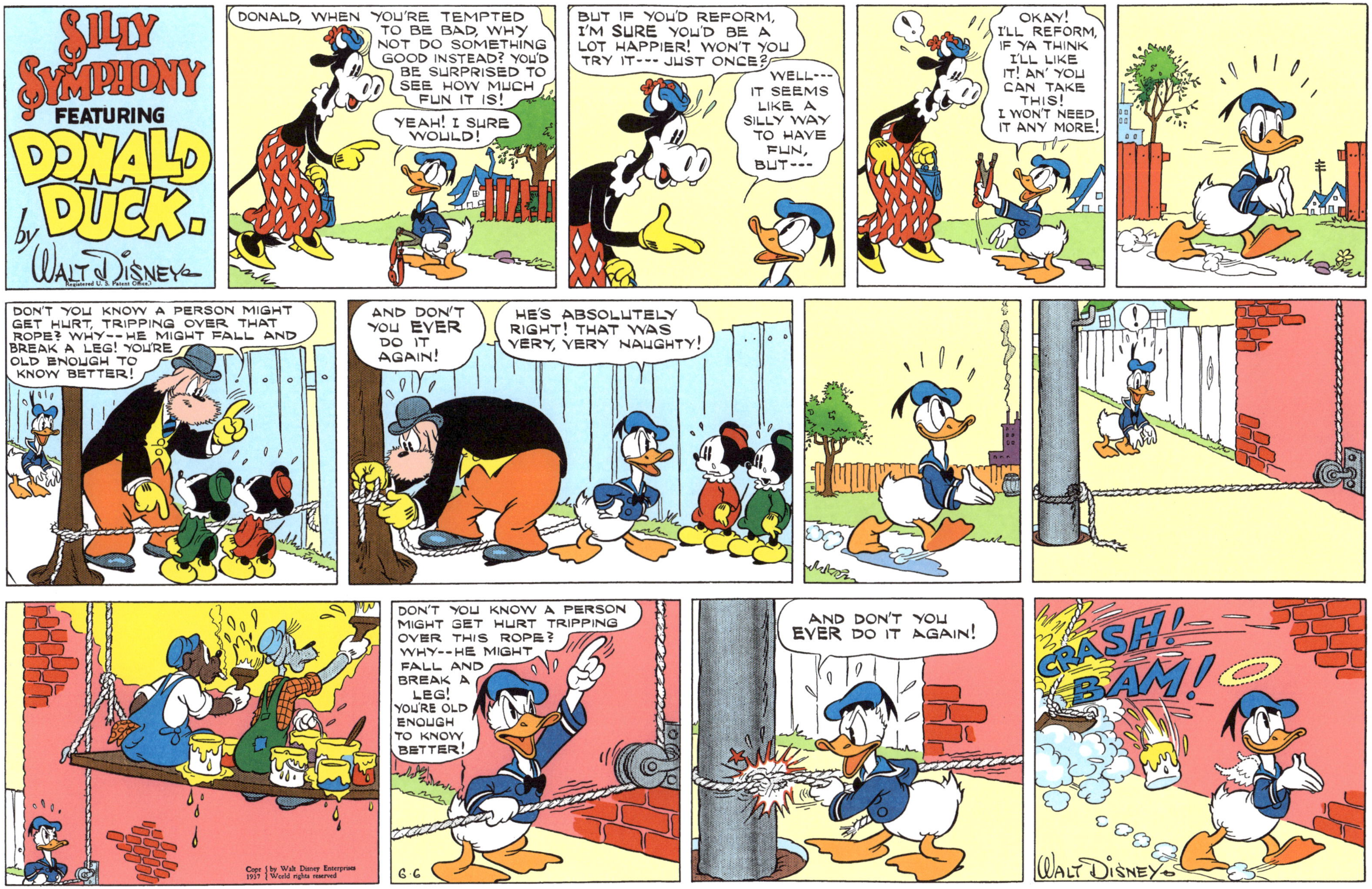
SILLY SYMPHONY
FEATURING
DONALD DUCK.
by WALT DISNEY
Registered U.S. Patent Office.
DONALD, WHEN YOU'RE TEMPTED TO BE BAD, WHY NOT DO SOMETHING GOOD INSTEAD? YOU'D BE SURPRISED TO SEE HOW MUCH FUN IT IS!
YEAH! I SURE WOULD!
BUT IF YOU'D REFORM, I'M SURE YOU'D BE A LOT HAPPIER! WON'T YOU TRY IT--- JUST ONCE?
WELL--- IT SEEMS LIKE A SILLY WAY TO HAVE FUN, BUT---
OKAY! I'LL REFORM, IF YA THINK I'LL LIKE IT! AN' YOU CAN TAKE THIS! I WON'T NEED IT ANY MORE!
DON'T YOU KNOW A PERSON MIGHT GET HURT, TRIPPING OVER THAT ROPE? WHY--HE MIGHT FALL AND BREAK A LEG! YOU'RE OLD ENOUGH TO KNOW BETTER!
AND DON'T YOU EVER DO IT AGAIN!
HE'S ABSOLUTELY RIGHT! THAT WAS VERY, VERY NAUGHTY!
Copr 1937 by Walt Disney Enterprises World rights reserved
DON'T YOU KNOW A PERSON MIGHT GET HURT TRIPPING OVER THIS ROPE? WHY--HE MIGHT FALL AND BREAK A LEG! YOU'RE OLD ENOUGH TO KNOW BETTER!
6-6
AND DON'T YOU EVER DO IT AGAIN!
CRASH! BAM!
WALT DISNEY

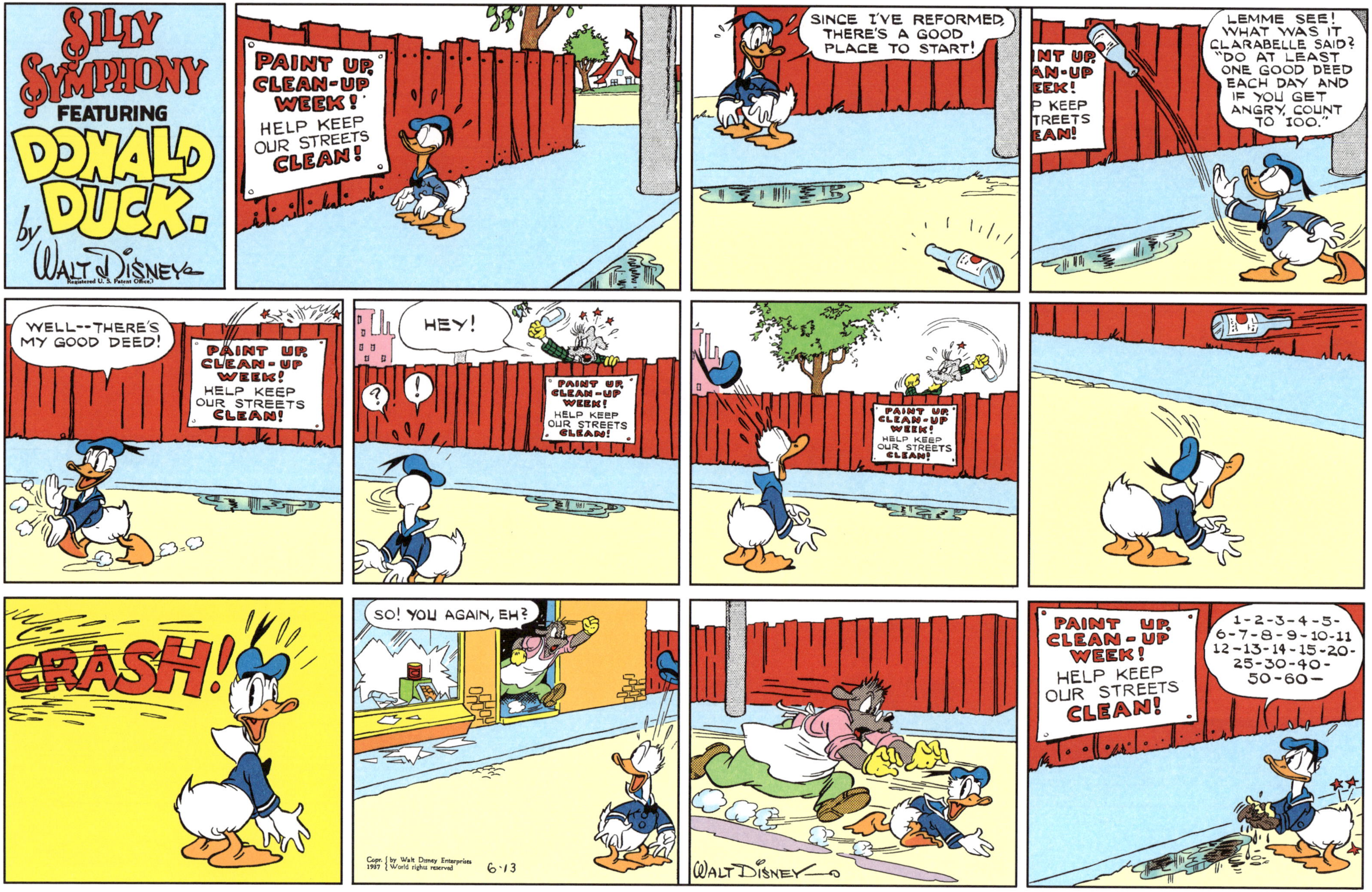
SILLY SYMPHONY
FEATURING
DONALD DUCK.
by WALT DISNEY
Registered U. S. Patent Office.
PAINT UP, CLEAN-UP WEEK! HELP KEEP OUR STREETS CLEAN!
SINCE I'VE REFORMED, THERE'S A GOOD PLACE TO START!
LEMME SEE! WHAT WAS IT CLARABELLE SAID? "DO AT LEAST ONE GOOD DEED EACH DAY AND IF YOU GET ANGRY, COUNT TO 100."
WELL--THERE'S MY GOOD DEED!
PAINT UP, CLEAN-UP WEEK! HELP KEEP OUR STREETS CLEAN!
HEY!
PAINT UP, CLEAN-UP WEEK! HELP KEEP OUR STREETS CLEAN!
PAINT UP, CLEAN-UP WEEK! HELP KEEP OUR STREETS CLEAN!
CRASH!
SO! YOU AGAIN, EH?
Copr. 1937 by Walt Disney Enterprises World rights reserved
6-13
WALT DISNEY
PAINT UP, CLEAN-UP WEEK! HELP KEEP OUR STREETS CLEAN!
1-2-3-4-5-6-7-8-9-10-11 12-13-14-15-20-25-30-40-50-60—

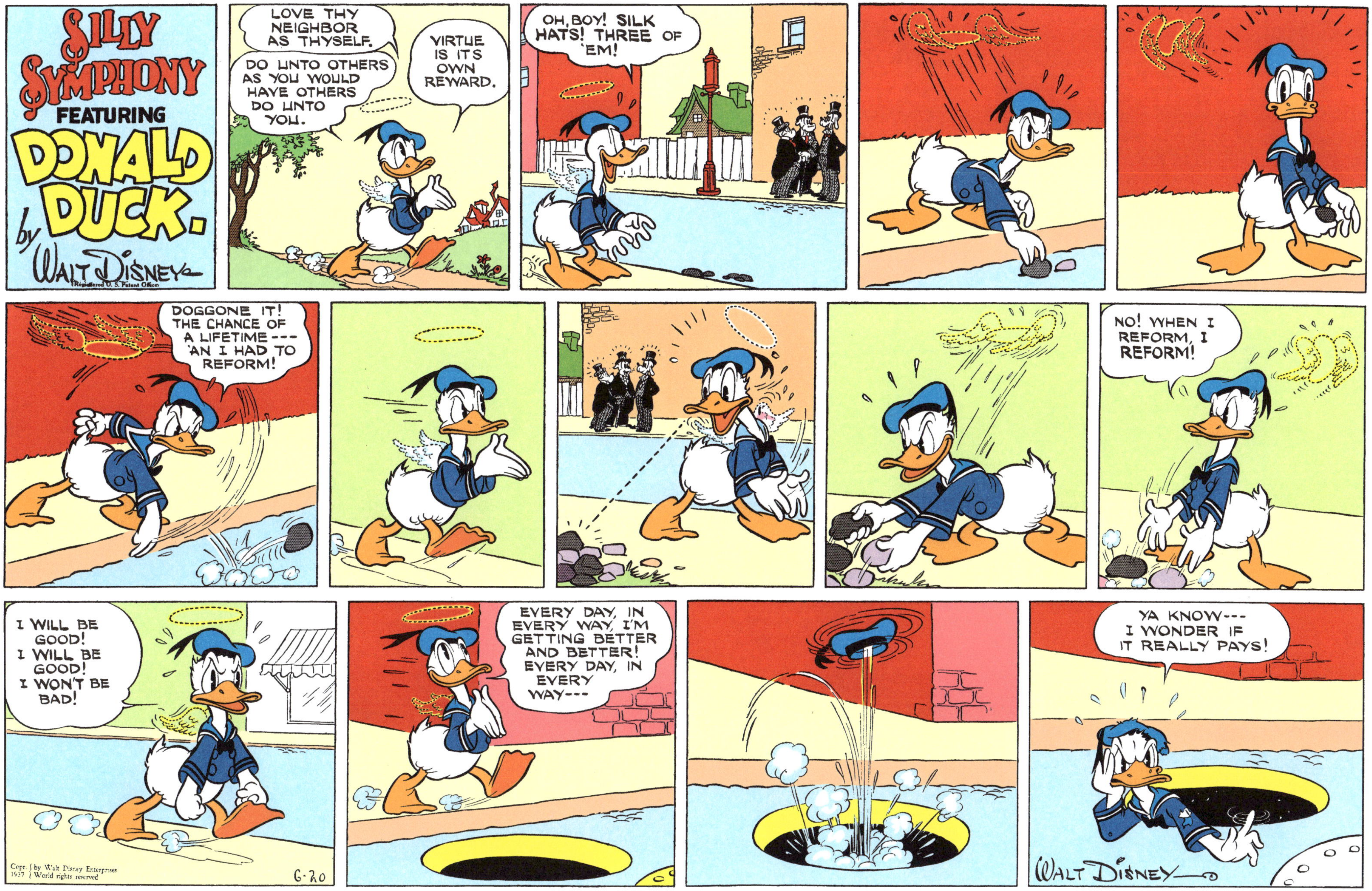
SILLY SYMPHONY
FEATURING
DONALD DUCK.
by WALT DISNEY
Registered U. S. Patent Office
LOVE THY NEIGHBOR AS THYSELF.
DO UNTO OTHERS AS YOU WOULD HAVE OTHERS DO UNTO YOU.
VIRTUE IS ITS OWN REWARD.
OH, BOY! SILK HATS! THREE OF 'EM!
DOGGONE IT! THE CHANCE OF A LIFETIME--- 'AN I HAD TO REFORM!
NO! WHEN I REFORM, I REFORM!
I WILL BE GOOD! I WILL BE GOOD! I WON'T BE BAD!
Copr. by Walt Disney Enterprises 1937 World rights reserved
6-20
EVERY DAY, IN EVERY WAY, I'M GETTING BETTER AND BETTER! EVERY DAY, IN EVERY WAY---
YA KNOW--- I WONDER IF IT REALLY PAYS!
WALT DISNEY

SILLY SYMPHONY
FEATURING
DONALD DUCK
by WALT DISNEY
Registered U. S. Patent Office.
?
!
?
?
?
!
?
CRASH!
Copr. by Walt Disney Enterprises 1937 World rights reserved
6-27
!
WALT DISNEY
HONESTY IS THE BEST POLICY--- A KIND DEED IS NEVER LOST--- ACTIONS SPEAK LOUDER THAN WORDS---
MAXIMS AND PROVERBS

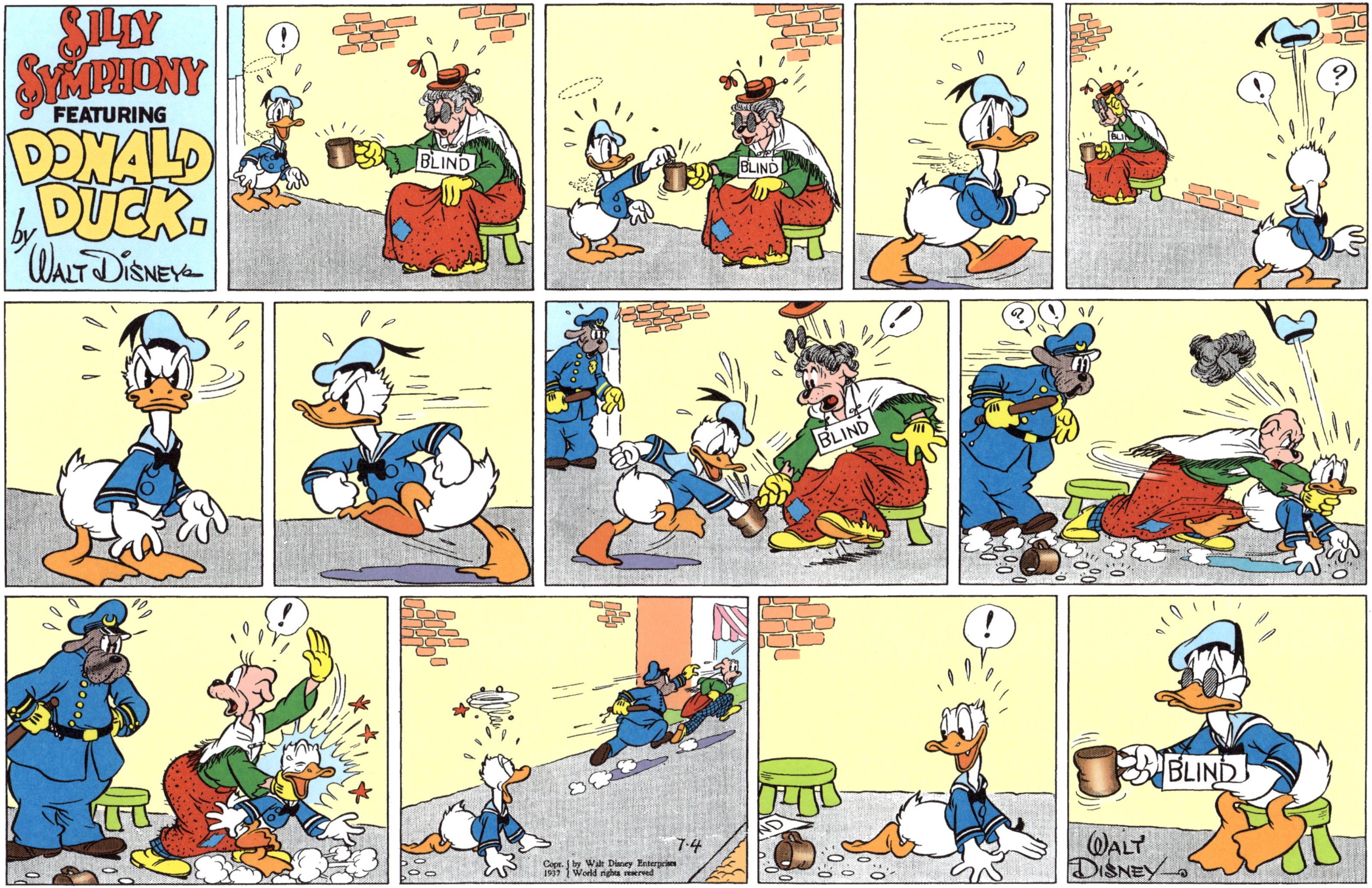
SILLY SYMPHONY
FEATURING
DONALD DUCK.
by WALT DISNEY
!
BLIND
BLIND
BLIND
!
?
!
BLIND
?
!
!
7-4
Copr. by Walt Disney Enterprises 1937 World rights reserved
!
BLIND
WALT DISNEY

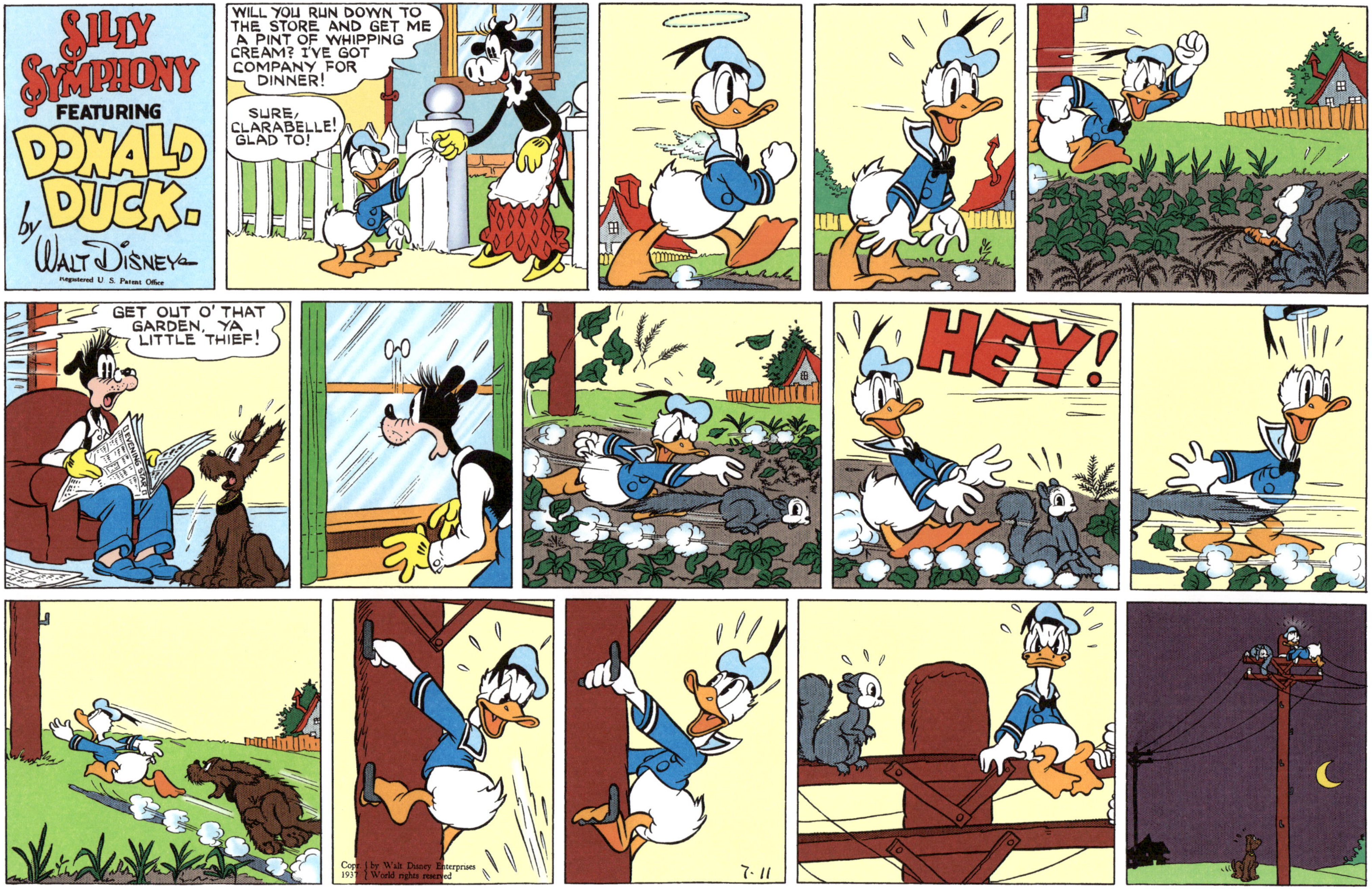
SILLY SYMPHONY
FEATURING
DONALD DUCK.
by WALT DISNEY
Registered U. S. Patent Office
WILL YOU RUN DOWN TO THE STORE AND GET ME A PINT OF WHIPPING CREAM? I'VE GOT COMPANY FOR DINNER!
SURE, CLARABELLE! GLAD TO!
GET OUT O' THAT GARDEN, YA LITTLE THIEF!
EVENING STAR
HEY!
Copr. 1937 by Walt Disney Enterprises
World rights reserved
7-11

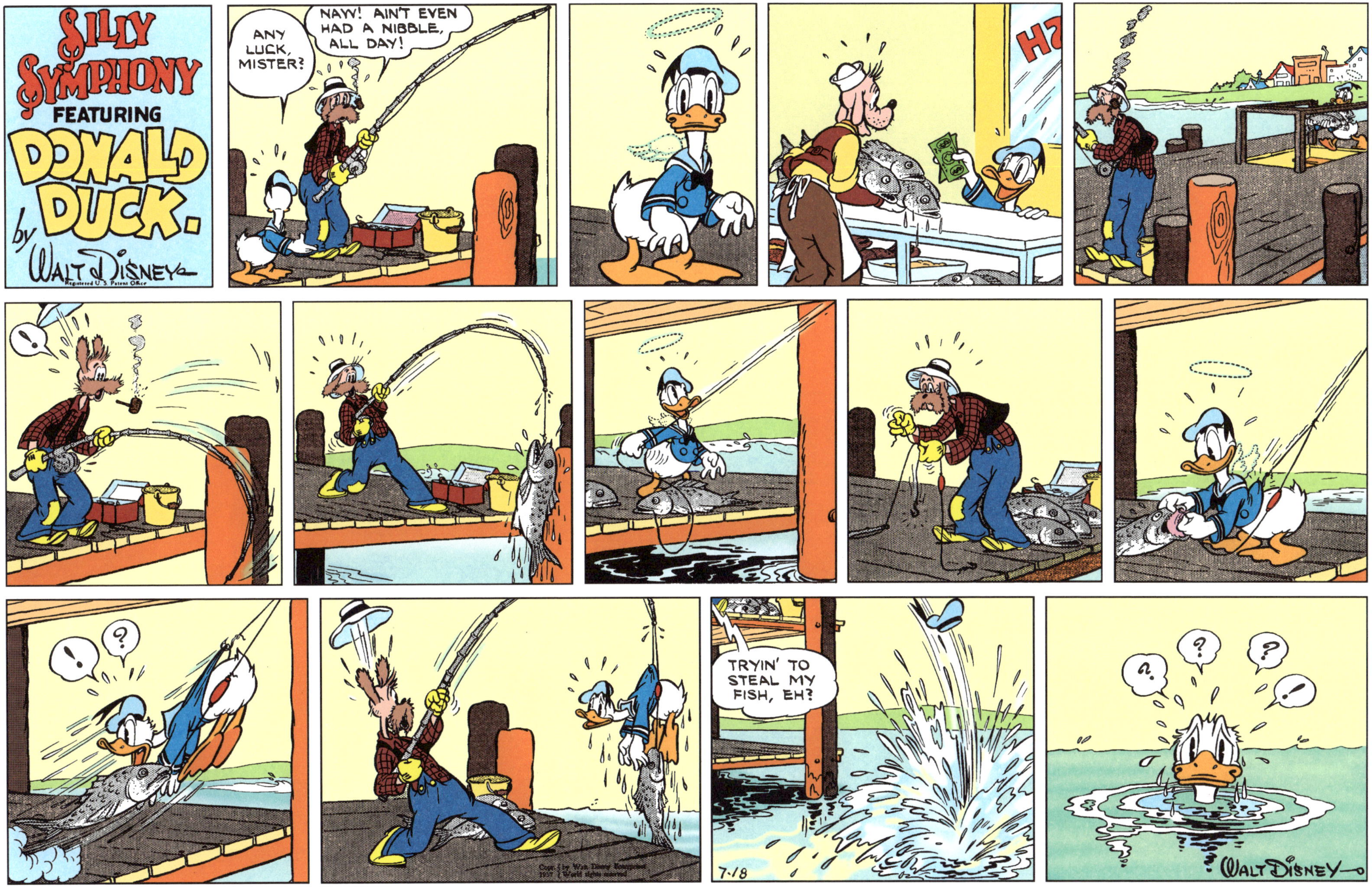
SILLY SYMPHONY
FEATURING
DONALD DUCK.
by WALT DISNEY
Registered U.S. Patent Office
ANY LUCK, MISTER?
NAW! AIN'T EVEN HAD A NIBBLE, ALL DAY!
!
!
?
TRYIN' TO STEAL MY FISH, EH?
7-18
?
?
?
!
WALT DISNEY

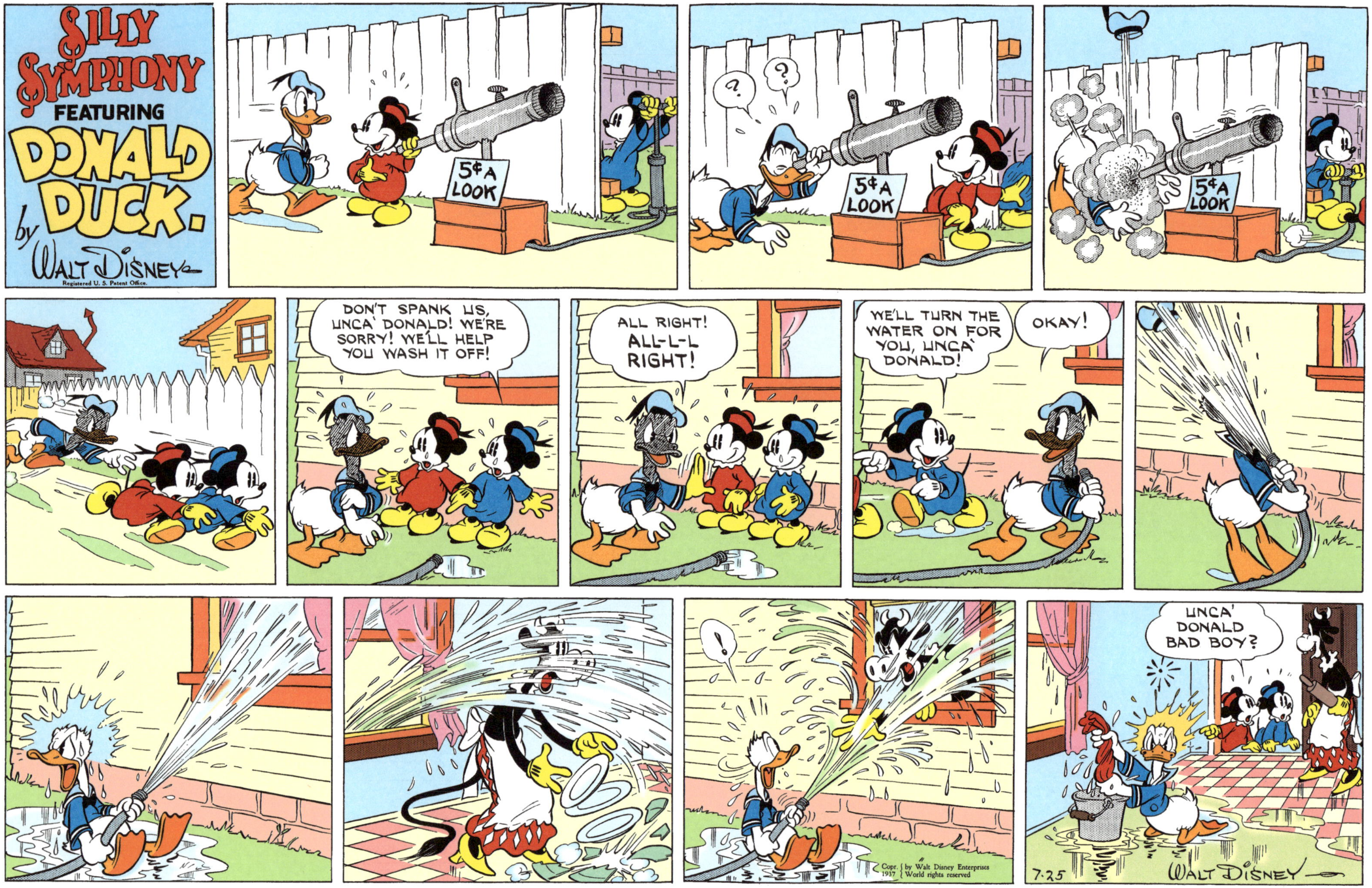
SILLY SYMPHONY
FEATURING
DONALD DUCK.
by WALT DISNEY
Registered U. S. Patent Office.
5¢ A LOOK
?
?
5¢ A LOOK
5¢ A LOOK
DON'T SPANK US, UNCA' DONALD! WE'RE SORRY! WE'LL HELP YOU WASH IT OFF!
ALL RIGHT! ALL-L-L RIGHT!
WE'LL TURN THE WATER ON FOR YOU, UNCA' DONALD!
OKAY!
!
Copr. 1937 by Walt Disney Enterprises World rights reserved
UNCA' DONALD BAD BOY?
7-25
WALT DISNEY

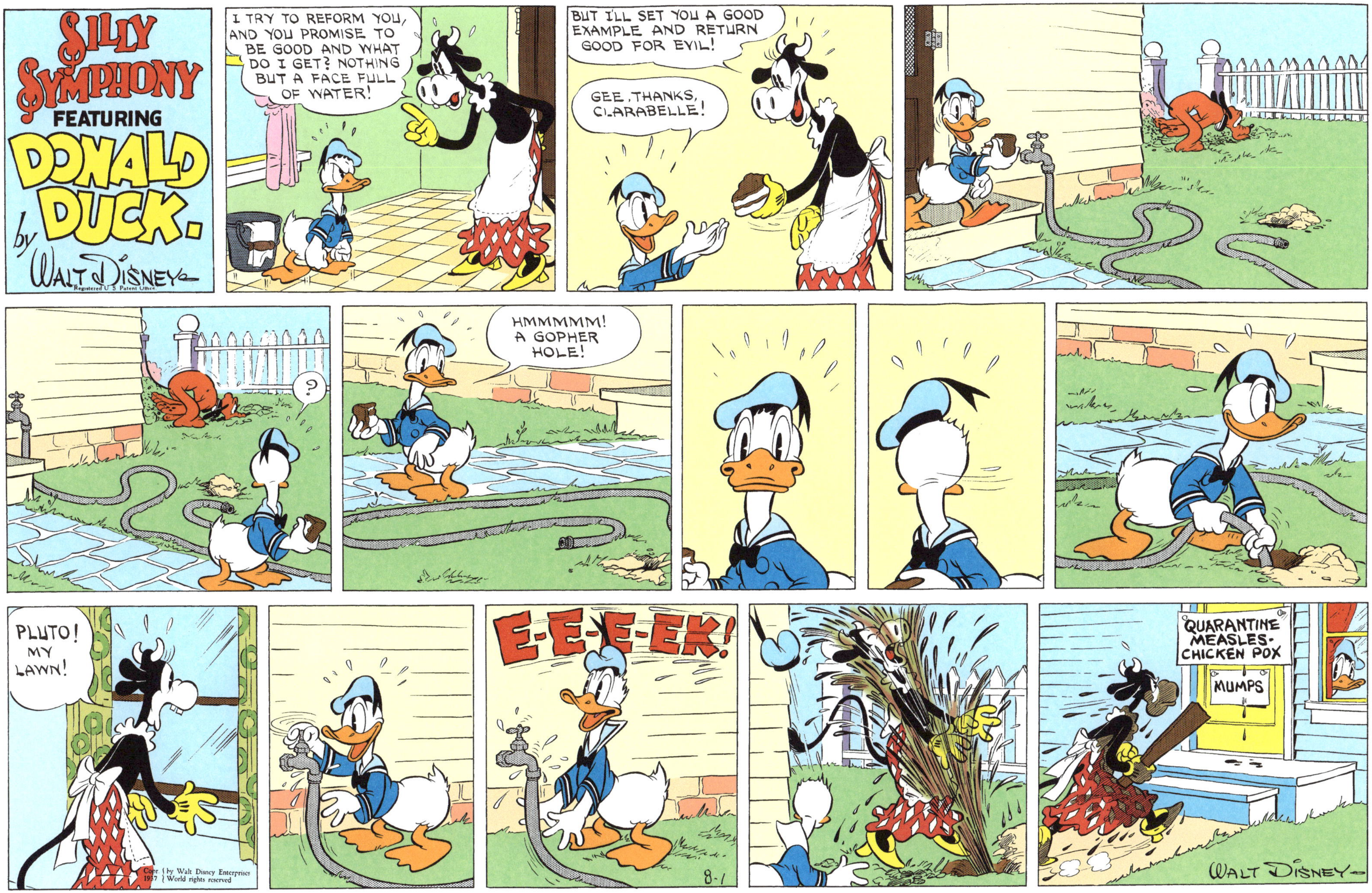
SILLY SYMPHONY
FEATURING
DONALD DUCK.
by WALT DISNEY
Registered U.S. Patent Office
I TRY TO REFORM YOU, AND YOU PROMISE TO BE GOOD AND WHAT DO I GET? NOTHING BUT A FACE FULL OF WATER!
BUT I'LL SET YOU A GOOD EXAMPLE AND RETURN GOOD FOR EVIL!
GEE, THANKS, CLARABELLE!
?
HMMMMM! A GOPHER HOLE!
PLUTO! MY LAWN!
Copr. 1937 by Walt Disney Enterprises World rights reserved
E-E-E-EK!
8-1
QUARANTINE MEASLES- CHICKEN POX
MUMPS
WALT DISNEY

SILLY SYMPHONY
FEATURING
DONALD DUCK.
by WALT DISNEY
Registered U. S. Patent Office
WHEEE-E-E!
HEY! LET ME DOWN!
8·8
WALT DISNEY

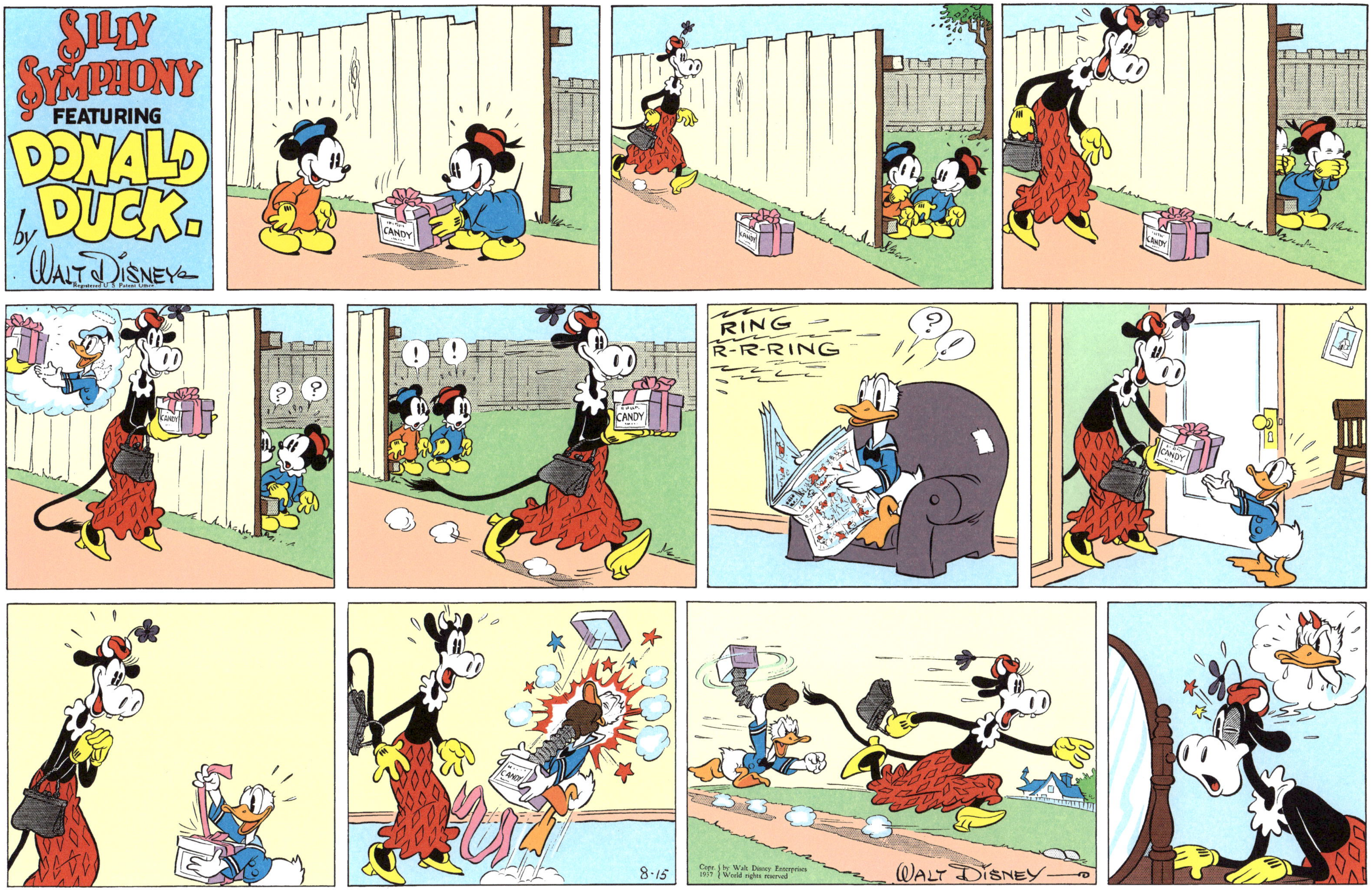
SILLY SYMPHONY
FEATURING
DONALD DUCK.
by WALT DISNEY
Registered U.S. Patent Office
CANDY
CANDY
CANDY
? ?
CANDY
! !
CANDY
RING
R-R-RING
? !
CANDY
CANDY
8-15
Copr. 1937 by Walt Disney Enterprises
World rights reserved
WALT DISNEY

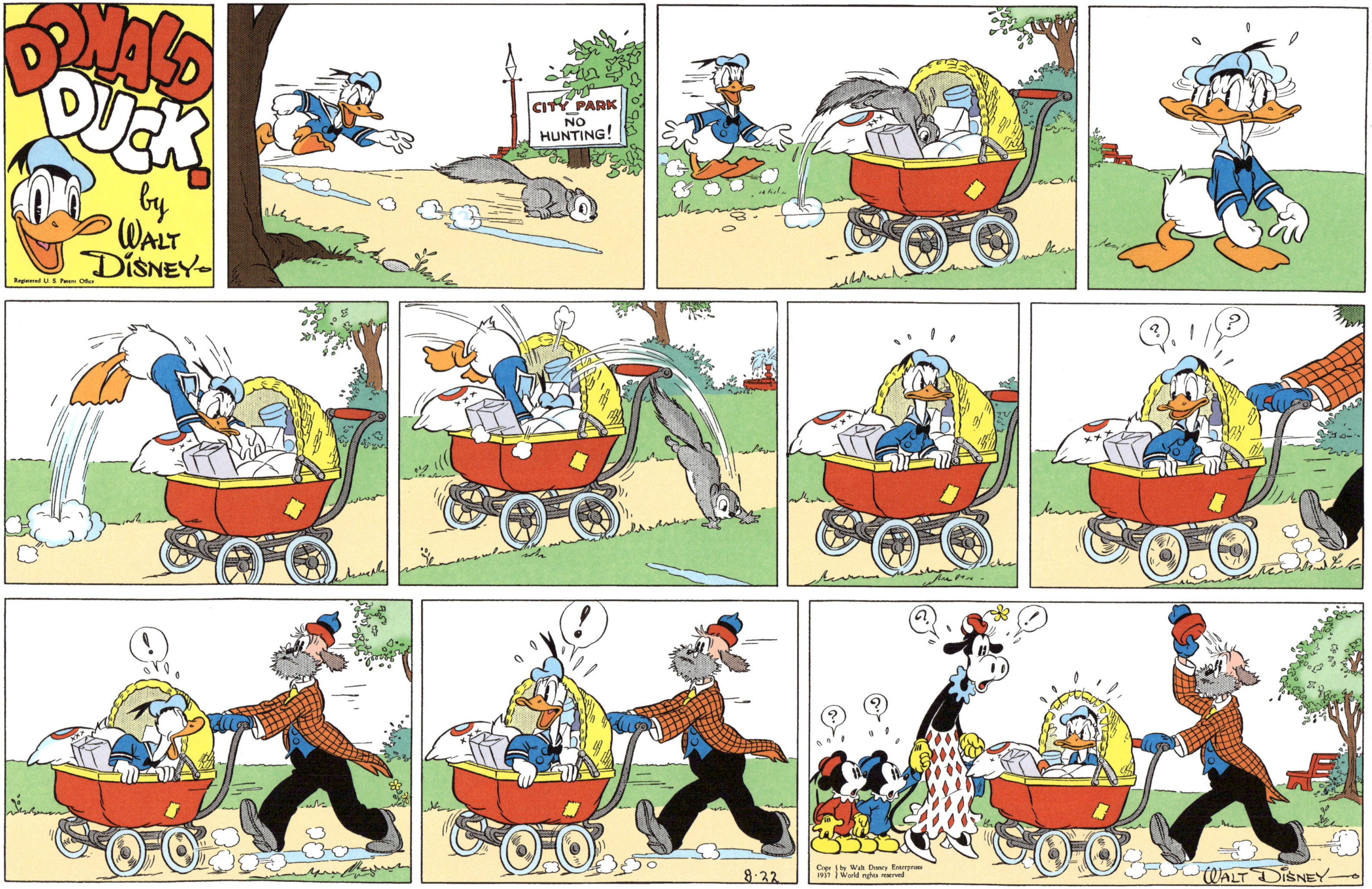
DONALD DUCK
by WALT DISNEY
Registered U. S. Patent Office
CITY PARK
NO HUNTING!
?
?
!
!
?
?
?
!
8·22
Copr 1937 by Walt Disney Enterprises World rights reserved
WALT DISNEY

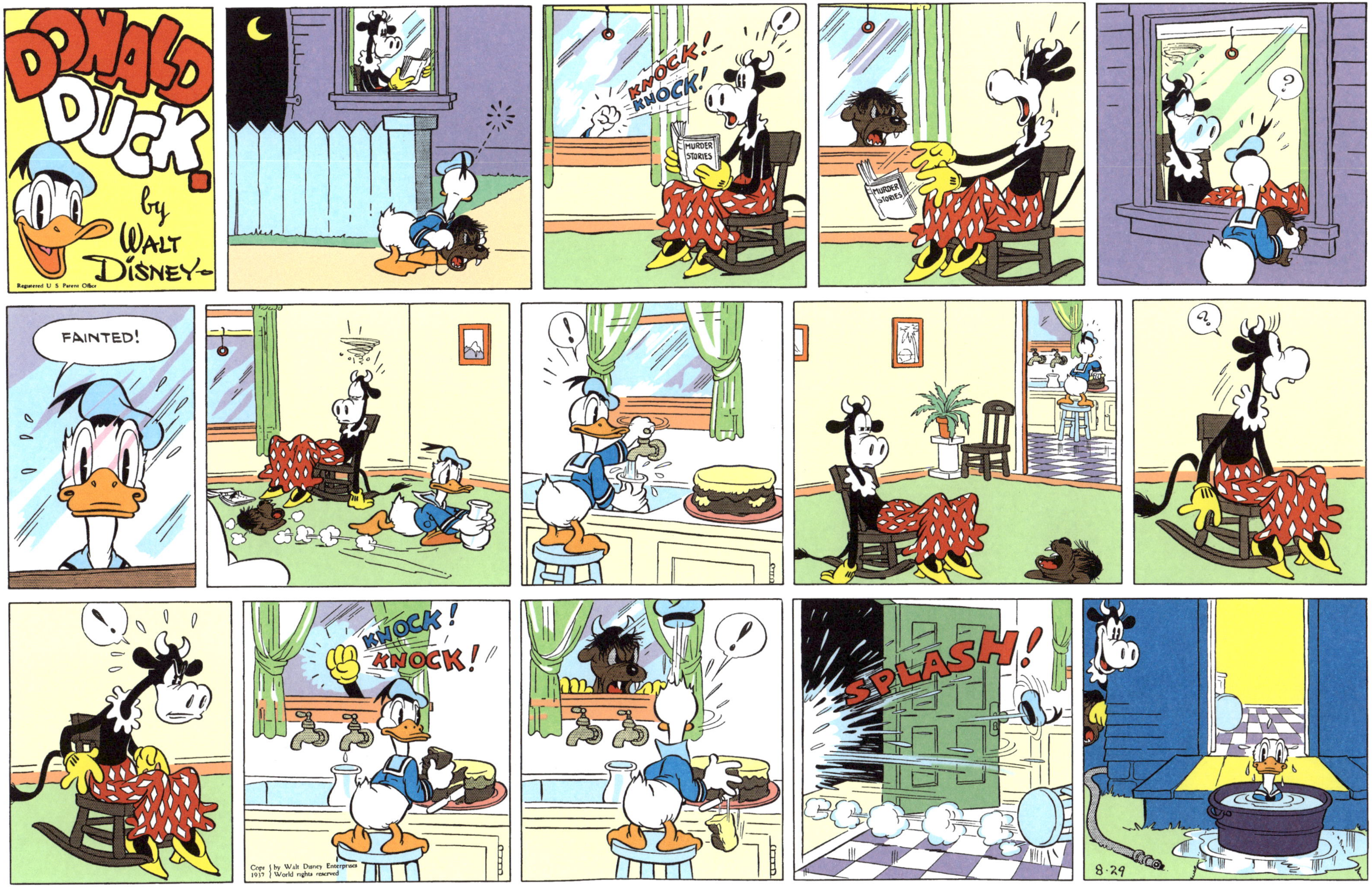
DONALD DUCK
by WALT DISNEY
Registered U S Patent Office
KNOCK! KNOCK!
MURDER STORIES
!
MURDER STORIES
?
FAINTED!
!
?
!
KNOCK! KNOCK!
Copr 1937 by Walt Disney Enterprises World rights reserved
!
SPLASH!
8·29

DONALD DUCK
by WALT DISNEY
Registered U. S. Patent Office
!
!
?
?
!
?
?
Copr 1937 by Walt Disney Enterprises World rights reserved
WALT DISNEY
9-5

DONALD DUCK
by WALT DISNEY
Registered U. S. Patent Office
?
?
?
?
?
?
?
!
?
?
?
?
?
?
?
!
Copr. 1937 by Walt Disney Enterprises World rights reserved
WALT DISNEY 9-12

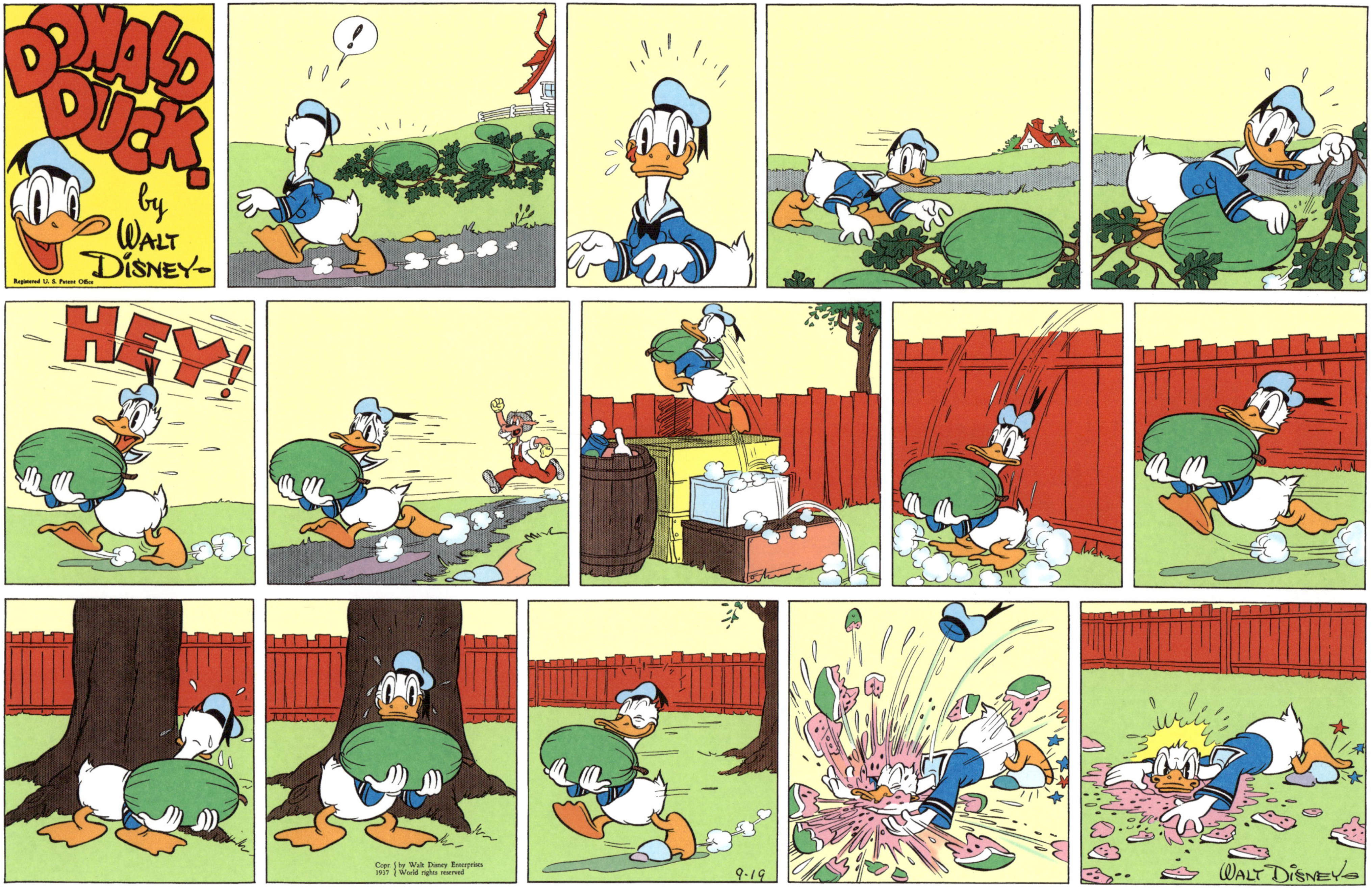
DONALD DUCK
by
WALT DISNEY
Registered U. S. Patent Office
!
HEY!
Copr. 1937 by Walt Disney Enterprises World rights reserved
9-19
WALT DISNEY

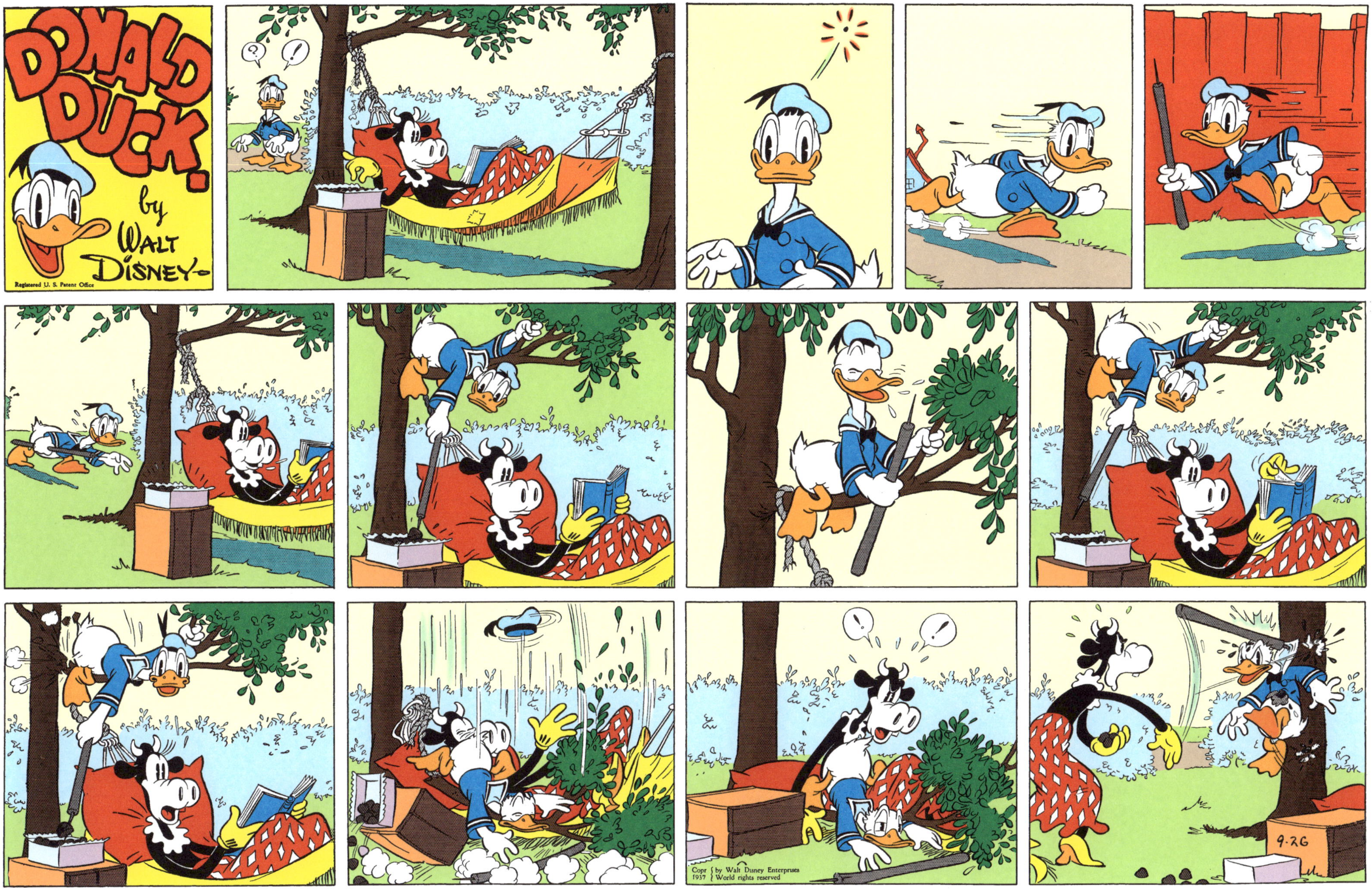
DONALD DUCK
by WALT DISNEY
Registered U. S. Patent Office
?
!
!
!
9·26
Copr 1937 by Walt Disney Enterprises World rights reserved

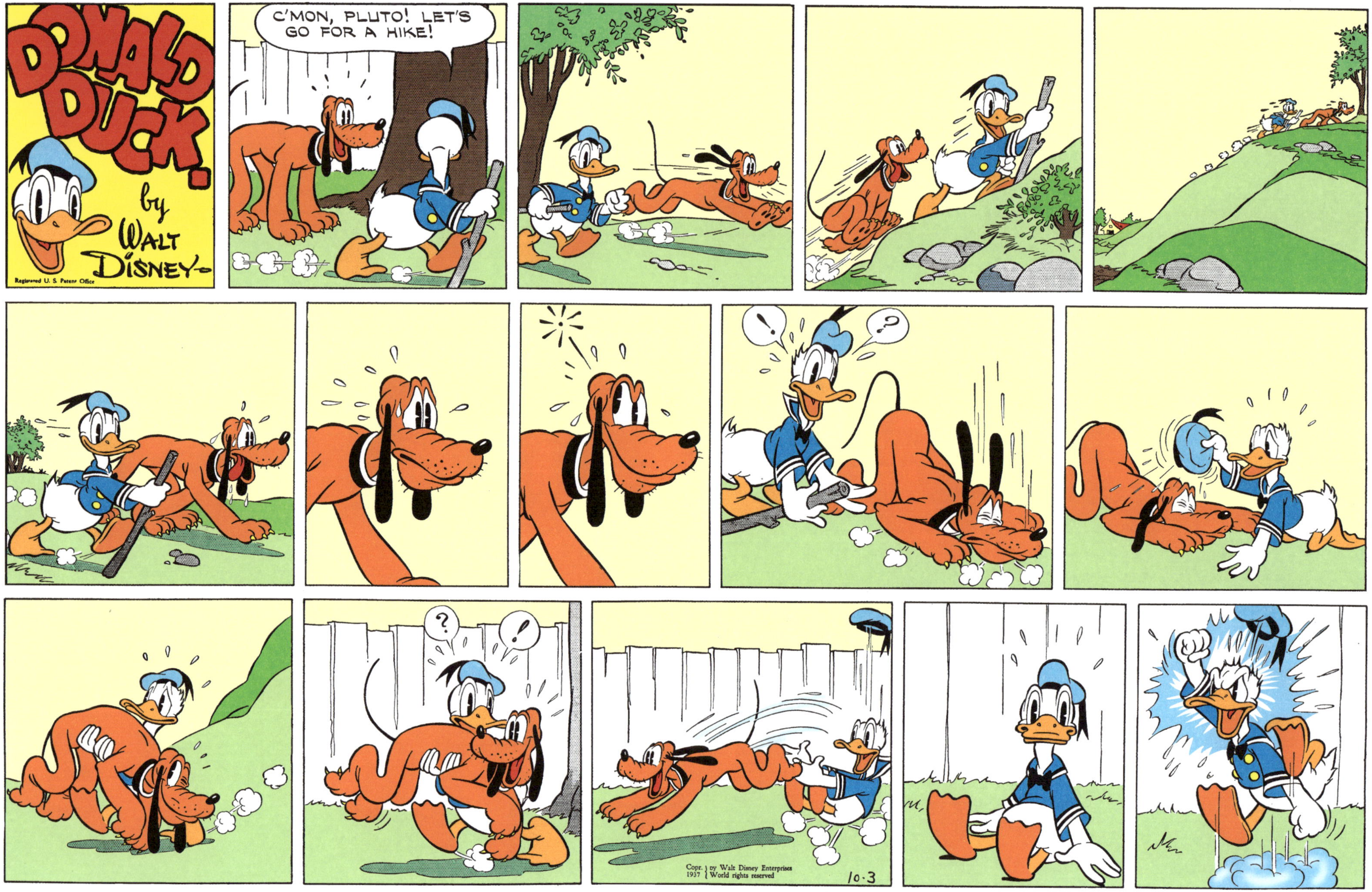
DONALD DUCK
by WALT DISNEY
Registered U. S. Patent Office
C'MON, PLUTO! LET'S GO FOR A HIKE!
!
?
?
!
Copr. 1937 by Walt Disney Enterprises World rights reserved
10-3

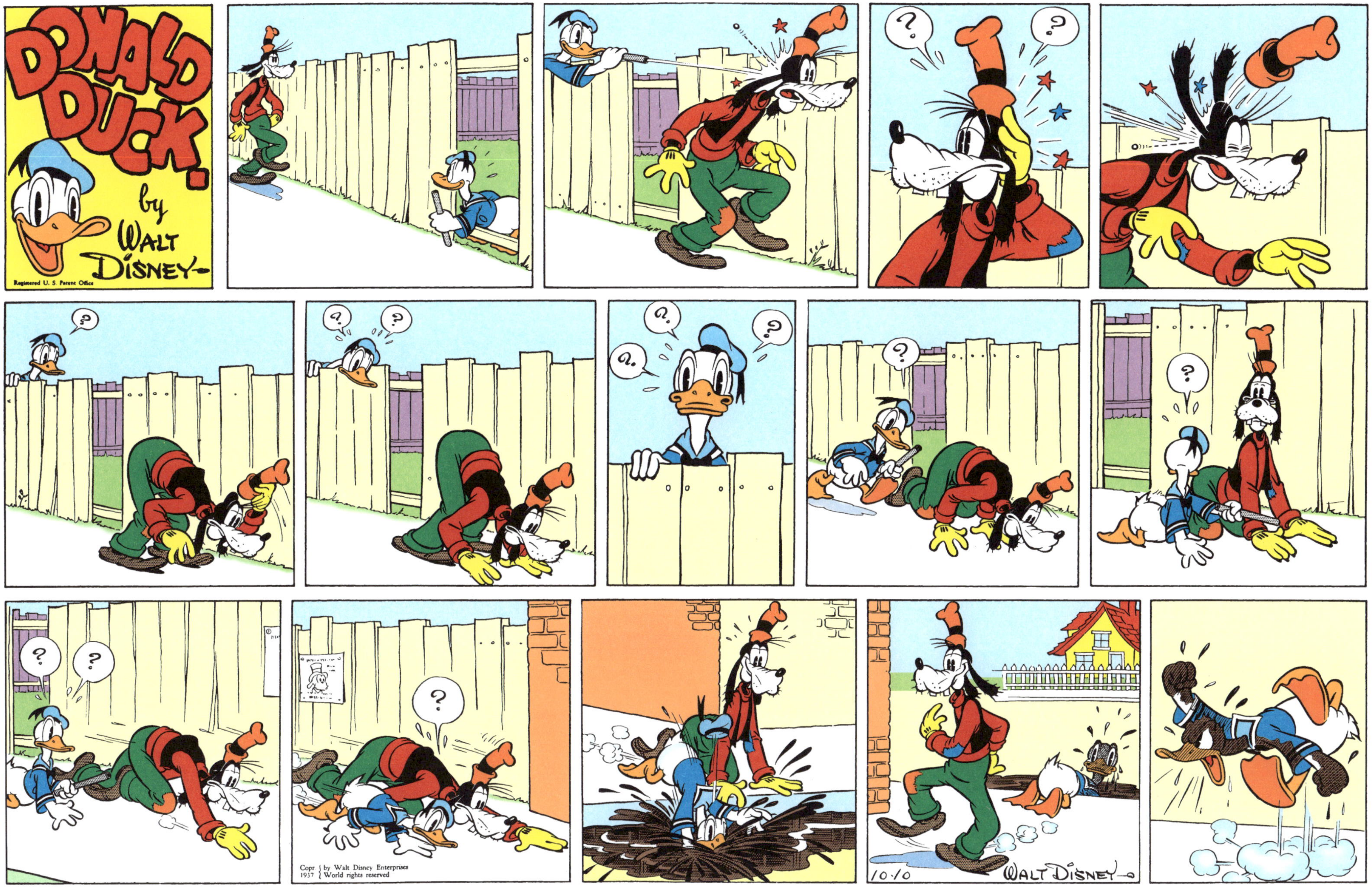
DONALD DUCK
by WALT DISNEY
Registered U. S. Patent Office
?
?
?
?
?
?
?
?
?
?
?
?
?
?
Copr 1937 { by Walt Disney Enterprises
World rights reserved
10·10
WALT DISNEY

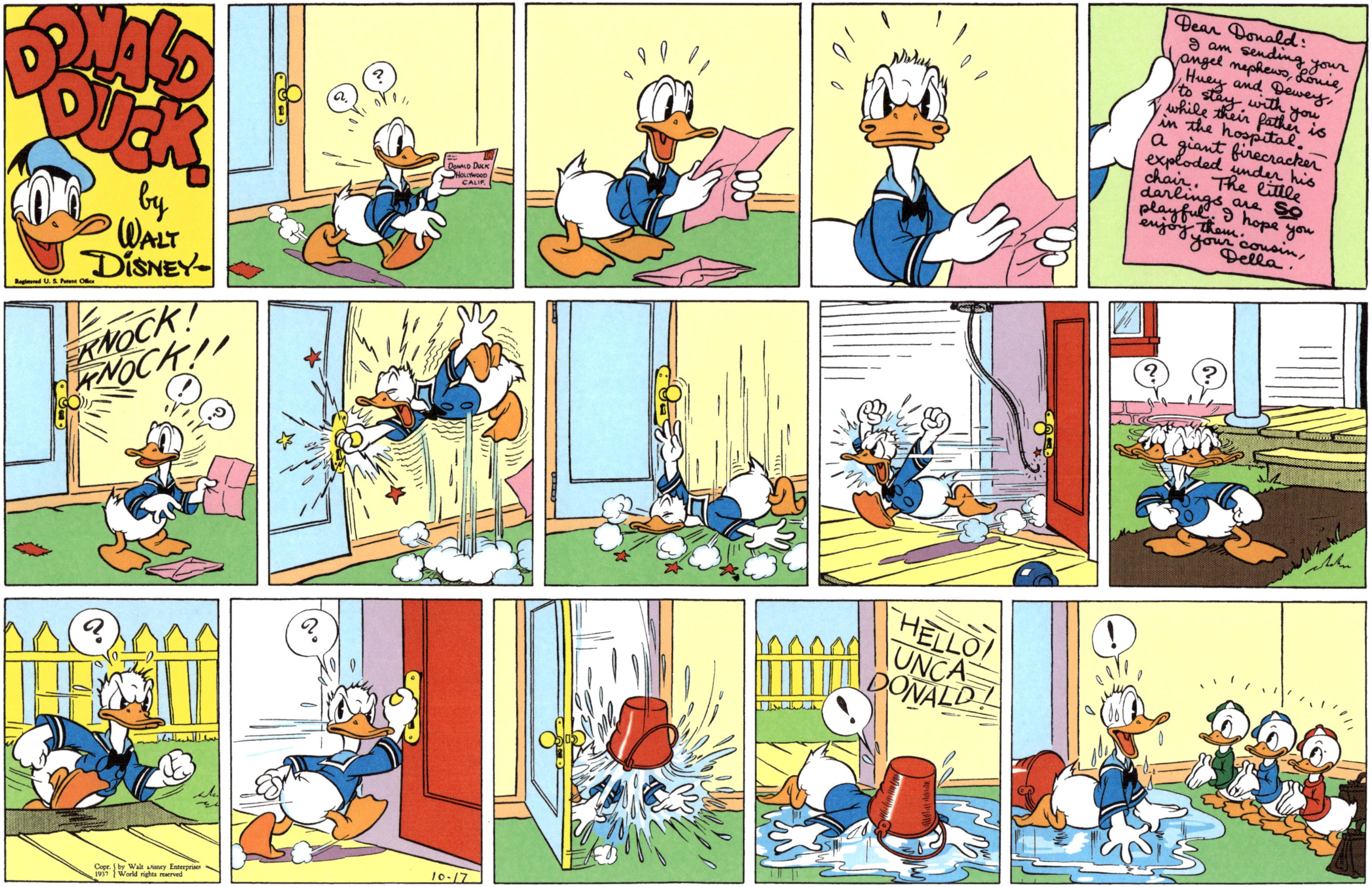
DONALD DUCK
by WALT DISNEY
Registered U. S. Patent Office
DONALD DUCK HOLLYWOOD CALIF.
Dear Donald:
I am sending your angel nephews, Louie, Huey and Dewey, to stay with you while their father is in the hospital. A giant firecracker exploded under his chair. The little darlings are SO playful. I hope you enjoy them.
Your cousin,
Della.
KNOCK! KNOCK!!
Copr. 1937 by Walt Disney Enterprises World rights reserved
10-17
HELLO! UNCA DONALD!

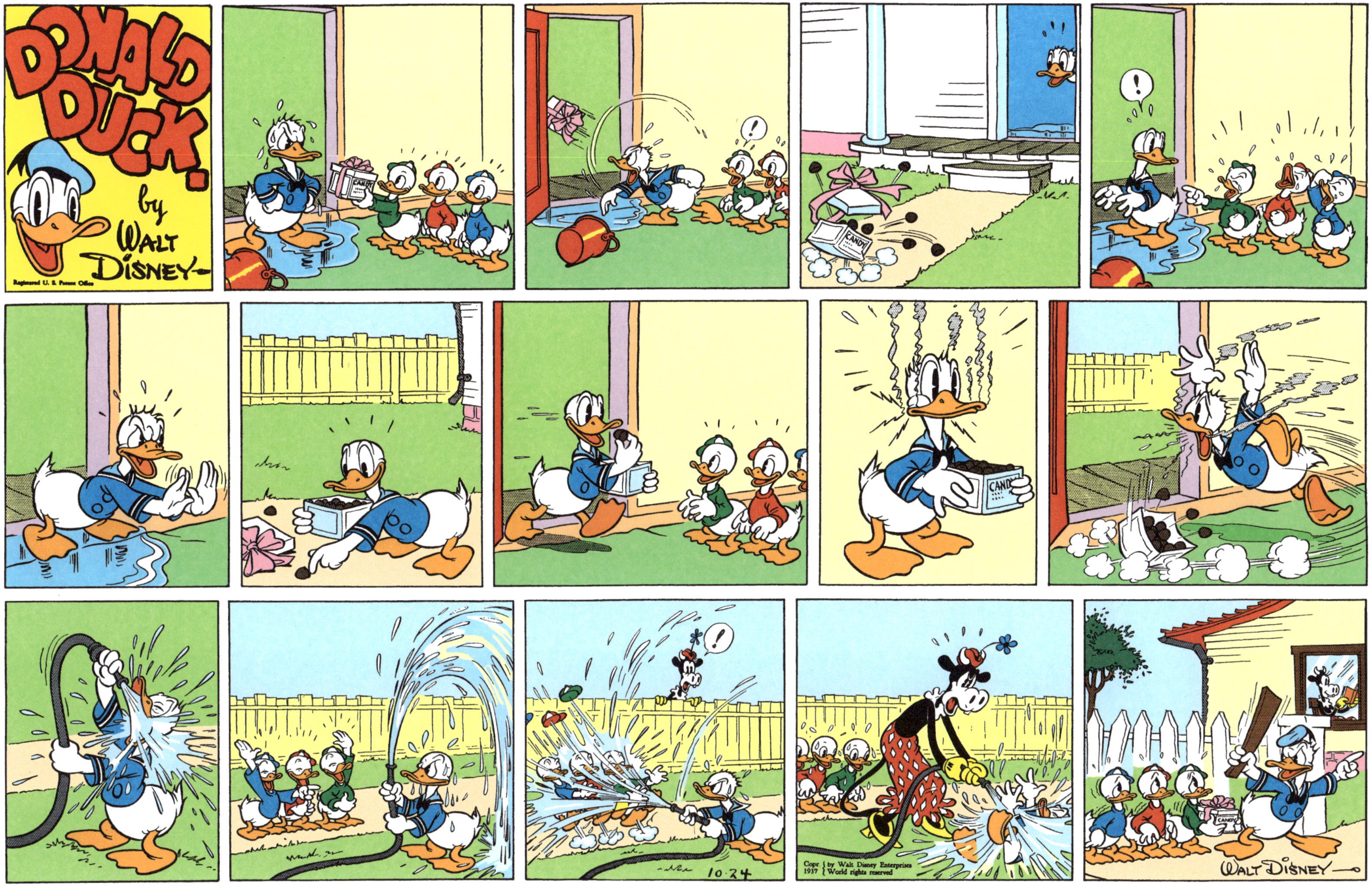
DONALD DUCK
by WALT DISNEY
Registered U. S. Patent Office
CANDY
!
CANDY
!
CANDY
!
10-24
Copr. 1937 by Walt Disney Enterprises World rights reserved
CANDY
WALT DISNEY

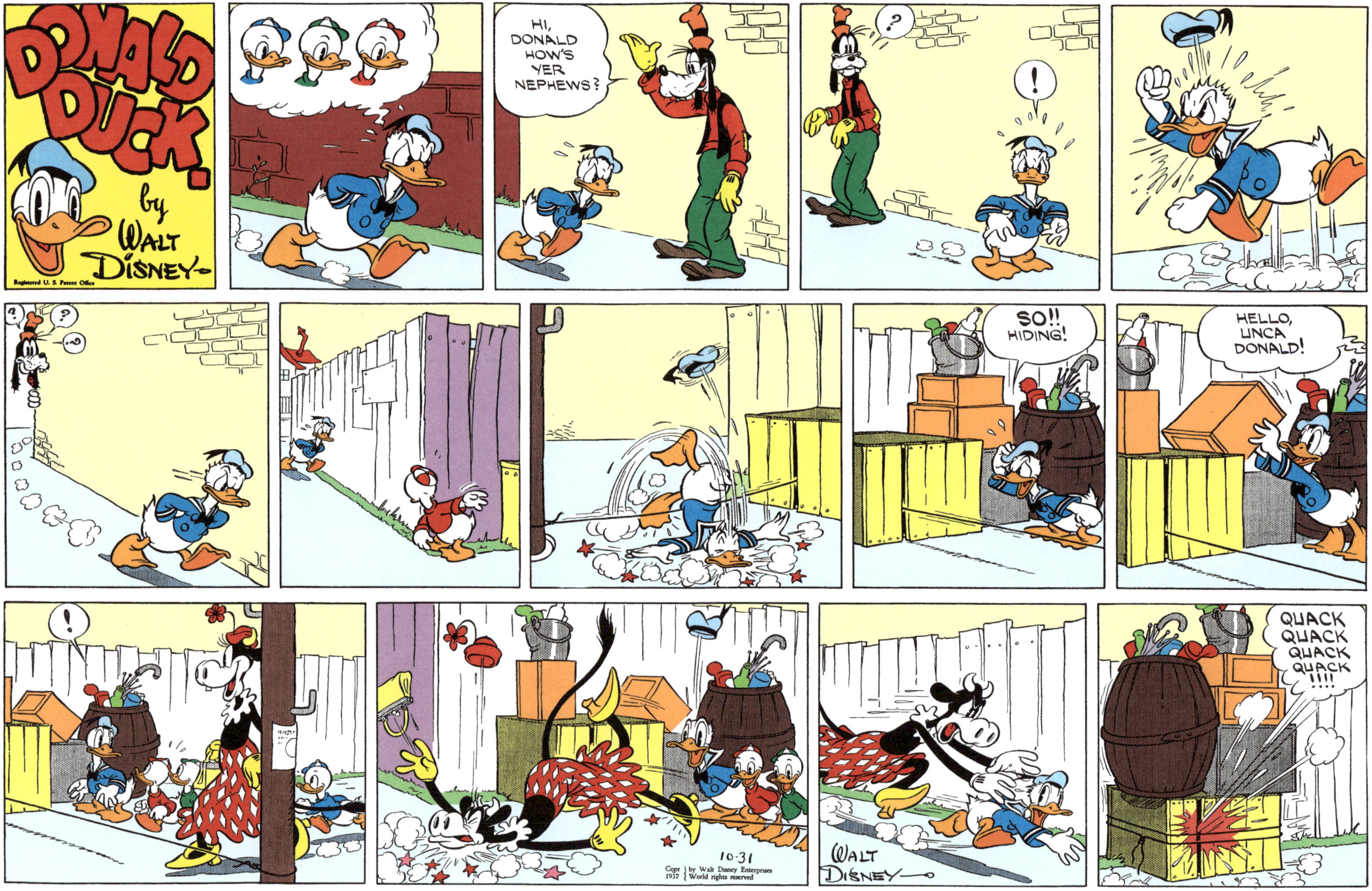
DONALD DUCK
by WALT DISNEY
Registered U. S. Patent Office
HI, DONALD HOW'S YER NEPHEWS?
?
!
SO!! HIDING!
HELLO, UNCA DONALD!
!
10-31
Copr 1937 by Walt Disney Enterprises World rights reserved
WALT DISNEY
QUACK QUACK QUACK QUACK !!!!

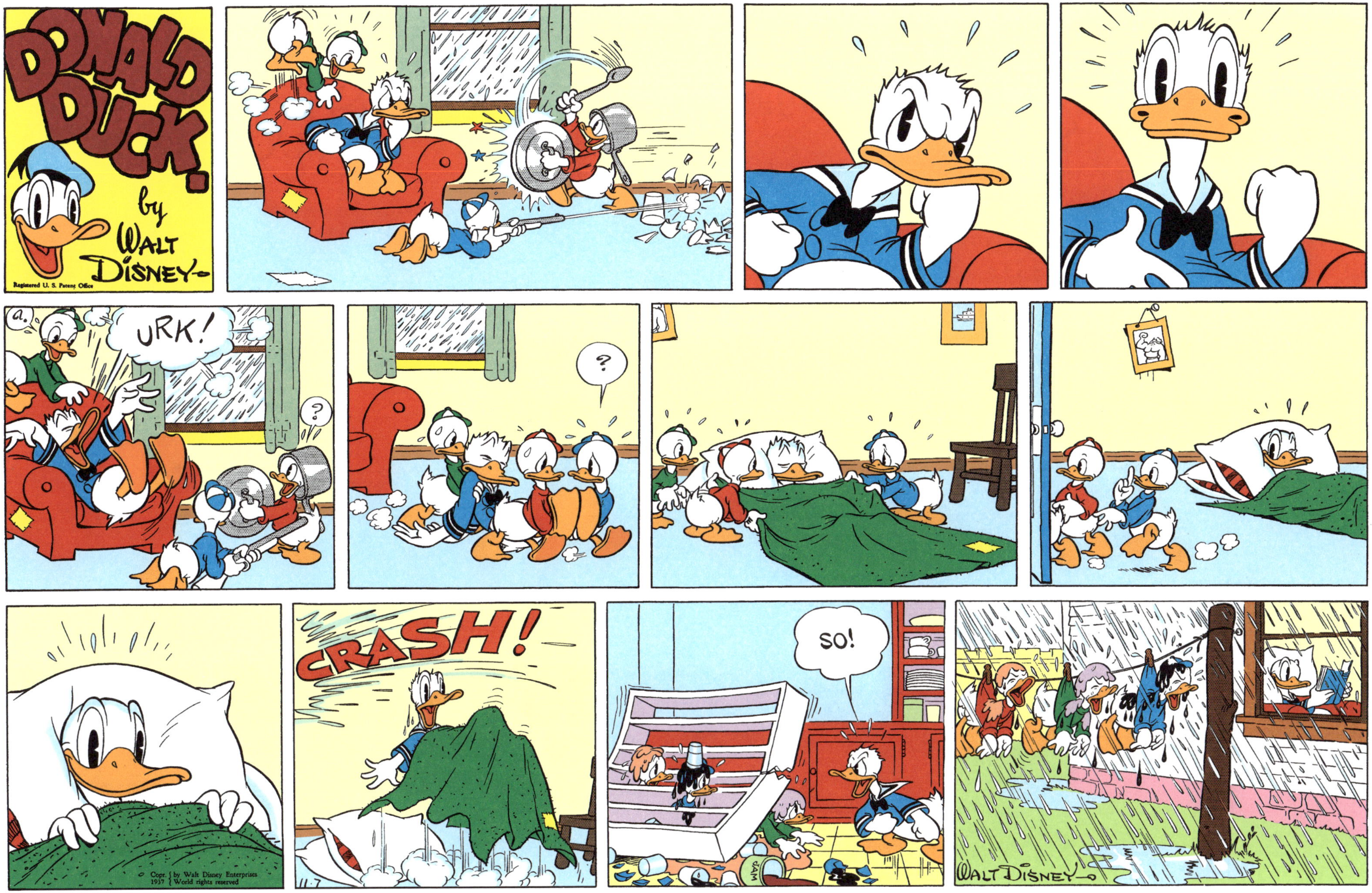
DONALD DUCK
by WALT DISNEY
Registered U. S. Patent Office
a.
URK!
?
?
CRASH!
11-7
Copr. 1937 by Walt Disney Enterprises World rights reserved
SO!
JAM
WALT DISNEY

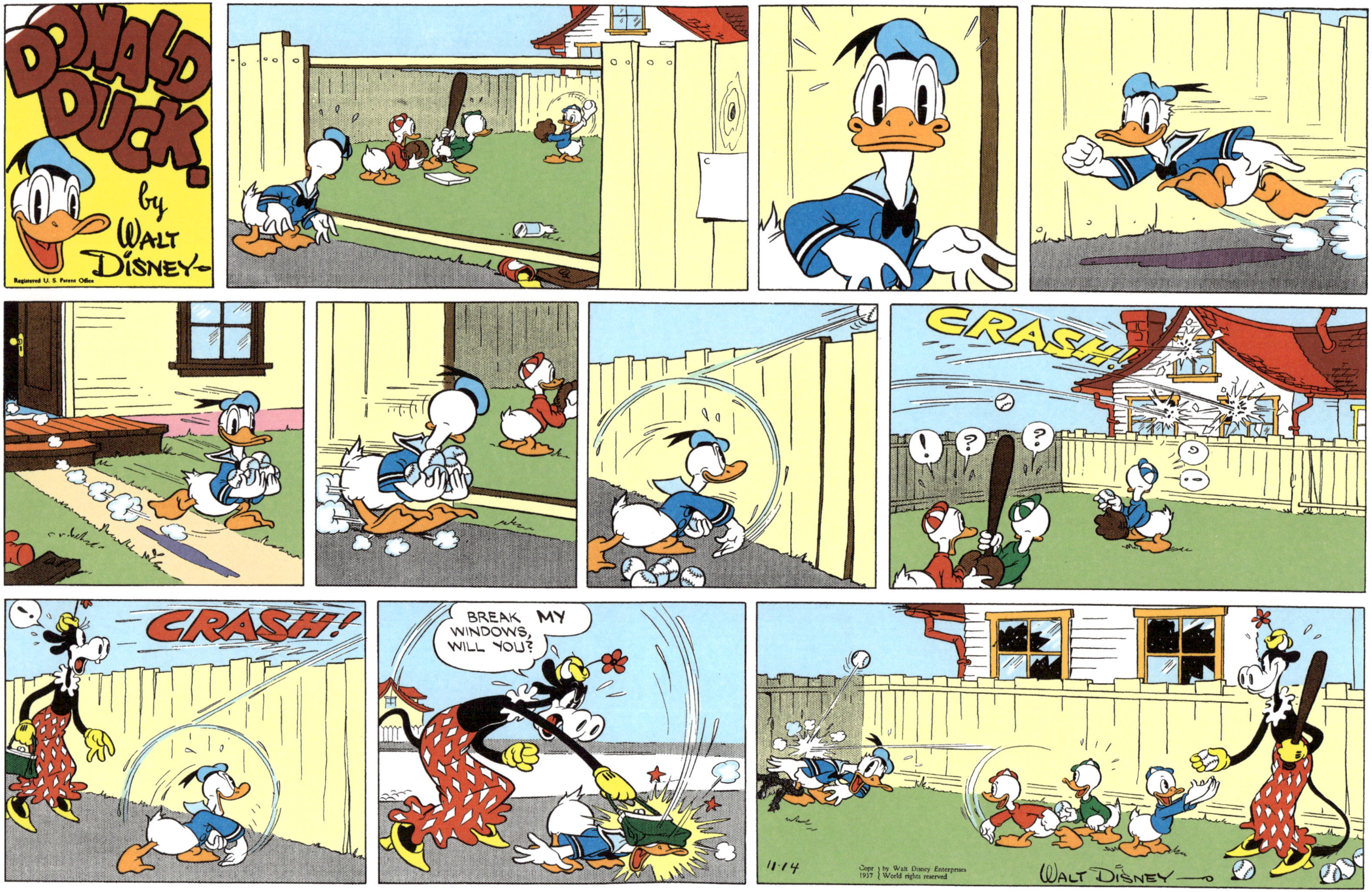
DONALD DUCK
by WALT DISNEY
Registered U. S. Patent Office
CRASH!
CRASH!
BREAK MY WINDOWS, WILL YOU?
11-14
Copr 1937 by Walt Disney Enterprises World rights reserved
WALT DISNEY

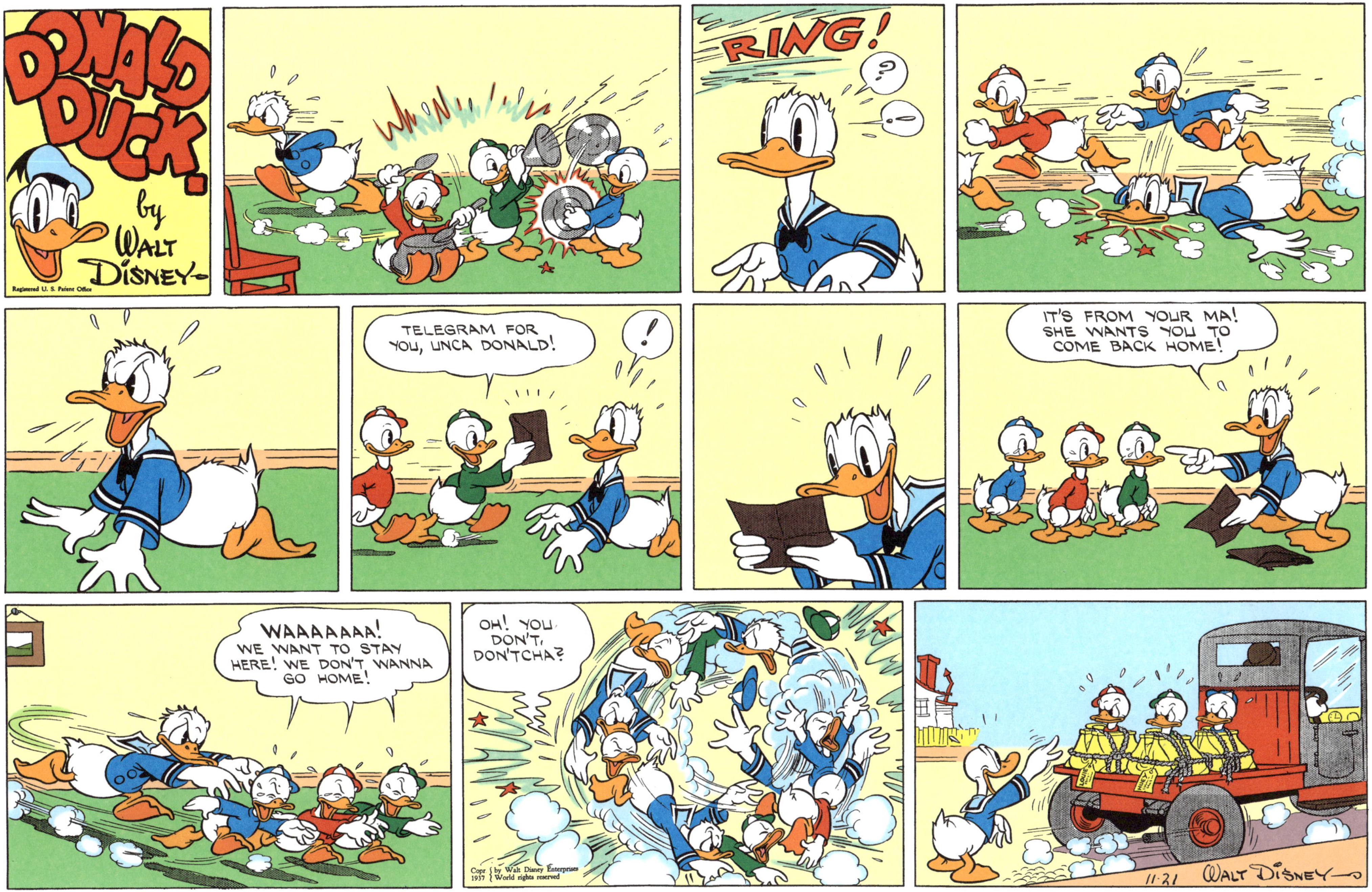
DONALD DUCK.
by WALT DISNEY
Registered U. S. Patent Office
RING!
?
!
TELEGRAM FOR YOU, UNCA DONALD!
!
IT'S FROM YOUR MA! SHE WANTS YOU TO COME BACK HOME!
WAAAAAAA! WE WANT TO STAY HERE! WE DON'T WANNA GO HOME!
OH! YOU DON'T, DON'TCHA?
Copr 1937 by Walt Disney Enterprises World rights reserved
11-21
WALT DISNEY

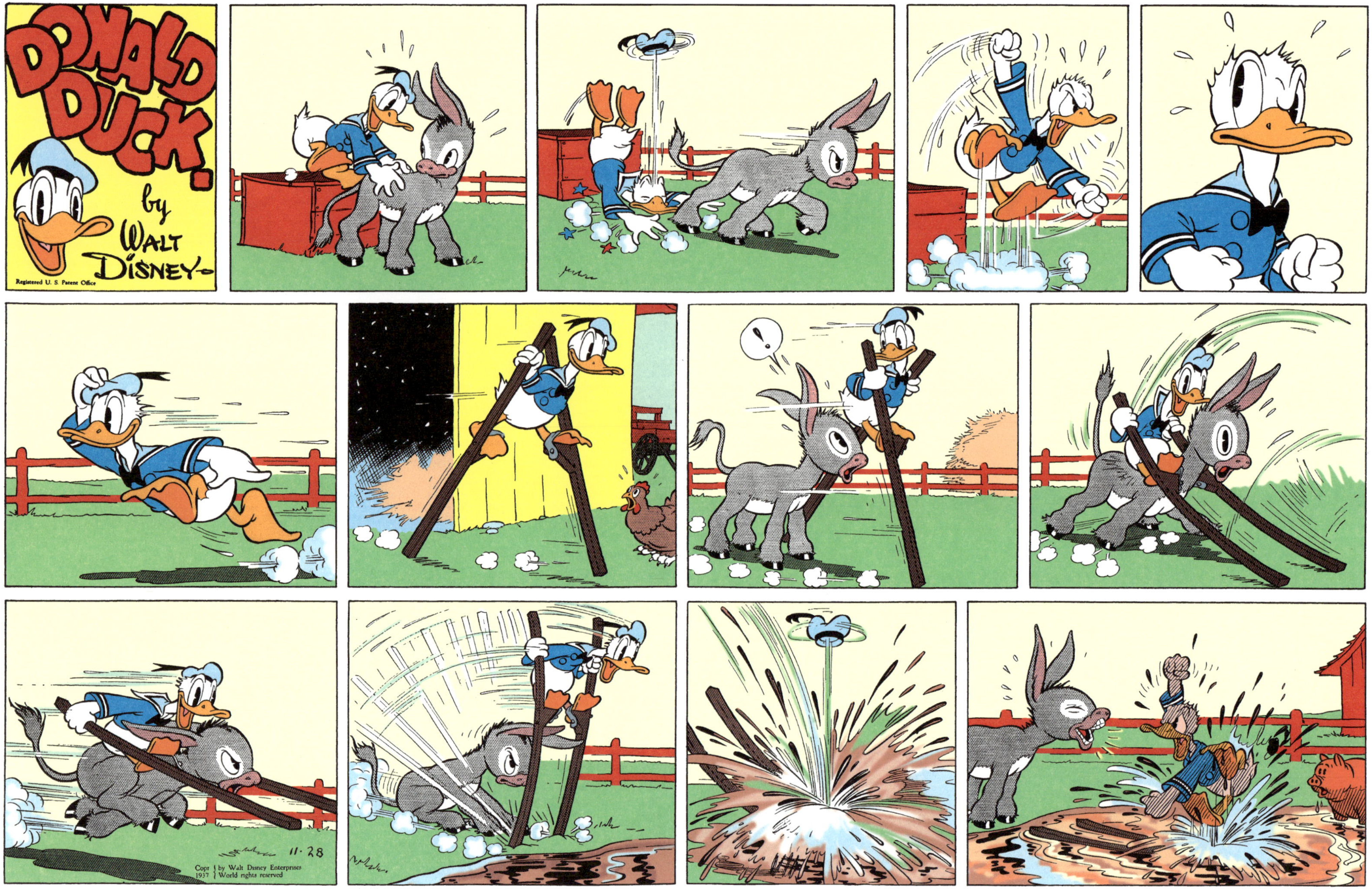
DONALD DUCK
by WALT DISNEY
Registered U. S. Patent Office
!
11-28
Copr 1937 by Walt Disney Enterprises World rights reserved

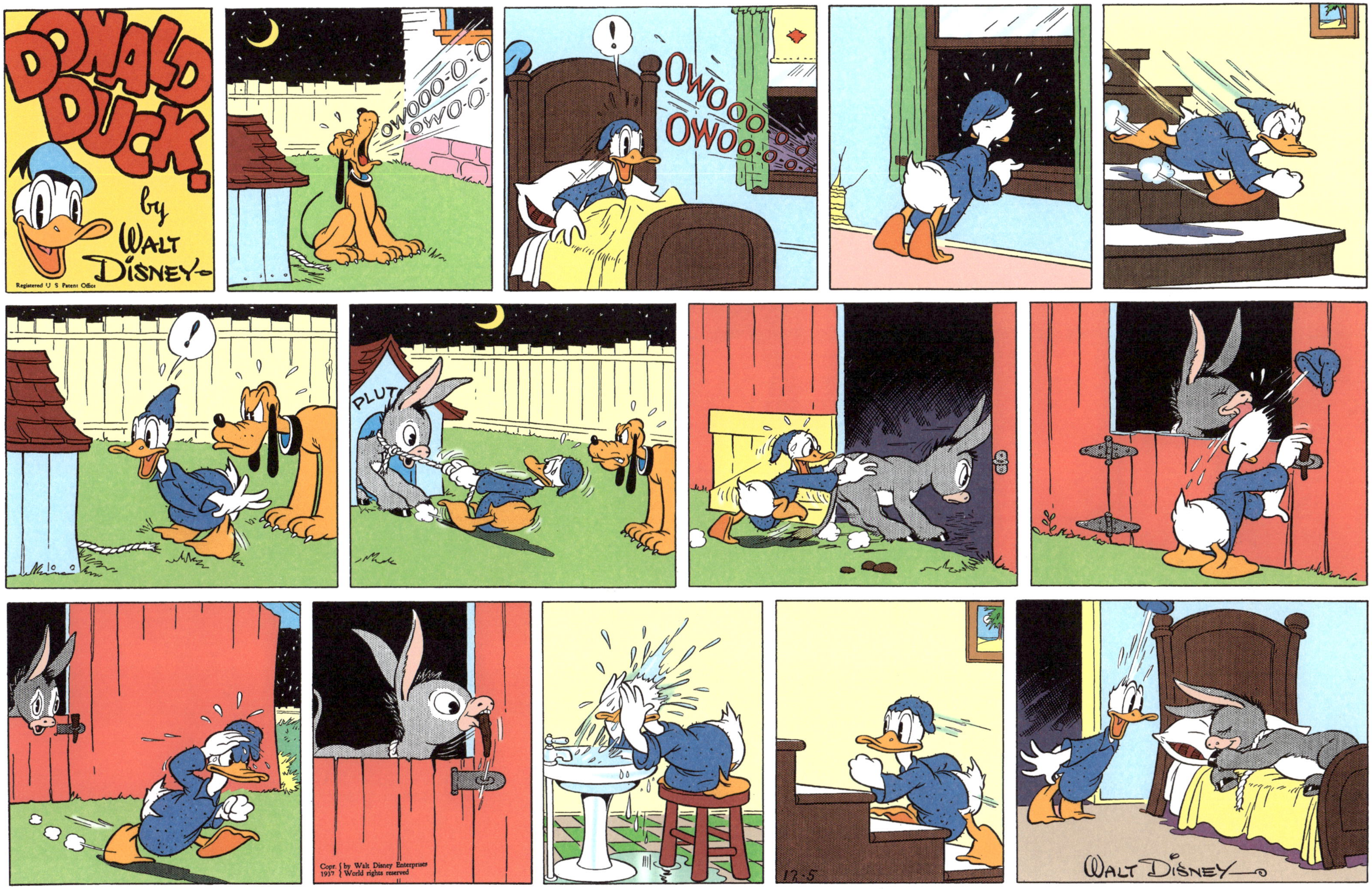
DONALD DUCK
by
WALT DISNEY
Registered U S Patent Office
OWOOO-O-O
OWO-O
!
OWOOO
OWOO-O-O
!
PLUT
Copr. 1937 by Walt Disney Enterprises World rights reserved
12-5
WALT DISNEY

SNOW WHITE AND THE SEVEN DWARFS

December 12, 1937 - April 24, 1938
Written by Merrill de Maris, drawn by Hank Porter, assisted by Bob Grant

After five years, the *Silly Symphony* comic page had become a flexible arena in which the Disney studio could display a variety of artistic wares. Now it was pressed into service to help promote the studio's historic feature-length film. By the time the movie began to open in theaters, readers were already getting to know Snow White, the Dwarfs, and the rest of the cast in weekly comic installments. Carefully coordinated with the rest of the *Snow White* promotional campaign, the strip retold the story in a more or less faithful adaptation. Here, as in the film, Snow White fell in love with her Prince, fled into the forest to escape the Queen's murderous jealousy, and was sheltered by the Dwarfs; here the Queen disguised herself, attempted to dispatch her victim with a poisoned apple and met her own demise, clearing the way for a happy ending for Snow White and the Prince.

But the *similarities* between strip and film serve to make the *differences* even more interesting. Some variations were dictated by the medium. In the film, the frightened Dwarfs search their house for the monster they think is hiding inside—a scene ideally suited for an extended set-piece of expressive character animation, but less adaptable to static comic panels. Here it's skimmed over quickly. Later in the film, confined downstairs after giving up their bedroom for Snow White's use, the Dwarfs fight over the one available pillow in a slapstick episode, then find comically uncomfortable ways to bed down for the night. In the comic page, again, each of these scenes is disposed of in a single panel.

The film's songs, several of which became standards in the popular-music market, similarly were of little use in the comics. In this continuity, only "Heigh-Ho," the Dwarfs' marching song (here rendered "Hi Ho"), was repeated; all the other songs in the score were eliminated. One of the highlights of the film is the sequence in which the Dwarfs ask Snow White to tell them a story; she responds by singing the romantic ballad "Some Day My Prince Will Come." In the comics, not only the song but the storytelling scene were cut altogether.

On the other hand, the comic strip offers intriguing plot elements that did *not* appear on the screen. Early in story development of the film, the writers had suggested an opening scene in which Snow White might construct an imaginary prince from garden implements, dub the effigy "Prince Buckethead," and play a mock-romantic scene with it until the real Prince overheard her and made a surprise appearance. This idea was soon dropped from the film, but it reappears in the comics version. Even more strikingly, the Disney story crew had considered an elaborate plot thread in which the jealous Queen had the Prince seized and imprisoned in a dungeon, from which he later made a heroic escape. These scenes, too, were cut from the film but survived intact on the comic page.

Thus discarding some elements from the film and adding some new ones of its own, this continuity stands as a distinct *Snow White* adaptation in its own right. Note, too, the marked shift in graphic style that appears in this story. In place of Al Taliaferro's clean, uncluttered line, previously the standard in the *Silly Symphony* comics, Hank Porter and Bob Grant introduce a quaint, shadowy storybook atmosphere—translating the rich texture of the film's visuals into the terms of the newspaper comic page.

Snow White
and the Seven Dwarfs
by Walt Disney
ONCE UPON A TIME THERE WAS A LOVELY LITTLE PRINCESS NAMED SNOW WHITE -----
---- WHO WAS FORCED TO DRESS IN RAGS AND DO MENIAL WORK AROUND THE CASTLE -------
-----BY HER WICKED STEP-MOTHER, THE QUEEN!
QUEEN GRIMHILDE HAD A MAGIC MIRROR WHICH WOULD ANSWER ANY QUESTION SHE ASKED! AND, BEING VERY VAIN, SHE ALWAYS ASKED THE SAME QUESTION:
MIRROR, MIRROR, ON THE WALL, WHO IS THE FAIREST ONE OF ALL?
AND ALWAYS THE FACE IN THE MIRROR GAVE THE SAME REPLY:
YOU, MY QUEEN, ARE THE FAIREST ONE OF ALL!
SO THE QUEEN WOULD GO BACK TO HER THRONE, WHERE SHE SAT, ADMIRING HER BEAUTY!
I WON'T ALWAYS HAVE TO WORK SO HARD! SOME DAY A PRINCE WILL COME FOR ME!
DO YOU WANT TO SEE WHAT MY PRINCE WILL LOOK LIKE?
THERE HE IS! MY PRINCE! PRINCE BUCKETHEAD!
12-12
BUT, FROM A FAR COUNTRY, COMES AN ADVENTUROUS PRINCE WHO HAS HEARD OF SNOW WHITE'S BEAUTY!
WITHIN AN HOUR WE SHALL BE AT THE CASTLE--- AND OUR GREATEST ADVENTURE WILL START!
Copr. 1937 by Walt Disney Enterprises World rights reserved
TO BE CONTINUED--

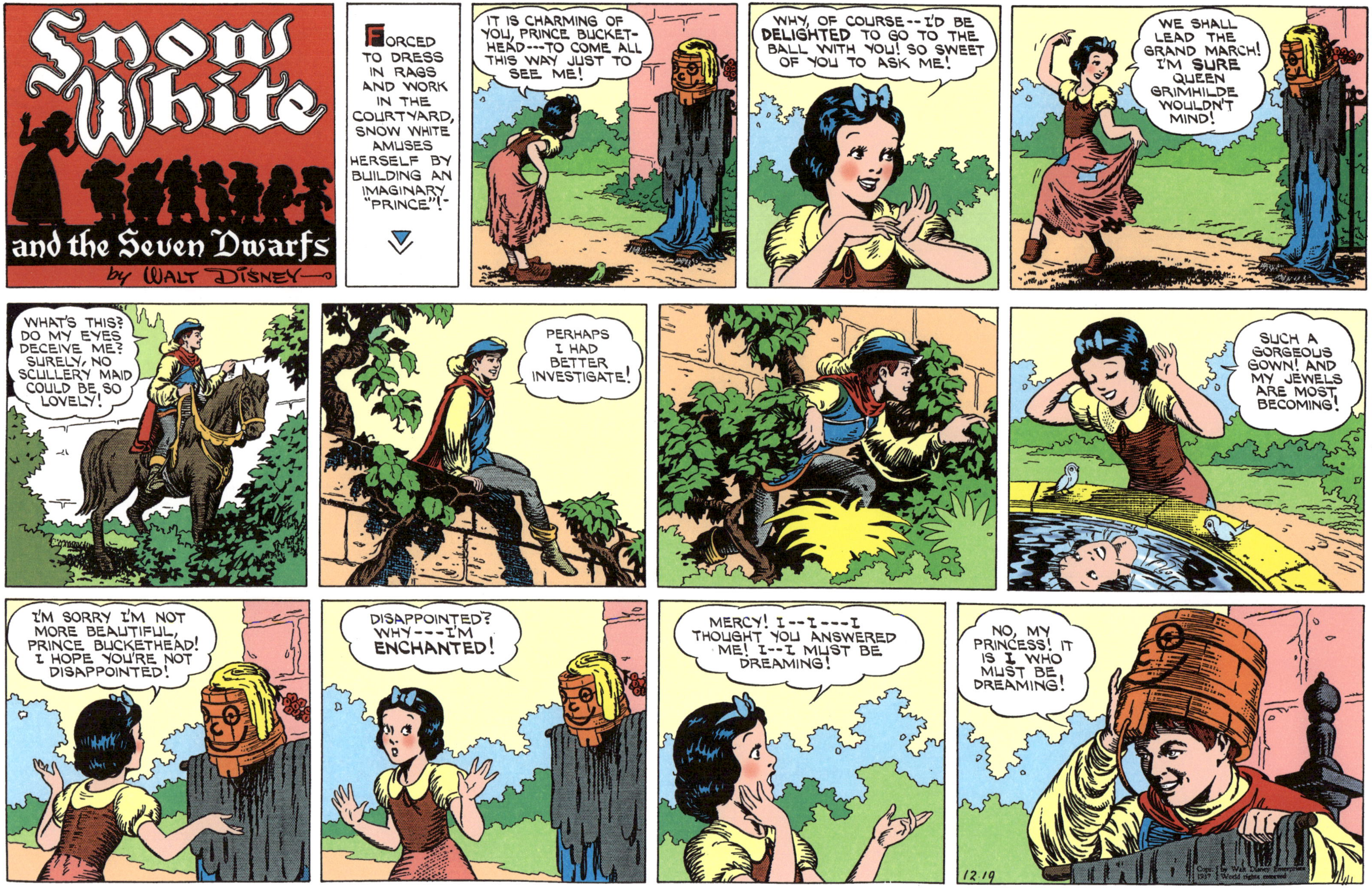
Snow White
and the Seven Dwarfs
by Walt Disney
Forced to dress in rags and work in the courtyard, Snow White amuses herself by building an imaginary "prince"!
IT IS CHARMING OF YOU, PRINCE BUCKET-HEAD---TO COME ALL THIS WAY JUST TO SEE ME!
WHY, OF COURSE--I'D BE DELIGHTED TO GO TO THE BALL WITH YOU! SO SWEET OF YOU TO ASK ME!
WE SHALL LEAD THE GRAND MARCH! I'M SURE QUEEN GRIMHILDE WOULDN'T MIND!
WHAT'S THIS? DO MY EYES DECEIVE ME? SURELY, NO SCULLERY MAID COULD BE SO LOVELY!
PERHAPS I HAD BETTER INVESTIGATE!
SUCH A GORGEOUS GOWN! AND MY JEWELS ARE MOST BECOMING!
I'M SORRY I'M NOT MORE BEAUTIFUL, PRINCE BUCKETHEAD! I HOPE YOU'RE NOT DISAPPOINTED!
DISAPPOINTED? WHY---I'M ENCHANTED!
MERCY! I--I---I THOUGHT YOU ANSWERED ME! I--I MUST BE DREAMING!
NO, MY PRINCESS! IT IS I WHO MUST BE DREAMING!
12-19

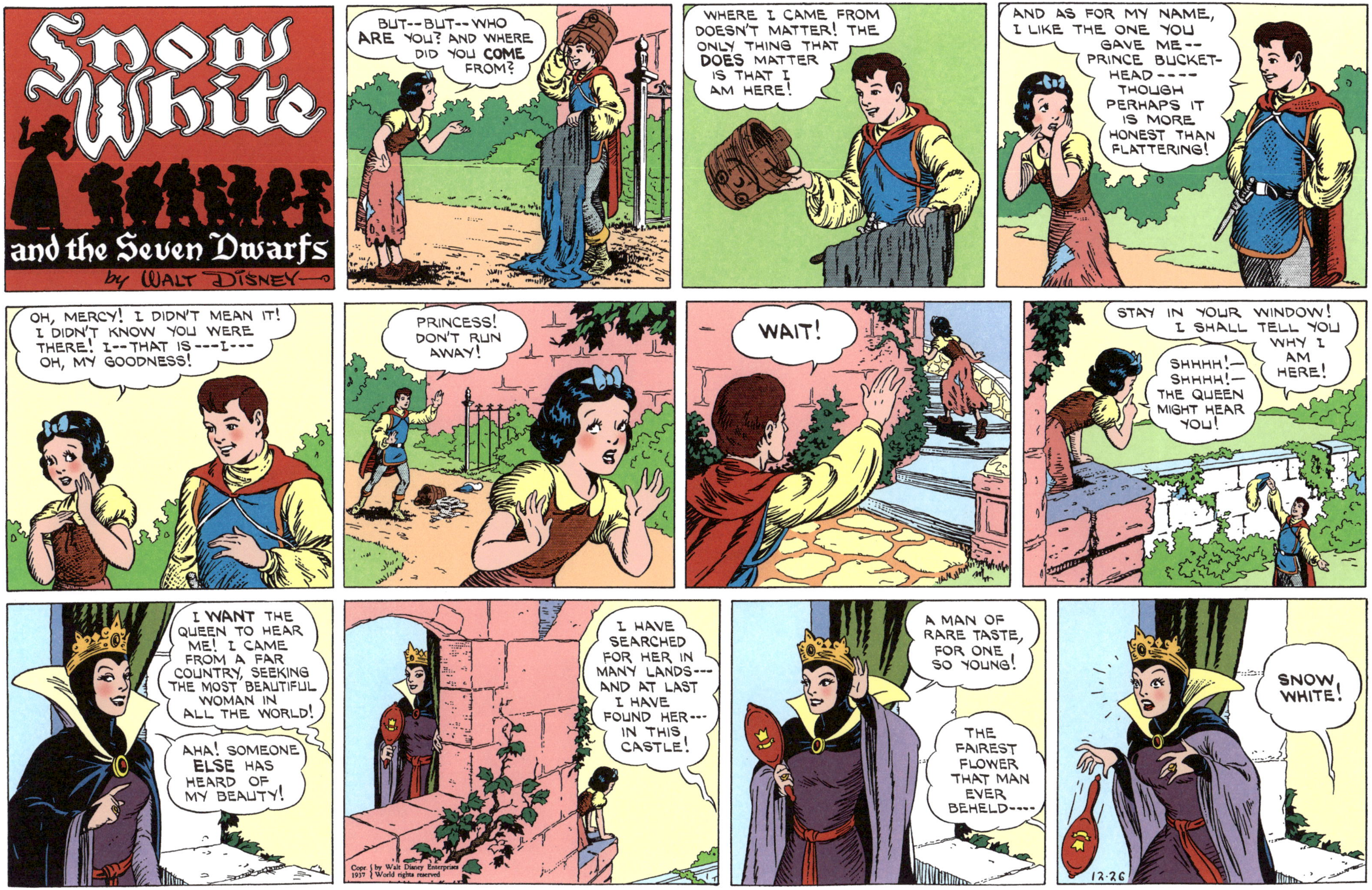
Snow White
and the Seven Dwarfs
by Walt Disney
BUT--BUT--WHO ARE YOU? AND WHERE DID YOU COME FROM?
WHERE I CAME FROM DOESN'T MATTER! THE ONLY THING THAT DOES MATTER IS THAT I AM HERE!
AND AS FOR MY NAME, I LIKE THE ONE YOU GAVE ME-- PRINCE BUCKET-HEAD---- THOUGH PERHAPS IT IS MORE HONEST THAN FLATTERING!
OH, MERCY! I DIDN'T MEAN IT! I DIDN'T KNOW YOU WERE THERE! I--THAT IS---I--- OH, MY GOODNESS!
PRINCESS! DON'T RUN AWAY!
WAIT!
STAY IN YOUR WINDOW! I SHALL TELL YOU WHY I AM HERE!
SHHHH!— SHHHH!— THE QUEEN MIGHT HEAR YOU!
I WANT THE QUEEN TO HEAR ME! I CAME FROM A FAR COUNTRY, SEEKING THE MOST BEAUTIFUL WOMAN IN ALL THE WORLD!
AHA! SOMEONE ELSE HAS HEARD OF MY BEAUTY!
I HAVE SEARCHED FOR HER IN MANY LANDS--- AND AT LAST I HAVE FOUND HER--- IN THIS CASTLE!
Copr. 1937 by Walt Disney Enterprises World rights reserved
A MAN OF RARE TASTE, FOR ONE SO YOUNG!
THE FAIREST FLOWER THAT MAN EVER BEHELD----
SNOW WHITE!
12-26

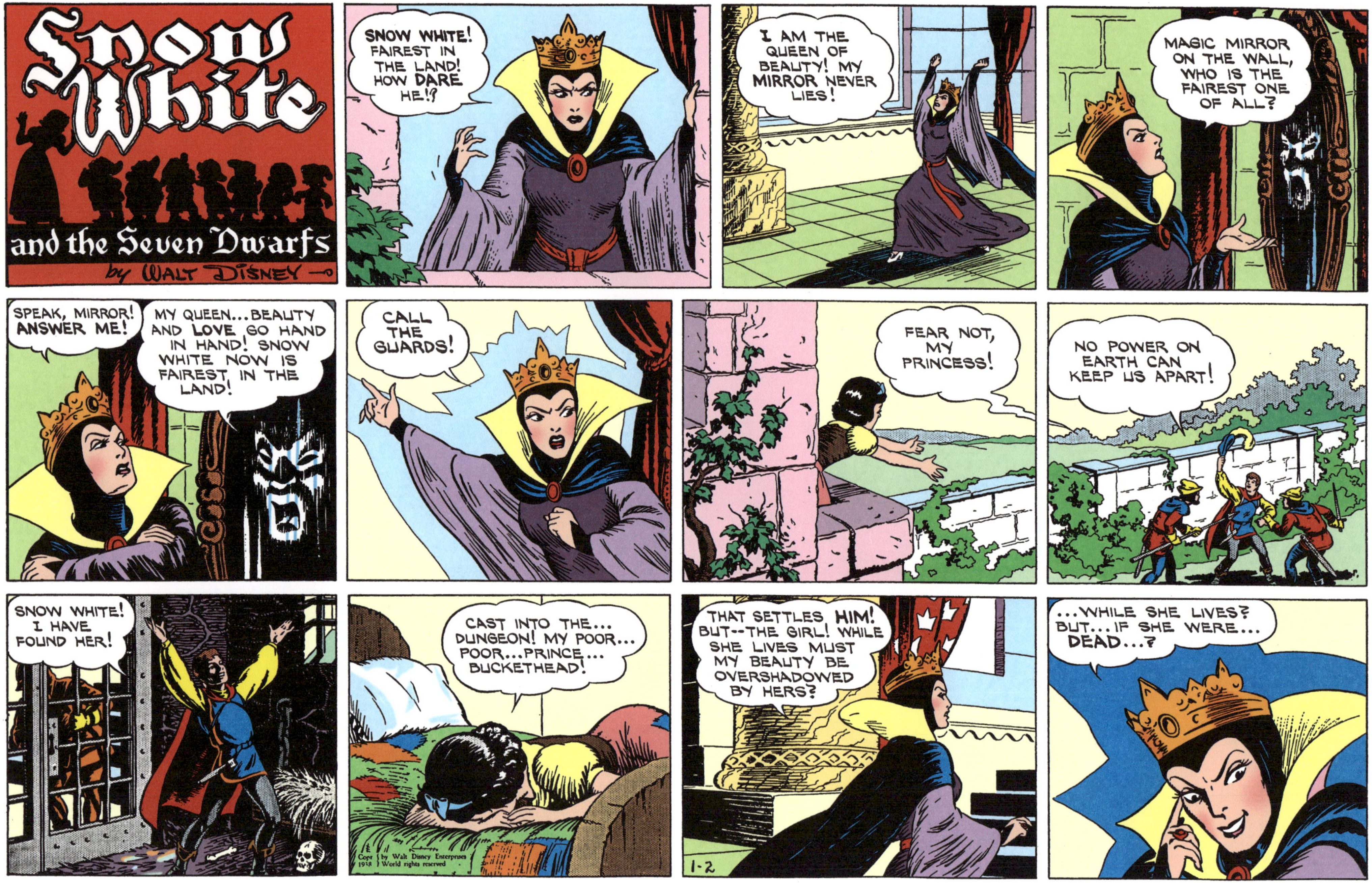
Snow White
and the Seven Dwarfs
by Walt Disney
SNOW WHITE! FAIREST IN THE LAND! HOW DARE HE!?
I AM THE QUEEN OF BEAUTY! MY MIRROR NEVER LIES!
MAGIC MIRROR ON THE WALL, WHO IS THE FAIREST ONE OF ALL?
SPEAK, MIRROR! ANSWER ME!
MY QUEEN...BEAUTY AND LOVE GO HAND IN HAND! SNOW WHITE NOW IS FAIREST IN THE LAND!
CALL THE GUARDS!
FEAR NOT, MY PRINCESS!
NO POWER ON EARTH CAN KEEP US APART!
SNOW WHITE! I HAVE FOUND HER!
CAST INTO THE... DUNGEON! MY POOR... POOR...PRINCE... BUCKETHEAD!
Copr 1938 by Walt Disney Enterprises World rights reserved
THAT SETTLES HIM! BUT--THE GIRL! WHILE SHE LIVES MUST MY BEAUTY BE OVERSHADOWED BY HERS?
1-2
...WHILE SHE LIVES? BUT... IF SHE WERE... DEAD...?

Snow White
and the Seven Dwarfs
by Walt Disney
THE WICKED QUEEN, INSANELY JEALOUS OVER SNOW WHITE'S BEAUTY, HAS CAST THE LITTLE PRINCESS' LOVER INTO THE DUNGEON. SHE THEN CALLS HER HUNTSMAN BEFORE HER.
YOU SENT FOR ME, YOUR MAJESTY?
I WISH YOU TO TAKE SNOW WHITE FOR A WALK--DEEP INTO THE FOREST!
YOU WILL FIND SOME SECLUDED GLADE -- AND THERE ---
--- YOU WILL KILL HER!
YOUR MAJESTY! I CANNOT DO THAT! THE LITTLE PRINCESS---!
THE LIVES OF YOUR OWN CHILDREN ARE FORFEIT, IF YOU FAIL! DO YOU UNDERSTAND?
BUT TO MAKE DOUBLY SURE YOU DO NOT FAIL--- BRING BACK HER HEART IN THIS!
AS YOUR MAJESTY COMMANDS!
WHO KNOCKS?
IT IS HUMBERT, THE QUEEN'S HUNTSMAN, YOUR HIGHNESS!
HER MAJESTY THINKS YOU HAVE BEEN WORKING TOO HARD! SHE SUGGESTS A HOLIDAY--- A STROLL IN THE FOREST!
THE QUEEN-- SAID THAT?
1-9
I MIGHT DISTRUST THE QUEEN IF YOU WERE NOT WITH ME, HUMBERT! BUT I KNOW THAT YOU WILL LET NOTHING HARM ME!
Copr. 1938 by Walt Disney Enterprises World rights reserved

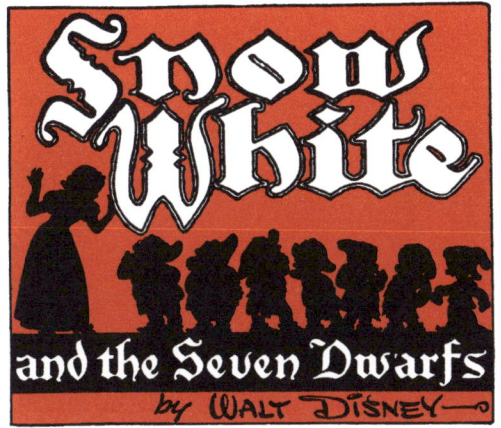

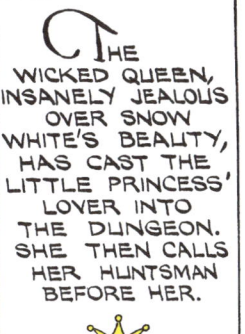

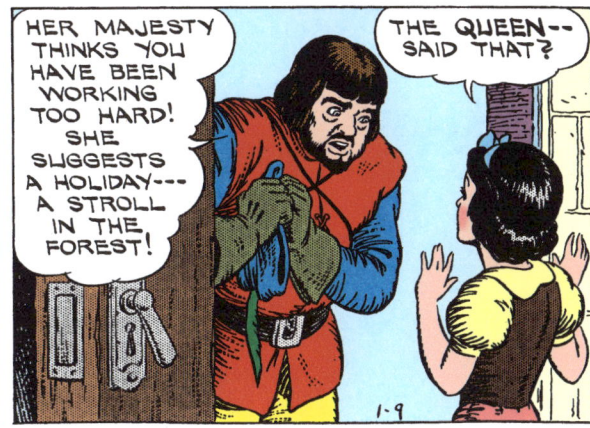

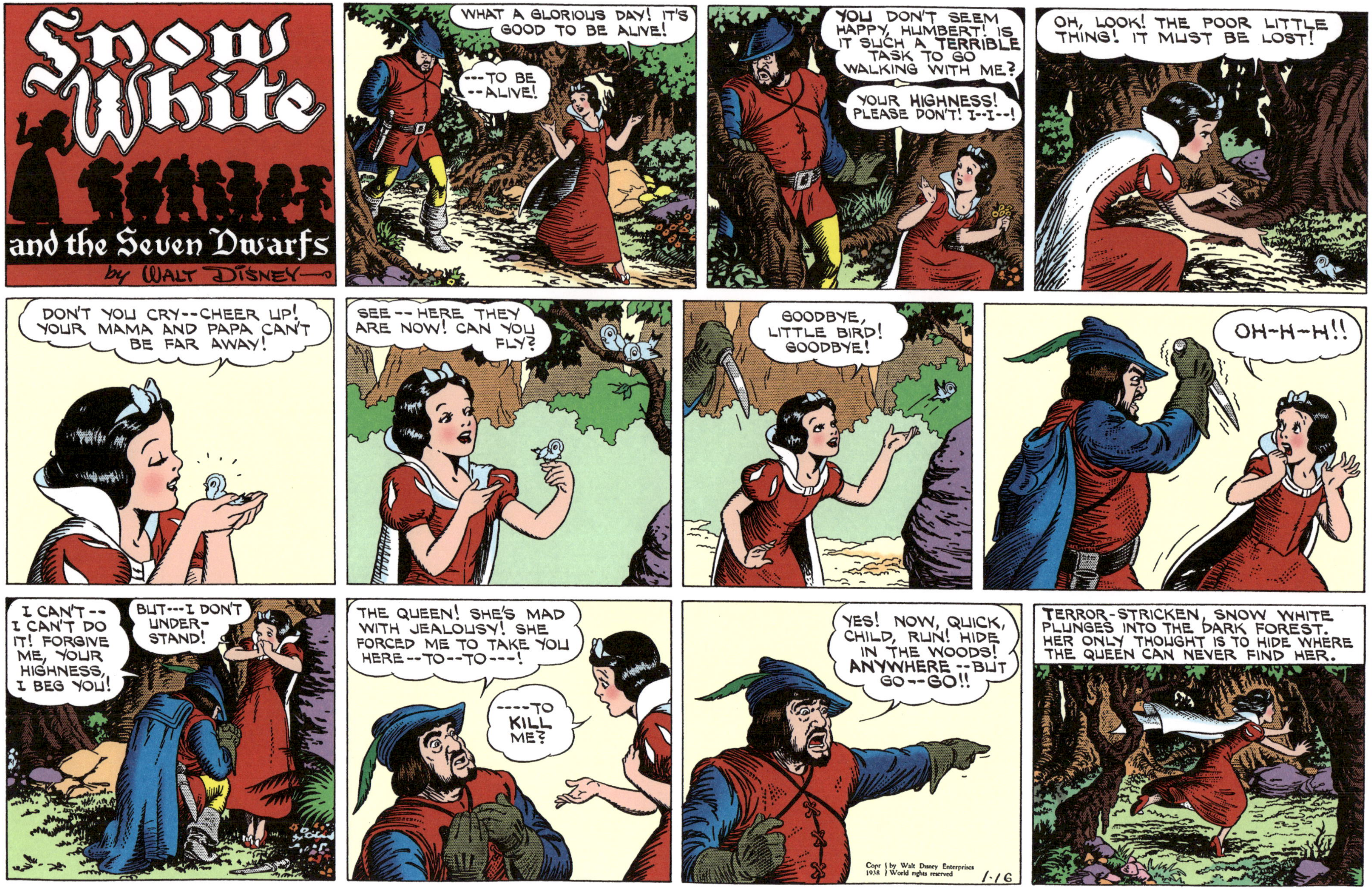

Snow White and the Seven Dwarfs
by Walt Disney
WHAT A GLORIOUS DAY! IT'S GOOD TO BE ALIVE!
---TO BE --ALIVE!
YOU DON'T SEEM HAPPY, HUMBERT! IS IT SUCH A TERRIBLE TASK TO GO WALKING WITH ME?
YOUR HIGHNESS! PLEASE DON'T! I--I--!
OH, LOOK! THE POOR LITTLE THING! IT MUST BE LOST!
DON'T YOU CRY--CHEER UP! YOUR MAMA AND PAPA CAN'T BE FAR AWAY!
SEE--HERE THEY ARE NOW! CAN YOU FLY?
GOODBYE, LITTLE BIRD! GOODBYE!
OH-H-H!!
I CAN'T--I CAN'T DO IT! FORGIVE ME, YOUR HIGHNESS, I BEG YOU!
BUT---I DON'T UNDER-STAND!
THE QUEEN! SHE'S MAD WITH JEALOUSY! SHE FORCED ME TO TAKE YOU HERE--TO--TO---!
----TO KILL ME?
YES! NOW, QUICK, CHILD, RUN! HIDE IN THE WOODS! ANYWHERE--BUT GO--GO!!
Copr. 1938 by Walt Disney Enterprises World rights reserved
1-16
TERROR-STRICKEN, SNOW WHITE PLUNGES INTO THE DARK FOREST. HER ONLY THOUGHT IS TO HIDE WHERE THE QUEEN CAN NEVER FIND HER.

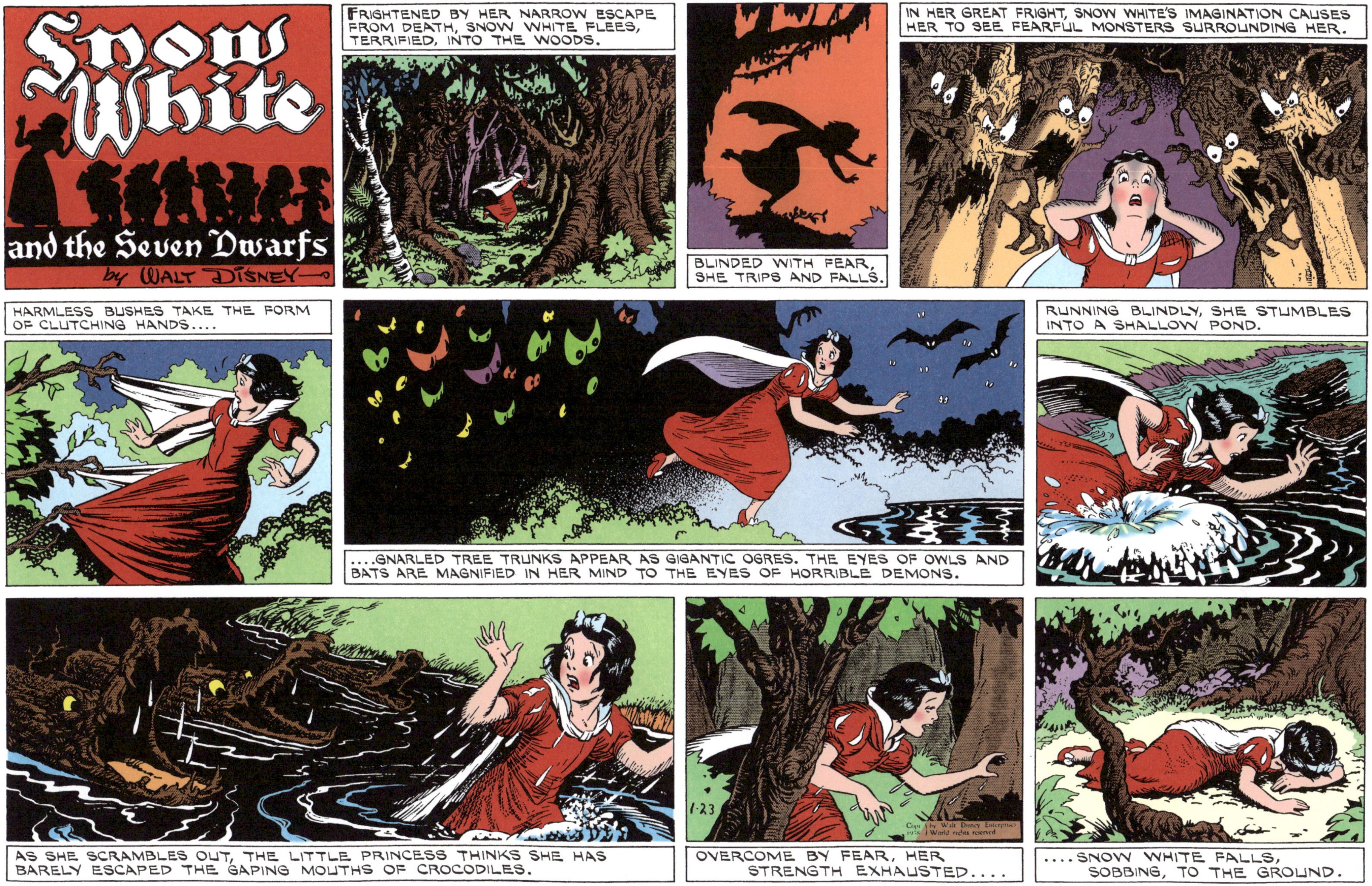
Snow White
and the Seven Dwarfs
by WALT DISNEY
FRIGHTENED BY HER NARROW ESCAPE FROM DEATH, SNOW WHITE FLEES, TERRIFIED, INTO THE WOODS.
BLINDED WITH FEAR, SHE TRIPS AND FALLS.
IN HER GREAT FRIGHT, SNOW WHITE'S IMAGINATION CAUSES HER TO SEE FEARFUL MONSTERS SURROUNDING HER.
HARMLESS BUSHES TAKE THE FORM OF CLUTCHING HANDS....
....GNARLED TREE TRUNKS APPEAR AS GIGANTIC OGRES. THE EYES OF OWLS AND BATS ARE MAGNIFIED IN HER MIND TO THE EYES OF HORRIBLE DEMONS.
RUNNING BLINDLY, SHE STUMBLES INTO A SHALLOW POND.
AS SHE SCRAMBLES OUT, THE LITTLE PRINCESS THINKS SHE HAS BARELY ESCAPED THE GAPING MOUTHS OF CROCODILES.
1-23
OVERCOME BY FEAR, HER STRENGTH EXHAUSTED....
....SNOW WHITE FALLS, SOBBING, TO THE GROUND.

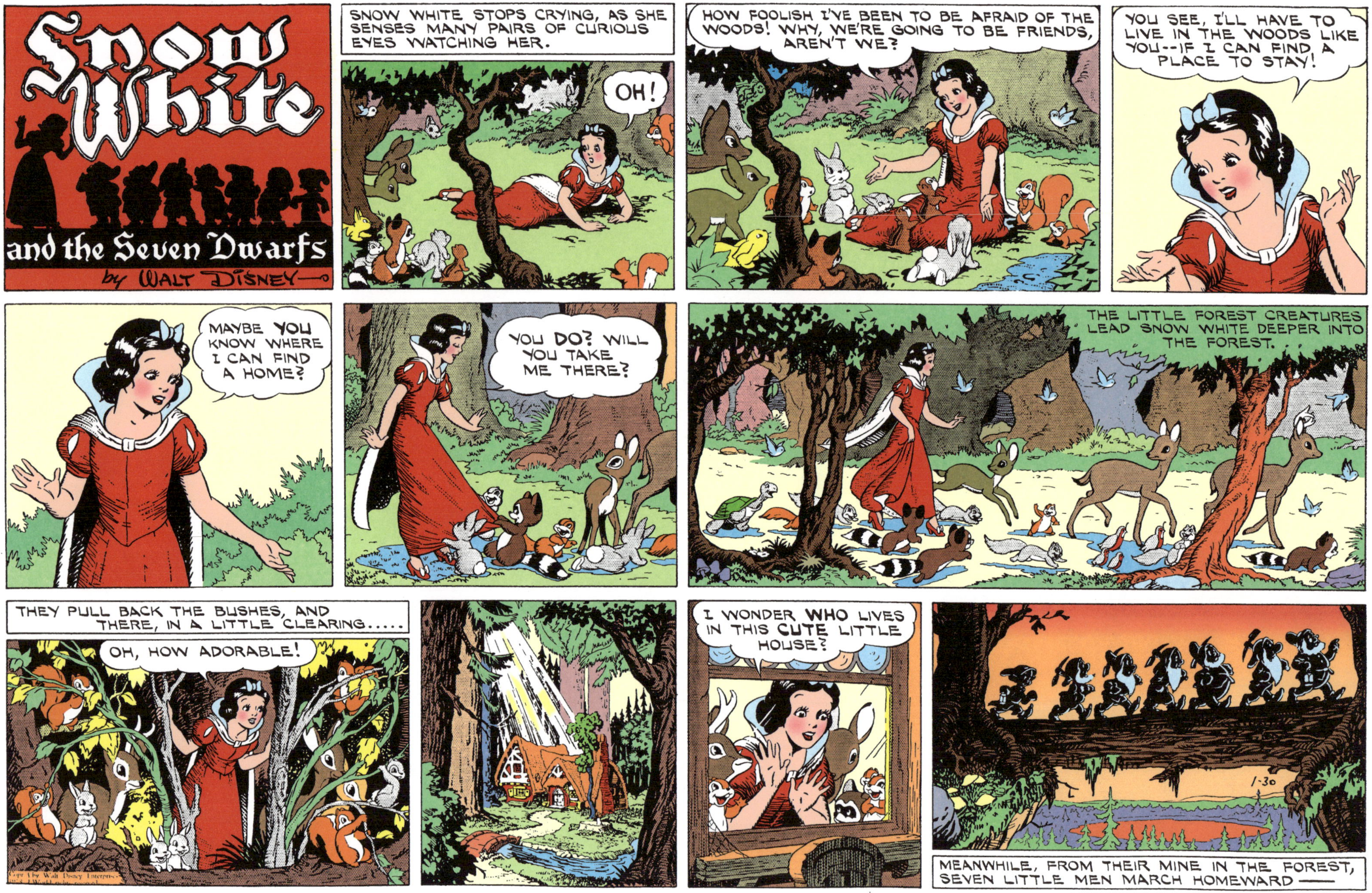
Snow White and the Seven Dwarfs
by WALT DISNEY
SNOW WHITE STOPS CRYING, AS SHE SENSES MANY PAIRS OF CURIOUS EYES WATCHING HER.
OH!
HOW FOOLISH I'VE BEEN TO BE AFRAID OF THE WOODS! WHY, WE'RE GOING TO BE FRIENDS, AREN'T WE?
YOU SEE, I'LL HAVE TO LIVE IN THE WOODS LIKE YOU--IF I CAN FIND A PLACE TO STAY!
MAYBE YOU KNOW WHERE I CAN FIND A HOME?
YOU DO? WILL YOU TAKE ME THERE?
THE LITTLE FOREST CREATURES LEAD SNOW WHITE DEEPER INTO THE FOREST.
THEY PULL BACK THE BUSHES, AND THERE, IN A LITTLE CLEARING.....
OH, HOW ADORABLE!
I WONDER WHO LIVES IN THIS CUTE LITTLE HOUSE?
1-30
MEANWHILE, FROM THEIR MINE IN THE FOREST, SEVEN LITTLE MEN MARCH HOMEWARD ——

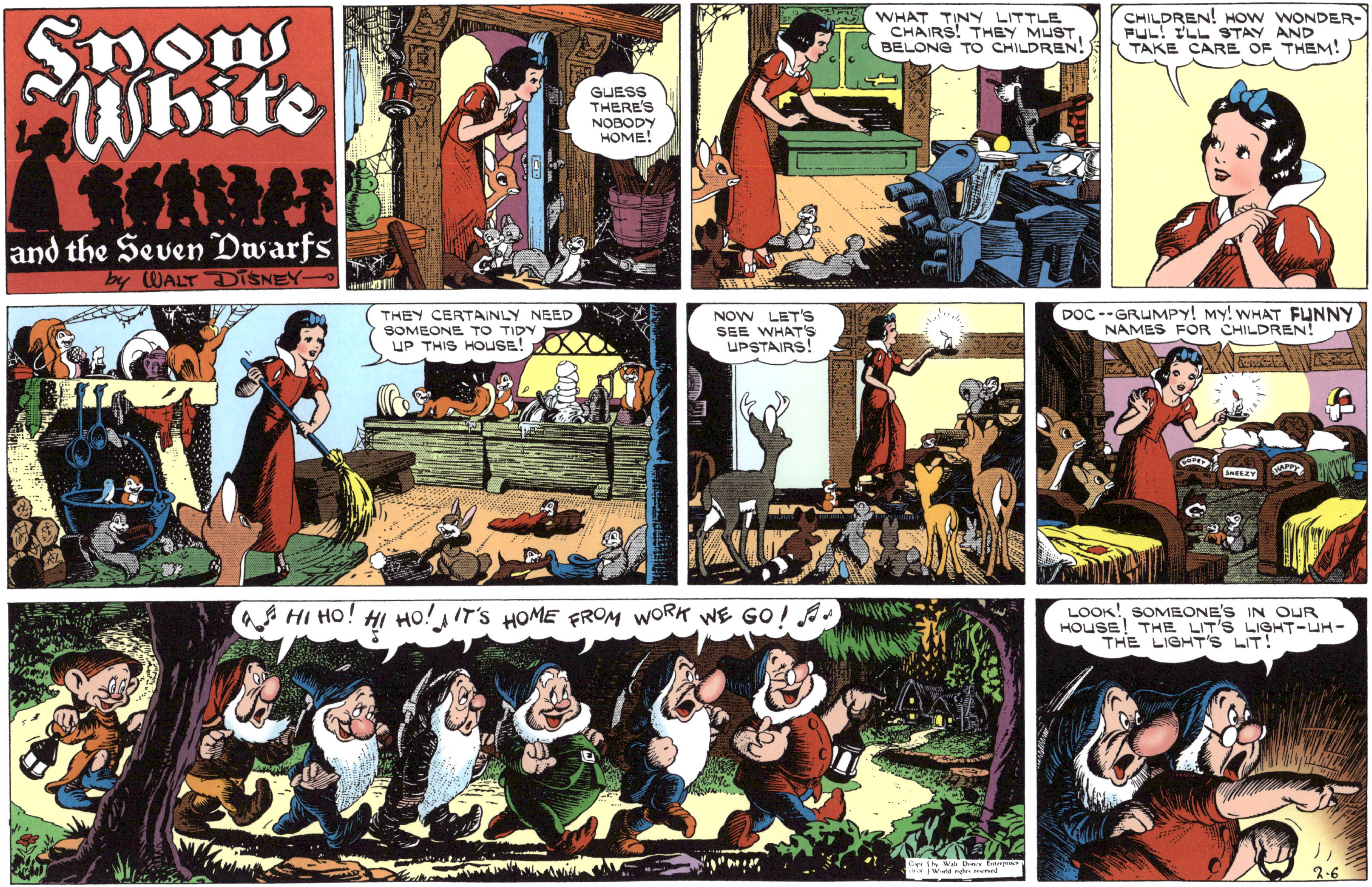
Snow White
and the Seven Dwarfs
by WALT DISNEY
GUESS THERE'S NOBODY HOME!
WHAT TINY LITTLE CHAIRS! THEY MUST BELONG TO CHILDREN!
CHILDREN! HOW WONDERFUL! I'LL STAY AND TAKE CARE OF THEM!
THEY CERTAINLY NEED SOMEONE TO TIDY UP THIS HOUSE!
NOW LET'S SEE WHAT'S UPSTAIRS!
DOC--GRUMPY! MY! WHAT FUNNY NAMES FOR CHILDREN!
DOPEY
SNEEZY
HAPPY
HI HO! HI HO! IT'S HOME FROM WORK WE GO!
Copr (by Walt Disney Enterprises 1938) World rights reserved
LOOK! SOMEONE'S IN OUR HOUSE! THE LIT'S LIGHT-UH-THE LIGHT'S LIT!
2-6

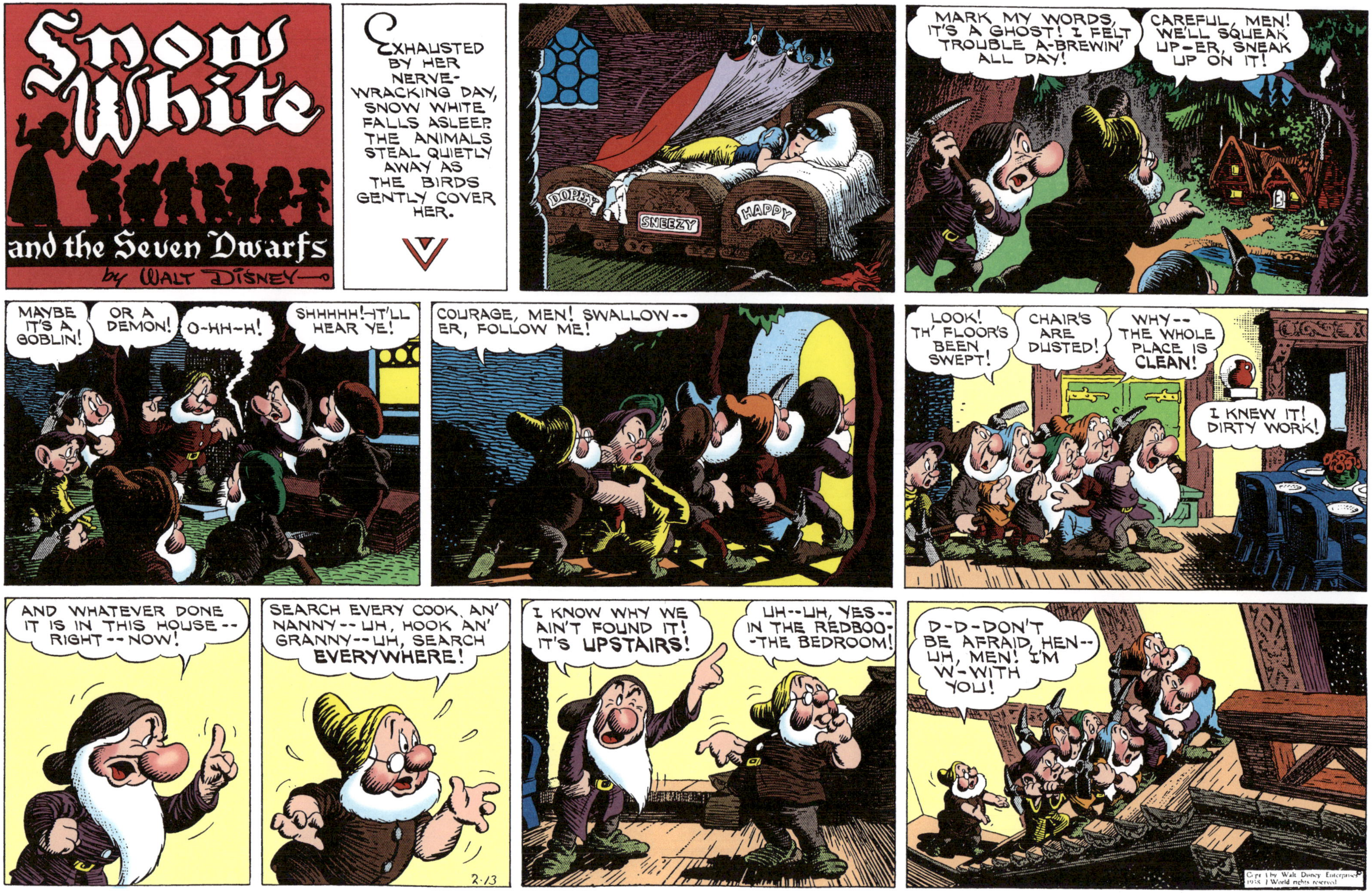
Snow White and the Seven Dwarfs
by Walt Disney
EXHAUSTED BY HER NERVE-WRACKING DAY, SNOW WHITE FALLS ASLEEP. THE ANIMALS STEAL QUIETLY AWAY AS THE BIRDS GENTLY COVER HER.
DOPEY
SNEEZY
HAPPY
MARK MY WORDS, IT'S A GHOST! I FELT TROUBLE A-BREWIN' ALL DAY!
CAREFUL, MEN! WE'LL SQUEAK UP—ER, SNEAK UP ON IT!
MAYBE IT'S A GOBLIN!
OR A DEMON!
O-HH-H!
SHHHHH!—IT'LL HEAR YE!
COURAGE, MEN! SWALLOW-- ER, FOLLOW ME!
LOOK! TH' FLOOR'S BEEN SWEPT!
CHAIR'S ARE DUSTED!
WHY-- THE WHOLE PLACE IS CLEAN!
I KNEW IT! DIRTY WORK!
AND WHATEVER DONE IT IS IN THIS HOUSE-- RIGHT--NOW!
SEARCH EVERY COOK AN' NANNY--UH, HOOK AN' GRANNY--UH, SEARCH EVERYWHERE!
2-13
I KNOW WHY WE AIN'T FOUND IT! IT'S UPSTAIRS!
UH--UH, YES-- IN THE REDBOO- -THE BEDROOM!
D-D-DON'T BE AFRAID, HEN-- UH, MEN! I'M W-WITH YOU!
Copr 1938 by Walt Disney Enterprises
World rights reserved

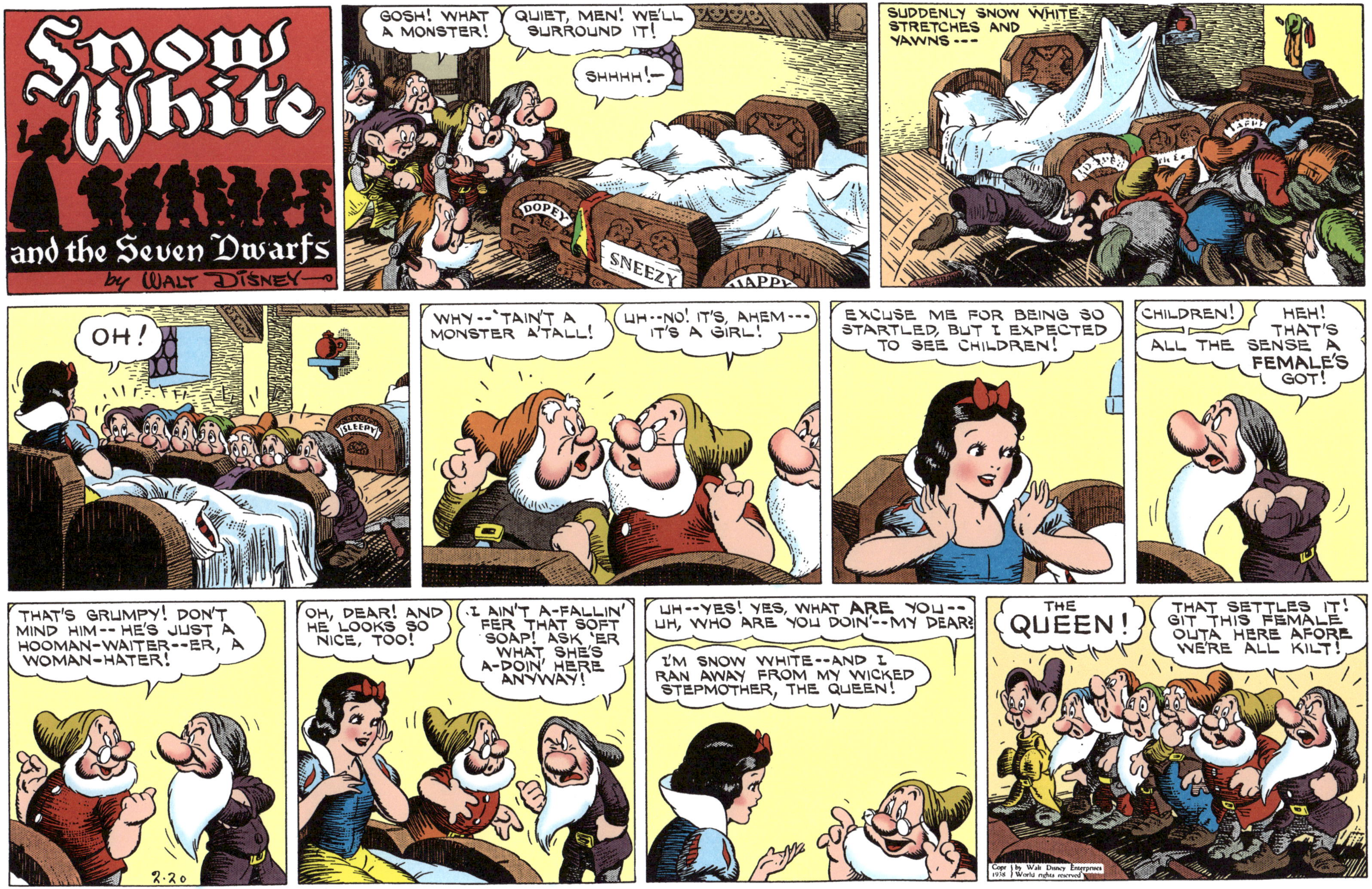
Snow White and the Seven Dwarfs
by Walt Disney
GOSH! WHAT A MONSTER!
QUIET, MEN! WE'LL SURROUND IT!
SHHHH!—
DOPEY
SNEEZY
HAPPY
SUDDENLY SNOW WHITE STRETCHES AND YAWNS---
OH!
SLEEPY
WHY--'TAIN'T A MONSTER A'TALL!
UH--NO! IT'S, AHEM--- IT'S A GIRL!
EXCUSE ME FOR BEING SO STARTLED, BUT I EXPECTED TO SEE CHILDREN!
CHILDREN!
HEH! THAT'S ALL THE SENSE A FEMALE'S GOT!
THAT'S GRUMPY! DON'T MIND HIM--HE'S JUST A HOOMAN-WAITER--ER, A WOMAN-HATER!
2·20
OH, DEAR! AND HE LOOKS SO NICE, TOO!
I AIN'T A-FALLIN' FER THAT SOFT SOAP! ASK 'ER WHAT SHE'S A-DOIN' HERE ANYWAY!
UH--YES! YES, WHAT ARE YOU--UH, WHO ARE YOU DOIN'--MY DEAR?
I'M SNOW WHITE--AND I RAN AWAY FROM MY WICKED STEPMOTHER, THE QUEEN!
THE QUEEN!
THAT SETTLES IT! GIT THIS FEMALE OUTA HERE AFORE WE'RE ALL KILT!
Copr 1938 by Walt Disney Enterprises World rights reserved

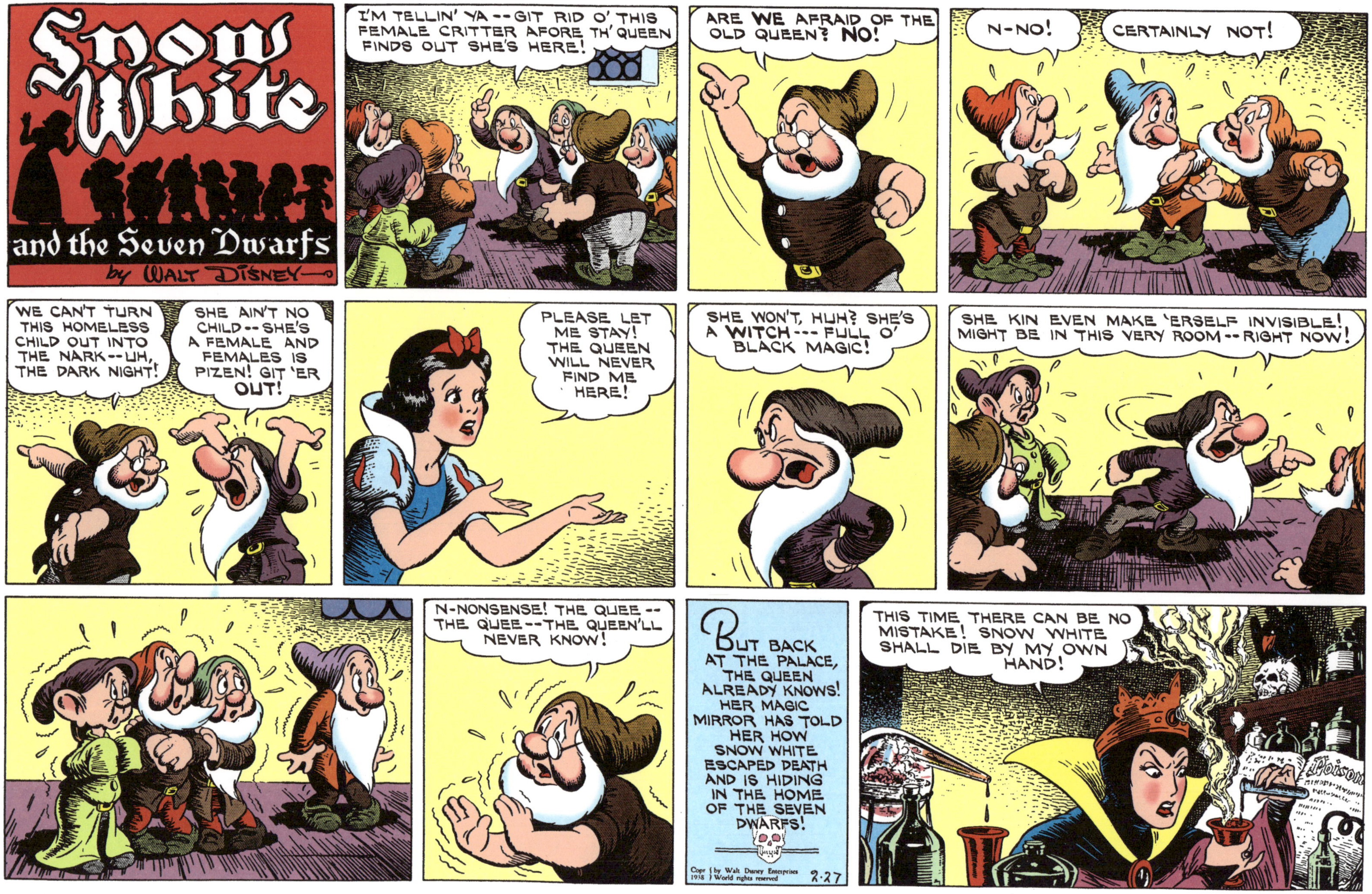
Snow White
and the Seven Dwarfs
by Walt Disney
I'M TELLIN' YA -- GIT RID O' THIS FEMALE CRITTER AFORE TH' QUEEN FINDS OUT SHE'S HERE!
ARE WE AFRAID OF THE OLD QUEEN? NO!
N-NO!
CERTAINLY NOT!
WE CAN'T TURN THIS HOMELESS CHILD OUT INTO THE NARK -- UH, THE DARK NIGHT!
SHE AIN'T NO CHILD -- SHE'S A FEMALE AND FEMALES IS PIZEN! GIT 'ER OUT!
PLEASE LET ME STAY! THE QUEEN WILL NEVER FIND ME HERE!
SHE WON'T, HUH? SHE'S A WITCH --- FULL O' BLACK MAGIC!
SHE KIN EVEN MAKE 'ERSELF INVISIBLE! MIGHT BE IN THIS VERY ROOM -- RIGHT NOW!
N-NONSENSE! THE QUEE -- THE QUEE -- THE QUEEN'LL NEVER KNOW!
BUT BACK AT THE PALACE, THE QUEEN ALREADY KNOWS! HER MAGIC MIRROR HAS TOLD HER HOW SNOW WHITE ESCAPED DEATH AND IS HIDING IN THE HOME OF THE SEVEN DWARFS!
Copr. 1938 by Walt Disney Enterprises World rights reserved
2-27
THIS TIME THERE CAN BE NO MISTAKE! SNOW WHITE SHALL DIE BY MY OWN HAND!
Poison

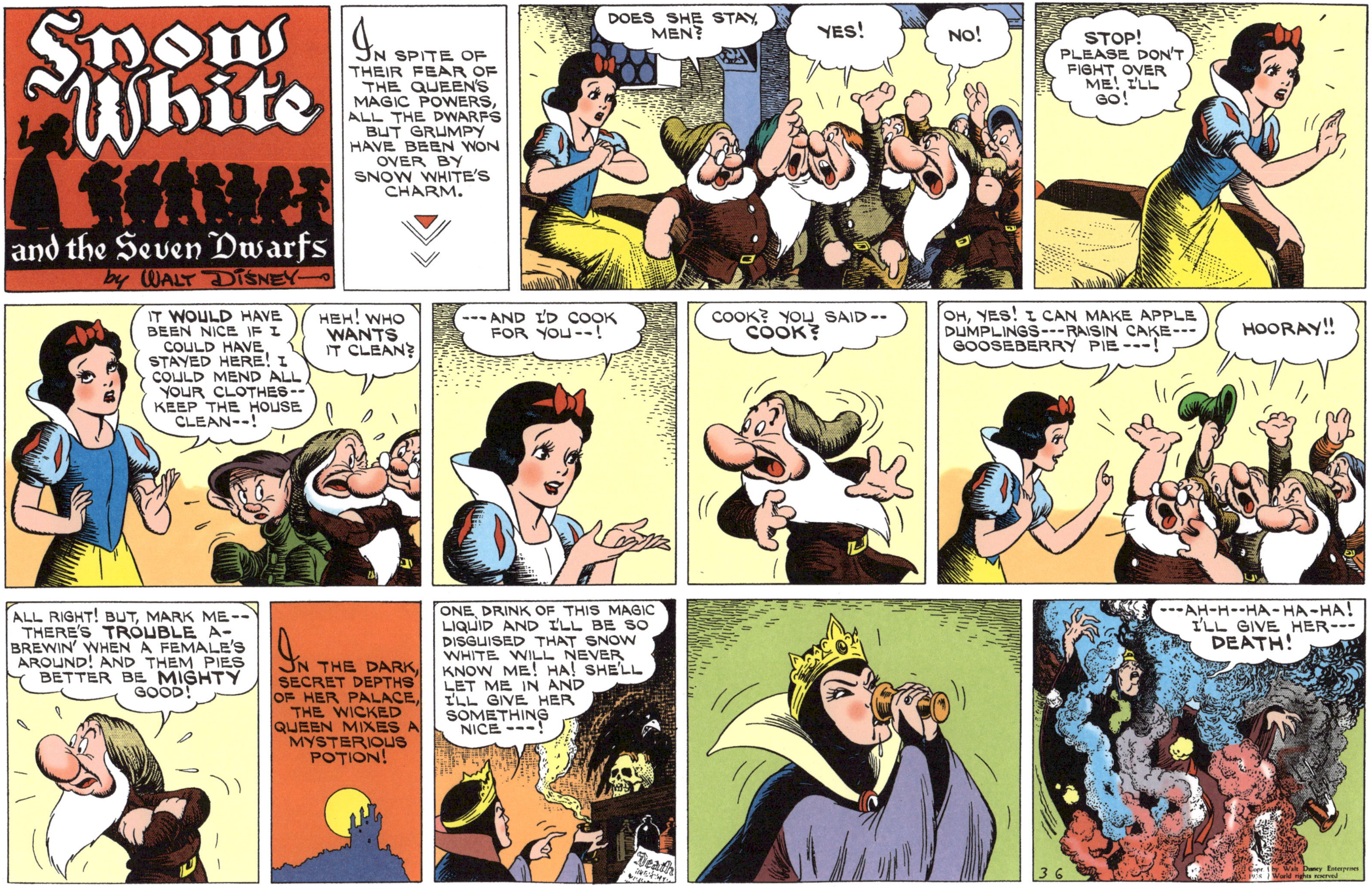

Snow White
and the Seven Dwarfs
by Walt Disney
In spite of their fear of the Queen's magic powers, all the dwarfs but Grumpy have been won over by Snow White's charm.
Does she stay, men?
Yes!
No!
Stop! Please don't fight over me! I'll go!
It would have been nice if I could have stayed here! I could mend all your clothes -- keep the house clean--!
Heh! Who wants it clean?
---and I'd cook for you--!
Cook? You said -- cook?
Oh, yes! I can make apple dumplings---raisin cake---gooseberry pie---!
Hooray!!
All right! But, mark me-- there's trouble a-brewin' when a female's around! And them pies better be mighty good!
In the dark, secret depths of her palace, the wicked Queen mixes a mysterious potion!
One drink of this magic liquid and I'll be so disguised that Snow White will never know me! Ha! She'll let me in and I'll give her something nice---!
---Ah-h--ha-ha-ha! I'll give her--- death!
3 6
Copr. 1938 by Walt Disney Enterprises World rights reserved

Snow White and the Seven Dwarfs
by WALT DISNEY
TO FURTHER HER PLOT AGAINST SNOW WHITE'S LIFE THE QUEEN DRINKS A MAGIC POTION WHICH CHANGES HER INTO AN OLD AND FEEBLE PEDDLER WOMAN
HEH-HEH-HEH! A PERFECT DISGUISE! SHE'LL THINK I'M A HARMLESS OLD WOMAN --- HARMLESS! HEH-HEH-HEH!
AND NOW--SOMETHING TO TAKE TO LITTLE SNOW WHITE! SOMETHING SHE'LL LIKE---AH! THE VERY THING!
THE POISONED APPLE---SLEEPING DEATH!
ONE BITE--AND HER EYES WILL CLOSE IN THE SLEEPING DEATH! THEN I'LL BE FAIREST IN THE LAND!
MEANWHILE, THE SEVEN LITTLE MEN HAVE ACCEPTED SNOW WHITE AS THEIR HOUSEKEEPER AND SHE IS HAPPILY COOKING THEIR DINNER.
SOUP!
JIMINY CRICKETS!
GRACIOUS! WHAT TERRIBLE MANNERS!
SMELLS GOOD!
DINNER'S NOT QUITE READY! AND BESIDES, YOU HAVEN'T WASHED YET!
W-WASH?
WHAT FER? 'TAIN'T NEW YEARS!
WE AIN'T GOIN' NO PLACE!
NOW! NOW! GO RIGHT OUT AND WASH!
COURAGE, MEN! IT WON'T HURT ---MUCH!
GOSH-- IT'S COLD!
AND WET, TOO!
FINE BUNCH O' WATER-LILIES! WASHIN'---JEST TO PLEASE A WOMAN! HEH! LIKE TO SEE ANYBODY MAKE ME WASH!
3-13
LEMME GO! LEMME LOOSE, Y' IDJUTS! YOU'LL PAY FER THIS!
HOLD HIM, MEN! STRING, UH--- BRING HIM TO THE TUB!
SOUSE HIS WHISKERS!
DON'T SPARE THE SOAP!
I'LL--BLUB-B---YOU OLD--BLUBBLE---JEST WAIT---GLUB--BUB-B!
DINNER!
HOORAY!

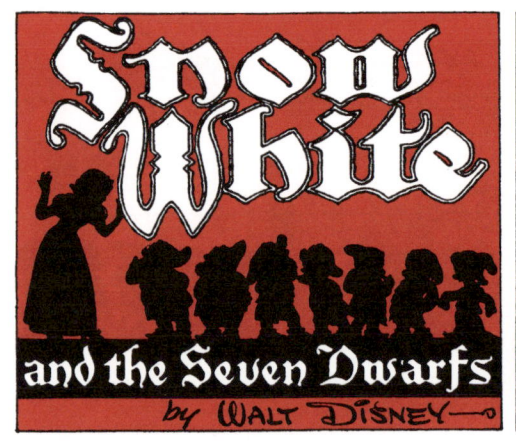

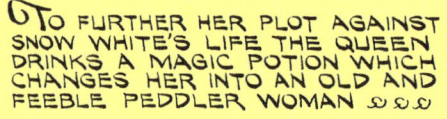

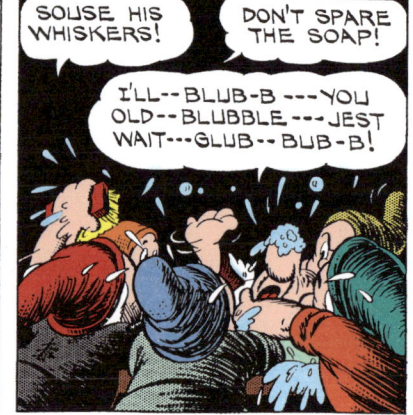

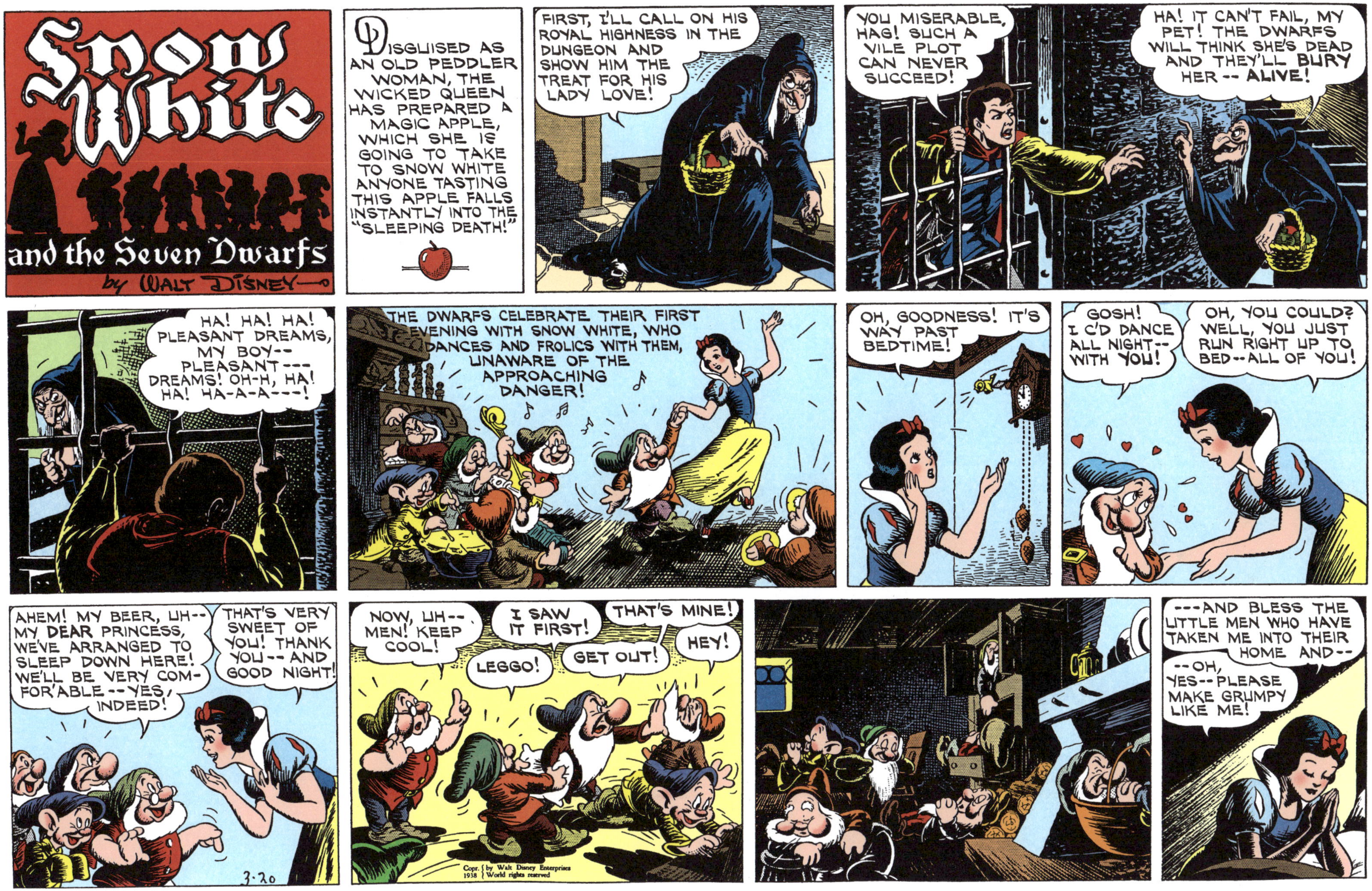
Snow White
and the Seven Dwarfs
by Walt Disney
Disguised as an old peddler woman, the wicked queen has prepared a magic apple, which she is going to take to Snow White. Anyone tasting this apple falls instantly into the "sleeping death!"
First, I'll call on his royal highness in the dungeon and show him the treat for his lady love!
You miserable hag! Such a vile plot can never succeed!
Ha! It can't fail, my pet! The dwarfs will think she's dead and they'll **bury** her -- **alive!**
Ha! Ha! Ha! Pleasant dreams, my boy-- pleasant--- dreams! Oh-h, ha! Ha! Ha-a-a---!
The dwarfs celebrate their first evening with Snow White, who dances and frolics with them, unaware of the approaching danger!
Oh, goodness! It's way past bedtime!
Gosh! I c'd dance all night-- with **you**!
Oh, you could? Well, you just run right up to bed--all of you!
Ahem! My beer, uh-- my **dear** princess, we've arranged to sleep down here! We'll be very com-for'able--yes, indeed!
That's very sweet of you! Thank you--and good night!
3-20
Now, uh-- men! Keep cool!
I saw it first!
That's mine!
Leggo!
Get out!
Hey!
Copr. 1938 by Walt Disney Enterprises World rights reserved
---And bless the little men who have taken me into their home and--
--Oh, yes--please make Grumpy like me!

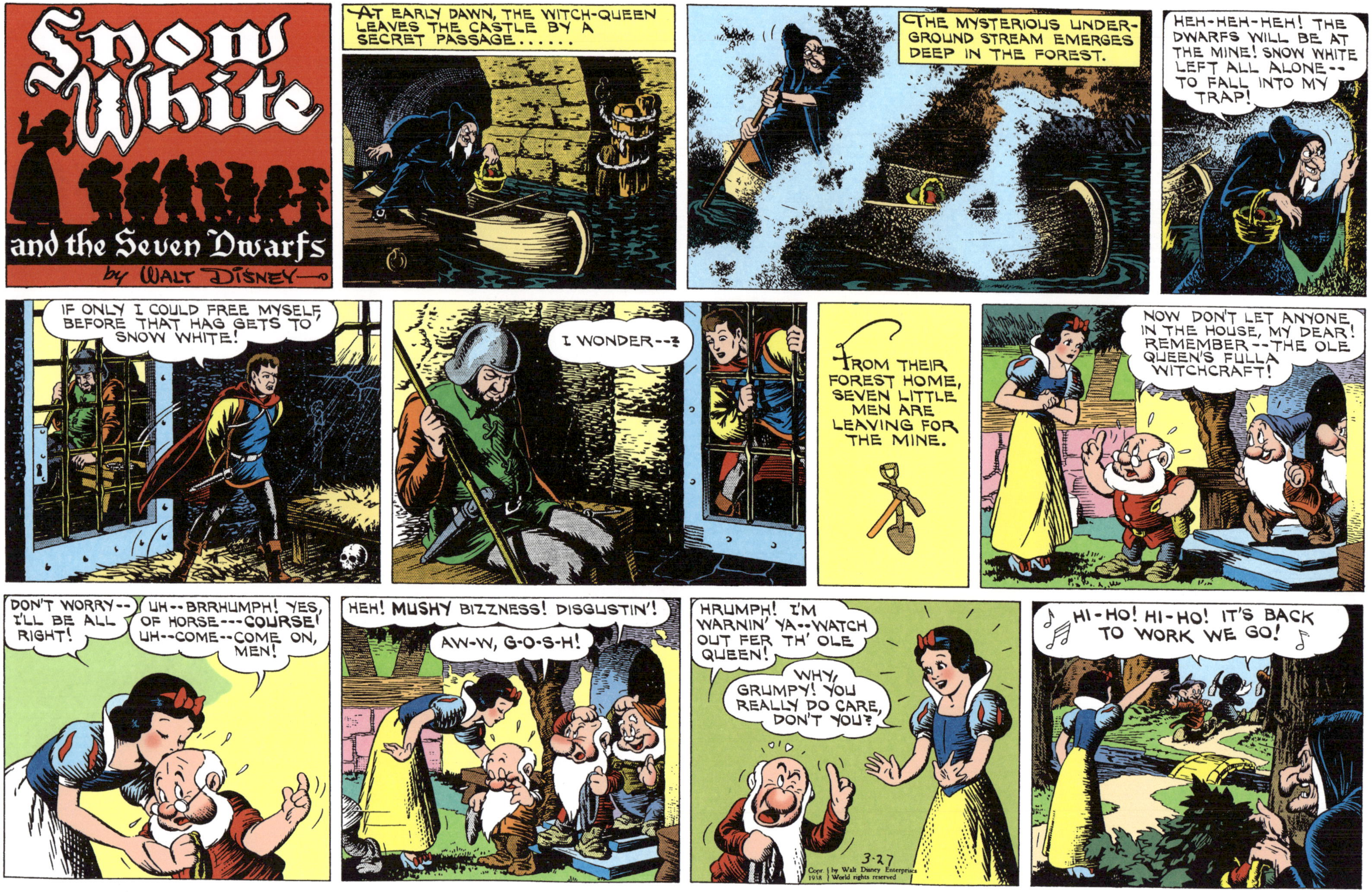

Snow White
and the Seven Dwarfs
by WALT DISNEY
AT EARLY DAWN, THE WITCH-QUEEN LEAVES THE CASTLE BY A SECRET PASSAGE......
THE MYSTERIOUS UNDER-GROUND STREAM EMERGES DEEP IN THE FOREST.
HEH-HEH-HEH! THE DWARFS WILL BE AT THE MINE! SNOW WHITE LEFT ALL ALONE-- TO FALL INTO MY TRAP!
IF ONLY I COULD FREE MYSELF BEFORE THAT HAG GETS TO SNOW WHITE!
I WONDER--?
FROM THEIR FOREST HOME, SEVEN LITTLE MEN ARE LEAVING FOR THE MINE.
NOW DON'T LET ANYONE IN THE HOUSE, MY DEAR! REMEMBER--THE OLE QUEEN'S FULLA WITCHCRAFT!
DON'T WORRY-- I'LL BE ALL RIGHT!
UH--BRRHUMPH! YES, OF HORSE---COURSE! UH--COME--COME ON, MEN!
HEH! MUSHY BIZZNESS! DISGUSTIN'!
AW-W, G-O-S-H!
HRUMPH! I'M WARNIN' YA--WATCH OUT FER TH' OLE QUEEN!
WHY, GRUMPY! YOU REALLY DO CARE, DON'T YOU?
3-27
Copr. 1938 by Walt Disney Enterprises World rights reserved
HI-HO! HI-HO! IT'S BACK TO WORK WE GO!

Snow White
and the Seven Dwarfs
by Walt Disney
HA! THE DWARFS ARE FAR AWAY BY NOW! SNOW WHITE WILL BE ALONE!
IN THE CASTLE DUNGEON, THE PRINCE TRIES DESPERATELY TO ESCAPE IN TIME TO SAVE SNOW WHITE FROM THE POISONED APPLE!
SLEEP ONE MORE SECOND, MY FRIEND, AND I'LL BE FREE!
STOP --IN THE NAME OF THE QUEEN!
THAT FOR YOUR QUEEN!
WHAT GOES ON HERE?
MOUNTING HIS FAITHFUL HORSE, THE PRINCE COMPLETES HIS ESCAPE AND SPEEDS FOR THE FOREST!
OH-H!
DON'T BE FRIGHTENED! I'M JUST AN OLD APPLE WOMAN, DEARIE!
MY APPLES MAKE GRAND PIES--- THE KIND THE LITTLE MEN LIKE! TRY ONE, DEARIE! JUST TAKE A BITE!
IT LOOKS AWFULLY GOOD!
OH! OUCH! GET AWAY!
SHOO! STOP THAT! SHOO!
4/3
Copr 1938 by Walt Disney Enterprises World rights reserved

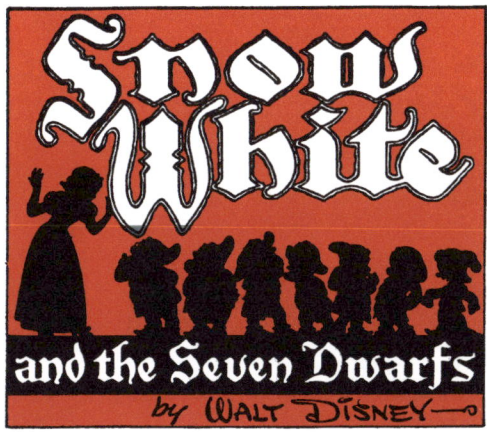

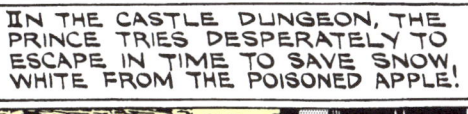

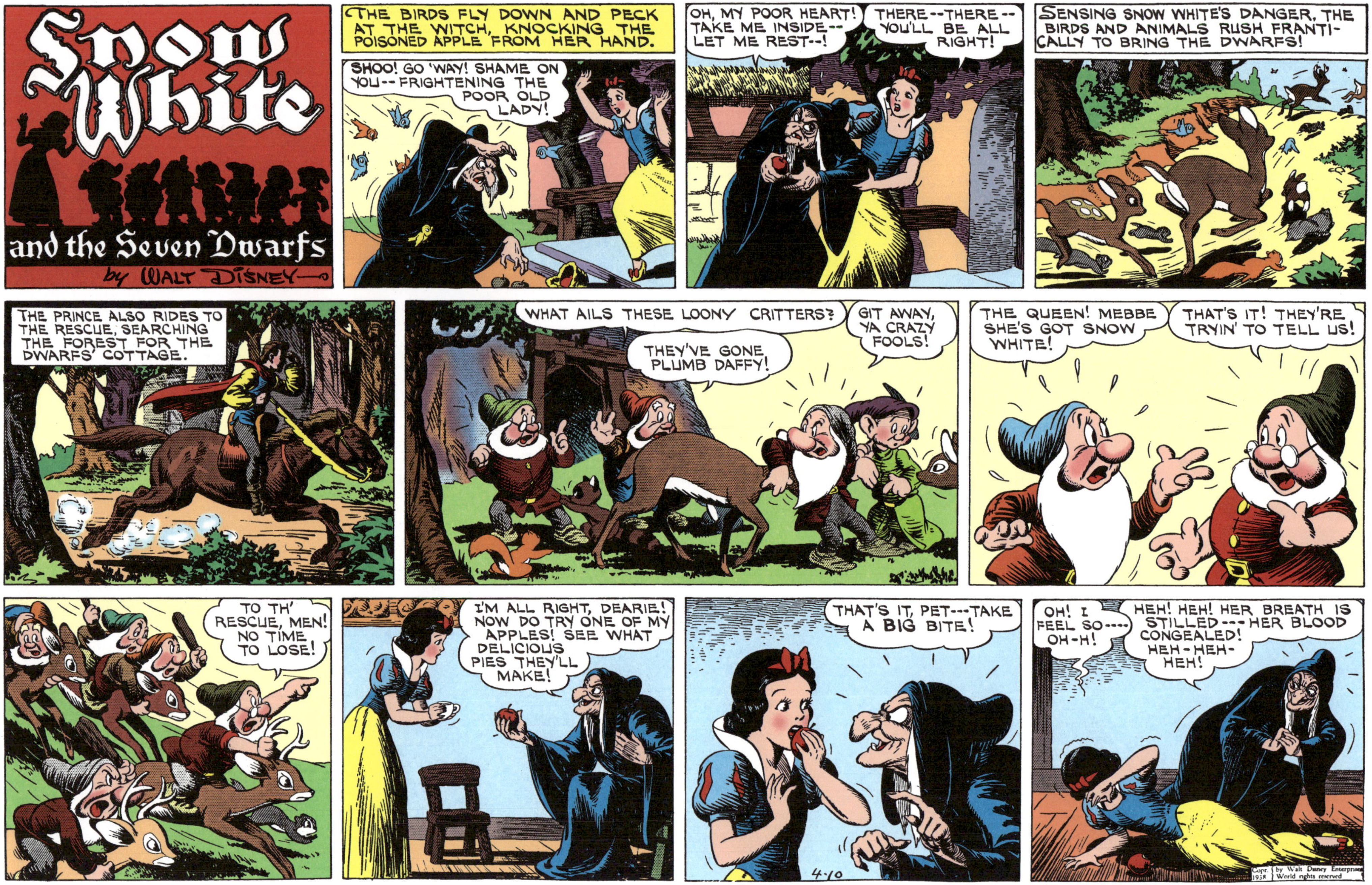
Snow White
and the Seven Dwarfs
by Walt Disney
THE BIRDS FLY DOWN AND PECK AT THE WITCH, KNOCKING THE POISONED APPLE FROM HER HAND.
SHOO! GO 'WAY! SHAME ON YOU-- FRIGHTENING THE POOR OLD LADY!
OH, MY POOR HEART! TAKE ME INSIDE-- LET ME REST--!
THERE--THERE-- YOU'LL BE ALL RIGHT!
SENSING SNOW WHITE'S DANGER, THE BIRDS AND ANIMALS RUSH FRANTICALLY TO BRING THE DWARFS!
THE PRINCE ALSO RIDES TO THE RESCUE, SEARCHING THE FOREST FOR THE DWARFS' COTTAGE.
WHAT AILS THESE LOONY CRITTERS?
THEY'VE GONE PLUMB DAFFY!
GIT AWAY, YA CRAZY FOOLS!
THE QUEEN! MEBBE SHE'S GOT SNOW WHITE!
THAT'S IT! THEY'RE TRYIN' TO TELL US!
TO TH' RESCUE, MEN! NO TIME TO LOSE!
I'M ALL RIGHT, DEARIE! NOW DO TRY ONE OF MY APPLES! SEE WHAT DELICIOUS PIES THEY'LL MAKE!
THAT'S IT, PET---TAKE A BIG BITE!
4-10
OH! I FEEL SO---- OH-H!
HEH! HEH! HER BREATH IS STILLED---HER BLOOD CONGEALED! HEH-HEH-HEH!
Copr. 1938 by Walt Disney Enterprises World rights reserved

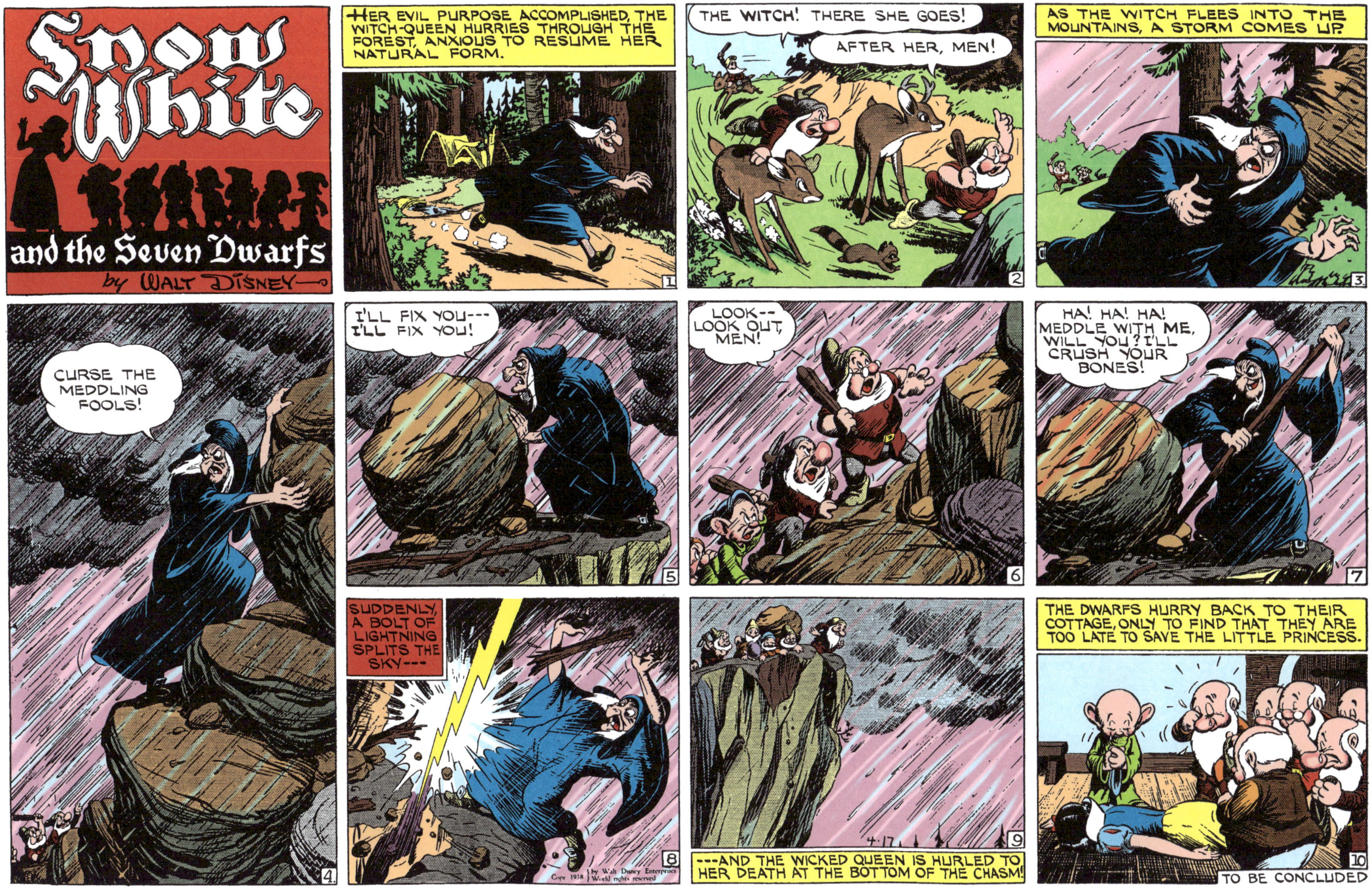
Snow White and the Seven Dwarfs
by Walt Disney
HER EVIL PURPOSE ACCOMPLISHED, THE WITCH-QUEEN HURRIES THROUGH THE FOREST, ANXIOUS TO RESUME HER NATURAL FORM.
THE WITCH! THERE SHE GOES!
AFTER HER, MEN!
AS THE WITCH FLEES INTO THE MOUNTAINS, A STORM COMES UP.
CURSE THE MEDDLING FOOLS!
I'LL FIX YOU--- I'LL FIX YOU!
LOOK-- LOOK OUT, MEN!
HA! HA! HA! MEDDLE WITH ME, WILL YOU? I'LL CRUSH YOUR BONES!
SUDDENLY, A BOLT OF LIGHTNING SPLITS THE SKY---
Copr. 1938 by Walt Disney Enterprises World rights reserved
4-17
---AND THE WICKED QUEEN IS HURLED TO HER DEATH AT THE BOTTOM OF THE CHASM!
THE DWARFS HURRY BACK TO THEIR COTTAGE, ONLY TO FIND THAT THEY ARE TOO LATE TO SAVE THE LITTLE PRINCESS.
TO BE CONCLUDED

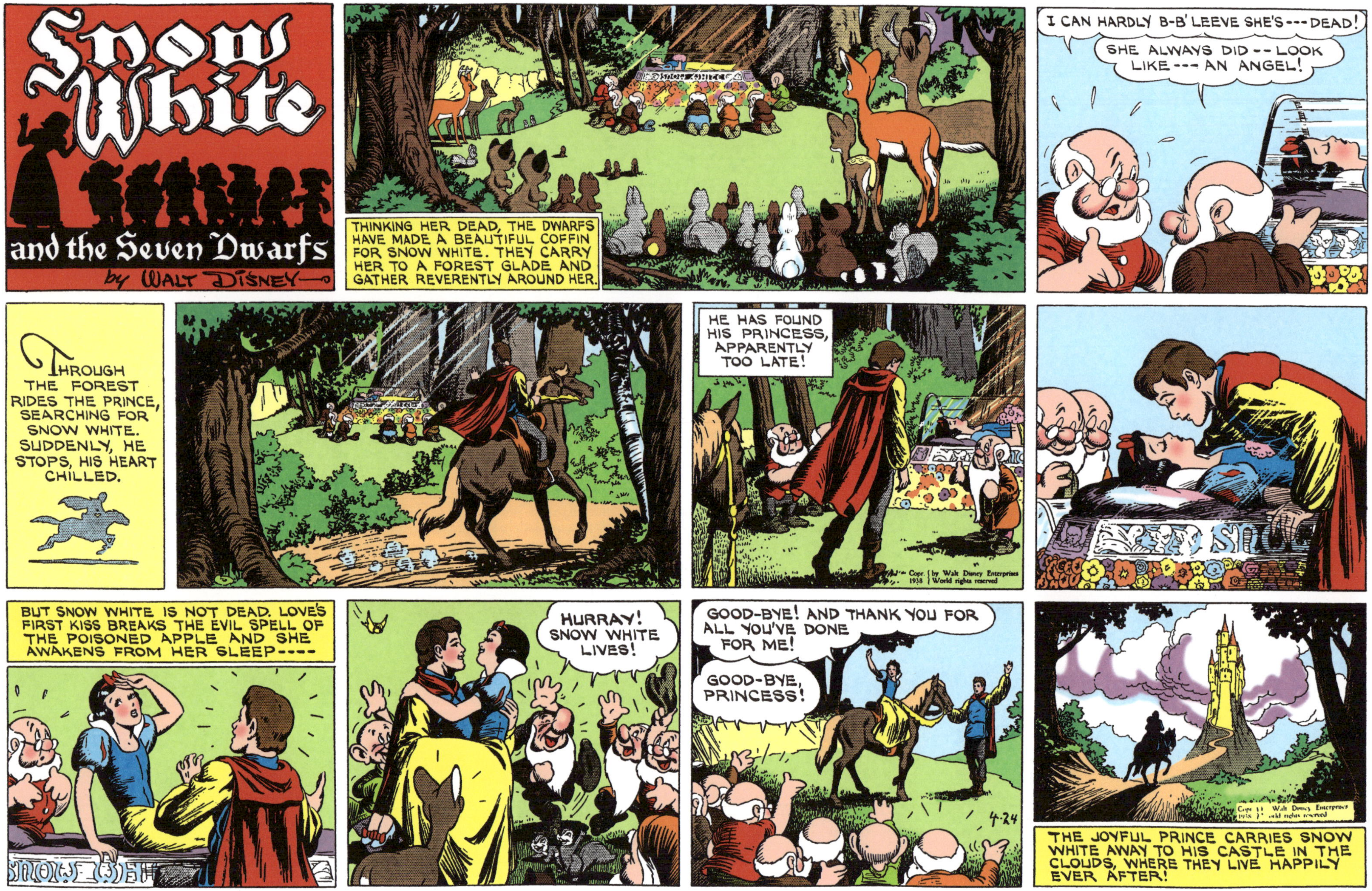
Snow White
and the Seven Dwarfs
by Walt Disney
THINKING HER DEAD, THE DWARFS HAVE MADE A BEAUTIFUL COFFIN FOR SNOW WHITE. THEY CARRY HER TO A FOREST GLADE AND GATHER REVERENTLY AROUND HER.
I CAN HARDLY B-B'LEEVE SHE'S---DEAD!
SHE ALWAYS DID--LOOK LIKE---AN ANGEL!
THROUGH THE FOREST RIDES THE PRINCE, SEARCHING FOR SNOW WHITE. SUDDENLY, HE STOPS, HIS HEART CHILLED.
HE HAS FOUND HIS PRINCESS, APPARENTLY TOO LATE!
Copr. 1938 by Walt Disney Enterprises World rights reserved
BUT SNOW WHITE IS NOT DEAD. LOVE'S FIRST KISS BREAKS THE EVIL SPELL OF THE POISONED APPLE AND SHE AWAKENS FROM HER SLEEP----
HURRAY! SNOW WHITE LIVES!
GOOD-BYE! AND THANK YOU FOR ALL YOU'VE DONE FOR ME!
GOOD-BYE, PRINCESS!
4-24
THE JOYFUL PRINCE CARRIES SNOW WHITE AWAY TO HIS CASTLE IN THE CLOUDS, WHERE THEY LIVE HAPPILY EVER AFTER!

SILLY SYMPHONIES

THE PRACTICAL PIG

May 1 - August 7, 1938
Written by Merrill de Maris, drawn by Al Taliaferro

For the first time in nearly two years—after detouring into unfamiliar territory with *Donald Duck* and *Snow White*—the Sunday comic feature returned in May 1938 to its original mission: adapting and retelling stories from the *Silly Symphonies*. The last previous *Symphony* continuity in 1936 had been based on a story featuring the Three Little Pigs and the Big Bad Wolf; now, fittingly, the strip picked up where it had left off. Production of *The Practical Pig*, the studio's latest Pig sequel, was essentially complete by May 1938, but most movie audiences would not see it until the following year.

By 1938 Al Taliaferro was installed as the artist behind the new *Donald Duck* daily strip, but he returned to his *Silly Symphony* post and carried a double workload, continuing to draw both strips. Merrill de Maris, who had written the *Snow White* continuity, remained in place as the Sunday page's writer when the *Silly Symphony* stories resumed. It's worth noting that he did not revive the convention of rhyming dialogue, previously a regular practice in the strip. Otherwise de Maris and Taliaferro proceeded along familiar lines, loosely adapting the film's story but also introducing some new ideas of their own. Practical Pig's latest invention, an intricately designed "lie detector," is a highlight of the film and survives in the comic adaptation. So does the Wolf's disguise as a comically lisping messenger boy. On the other hand, the Wolf's most preposterous disguise yet—as a mermaid, complete with portable island—does *not* reappear in the strip. Instead he masquerades as a gypsy fortune-teller, his advice to the pigs laced with double-entendres that telegraph his true intentions.

Like the earlier Pig story, this one includes a bonus for Disney enthusiasts: the continuity is primarily based on *The Practical Pig* but is also sprinkled with images and gags from the earlier films. Not least among these is an appearance by the Three Little Wolves, who had made their debut in the 1936 short of the same title.

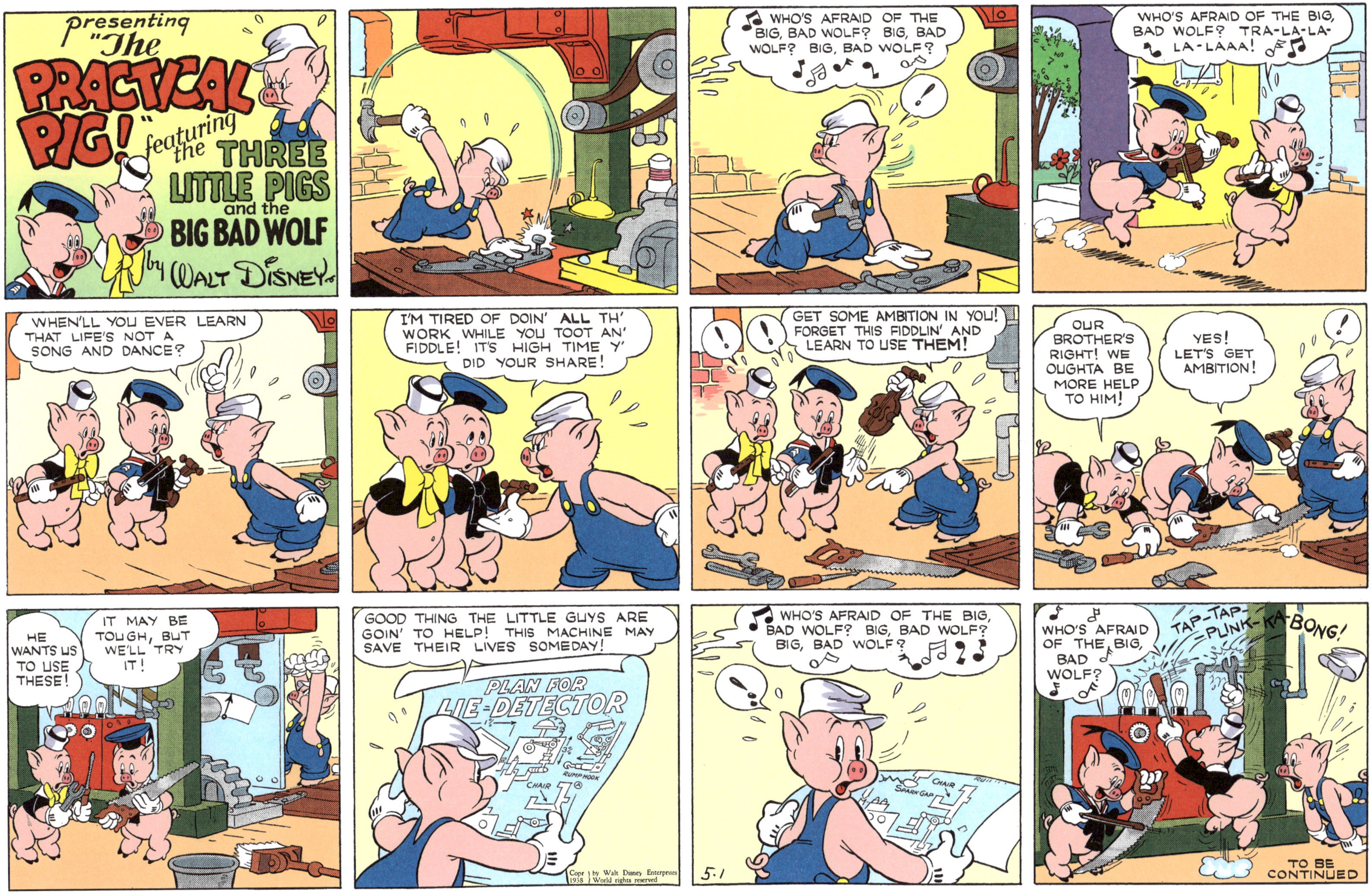
presenting "The PRACTICAL PIG!" featuring the THREE LITTLE PIGS and the BIG BAD WOLF
by WALT DISNEY
WHO'S AFRAID OF THE BIG, BAD WOLF? BIG, BAD WOLF? BIG, BAD WOLF?
!
WHO'S AFRAID OF THE BIG, BAD WOLF? TRA-LA-LA-LA-LAAA!
WHEN'LL YOU EVER LEARN THAT LIFE'S NOT A SONG AND DANCE?
I'M TIRED OF DOIN' ALL TH' WORK WHILE YOU TOOT AN' FIDDLE! IT'S HIGH TIME Y' DID YOUR SHARE!
! !
GET SOME AMBITION IN YOU! FORGET THIS FIDDLIN' AND LEARN TO USE THEM!
OUR BROTHER'S RIGHT! WE OUGHTA BE MORE HELP TO HIM!
YES! LET'S GET AMBITION!
!
HE WANTS US TO USE THESE!
IT MAY BE TOUGH, BUT WE'LL TRY IT!
GOOD THING THE LITTLE GUYS ARE GOIN' TO HELP! THIS MACHINE MAY SAVE THEIR LIVES SOMEDAY!
PLAN FOR LIE-DETECTOR
RUMP HOOK
CHAIR
Copr. 1938 by Walt Disney Enterprises World rights reserved
WHO'S AFRAID OF THE BIG, BAD WOLF? BIG, BAD WOLF? BIG, BAD WOLF?
!
CHAIR
SPARK GAP
5-1
WHO'S AFRAID OF THE BIG, BAD WOLF?
TAP-TAP-PLINK-KA-BONG!
TO BE CONTINUED

THE PRACTICAL PIG! featuring the 3 LITTLE PIGS by WALT DISNEY
I GIVE UP! WHEN IT COMES TO WORK, YOU GUYS ARE JUST HOPELESS!
GO AHEAD-- SING AN' DANCE! TOOT AN' FIDDLE TILL THE WOLF GETS Y' AGAIN! AND WHEN HE DOES---
FATHER
---I S'POSE I'LL BE CRAZY ENOUGH TO SAVE YOUR WORTHLESS HIDES--IF I CAN!
NOW BEAT IT! SCRAM! YOU'RE NO GOOD HERE, SO KEEP OUT AND LET ME WORK!
WHAT DID WE DO? NUTHIN' AT ALL!
HE CAN'T TALK TO US LIKE THAT!
I'VE A GOOD NOTION TO LEAVE HOME AN' BE A BANDIT OR--- OR SOMEP'N!
YES! LET'S MAKE HIM SORRY HE DON'T TREAT US RIGHT!
I'VE GOT IT! WE'LL GO IN THE WOODS AND LIVE WITH THE GYPSIES!
SWELL! GYPSIES NEVER HAFTA WORK!
OH, JOLLY GYPSY BOYS ARE WE!
WE KICK OUR HEELS AND DANCE WITH GLEE!
TRA-LA! TRA-LA! TRA-LAA-A-A!
Copr 1938 by Walt Disney Enterprises World rights reserved
BUT S'POSE THE WOLF IS IN THE WOODS!
AW, SHUCKS! WE'VE SCARED HIM AWAY FOREVER!
5-8
REMEMBER! YOU KIDS WAIT HERE! POP'S GONTER DO A BIT O' PLAIN AND FANCY SPYIN'!
HURRY UP, POP! WE'RE HUNGRY!
FIRST, TO SEE WHAT THE LI'L PORKERS ARE UP TO--THEN I'LL LAY ME PLANS TO NAB 'EM! HEH-HEH-HEH!

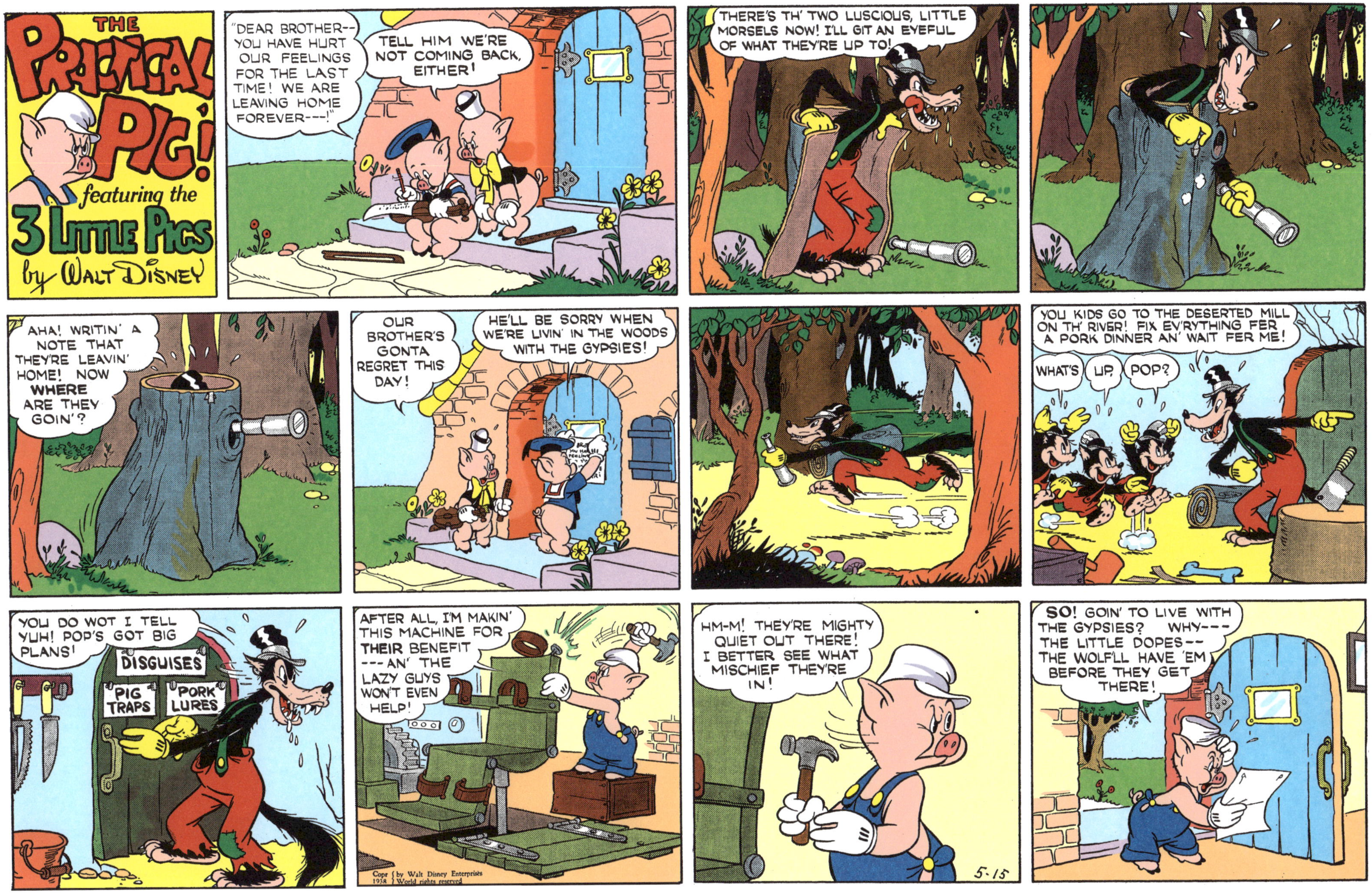
THE PRACTICAL PIG!
featuring the 3 LITTLE PIGS
by WALT DISNEY
"DEAR BROTHER-- YOU HAVE HURT OUR FEELINGS FOR THE LAST TIME! WE ARE LEAVING HOME FOREVER---!"
TELL HIM WE'RE NOT COMING BACK, EITHER!
THERE'S TH' TWO LUSCIOUS, LITTLE MORSELS NOW! I'LL GIT AN EYEFUL OF WHAT THEY'RE UP TO!
AHA! WRITIN' A NOTE THAT THEY'RE LEAVIN' HOME! NOW **WHERE** ARE THEY GOIN'?
OUR BROTHER'S GONTA REGRET THIS DAY!
HE'LL BE SORRY WHEN WE'RE LIVIN' IN THE WOODS WITH THE GYPSIES!
YOU KIDS GO TO THE DESERTED MILL ON TH' RIVER! FIX EV'RYTHING FER A PORK DINNER AN' WAIT FER ME!
WHAT'S
UP
POP?
YOU DO WOT I TELL YUH! POP'S GOT BIG PLANS!
DISGUISES
PIG TRAPS
PORK LURES
AFTER ALL, I'M MAKIN' THIS MACHINE FOR **THEIR** BENEFIT ---AN' THE LAZY GUYS WON'T EVEN HELP!
Copr 1938 by Walt Disney Enterprises World rights reserved
HM-M! THEY'RE MIGHTY QUIET OUT THERE! I BETTER SEE WHAT MISCHIEF THEY'RE IN!
5-15
SO! GOIN' TO LIVE WITH THE GYPSIES? WHY--- THE LITTLE DOPES-- THE WOLF'LL HAVE 'EM BEFORE THEY GET THERE!

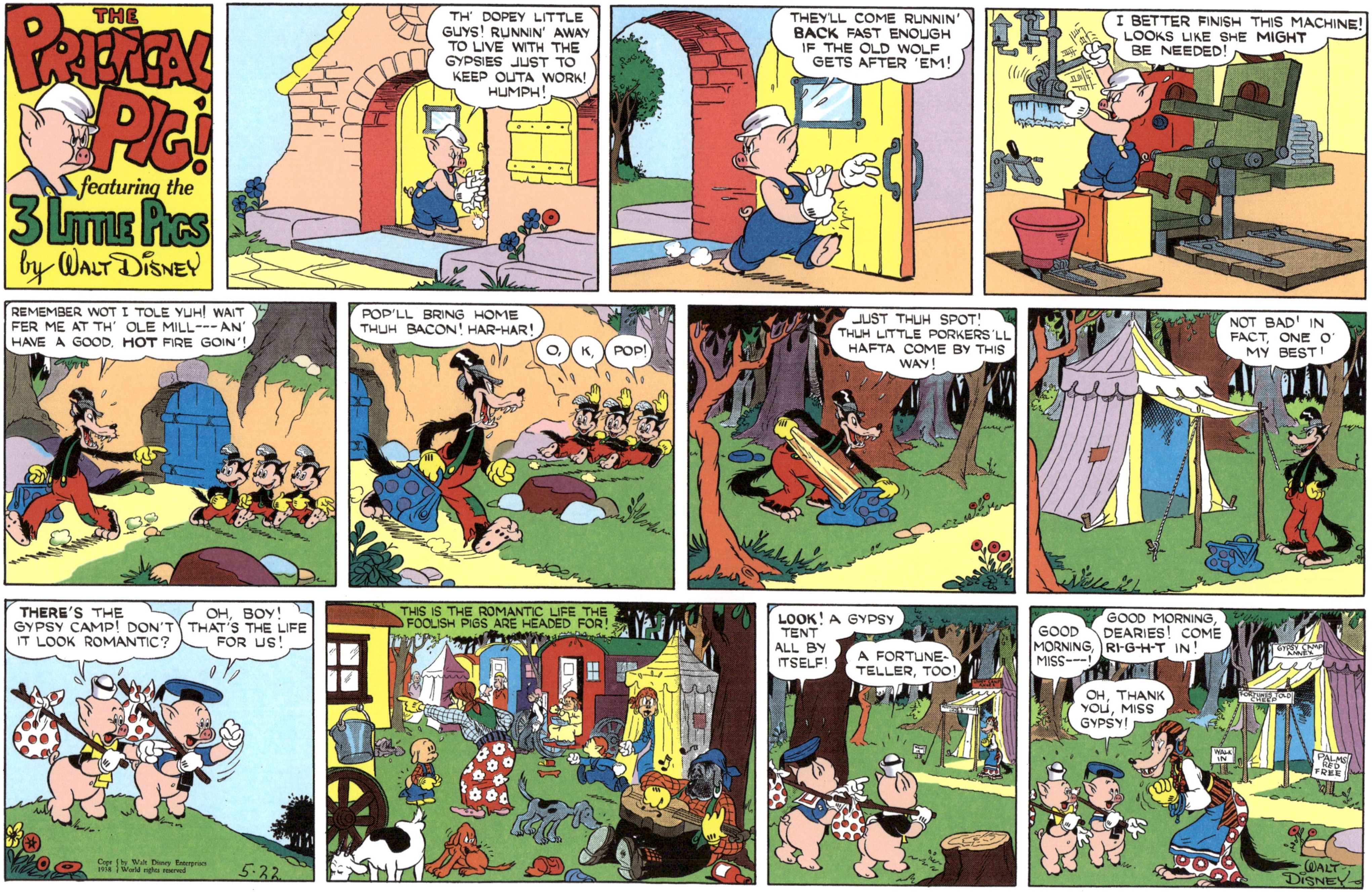
THE PRACTICAL PIG!
featuring the 3 LITTLE PIGS
by WALT DISNEY
TH' DOPEY LITTLE GUYS! RUNNIN' AWAY TO LIVE WITH THE GYPSIES JUST TO KEEP OUTA WORK! HUMPH!
THEY'LL COME RUNNIN' BACK FAST ENOUGH IF THE OLD WOLF GETS AFTER 'EM!
I BETTER FINISH THIS MACHINE! LOOKS LIKE SHE MIGHT BE NEEDED!
REMEMBER WOT I TOLE YUH! WAIT FER ME AT TH' OLE MILL---AN' HAVE A GOOD, HOT FIRE GOIN'!
POP'LL BRING HOME THUH BACON! HAR-HAR!
O,
K,
POP!
JUST THUH SPOT! THUH LITTLE PORKERS'LL HAFTA COME BY THIS WAY!
NOT BAD! IN FACT, ONE O' MY BEST!
THERE'S THE GYPSY CAMP! DON'T IT LOOK ROMANTIC?
OH, BOY! THAT'S THE LIFE FOR US!
Copr. 1938 by Walt Disney Enterprises World rights reserved
5-22
THIS IS THE ROMANTIC LIFE THE FOOLISH PIGS ARE HEADED FOR!
LOOK! A GYPSY TENT ALL BY ITSELF!
A FORTUNE-TELLER, TOO!
GOOD MORNING, MISS---!
GOOD MORNING, DEARIES! COME RI-G-H-T IN!
OH, THANK YOU, MISS GYPSY!
GYPSY CAMP ANNEX
FORTUNES TOLD CHEEP
WALK IN
PALMS RED FREE
WALT DISNEY

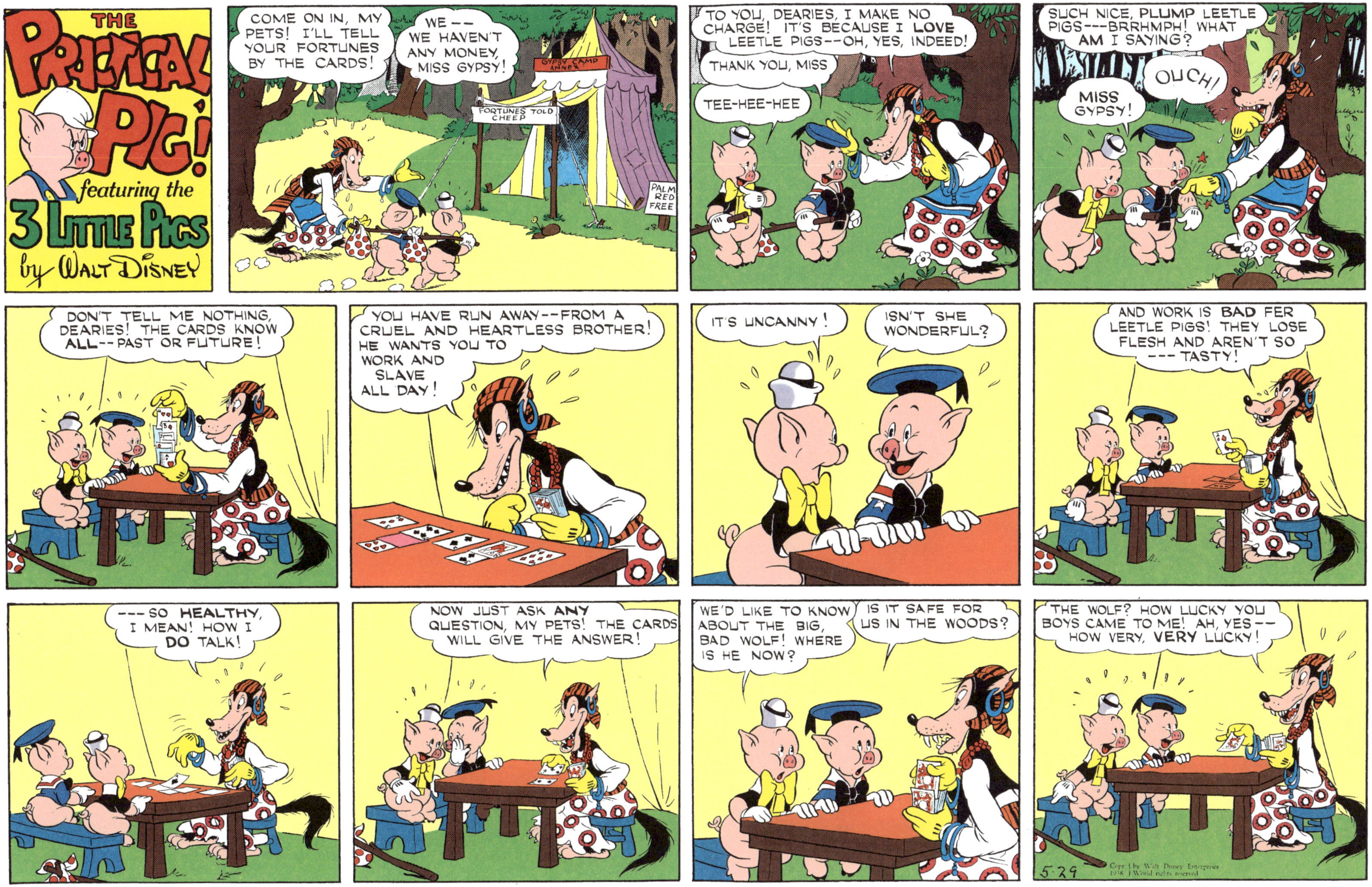
THE PRACTICAL PIG!
featuring the 3 LITTLE PIGS
by WALT DISNEY
COME ON IN, MY PETS! I'LL TELL YOUR FORTUNES BY THE CARDS!
WE -- WE HAVEN'T ANY MONEY, MISS GYPSY!
GYPSY CAMP ANNEX
FORTUNES TOLD CHEEP
PALM RED FREE
TO YOU, DEARIES, I MAKE NO CHARGE! IT'S BECAUSE I LOVE LEETLE PIGS--OH, YES, INDEED!
THANK YOU, MISS
TEE-HEE-HEE
SUCH NICE, PLUMP LEETLE PIGS---BRRHMPH! WHAT AM I SAYING?
MISS GYPSY!
OUCH!
DON'T TELL ME NOTHING, DEARIES! THE CARDS KNOW ALL--PAST OR FUTURE!
YOU HAVE RUN AWAY--FROM A CRUEL AND HEARTLESS BROTHER! HE WANTS YOU TO WORK AND SLAVE ALL DAY!
IT'S UNCANNY!
ISN'T SHE WONDERFUL?
AND WORK IS BAD FER LEETLE PIGS! THEY LOSE FLESH AND AREN'T SO ---TASTY!
---SO HEALTHY, I MEAN! HOW I DO TALK!
NOW JUST ASK ANY QUESTION, MY PETS! THE CARDS WILL GIVE THE ANSWER!
WE'D LIKE TO KNOW ABOUT THE BIG, BAD WOLF! WHERE IS HE NOW?
IS IT SAFE FOR US IN THE WOODS?
THE WOLF? HOW LUCKY YOU BOYS CAME TO ME! AH, YES-- HOW VERY, VERY LUCKY!
5-29
Copr. 1938 by Walt Disney Enterprises World rights reserved

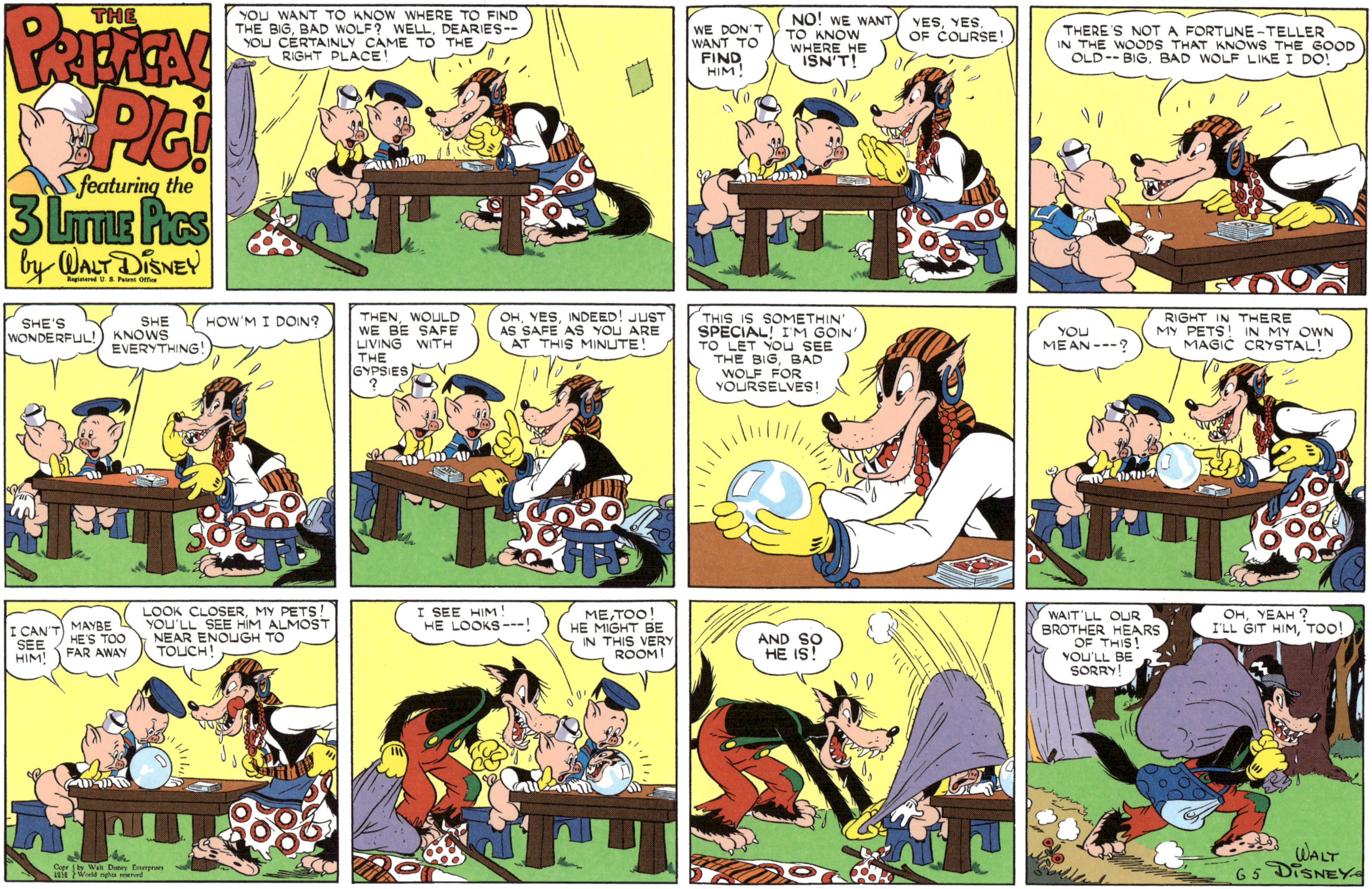
THE PRACTICAL PIG!
featuring the
3 LITTLE PIGS
by WALT DISNEY
Registered U. S. Patent Office
YOU WANT TO KNOW WHERE TO FIND THE BIG, BAD WOLF? WELL, DEARIES-- YOU CERTAINLY CAME TO THE RIGHT PLACE!
WE DON'T WANT TO FIND HIM!
NO! WE WANT TO KNOW WHERE HE ISN'T!
YES, YES, OF COURSE!
THERE'S NOT A FORTUNE-TELLER IN THE WOODS THAT KNOWS THE GOOD OLD--BIG, BAD WOLF LIKE I DO!
SHE'S WONDERFUL!
SHE KNOWS EVERYTHING!
HOW'M I DOIN?
THEN, WOULD WE BE SAFE LIVING WITH THE GYPSIES?
OH, YES, INDEED! JUST AS SAFE AS YOU ARE AT THIS MINUTE!
THIS IS SOMETHIN' SPECIAL! I'M GOIN' TO LET YOU SEE THE BIG, BAD WOLF FOR YOURSELVES!
YOU MEAN---?
RIGHT IN THERE MY PETS! IN MY OWN MAGIC CRYSTAL!
I CAN'T SEE HIM!
MAYBE HE'S TOO FAR AWAY
LOOK CLOSER, MY PETS! YOU'LL SEE HIM ALMOST NEAR ENOUGH TO TOUCH!
Copr 1938 by Walt Disney Enterprises World rights reserved
I SEE HIM! HE LOOKS---!
ME, TOO! HE MIGHT BE IN THIS VERY ROOM!
AND SO HE IS!
WAIT'LL OUR BROTHER HEARS OF THIS! YOU'LL BE SORRY!
OH, YEAH? I'LL GIT HIM, TOO!
WALT DISNEY
6 5

THE PRACTICAL PIG! featuring the 3 LITTLE PIGS by WALT DISNEY
THOSE FOOLISH BROTHERS O' MINE! THEY'VE PROBABLY WALKED RIGHT INTO SOME TRAP THE WOLF'S SET FOR 'EM!
WELL, I'M READY FOR HIM, IF HE TRIES HIS TRICKS AROUND HERE!
WELCOME
I WANTA EAT!
YEH! WHERE TH' HECK IS POP?
HE SAID WE'D HAVE PORK FER DINNER!
HERE HE COMES NOW!
HAS HE GOT 'EM?
DIDJA GET 'EM, POP?
DO WE EAT?
I TOLE YUH I'D BRING HOME THUH BACON, DIDN' I?
TAKE IT EASY! WE DON'T EAT 'TIL I GIVE THUH WORD --SEE!?
SPLAT!
AW-- GEE, POP!
WE'RE HUNGRY!
WOT'S TH' IDEA?
I'M GONTER GIT TH' OTHER ONE--THAT'S WOT! I GOT BIG PLANS!
THAT THIRD PIG'S TOUGH TO KETCH, BUT HE'LL FALL FER THIS TRICK! HAR-HAR-HAR!
HEY!! GIT AWAY FROM THEM OR I'LL BLOW YER TEETH IN!
G-12
REMEMBER! WE EAT WHEN I GIT BACK WITH TH' OTHER PIG! NOT BEFORE--SEE?
OKAY,
PAPA,
DEAR!

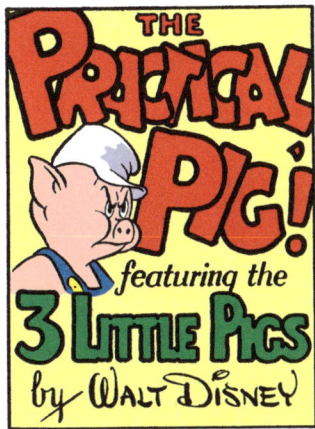

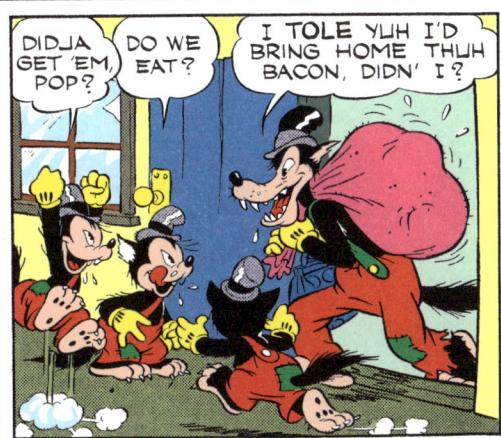

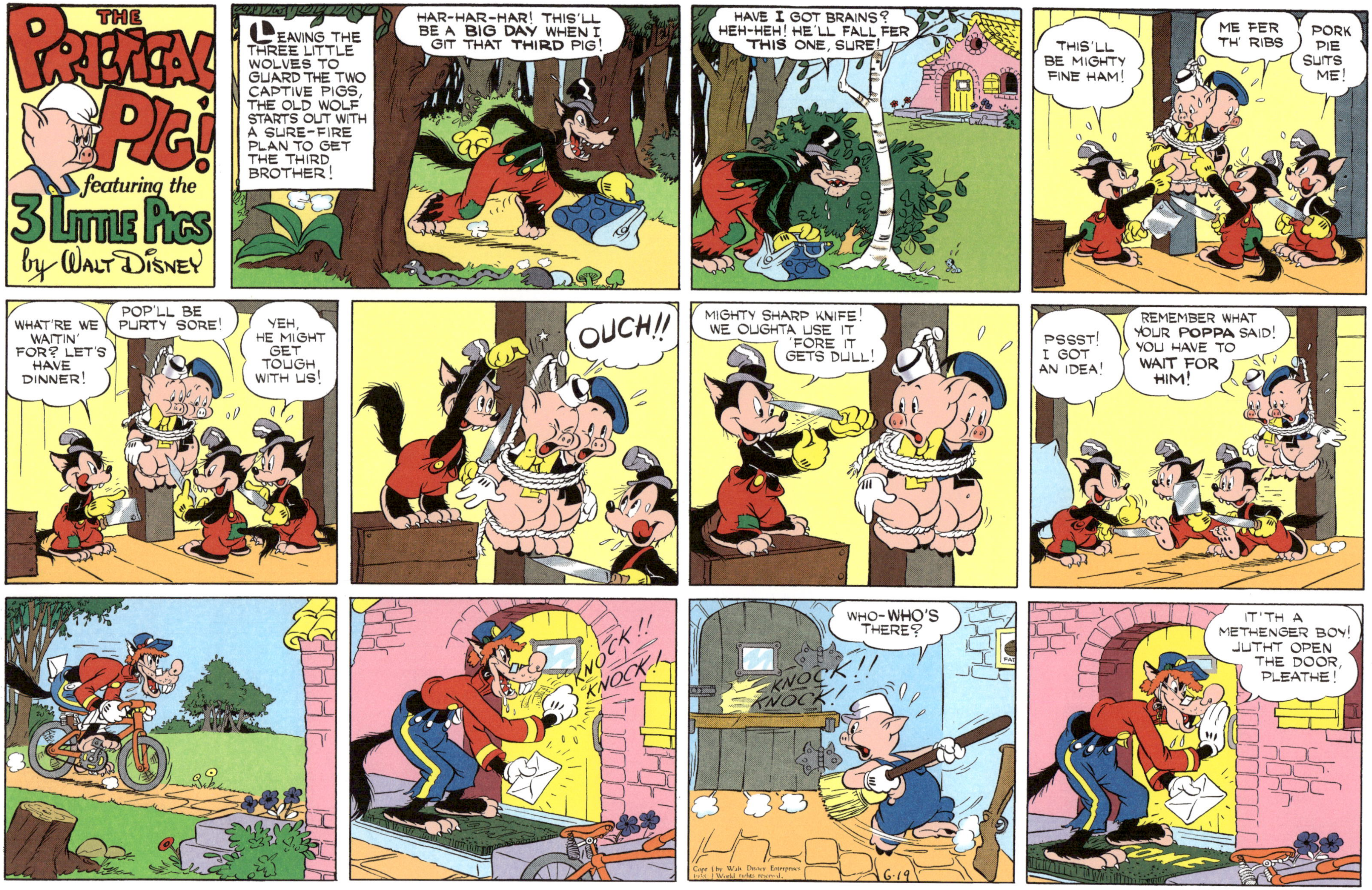
THE PRACTICAL PIG!
featuring the 3 LITTLE PIGS
by WALT DISNEY
LEAVING THE THREE LITTLE WOLVES TO GUARD THE TWO CAPTIVE PIGS, THE OLD WOLF STARTS OUT WITH A SURE-FIRE PLAN TO GET THE THIRD BROTHER!
HAR-HAR-HAR! THIS'LL BE A BIG DAY WHEN I GIT THAT THIRD PIG!
HAVE I GOT BRAINS? HEH-HEH! HE'LL FALL FER THIS ONE, SURE!
THIS'LL BE MIGHTY FINE HAM!
ME FER TH' RIBS
PORK PIE SUITS ME!
WHAT'RE WE WAITIN' FOR? LET'S HAVE DINNER!
POP'LL BE PURTY SORE!
YEH, HE MIGHT GET TOUGH WITH US!
OUCH!!
MIGHTY SHARP KNIFE! WE OUGHTA USE IT 'FORE IT GETS DULL!
PSSST! I GOT AN IDEA!
REMEMBER WHAT YOUR POPPA SAID! YOU HAVE TO WAIT FOR HIM!
KNOCK!! KNOCK!
WHO-WHO'S THERE?
KNOCK!! KNOCK!
6-19
IT'TH A METHENGER BOY! JUTHT OPEN THE DOOR, PLEATHE!

THE
PRACTICAL PIG!
featuring the
3 LITTLE PIGS
by WALT DISNEY
HAVING CAPTURED THE TWO FOOLISH PIGS, THE BIG, BAD WOLF DONS A MESSENGER BOY DISGUISE AND CALLS ON THE PRACTICAL BROTHER.
YETH, THIR! IT'TH A VERY IMPORTANT METHAGE!
P-PUT IT UNDER THE DOOR!
DAD
HEH-HEH! THIS'LL GET 'IM!
JUST AS I THOUGHT! IT'S TH' WOLF!
DERE BRUTHER We Have Bin kid-NAPPED BY THE GIPSYS. cum At ONCE. YURE DERE BRUTHERS
AHEM! ANY ANTHER, THIR?
I--I'LL BE WITH Y' IN A MINUTE!
HEY!! WOT TH---?
TRUTH
YUH LITTLE !!!
I'LL SKIN Y' ALIVE---I'LL---!!
MEANWHILE—IN THE DESERTED MILL.
SWELL!
GREAT IDEA!
WE'LL GIVE 'EM AN EVEN BREAK!
HEADS, WE EAT NOW---!
---AND TAILS. WE WAIT FER POP!
HEADS! WE EAT!
HURRAY!
PORK PIE!
YUM! YUM!
WALT DISNEY
6-26

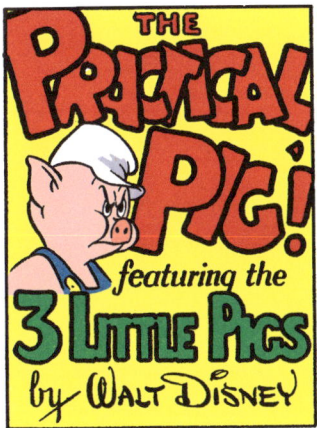

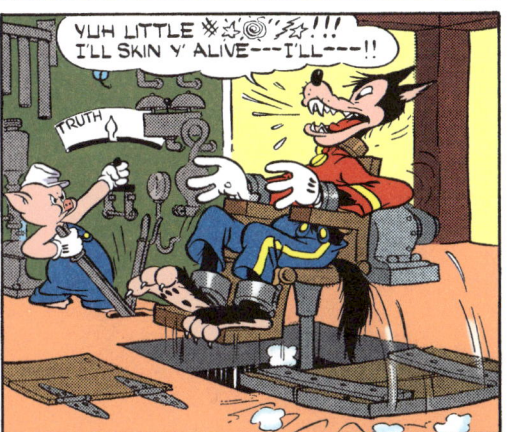

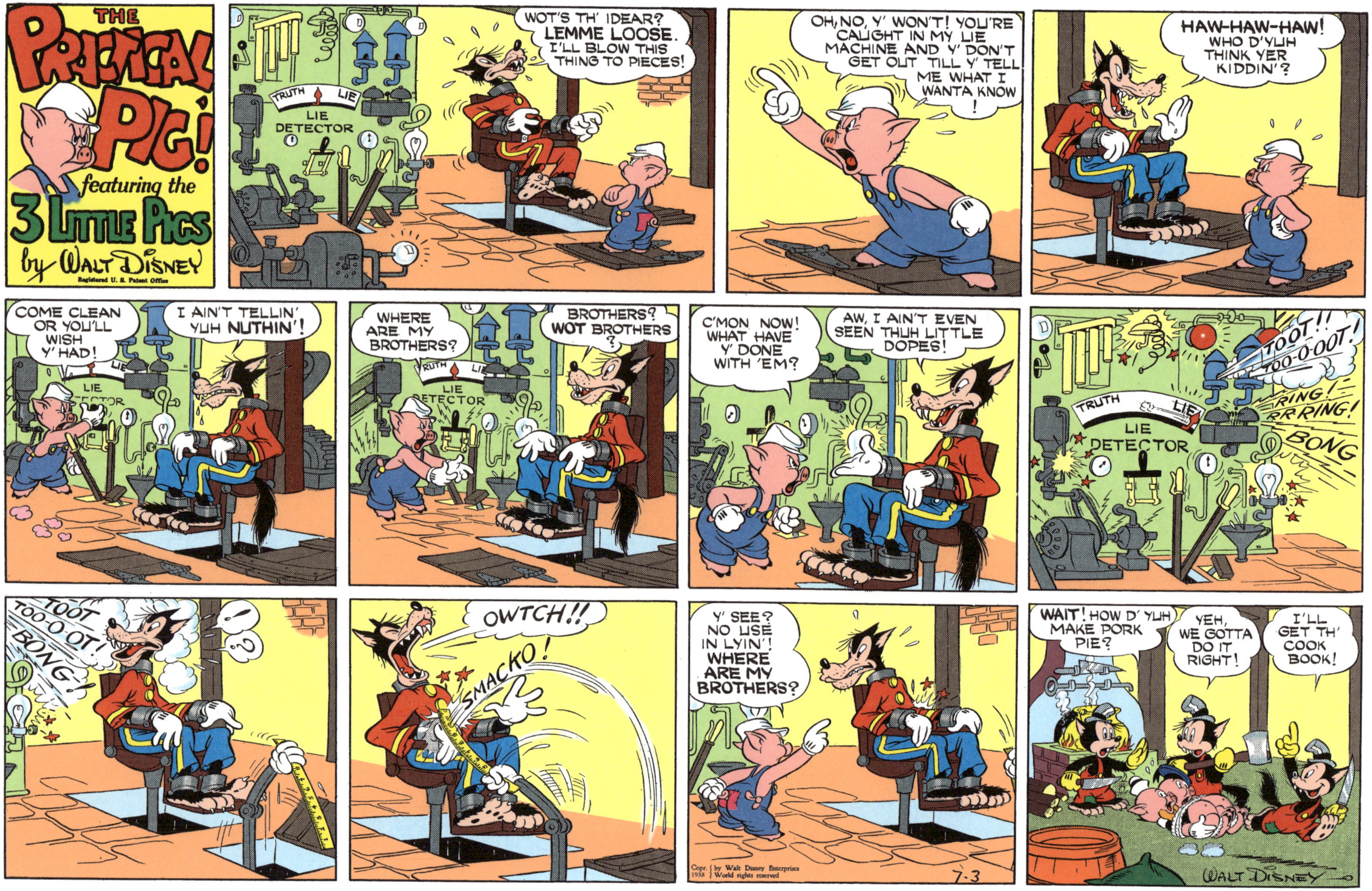
THE PRACTICAL PIG!
featuring the 3 LITTLE PIGS
by WALT DISNEY
Registered U. S. Patent Office
TRUTH LIE
LIE DETECTOR
WOT'S TH' IDEAR? LEMME LOOSE. I'LL BLOW THIS THING TO PIECES!
OH, NO, Y' WON'T! YOU'RE CAUGHT IN MY LIE MACHINE AND Y' DON'T GET OUT TILL Y' TELL ME WHAT I WANTA KNOW!
HAW-HAW-HAW! WHO D'YUH THINK YER KIDDIN'?
COME CLEAN OR YOU'LL WISH Y' HAD!
I AIN'T TELLIN' YUH NUTHIN'!
WHERE ARE MY BROTHERS?
BROTHERS? WOT BROTHERS?
C'MON NOW! WHAT HAVE Y' DONE WITH 'EM?
AW, I AIN'T EVEN SEEN THUH LITTLE DOPES!
TOOT!! TOO-O-OOT!
RING! RRRING!
BONG
TOOT TOO-O-OT! BONG-!
OWTCH!!
SMACKO!
Y' SEE? NO USE IN LYIN'! WHERE ARE MY BROTHERS?
Copr. 1938 by Walt Disney Enterprises World rights reserved
7-3
WAIT! HOW D' YUH MAKE PORK PIE?
YEH, WE GOTTA DO IT RIGHT!
I'LL GET TH' COOK BOOK!
WALT DISNEY

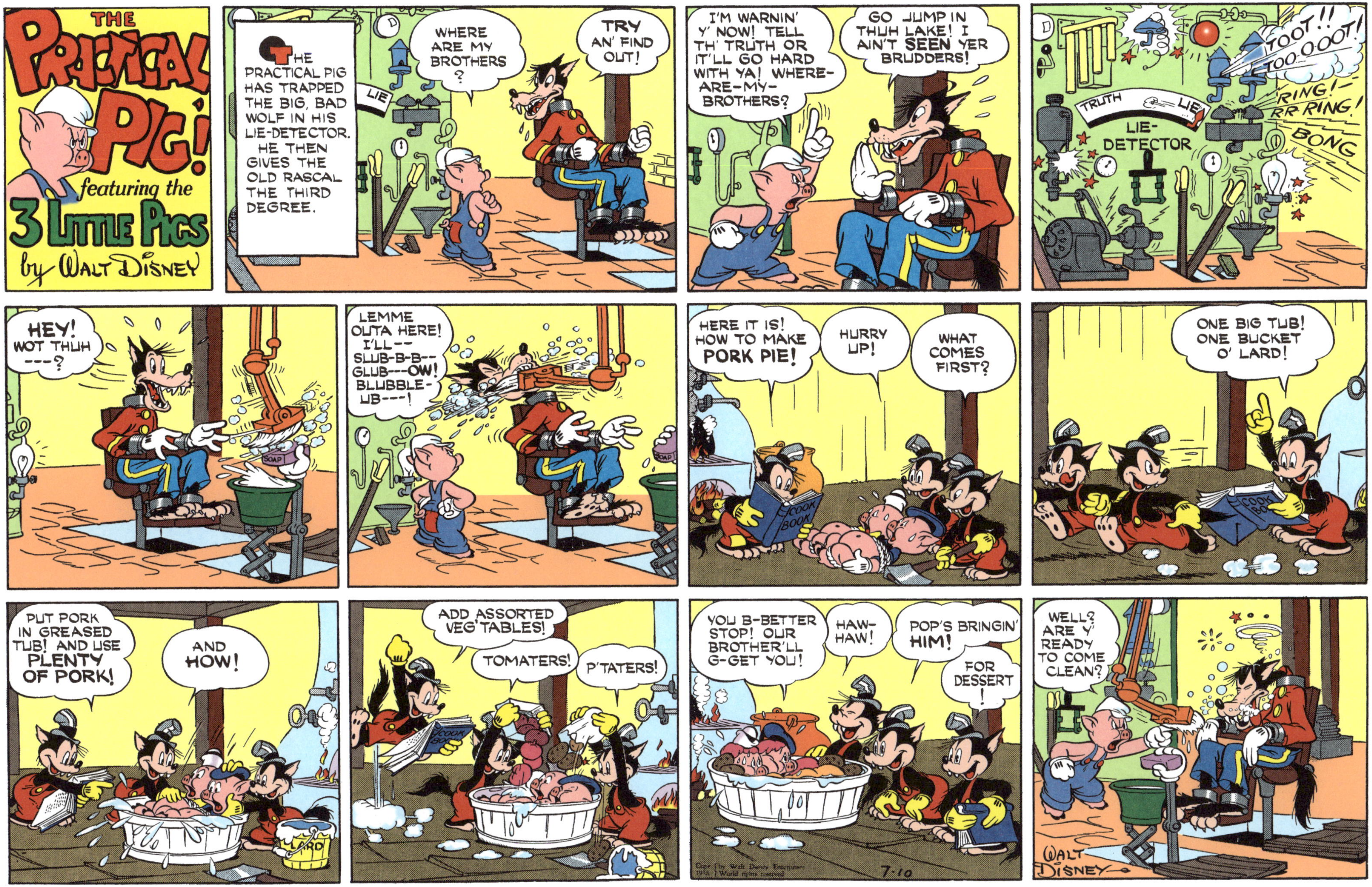
THE PRACTICAL PIG!
featuring the 3 LITTLE PIGS
by WALT DISNEY
THE PRACTICAL PIG HAS TRAPPED THE BIG, BAD WOLF IN HIS LIE-DETECTOR. HE THEN GIVES THE OLD RASCAL THE THIRD DEGREE.
LIE
WHERE ARE MY BROTHERS?
TRY AN' FIND OUT!
I'M WARNIN' Y' NOW! TELL TH' TRUTH OR IT'LL GO HARD WITH YA! WHERE-ARE-MY-BROTHERS?
GO JUMP IN THUH LAKE! I AIN'T SEEN YER BRUDDERS!
TRUTH
LIE
LIE-DETECTOR
TOOT!! TOO-O-OOT!
RING!- RR RING!
BONG
HEY! WOT THUH ---?
SOAP
LEMME OUTA HERE! I'LL-- SLUB-B-B-- GLUB---OW! BLUBBLE-UB---!
SOAP
HERE IT IS! HOW TO MAKE PORK PIE!
HURRY UP!
WHAT COMES FIRST?
COOK BOOK
ONE BIG TUB! ONE BUCKET O' LARD!
COOK BOOK
PUT PORK IN GREASED TUB! AND USE PLENTY OF PORK!
AND HOW!
LARD
ADD ASSORTED VEG'TABLES!
TOMATERS!
P'TATERS!
COOK BOOK
YOU B-BETTER STOP! OUR BROTHER'LL G-GET YOU!
HAW-HAW!
POP'S BRINGIN' HIM!
FOR DESSERT!
7-10
WELL? ARE Y' READY TO COME CLEAN?
WALT DISNEY

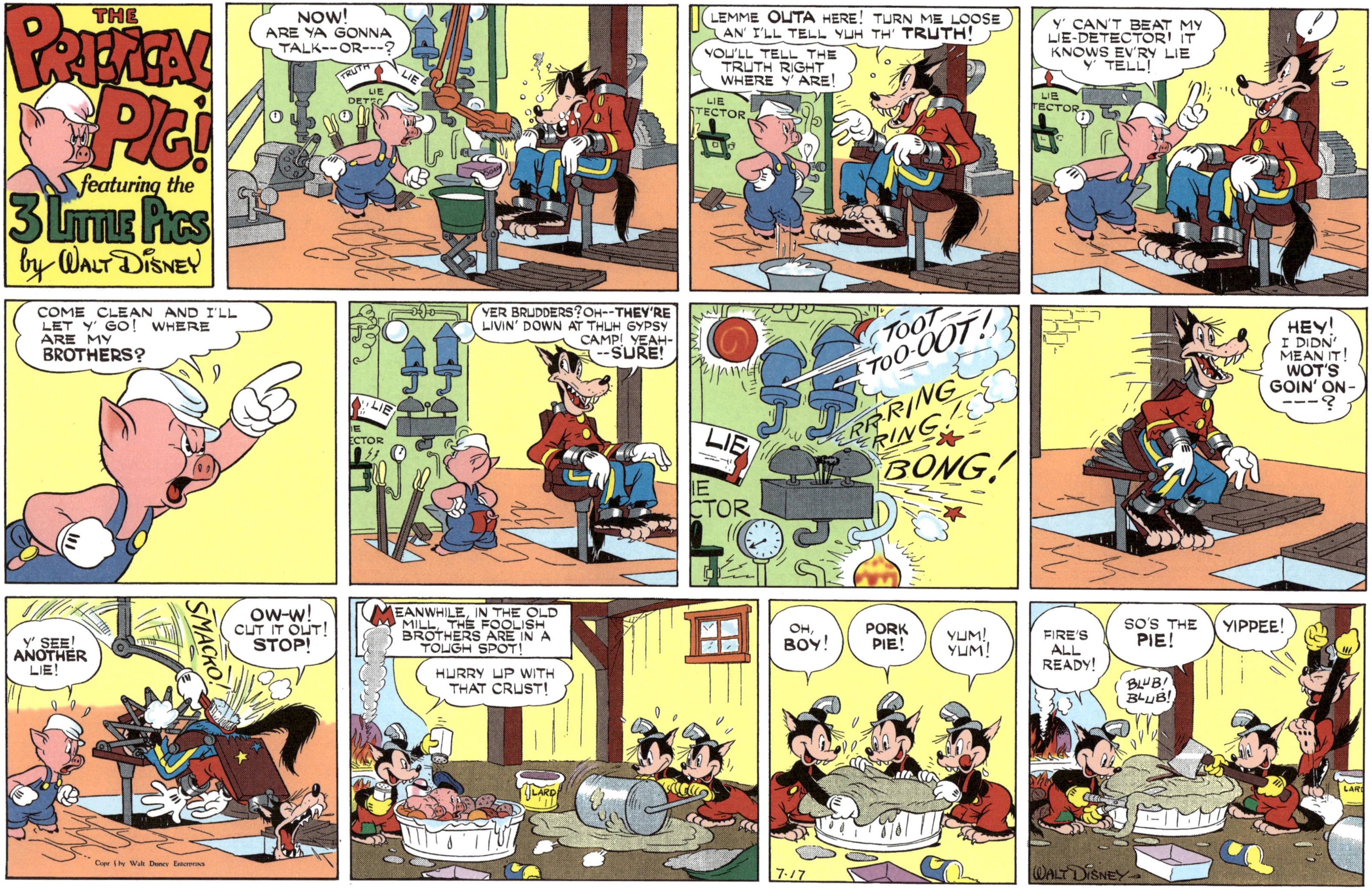
THE PRACTICAL PIG! featuring the 3 LITTLE PIGS
by WALT DISNEY
NOW! ARE YA GONNA TALK--OR---?
TRUTH LIE
LIE DETEC
SOAP
LEMME OUTA HERE! TURN ME LOOSE AN' I'LL TELL YUH TH' TRUTH!
YOU'LL TELL THE TRUTH RIGHT WHERE Y' ARE!
LIE DETECTOR
Y' CAN'T BEAT MY LIE-DETECTOR! IT KNOWS EV'RY LIE Y' TELL!
!
LIE TECTOR
COME CLEAN AND I'LL LET Y' GO! WHERE ARE MY BROTHERS?
YER BRUDDERS? OH--THEY'RE LIVIN' DOWN AT THUH GYPSY CAMP! YEAH- --SURE!
LIE
TOOT TOO-OOT!
RR-R-RING RING!
BONG!
LIE
HEY! I DIDN' MEAN IT! WOT'S GOIN' ON ---?
Y' SEE! ANOTHER LIE!
SMACKO!
OW-W! CUT IT OUT! STOP!
Copr by Walt Disney Enterprises
MEANWHILE, IN THE OLD MILL, THE FOOLISH BROTHERS ARE IN A TOUGH SPOT!
HURRY UP WITH THAT CRUST!
LARD
OH, BOY!
PORK PIE!
YUM! YUM!
7-17
FIRE'S ALL READY!
SO'S THE PIE!
YIPPEE!
BLUB! BLUB!
WALT DISNEY

THE PRACTICAL PIG! featuring the 3 LITTLE PIGS by WALT DISNEY
BOY-OH-BOY!
PORK PIE!
WITH ALL TH' TRIMMIN'S!
GIVE IT PLENTY O' HEAT!
COOK IT FAST!
BLUB! BLUB!
I KIN HARDLY WAIT!
YEE-OW-W!
I'M ON FIRE!!
HEY!
CATCH 'EM!
DON'T LOSE OUR PORK PIE!
WE GOTTA CATCH 'EM!
OR POP'LL MURDER US!
BUT "POP" ISN'T SITTING SO PRETTY, HIMSELF!
C'MON NOW! Y' CAN'T FOOL THIS MACHINE! WHERE ARE MY BROTHERS?
NOW LISSEN! YUH GOT ME ALL WRONG-- BUDDY!
I'M YER PAL, SEE? I WOULDN'T HARM THEM LI'L GUYS! WHY, THEY'RE LIKE ME OWN BRUDDERS, THEY ARE!
Copr. 1938 by Walt Disney Enterprises World rights reserved
LIE
LIE DETECTOR
TOOT TOO-OOT TOOT!
RING! RR-RING
BONG! BONG!
7-24
HALP! QUIT! STOP! I'LL TELL THE TRUTH! LET UP! I'LL TELL!
BANG!
SMACKO
SOAP
WALT DISNEY

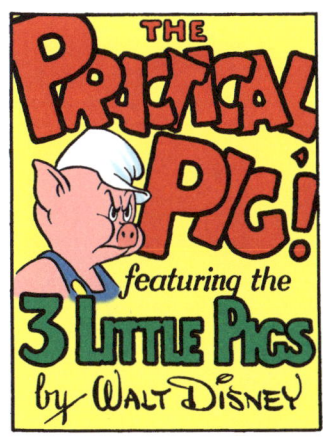

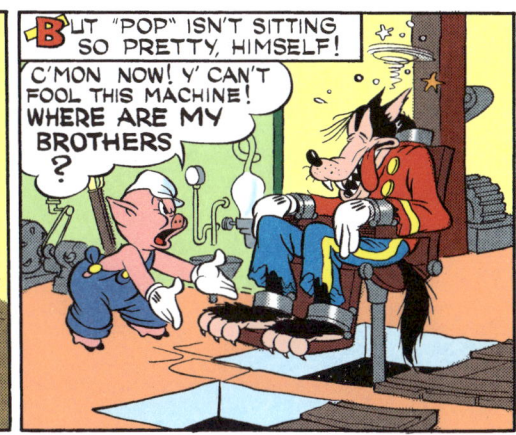

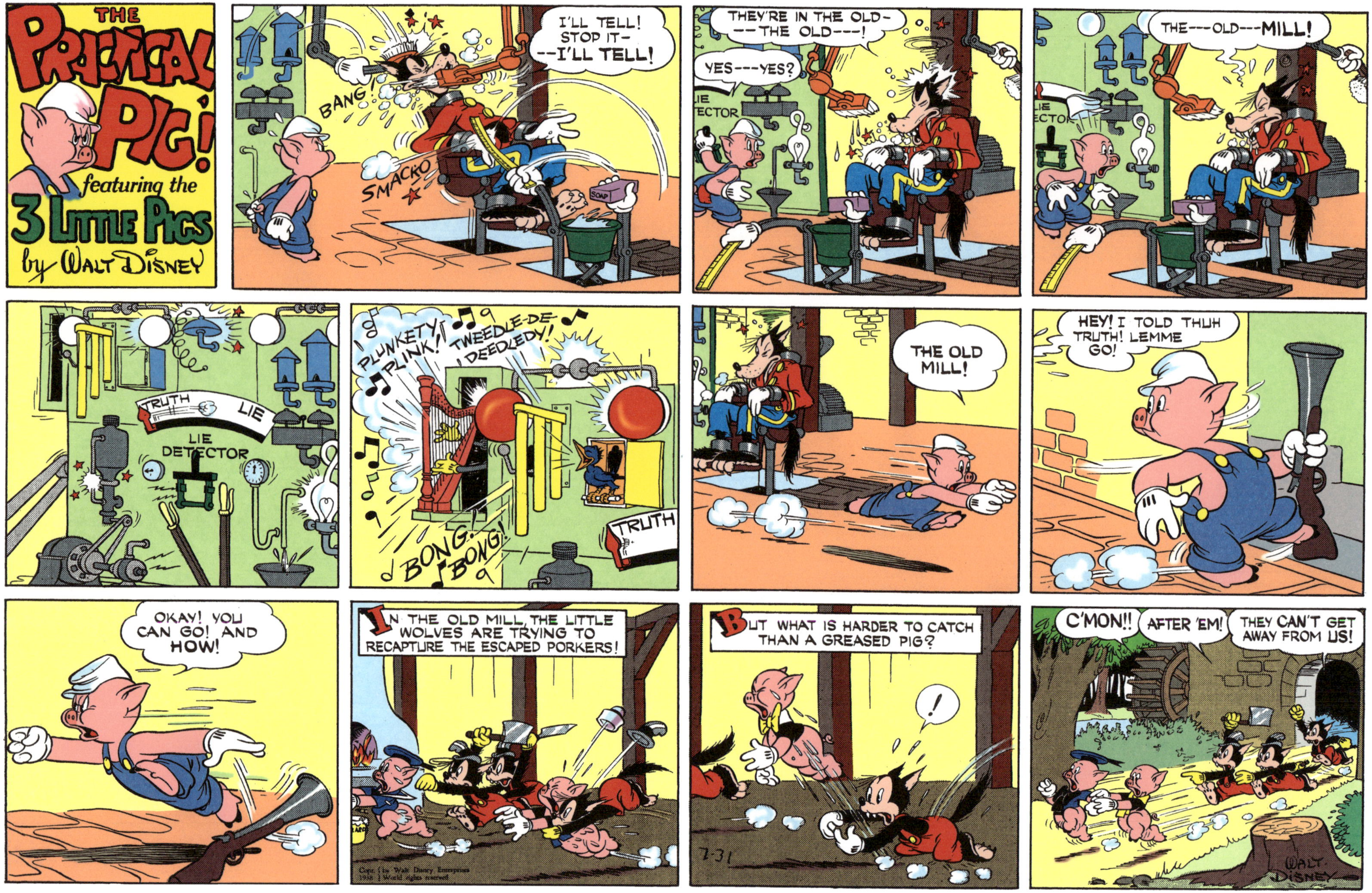
THE PRACTICAL PIG!
featuring the 3 LITTLE PIGS
by WALT DISNEY
I'LL TELL! STOP IT- --I'LL TELL!
BANG!
SMACKO
SOAP
THEY'RE IN THE OLD- --THE OLD---!
YES---YES?
THE---OLD---MILL!
TRUTH
LIE
LIE DETECTOR
PLUNKETY PLINK! TWEEDLE-DE DEEDLEDY!
BONG! BONG!
TRUTH
THE OLD MILL!
HEY! I TOLD THUH TRUTH! LEMME GO!
OKAY! YOU CAN GO! AND HOW!
IN THE OLD MILL, THE LITTLE WOLVES ARE TRYING TO RECAPTURE THE ESCAPED PORKERS!
BUT WHAT IS HARDER TO CATCH THAN A GREASED PIG?
!
7-31
C'MON!!
AFTER 'EM!
THEY CAN'T GET AWAY FROM US!
WALT DISNEY

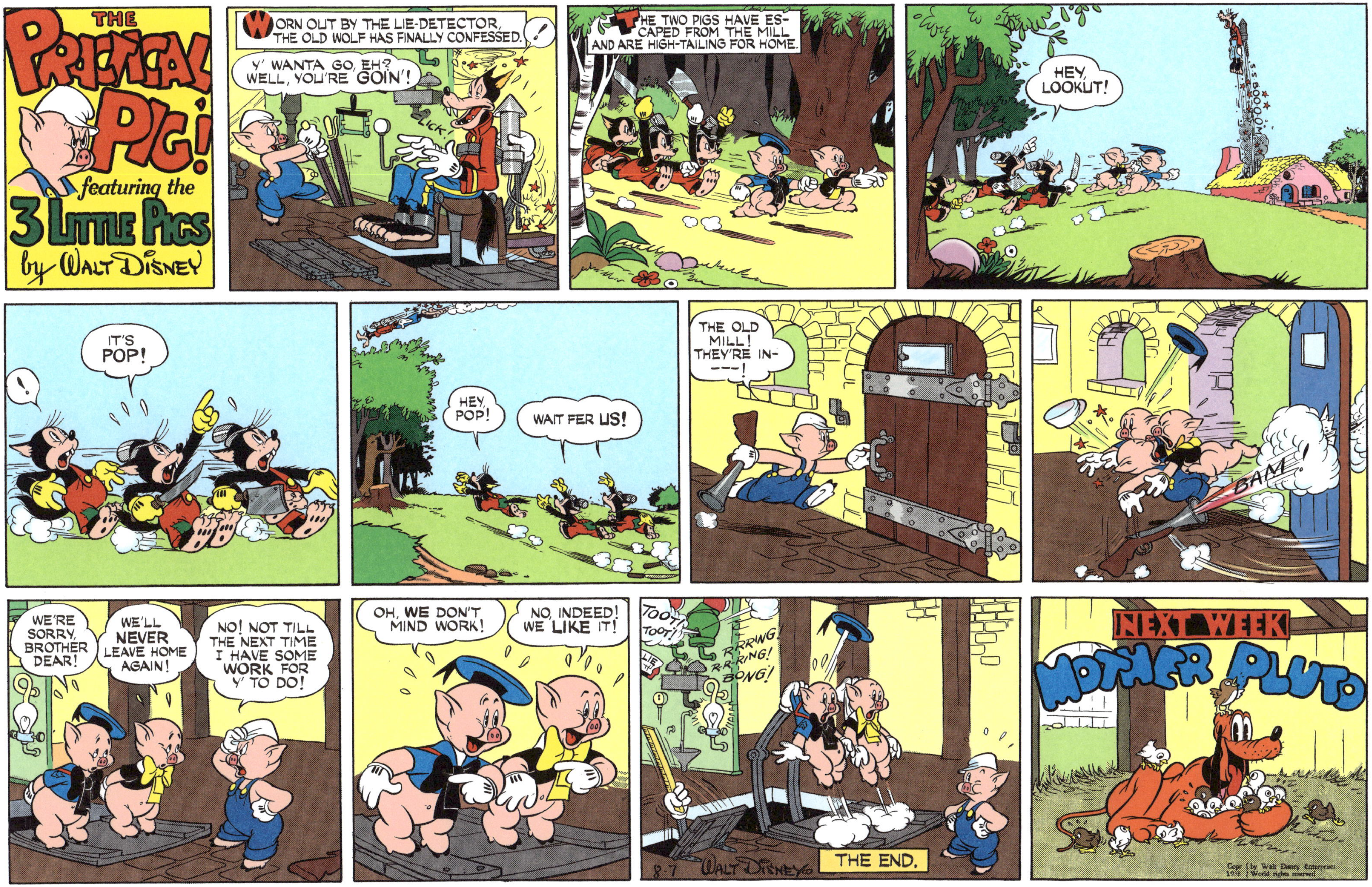
THE PRACTICAL PIG!
featuring the
3 LITTLE PIGS
by WALT DISNEY
WORN OUT BY THE LIE-DETECTOR, THE OLD WOLF HAS FINALLY CONFESSED.
!
Y' WANTA GO, EH? WELL, YOU'RE GOIN'!
LICK
THE TWO PIGS HAVE ESCAPED FROM THE MILL AND ARE HIGH-TAILING FOR HOME.
HEY, LOOKUT!
!
IT'S POP!
HEY, POP!
WAIT FER US!
THE OLD MILL! THEY'RE IN----!
BAM!
WE'RE SORRY, BROTHER DEAR!
WE'LL NEVER LEAVE HOME AGAIN!
NO! NOT TILL THE NEXT TIME I HAVE SOME WORK FOR Y' TO DO!
OH, WE DON'T MIND WORK!
NO, INDEED! WE LIKE IT!
TOOT! TOOT!
R-R-RING! R-R-RING! BONG!
8-7 WALT DISNEY
THE END.
NEXT WEEK
MOTHER PLUTO

MOTHER PLUTO

August 14 - October 16, 1938
Written by Merrill de Maris, drawn by Al Taliaferro

Released in 1936, *Mother Pluto* was a charming film and a gem of the animator's art. Today it is sometimes overlooked, but in the 1930s its story had a quiet staying power. It turned up again in Disney storybook adaptations, and, in 1938—nearly two years after the film's release—in the comics.

The *Silly Symphony* comic page routinely took creative liberties with its source stories, so it's not surprising that de Maris adapted this one for the purposes of the strip. Perhaps most strikingly, one of the baby chicks is isolated as a distinct character. In the film, the chicks are simply a gaggle of little interchangeable creatures; here the black chick wanders away, gets himself lost, and motivates a plot thread that doesn't appear in the film. In fact, if there's a precedent for this thread, it's in the *Symphony* comic page itself. Readers of *Silly Symphonies* Volume 1 may recall a 1934 continuity based on *The Wise Little Hen*, in which another little black runaway chick prompts an anxious search—also not reflecting anything in the film! Here, too, the end of the "Mother Pluto" strip resolves the story more or less as in the film, but discards the warmth of the film's ending and substitutes a gag finish in its place.

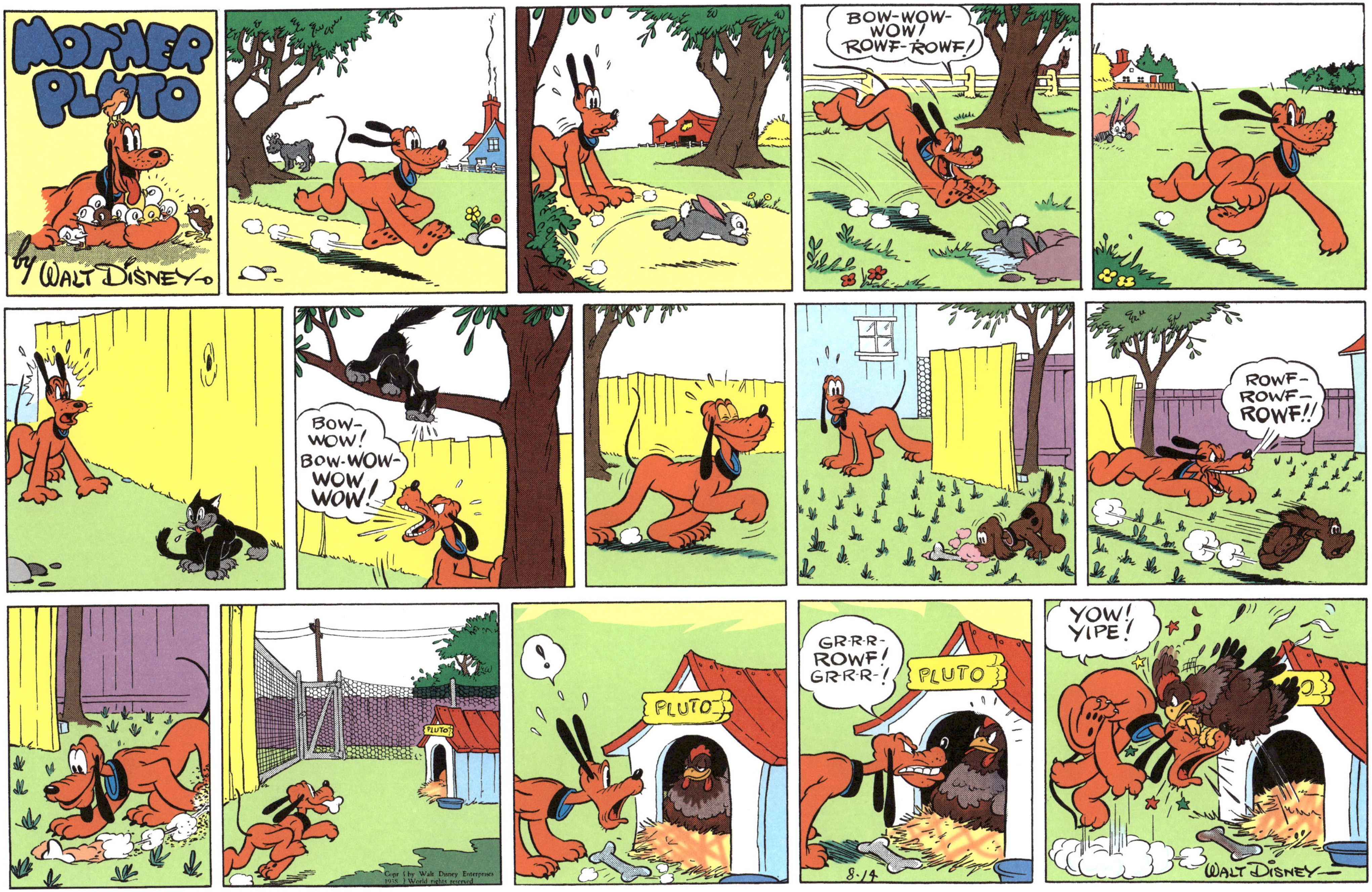
MOTHER PLUTO
by WALT DISNEY
BOW-WOW-WOW! ROWF-ROWF!
BOW-WOW! BOW-WOW-WOW WOW!
ROWF-ROWF-ROWF!!
Copr 1938 by Walt Disney Enterprises World rights reserved
!
PLUTO
GR-R-R-ROWF! GR-R-R-!
PLUTO
8-14
YOW! YIPE!
WALT DISNEY

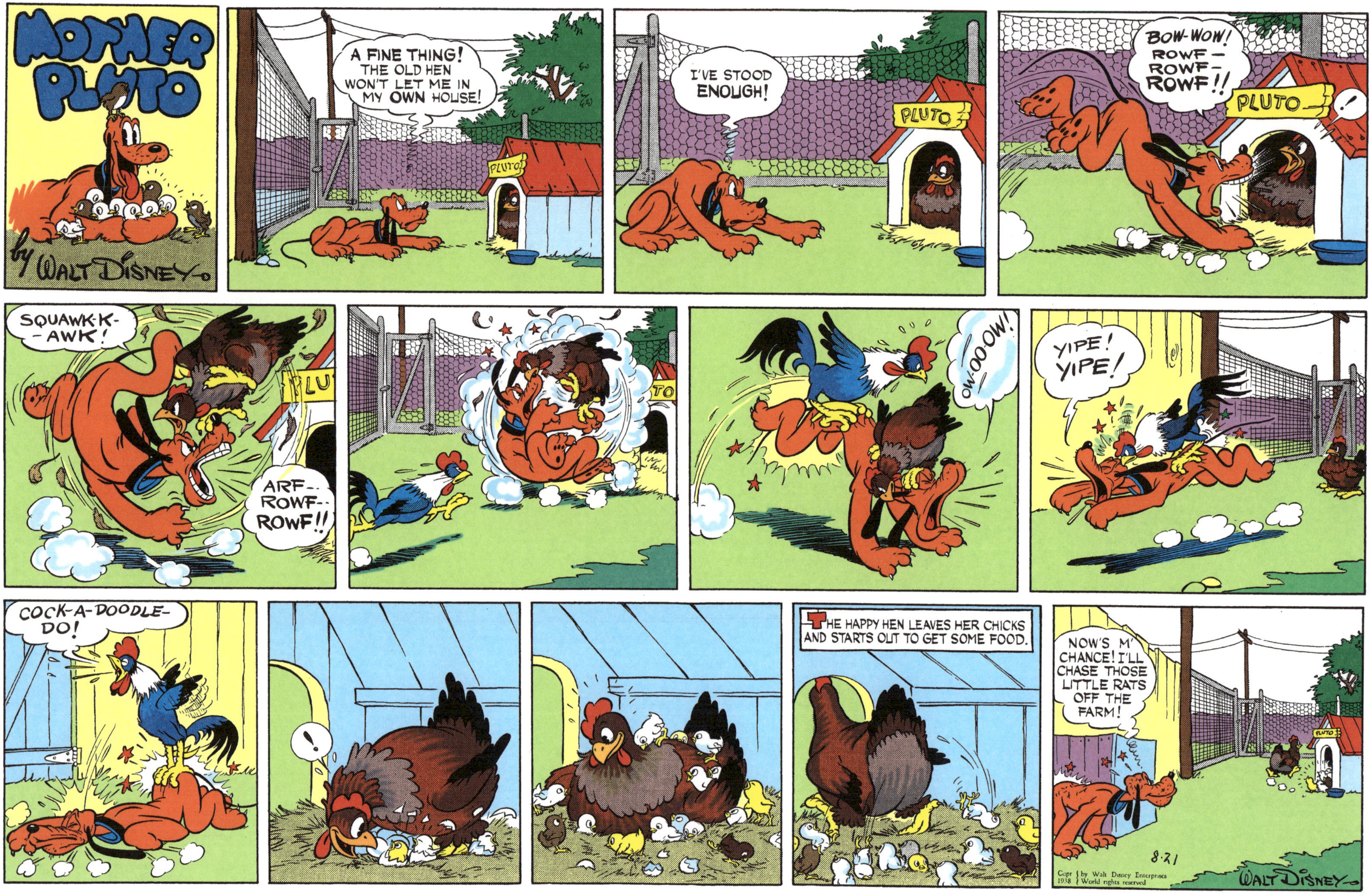
MOTHER PLUTO
by WALT DISNEY
A FINE THING! THE OLD HEN WON'T LET ME IN MY OWN HOUSE!
PLUTO
I'VE STOOD ENOUGH!
PLUTO
BOW-WOW! ROWF— ROWF— ROWF!!
PLUTO
!
SQUAWK-K -AWK!
ARF-- ROWF-- ROWF!!
OW-OO-OW!
YIPE! YIPE!
COCK-A-DOODLE-DO!
!
THE HAPPY HEN LEAVES HER CHICKS AND STARTS OUT TO GET SOME FOOD.
NOW'S M' CHANCE! I'LL CHASE THOSE LITTLE RATS OFF THE FARM!
PLUTO
8-21
Copr 1938 by Walt Disney Enterprises World rights reserved
WALT DISNEY

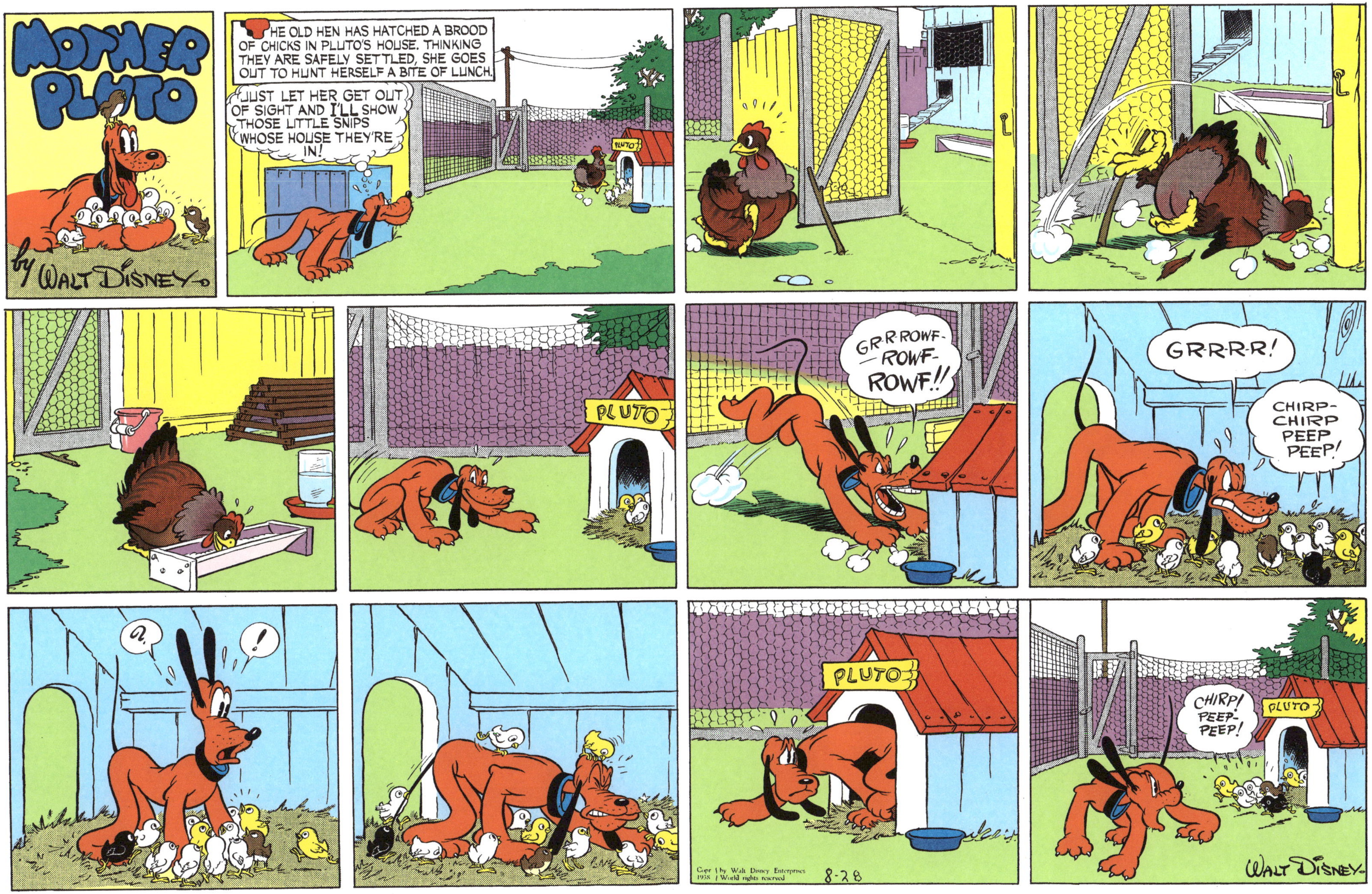

MOTHER PLUTO
by WALT DISNEY
THE OLD HEN HAS HATCHED A BROOD OF CHICKS IN PLUTO'S HOUSE. THINKING THEY ARE SAFELY SETTLED, SHE GOES OUT TO HUNT HERSELF A BITE OF LUNCH.
JUST LET HER GET OUT OF SIGHT AND I'LL SHOW THOSE LITTLE SNIPS WHOSE HOUSE THEY'RE IN!
PLUTO
PLUTO
GR-R-ROWF- ROWF- ROWF!!
GR-R-R-R!
CHIRP- CHIRP PEEP PEEP!
?
!
PLUTO
Copr by Walt Disney Enterprises 1938 World rights reserved
8-28
CHIRP! PEEP- PEEP!
PLUTO
WALT DISNEY

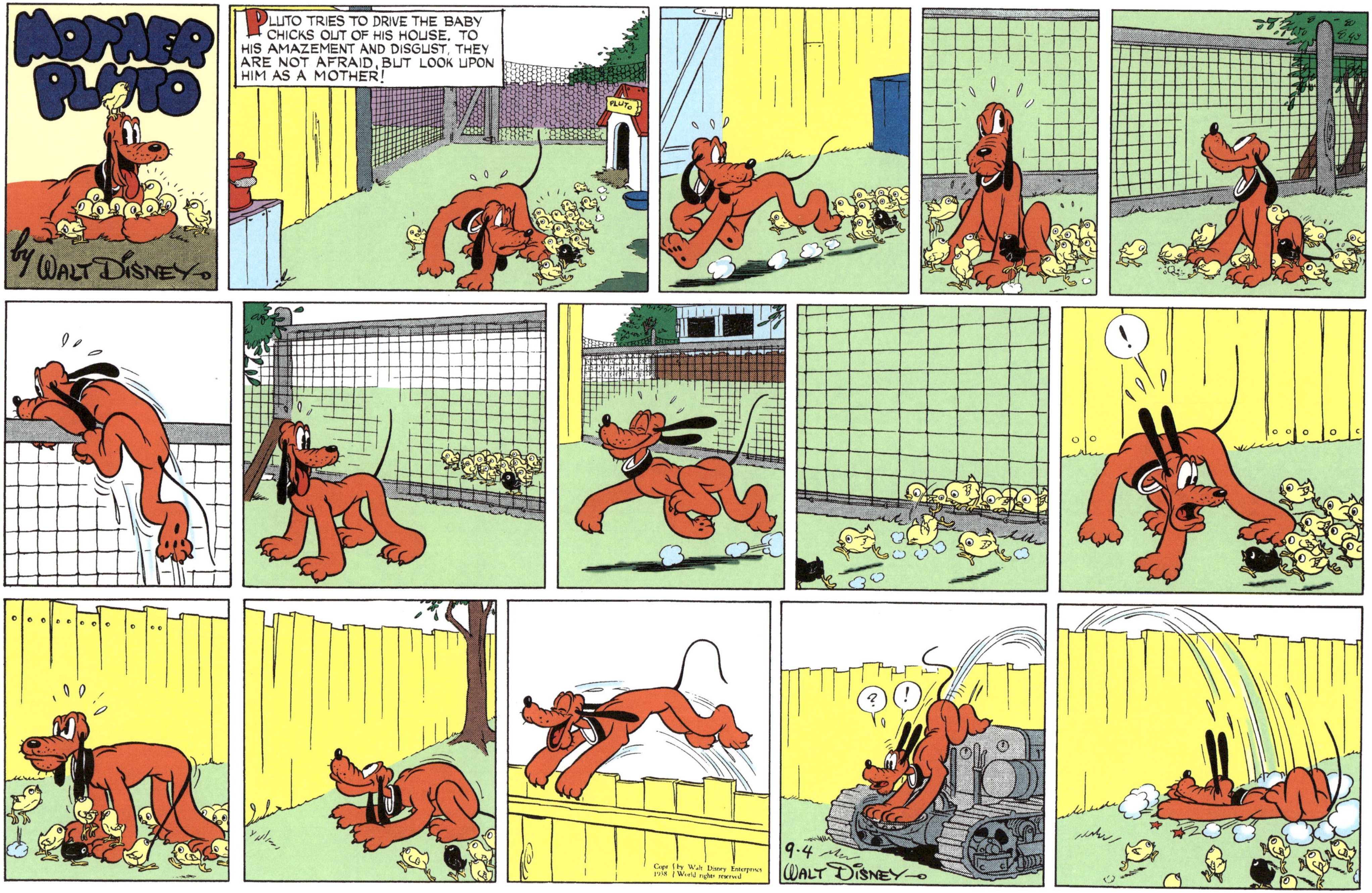
MOTHER PLUTO
by WALT DISNEY
PLUTO TRIES TO DRIVE THE BABY CHICKS OUT OF HIS HOUSE. TO HIS AMAZEMENT AND DISGUST, THEY ARE NOT AFRAID, BUT LOOK UPON HIM AS A MOTHER!
PLUTO
!
?
!
Copr 1938 by Walt Disney Enterprises World rights reserved
9-4
WALT DISNEY

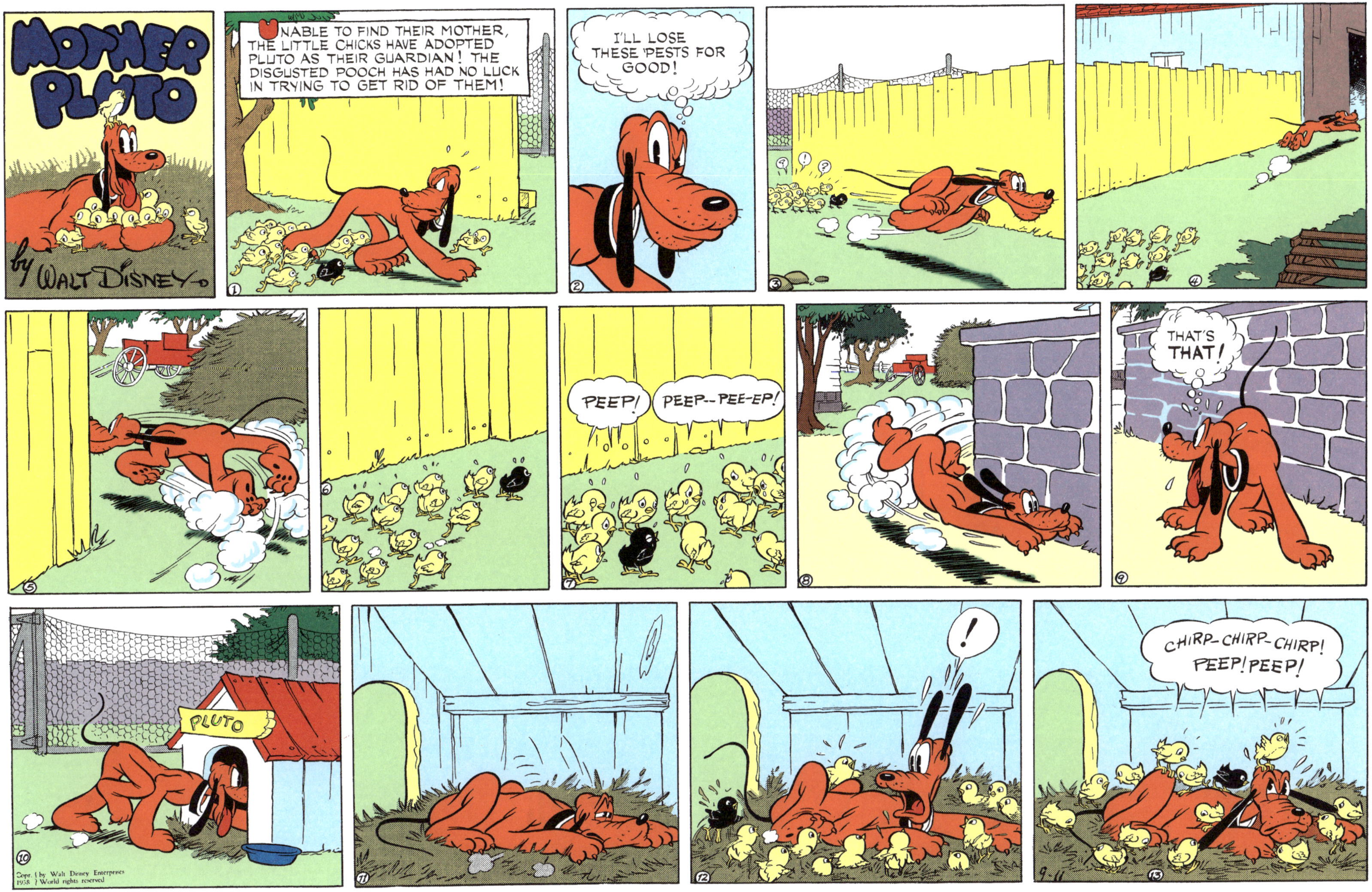
MOTHER PLUTO
by WALT DISNEY
UNABLE TO FIND THEIR MOTHER, THE LITTLE CHICKS HAVE ADOPTED PLUTO AS THEIR GUARDIAN! THE DISGUSTED POOCH HAS HAD NO LUCK IN TRYING TO GET RID OF THEM!
I'LL LOSE THESE 'PESTS FOR GOOD!
THAT'S THAT!
PEEP!
PEEP--PEE-EP!
PLUTO
Copr. 1938 by Walt Disney Enterprises World rights reserved
!
CHIRP-CHIRP-CHIRP! PEEP! PEEP!

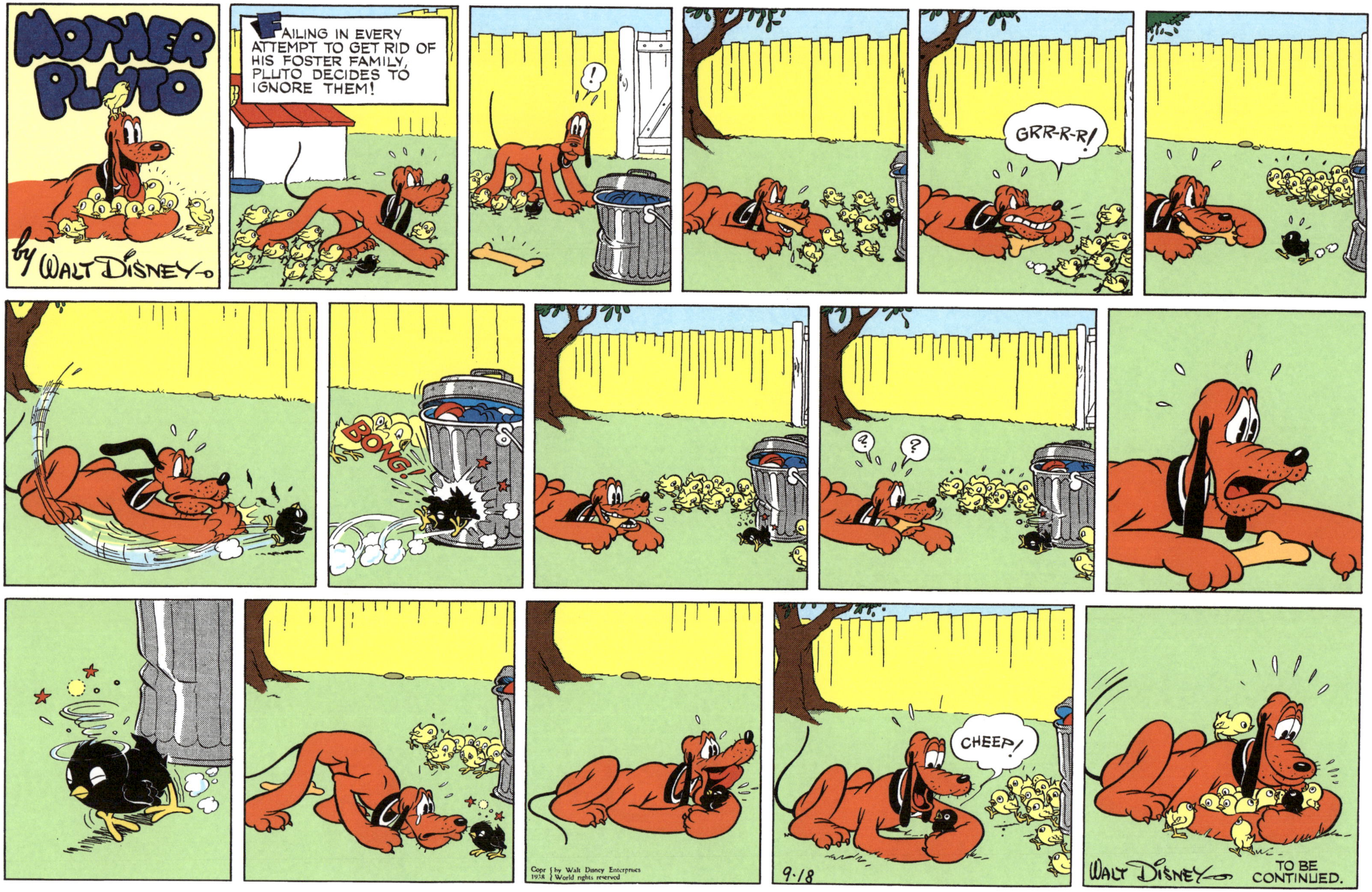
MOTHER PLUTO
by WALT DISNEY
FAILING IN EVERY ATTEMPT TO GET RID OF HIS FOSTER FAMILY, PLUTO DECIDES TO IGNORE THEM!
!
GRR-R-R!
BONG!
?
?
Copr 1938 by Walt Disney Enterprises World rights reserved
9·18
CHEEP!
WALT DISNEY
TO BE CONTINUED.

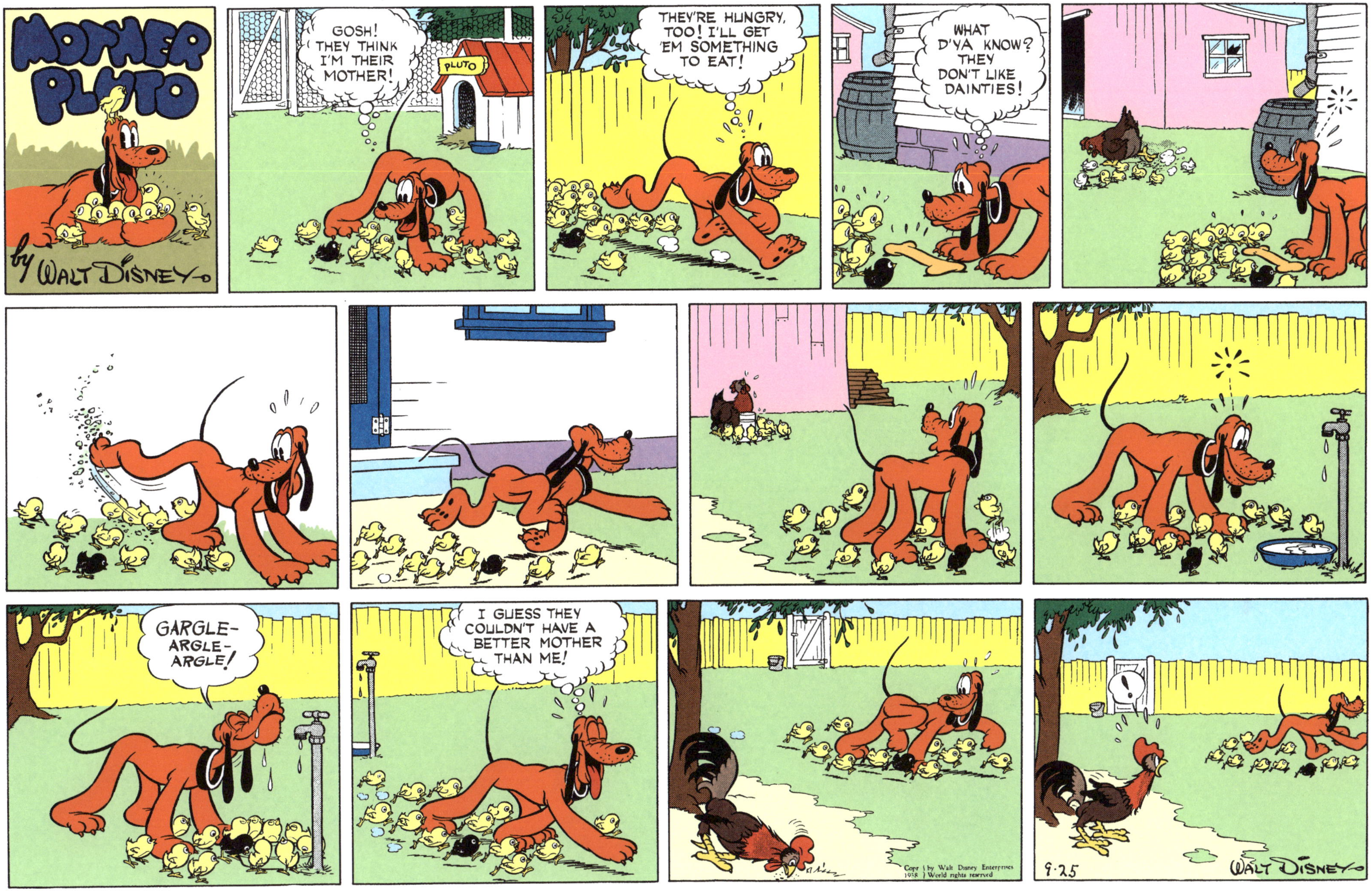
MOTHER PLUTO
by WALT DISNEY
GOSH! THEY THINK I'M THEIR MOTHER!
PLUTO
THEY'RE HUNGRY, TOO! I'LL GET 'EM SOMETHING TO EAT!
WHAT D'YA KNOW? THEY DON'T LIKE DAINTIES!
GARGLE-ARGLE-ARGLE!
I GUESS THEY COULDN'T HAVE A BETTER MOTHER THAN ME!
Copr. by Walt Disney Enterprises 1938 World rights reserved
9-25
WALT DISNEY

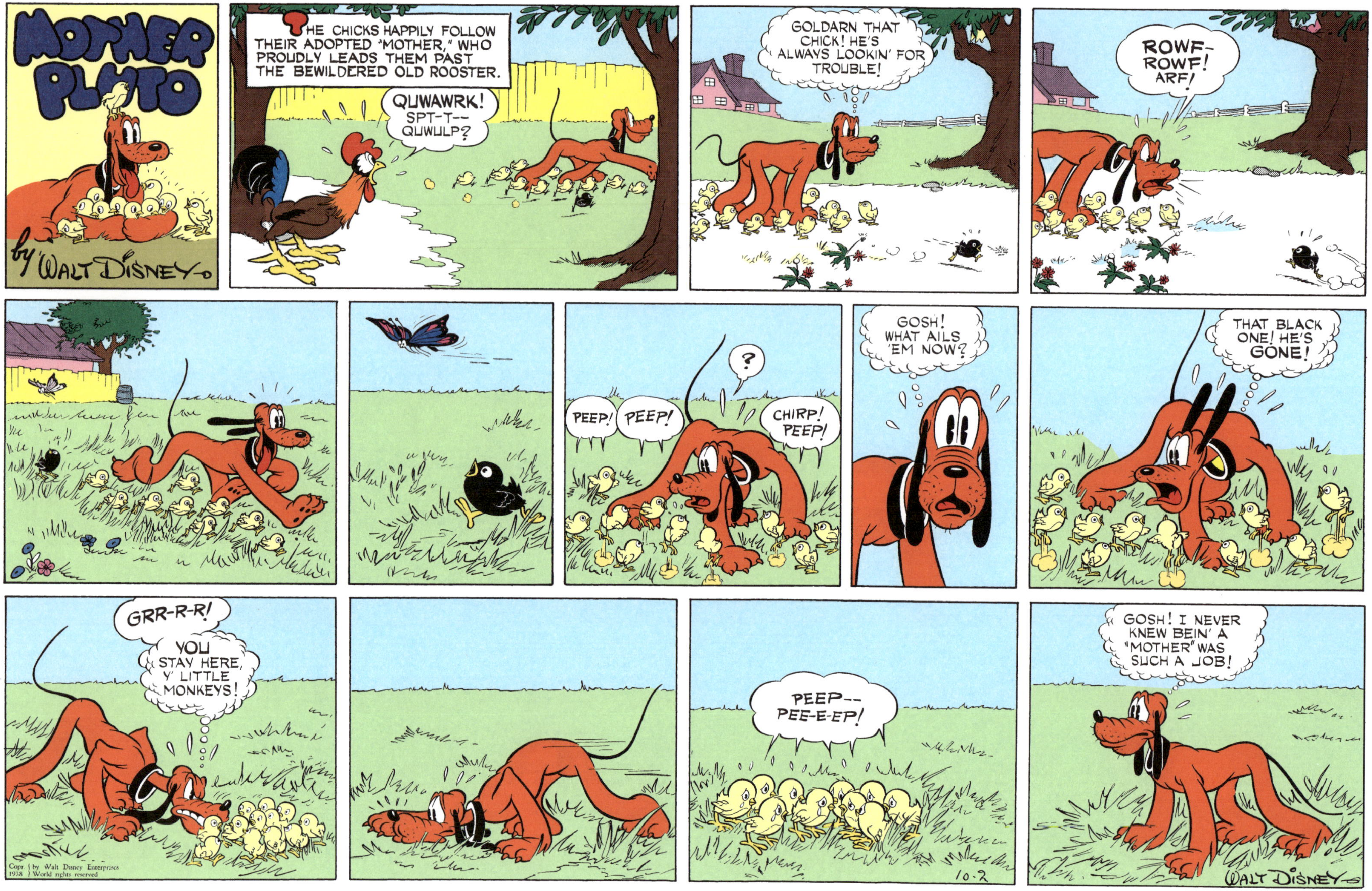
MOTHER PLUTO
by WALT DISNEY
THE CHICKS HAPPILY FOLLOW THEIR ADOPTED "MOTHER," WHO PROUDLY LEADS THEM PAST THE BEWILDERED OLD ROOSTER.
QUWAWRK! SPT-T-- QUWULP?
GOLDARN THAT CHICK! HE'S ALWAYS LOOKIN' FOR TROUBLE!
ROWF-ROWF! ARF!
PEEP! PEEP!
?
CHIRP! PEEP!
GOSH! WHAT AILS 'EM NOW?
THAT BLACK ONE! HE'S GONE!
GRR-R-R!
YOU STAY HERE, Y' LITTLE MONKEYS!
Copr. 1938 by Walt Disney Enterprises World rights reserved
PEEP-- PEE-E-EP!
10-2
GOSH! I NEVER KNEW BEIN' A "MOTHER" WAS SUCH A JOB!
WALT DISNEY

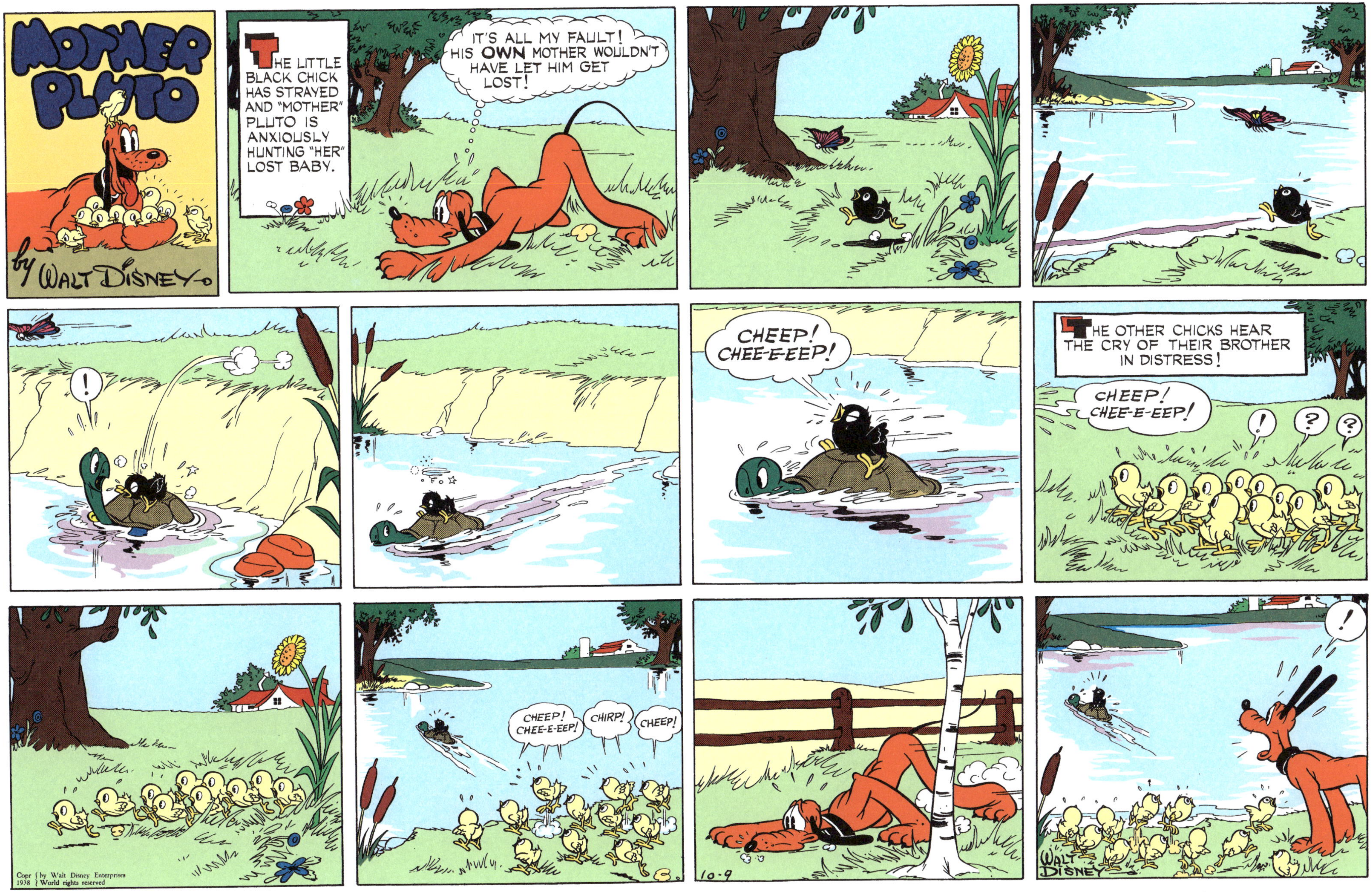
MOTHER PLUTO
by WALT DISNEY
THE LITTLE BLACK CHICK HAS STRAYED AND "MOTHER" PLUTO IS ANXIOUSLY HUNTING "HER" LOST BABY.
IT'S ALL MY FAULT! HIS OWN MOTHER WOULDN'T HAVE LET HIM GET LOST!
!
CHEEP! CHEE-E-EEP!
THE OTHER CHICKS HEAR THE CRY OF THEIR BROTHER IN DISTRESS!
CHEEP! CHEE-E-EEP!
!
?
?
Copr 1938 by Walt Disney Enterprises World rights reserved
CHEEP! CHEE-E-EEP!
CHIRP!
CHEEP!
10-9
!
WALT DISNEY

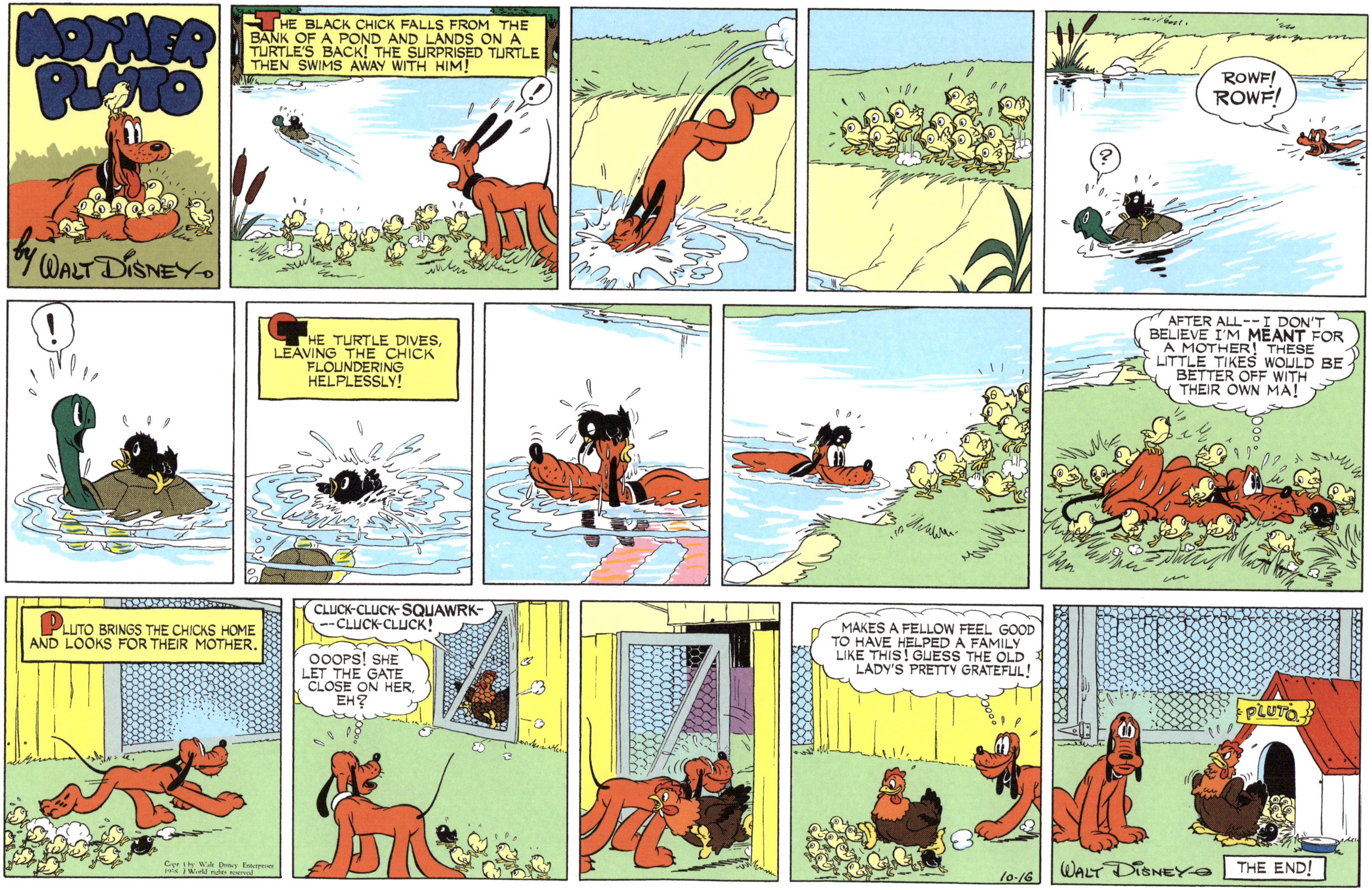
MOTHER PLUTO
by WALT DISNEY
THE BLACK CHICK FALLS FROM THE BANK OF A POND AND LANDS ON A TURTLE'S BACK! THE SURPRISED TURTLE THEN SWIMS AWAY WITH HIM!
!
ROWF! ROWF!
?
!
THE TURTLE DIVES, LEAVING THE CHICK FLOUNDERING HELPLESSLY!
AFTER ALL-- I DON'T BELIEVE I'M MEANT FOR A MOTHER! THESE LITTLE TIKES WOULD BE BETTER OFF WITH THEIR OWN MA!
PLUTO BRINGS THE CHICKS HOME AND LOOKS FOR THEIR MOTHER.
Copr 1938 by Walt Disney Enterprises World rights reserved
CLUCK-CLUCK-SQUAWRK- --CLUCK-CLUCK!
OOOPS! SHE LET THE GATE CLOSE ON HER, EH?
MAKES A FELLOW FEEL GOOD TO HAVE HELPED A FAMILY LIKE THIS! GUESS THE OLD LADY'S PRETTY GRATEFUL!
10-16
PLUTO
WALT DISNEY
THE END!

SILLY SYMPHONIES

THE FARMYARD SYMPHONY

October 23 - November 27, 1938
Written by Merrill de Maris, drawn by Al Taliaferro

Farmyard Symphony, one of the last entries in the *Silly Symphony* series, is a lovely film with practically no plot. Its premise is simple: the animals and people on a farm go about their daily routines while vocalizing, and accompanied by, classical music and operatic themes—a charming cinematic device, but unpromising material for a comic strip. Writer Merrill de Maris seizes on a running gag from the film, a hungry piglet's search for food, and expands it into a short (only six weeks) comic continuity, published concurrently with the film's release. Here the piglet is given distinctive markings and a name, and becomes the protagonist of the story.

By 1938 the Disney animation studio had grown so proficient that there was no single "Disney style"—each new film displayed a visual and storytelling approach tailored to the specific story and characters at hand. The *Silly Symphony* comics reflected the same versatility: the narrative style of one story might be discarded and replaced for the next one. Here the graphic format of "Mother Pluto"—predominantly visual, with only an occasional narrative comment or thought balloon—gives way to a quasi-storybook, with explanatory, and heavily moralizing, text in every panel. Al Taliaferro, too, maintains the impressive facility of his draftsmanship. *Farmyard Symphony*, the film, is distinguished partly by the lifelike appearance and movement of its animal characters; some of the same artists who would soon be working on *Bambi* sharpened their skills by animating the farmyard animals. Here Taliaferro keeps pace, rendering not only the pigs, but the other animals and the farmer, as they appear on the screen.

BEGINNING
"THE FARMYARD SYMPHONY"
BY WALT DISNEY
ONCE UPON A TIME, THERE LIVED IN A FARMYARD A MOTHER PIG AND HER FAMILY OF SIX LITTLE PIGLETS.
FIVE OF THESE PIGLETS WERE ALL PLAIN-COLORED, BUT THE SIXTH ONE HAD SPOTS ON HIS BACK.
FOR THIS REASON, HIS MOTHER HAD NAMED HIM SPOTTY.
WHEREAS HIS BROTHERS AND SISTERS WERE AS WELL-BEHAVED AS THEY COULD BE,
SPOTTY WAS AN ILL-MANNERED, GREEDY LITTLE FELLOW,
WHO WAS ALWAYS GETTING INTO TROUBLE!
HIS MOTHER DID HER BEST TO TRAIN HER CHILDREN AND KEEP THEM FROM ACTING TOO MUCH LIKE LITTLE PIGS!
!
BUT IN SPITE OF EVERYTHING,---
10-23
Copr. by Walt Disney Enterprises 1938 World rights reserved
---SPOTTY SEEMED TO HAVE A NATURAL GIFT FOR DOING WHAT HE SHOULDN'T DO!
CONTINUED.
WALT DISNEY

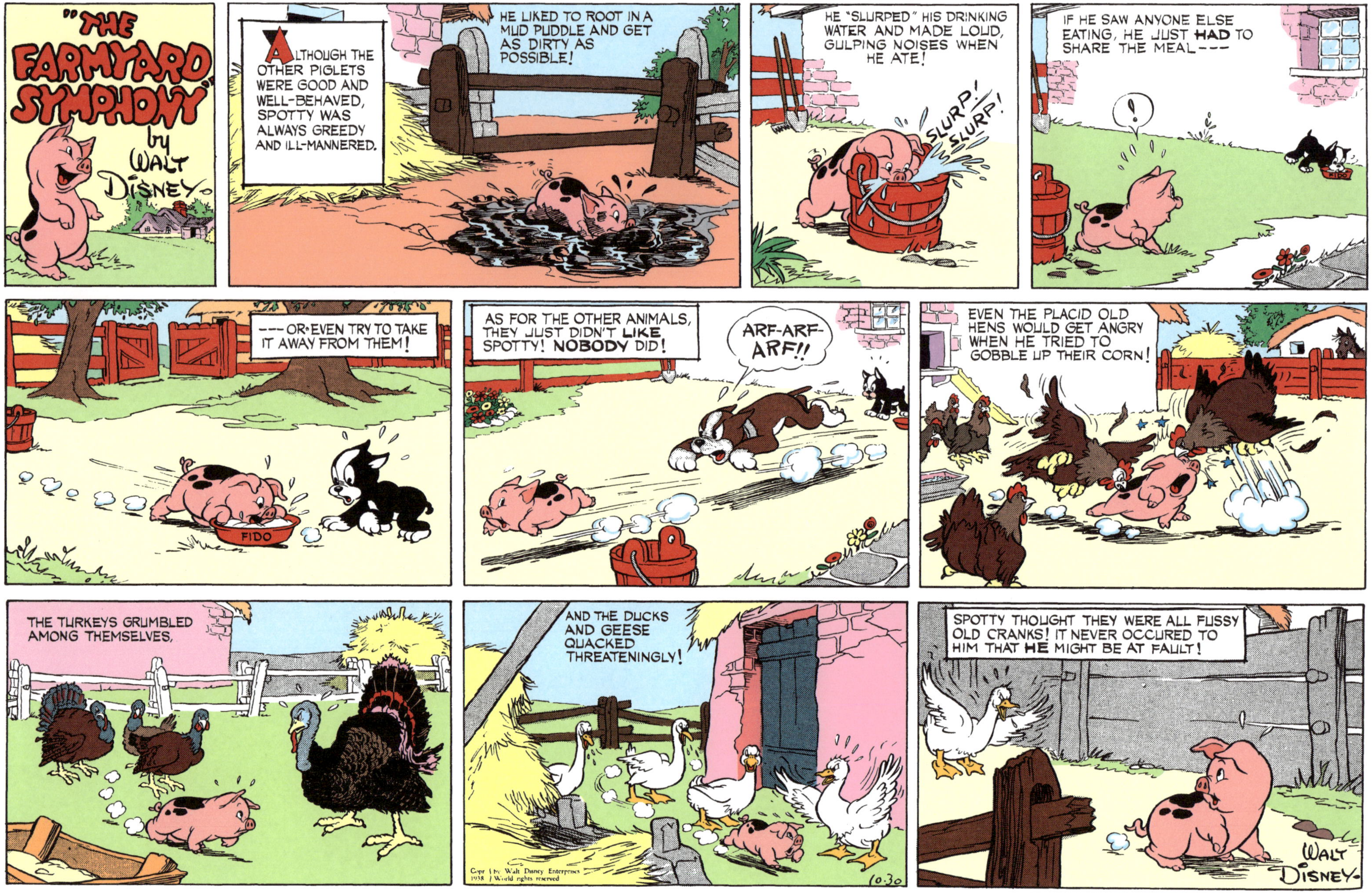
"THE FARMYARD SYMPHONY"
by WALT DISNEY
ALTHOUGH THE OTHER PIGLETS WERE GOOD AND WELL-BEHAVED, SPOTTY WAS ALWAYS GREEDY AND ILL-MANNERED.
HE LIKED TO ROOT IN A MUD PUDDLE AND GET AS DIRTY AS POSSIBLE!
HE "SLURPED" HIS DRINKING WATER AND MADE LOUD, GULPING NOISES WHEN HE ATE!
SLURP! SLURP!
IF HE SAW ANYONE ELSE EATING, HE JUST HAD TO SHARE THE MEAL---
!
FIDO
---OR EVEN TRY TO TAKE IT AWAY FROM THEM!
FIDO
AS FOR THE OTHER ANIMALS, THEY JUST DIDN'T LIKE SPOTTY! NOBODY DID!
ARF-ARF-ARF!!
EVEN THE PLACID OLD HENS WOULD GET ANGRY WHEN HE TRIED TO GOBBLE UP THEIR CORN!
THE TURKEYS GRUMBLED AMONG THEMSELVES,
AND THE DUCKS AND GEESE QUACKED THREATENINGLY!
Copr 1938 by Walt Disney Enterprises / World rights reserved
10-30
SPOTTY THOUGHT THEY WERE ALL FUSSY OLD CRANKS! IT NEVER OCCURED TO HIM THAT HE MIGHT BE AT FAULT!
WALT DISNEY

"The Farmyard Symphony" by Walt Disney

Panel 1: Spotty, the greedy little pig, was always so busy trying to get more than his share, that he never enjoyed what he had! One day at dinnertime---

Panel 2: ---Spotty nudged and pushed the others away from the trough! He thought they always got more than he did!

Panel 3: Then he saw the cows and horses munching contentedly and was sure they must have something extra special for dinner!

Panel 4: That was why they were so happy and contented, while he was still hungry---

Panel 5: ---Terribly hungry!

Panel 6: So, heedless of his mother's warning, Spotty nosed his way in where he shouldn't and, as usual---
OINK! OINK! OINK! OINK!

Panel 7: ---was thrown out before he had a single bite of food!

Panel 8: He finally got enough of being cuffed around and went back to his own meal.

Panel 9: But, alas--he was too late! Dinner was over!

Panel 10: Spotty complained in a loud, whining voice! But, of course, it was his own fault, as his mother told him!
O-I-N-K?
UNK-UNK-UNKH!

Panel 11: Just the same, Spotty sulked and felt very much abused. He decided to leave this mean old farmyard---

Panel 12: ---and find a more friendly place where a little pig would be treated right!

CONTINUED.

"THE FARMYARD SYMPHONY"
by WALT DISNEY
ALTHOUGH LIVING IN THE VERY NICEST FARMYARD ANY PIG COULD ASK FOR, SPOTTY WAS NEVER SATISFIED! SO ONE DAY HE CRAWLED THROUGH A HOLE IN THE FENCE AND RAN AWAY!
HE TROTTED ALONG A LITTLE LANE THAT RAN ACROSS THE BIG WORLD OUTSIDE THE FARMYARD---
---HIS MIND BUSY WITH THOUGHTS OF FINDING A NEW HOME, WHERE A PIGLET COULD EAT AND EAT ALL DAY LONG---
---AND MAYBE PART OF THE NIGHT, TOO!
SPOTTY'S MOTHER HAD MISSED HIM, ESPECIALLY AT MEALTIME, WHICH WAS SO MUCH QUIETER AND MORE PEACEFUL THAN USUAL.
SHE THOUGHT HE WAS AROUND THE FARMYARD SOMEWHERE AND SADLY WONDERED WHAT MISCHIEF THE LITTLE GLUTTON WAS INTO.
IN THE MEANTIME, SPOTTY, HIS APPETITE GROWING WITH EVERY STEP, CAME SUDDENLY UPON A HUGE FIELD OF CORN---MILES AND MILES OF IT!
NOW FRESH GREEN CORN WAS SPOTTY'S SPECIAL DELIGHT AND HERE WAS FAR MORE THAN HE HAD EVER DREAMED OF!
WHEN HE FIRST BEGAN TO EAT, HE WORRIED A LITTLE ABOUT THE EARS THAT WERE TOO HIGH TO REACH.
Copr. 1938 by Walt Disney Enterprises World rights reserved
11-13
BUT AFTER A WHILE HE WAS PRETTY SURE THAT THERE WOULD BE ENOUGH LOW ONES TO FILL HIM UP.
STILL LATER, IT OCCURRED TO HIM THAT HE OUGHT TO SAVE A FEW FOR TOMORROW, ANYWAY!
CONTINUED

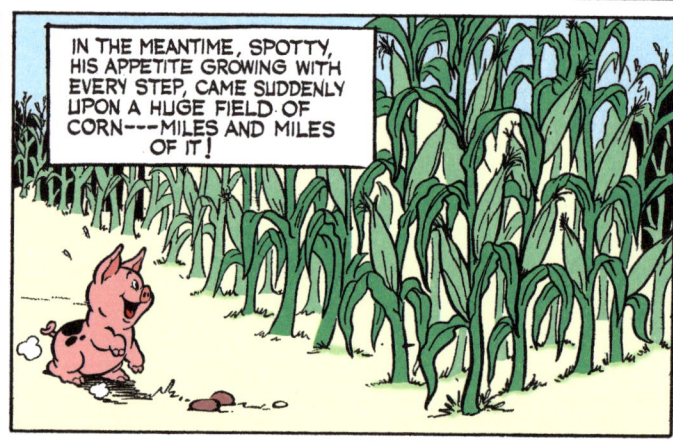

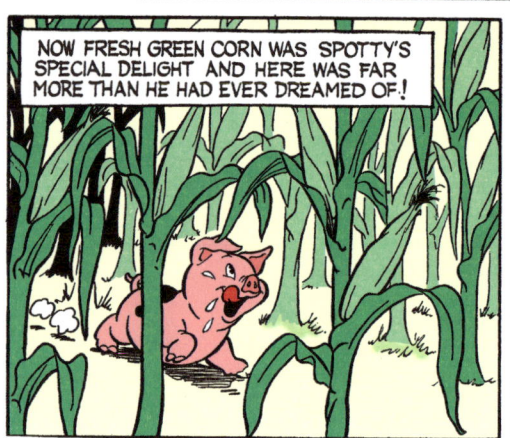

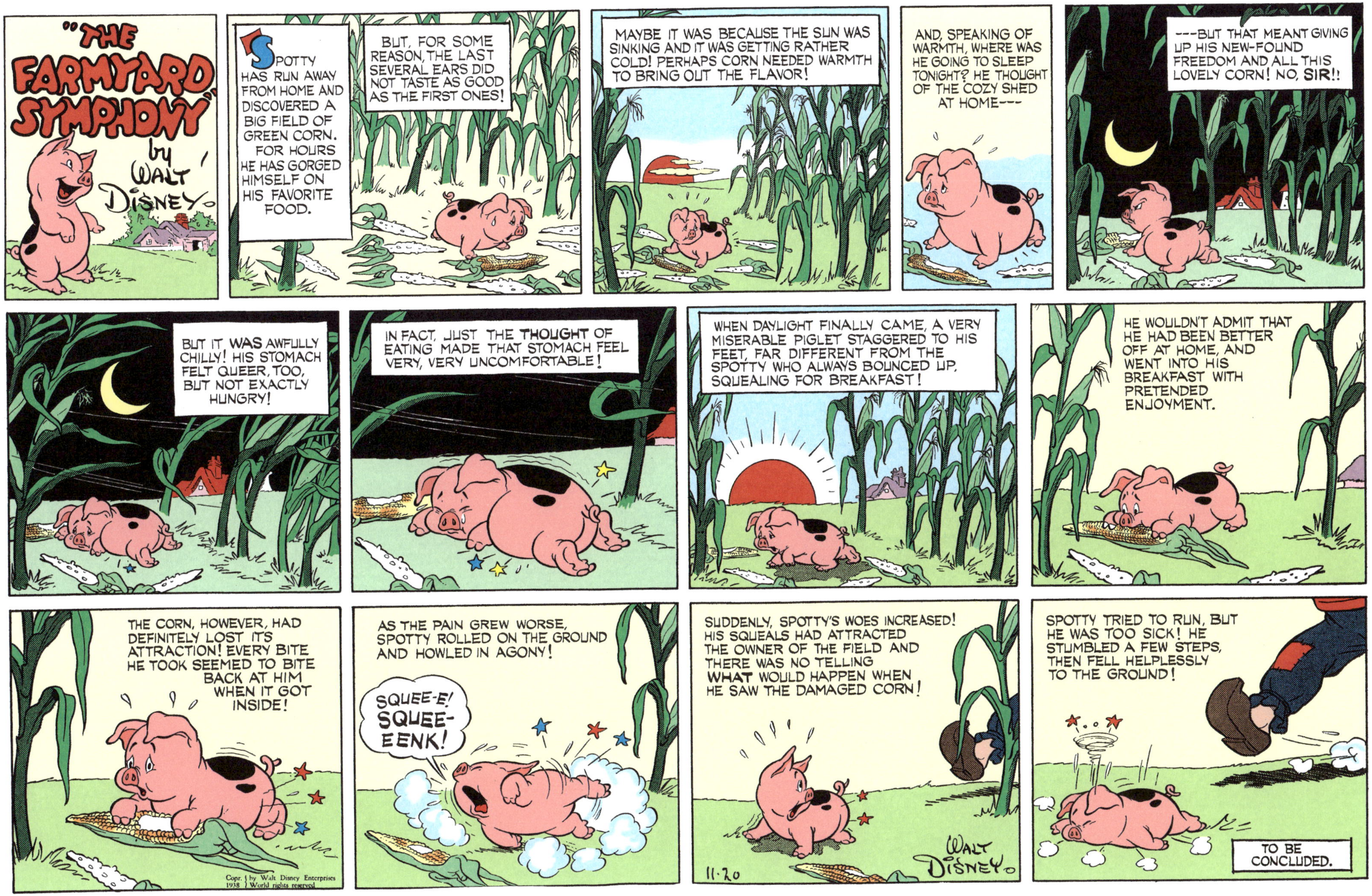
"THE FARMYARD SYMPHONY"
by WALT DISNEY
SPOTTY HAS RUN AWAY FROM HOME AND DISCOVERED A BIG FIELD OF GREEN CORN. FOR HOURS HE HAS GORGED HIMSELF ON HIS FAVORITE FOOD.
BUT, FOR SOME REASON, THE LAST SEVERAL EARS DID NOT TASTE AS GOOD AS THE FIRST ONES!
MAYBE IT WAS BECAUSE THE SUN WAS SINKING AND IT WAS GETTING RATHER COLD! PERHAPS CORN NEEDED WARMTH TO BRING OUT THE FLAVOR!
AND, SPEAKING OF WARMTH, WHERE WAS HE GOING TO SLEEP TONIGHT? HE THOUGHT OF THE COZY SHED AT HOME---
---BUT THAT MEANT GIVING UP HIS NEW-FOUND FREEDOM AND ALL THIS LOVELY CORN! NO, SIR!!
BUT IT WAS AWFULLY CHILLY! HIS STOMACH FELT QUEER, TOO, BUT NOT EXACTLY HUNGRY!
IN FACT, JUST THE THOUGHT OF EATING MADE THAT STOMACH FEEL VERY, VERY UNCOMFORTABLE!
WHEN DAYLIGHT FINALLY CAME, A VERY MISERABLE PIGLET STAGGERED TO HIS FEET, FAR DIFFERENT FROM THE SPOTTY WHO ALWAYS BOUNCED UP, SQUEALING FOR BREAKFAST!
HE WOULDN'T ADMIT THAT HE HAD BEEN BETTER OFF AT HOME, AND WENT INTO HIS BREAKFAST WITH PRETENDED ENJOYMENT.
THE CORN, HOWEVER, HAD DEFINITELY LOST ITS ATTRACTION! EVERY BITE HE TOOK SEEMED TO BITE BACK AT HIM WHEN IT GOT INSIDE!
Copr. 1938 by Walt Disney Enterprises World rights reserved
AS THE PAIN GREW WORSE, SPOTTY ROLLED ON THE GROUND AND HOWLED IN AGONY!
SQUEE-E! SQUEE-EENK!
SUDDENLY, SPOTTY'S WOES INCREASED! HIS SQUEALS HAD ATTRACTED THE OWNER OF THE FIELD AND THERE WAS NO TELLING WHAT WOULD HAPPEN WHEN HE SAW THE DAMAGED CORN!
11·20
WALT DISNEY
SPOTTY TRIED TO RUN, BUT HE WAS TOO SICK! HE STUMBLED A FEW STEPS, THEN FELL HELPLESSLY TO THE GROUND!
TO BE CONCLUDED.

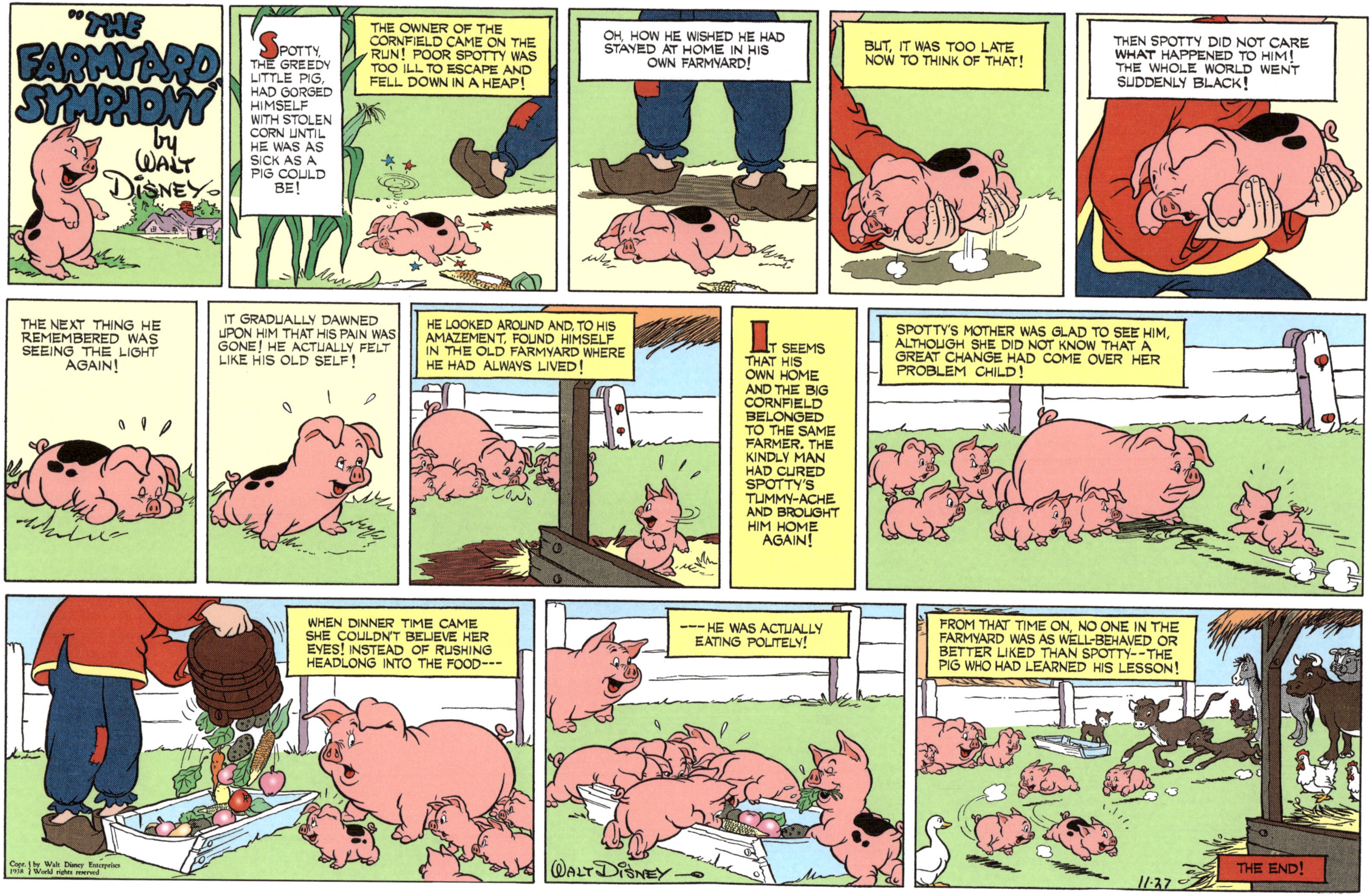
"THE FARMYARD SYMPHONY"
by WALT DISNEY
SPOTTY, THE GREEDY LITTLE PIG, HAD GORGED HIMSELF WITH STOLEN CORN UNTIL HE WAS AS SICK AS A PIG COULD BE!
THE OWNER OF THE CORNFIELD CAME ON THE RUN! POOR SPOTTY WAS TOO ILL TO ESCAPE AND FELL DOWN IN A HEAP!
OH, HOW HE WISHED HE HAD STAYED AT HOME IN HIS OWN FARMYARD!
BUT, IT WAS TOO LATE NOW TO THINK OF THAT!
THEN SPOTTY DID NOT CARE WHAT HAPPENED TO HIM! THE WHOLE WORLD WENT SUDDENLY BLACK!
THE NEXT THING HE REMEMBERED WAS SEEING THE LIGHT AGAIN!
IT GRADUALLY DAWNED UPON HIM THAT HIS PAIN WAS GONE! HE ACTUALLY FELT LIKE HIS OLD SELF!
HE LOOKED AROUND AND, TO HIS AMAZEMENT, FOUND HIMSELF IN THE OLD FARMYARD WHERE HE HAD ALWAYS LIVED!
IT SEEMS THAT HIS OWN HOME AND THE BIG CORNFIELD BELONGED TO THE SAME FARMER. THE KINDLY MAN HAD CURED SPOTTY'S TUMMY-ACHE AND BROUGHT HIM HOME AGAIN!
SPOTTY'S MOTHER WAS GLAD TO SEE HIM, ALTHOUGH SHE DID NOT KNOW THAT A GREAT CHANGE HAD COME OVER HER PROBLEM CHILD!
WHEN DINNER TIME CAME SHE COULDN'T BELIEVE HER EYES! INSTEAD OF RUSHING HEADLONG INTO THE FOOD---
Copr. 1938 by Walt Disney Enterprises World rights reserved
---HE WAS ACTUALLY EATING POLITELY!
WALT DISNEY
FROM THAT TIME ON, NO ONE IN THE FARMYARD WAS AS WELL-BEHAVED OR BETTER LIKED THAN SPOTTY--THE PIG WHO HAD LEARNED HIS LESSON!
11-27
THE END!

SILLY SYMPHONIES

TIMID ELMER

December 4, 1938 - February 12, 1939
Written by Merrill de Maris, drawn by Al Taliaferro

The concluding story in this volume is a historical treasure, based on a film that was planned but unfinished. Three years had passed since Disney fans had enjoyed *Elmer Elephant* and its comic adaptation, reproduced earlier in these pages. Now the studio story department planned to continue the little elephant's story in a sequel, "Timid Elmer." The film project was abandoned before completion, but its story, as adapted for the comics, is presented here.

Exactly what those adaptations were, we can only speculate. Like the earlier 1935-36 continuity, this one centers on the theme of Elmer's bravery or lack of it. The 1936 film had *not* concerned itself with questions of Elmer's courage, but production papers suggest that the sequel was planned along those lines. Taliaferro's art depicts the world of Elmer Elephant with seemingly effortless ease, even to reproducing specific poses that suggest scenes in the original film. Elmer and Tillie Tiger are back again, of course, as are the bullying kids (and a vicious bunch they are, too). There's also an appearance by the kindly old giraffe who had figured in the 1936 film. The giraffe had not appeared in the first comic continuity, but he takes a key role here.

What's perhaps even more interesting is the device introduced by the giraffe: the "magic acorn," a talisman that makes Elmer invincible because he *believes* it gives him special powers. Elmer never did return to the screen, but another little elephant did: in June 1939—a few months after this continuity appeared in newspapers—the Disney studio secured the rights to the story that would be produced as *Dumbo*. As developed for the screen, a key plot element in *Dumbo* is the "magic feather," an object that convinces Dumbo of his ability to fly. In the end, of course, both Elmer and Dumbo learn that those "magic" charms were only psychological props and that they had those powers all along. Historically fascinating in itself, Timid Elmer's story is also notable for its connections in the larger picture of Disney history.

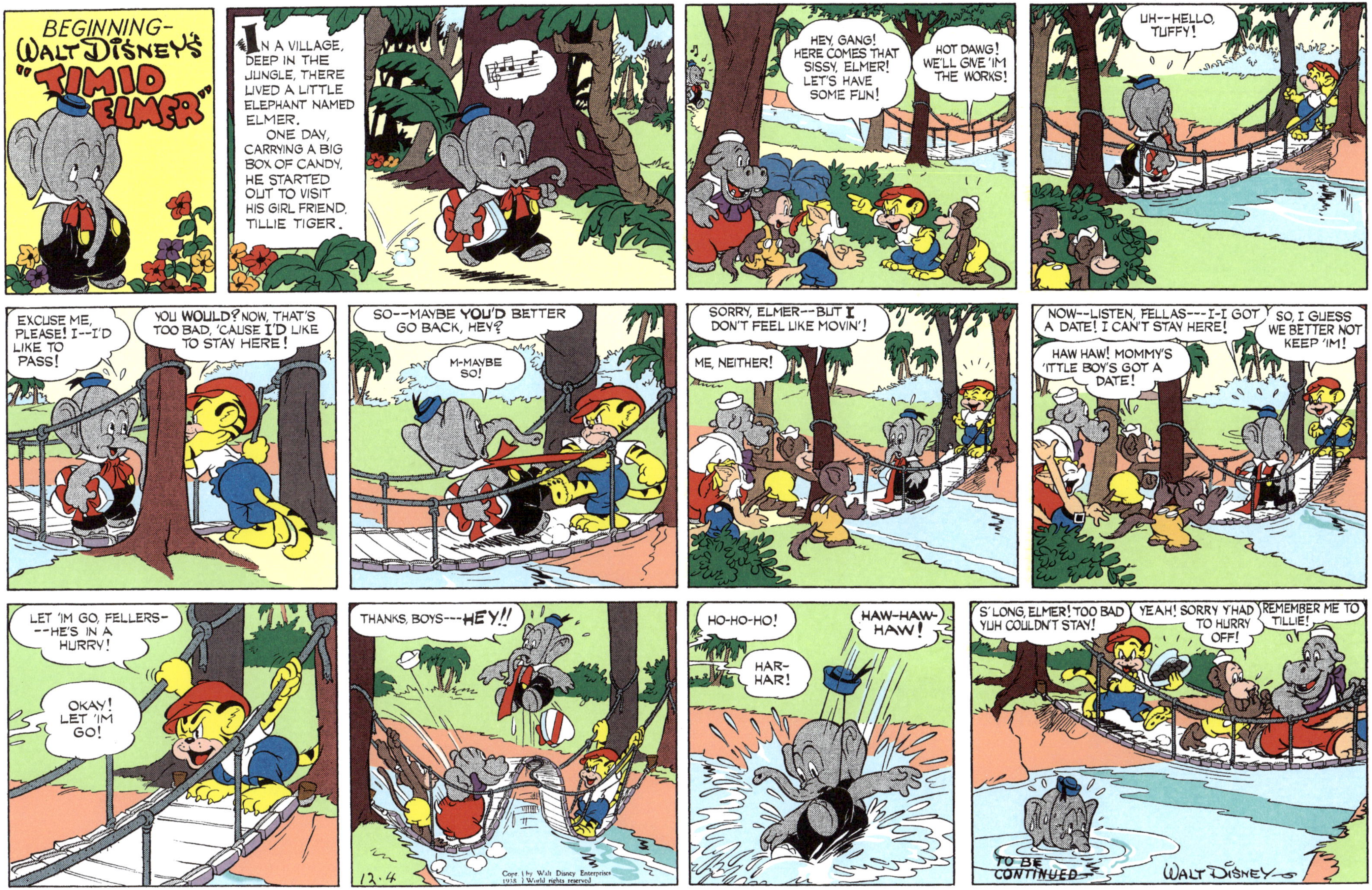
BEGINNING-
WALT DISNEY'S "TIMID ELMER"
IN A VILLAGE, DEEP IN THE JUNGLE, THERE LIVED A LITTLE ELEPHANT NAMED ELMER. ONE DAY, CARRYING A BIG BOX OF CANDY, HE STARTED OUT TO VISIT HIS GIRL FRIEND, TILLIE TIGER.
HEY, GANG! HERE COMES THAT SISSY, ELMER! LET'S HAVE SOME FUN!
HOT DAWG! WE'LL GIVE 'IM THE WORKS!
UH--HELLO, TUFFY!
EXCUSE ME, PLEASE! I--I'D LIKE TO PASS!
YOU WOULD? NOW, THAT'S TOO BAD, 'CAUSE I'D LIKE TO STAY HERE!
SO--MAYBE YOU'D BETTER GO BACK, HEY?
M-MAYBE SO!
SORRY, ELMER--BUT I DON'T FEEL LIKE MOVIN'!
ME, NEITHER!
NOW--LISTEN, FELLAS---I-I GOT A DATE! I CAN'T STAY HERE!
HAW HAW! MOMMY'S 'ITTLE BOY'S GOT A DATE!
SO, I GUESS WE BETTER NOT KEEP 'IM!
LET 'IM GO, FELLERS---HE'S IN A HURRY!
OKAY! LET 'IM GO!
THANKS, BOYS---HEY!!
12-4
Copr. 1938 by Walt Disney Enterprises World rights reserved
HO-HO-HO!
HAW-HAW-HAW!
HAR-HAR!
S'LONG, ELMER! TOO BAD YUH COULDN'T STAY!
YEAH! SORRY Y'HAD TO HURRY OFF!
REMEMBER ME TO TILLIE!
TO BE CONTINUED
WALT DISNEY

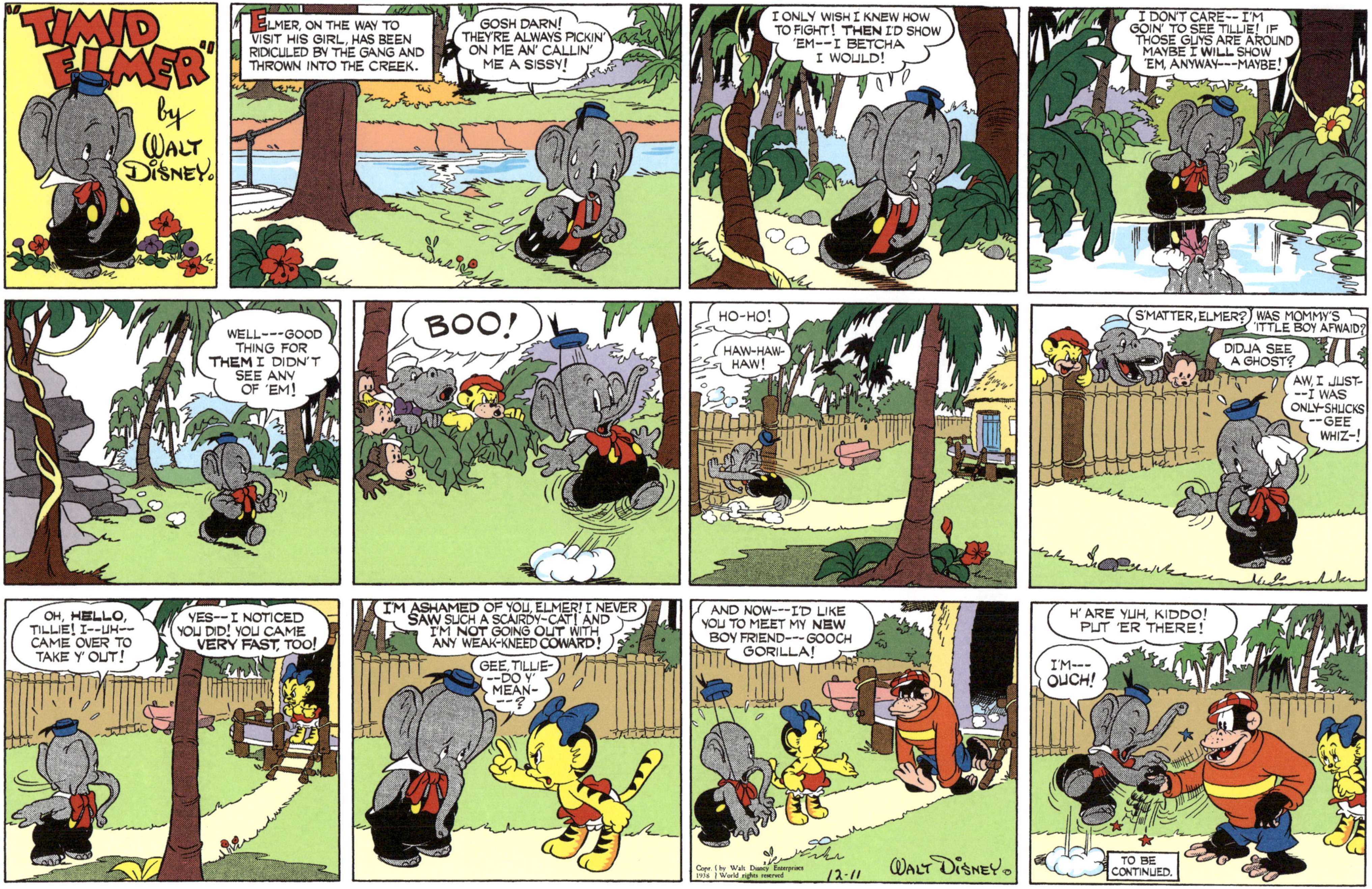
"TIMID ELMER"
by WALT DISNEY
ELMER, ON THE WAY TO VISIT HIS GIRL, HAS BEEN RIDICULED BY THE GANG AND THROWN INTO THE CREEK.
GOSH DARN! THEY'RE ALWAYS PICKIN' ON ME AN' CALLIN' ME A SISSY!
I ONLY WISH I KNEW HOW TO FIGHT! THEN I'D SHOW 'EM--I BETCHA I WOULD!
I DON'T CARE--I'M GOIN' TO SEE TILLIE! IF THOSE GUYS ARE AROUND MAYBE I WILL SHOW 'EM, ANYWAY---MAYBE!
WELL---GOOD THING FOR THEM I DIDN'T SEE ANY OF 'EM!
BOO!
HO-HO!
HAW-HAW-HAW!
S'MATTER, ELMER?
WAS MOMMY'S 'ITTLE BOY AFWAID?
DIDJA SEE A GHOST?
AW, I JUST--I WAS ONLY-SHUCKS--GEE WHIZ-!
OH, HELLO, TILLIE! I--UH--CAME OVER TO TAKE Y' OUT!
YES--I NOTICED YOU DID! YOU CAME VERY FAST, TOO!
I'M ASHAMED OF YOU, ELMER! I NEVER SAW SUCH A SCAIRDY-CAT! AND I'M NOT GOING OUT WITH ANY WEAK-KNEED COWARD!
GEE, TILLIE--DO Y' MEAN--?
AND NOW---I'D LIKE YOU TO MEET MY NEW BOY FRIEND---GOOCH GORILLA!
Copr. 1938 by Walt Disney Enterprises World rights reserved
12-11
WALT DISNEY
H' ARE YUH, KIDDO! PUT 'ER THERE!
I'M---OUCH!
TO BE CONTINUED.

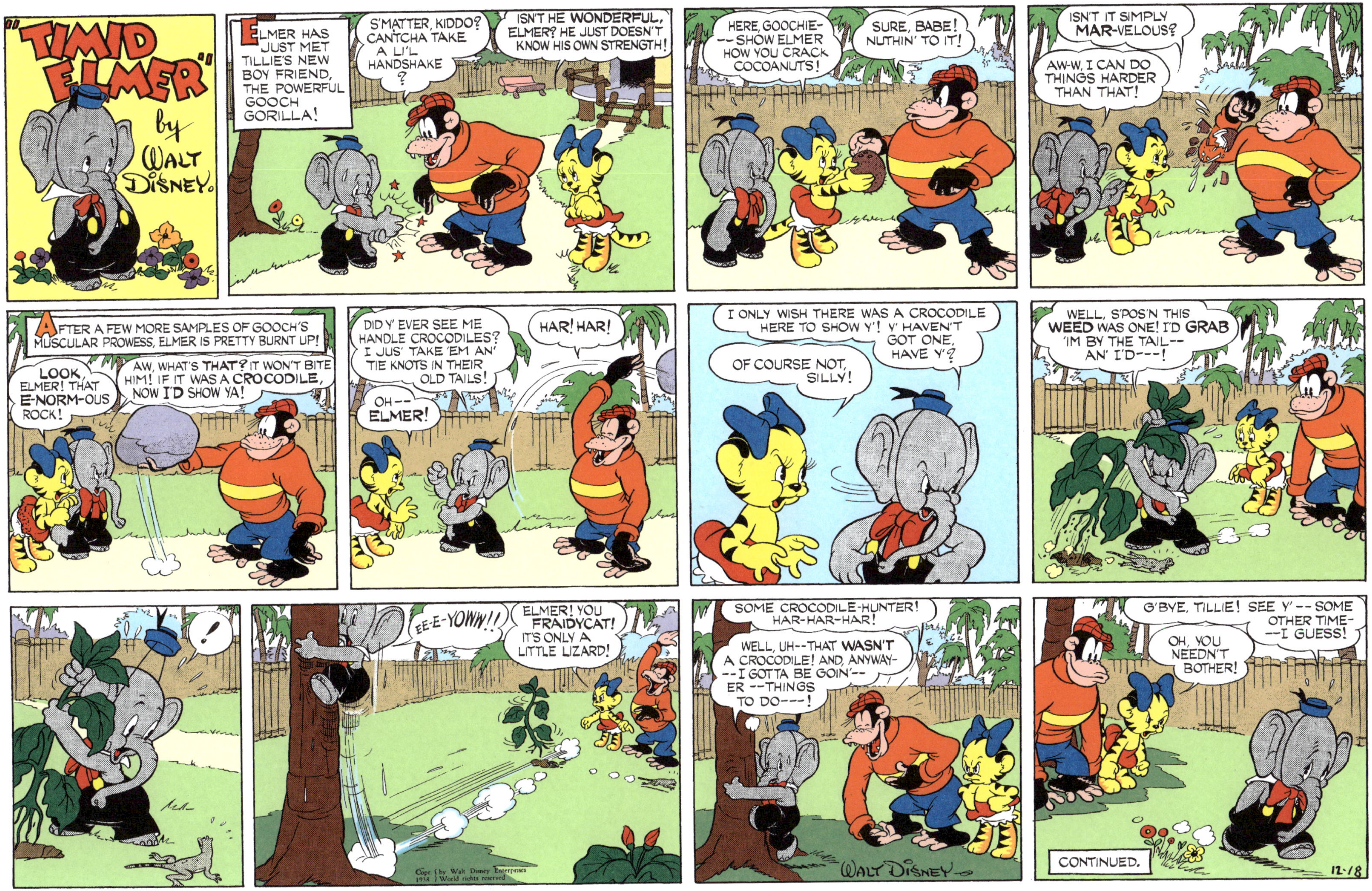
"TIMID ELMER"
by WALT DISNEY
ELMER HAS JUST MET TILLIE'S NEW BOY FRIEND, THE POWERFUL GOOCH GORILLA!
S'MATTER, KIDDO? CAN'TCHA TAKE A LI'L HANDSHAKE ?
ISN'T HE WONDERFUL, ELMER? HE JUST DOESN'T KNOW HIS OWN STRENGTH!
HERE, GOOCHIE--SHOW ELMER HOW YOU CRACK COCOANUTS!
SURE, BABE! NUTHIN' TO IT!
ISN'T IT SIMPLY MAR-VELOUS?
AW-W, I CAN DO THINGS HARDER THAN THAT!
AFTER A FEW MORE SAMPLES OF GOOCH'S MUSCULAR PROWESS, ELMER IS PRETTY BURNT UP!
LOOK, ELMER! THAT E-NORM-OUS ROCK!
AW, WHAT'S THAT? IT WON'T BITE HIM! IF IT WAS A CROCODILE, NOW I'D SHOW YA!
DID Y' EVER SEE ME HANDLE CROCODILES? I JUS' TAKE 'EM AN' TIE KNOTS IN THEIR OLD TAILS!
HAR! HAR!
OH-- ELMER!
I ONLY WISH THERE WAS A CROCODILE HERE TO SHOW Y'! Y' HAVEN'T GOT ONE, HAVE Y'?
OF COURSE NOT, SILLY!
WELL, S'POS'N THIS WEED WAS ONE! I'D GRAB 'IM BY THE TAIL-- AN' I'D---!
!
EE-E-YOWW!!
ELMER! YOU FRAIDYCAT! IT'S ONLY A LITTLE LIZARD!
Copr. by Walt Disney Enterprises 1938 World rights reserved
SOME CROCODILE-HUNTER! HAR-HAR-HAR!
WELL, UH--THAT WASN'T A CROCODILE! AND, ANYWAY---I GOTTA BE GOIN'-- ER --THINGS TO DO---!
WALT DISNEY
G'BYE, TILLIE! SEE Y'--SOME OTHER TIME---I GUESS!
OH, YOU NEEDN'T BOTHER!
CONTINUED.
12-18

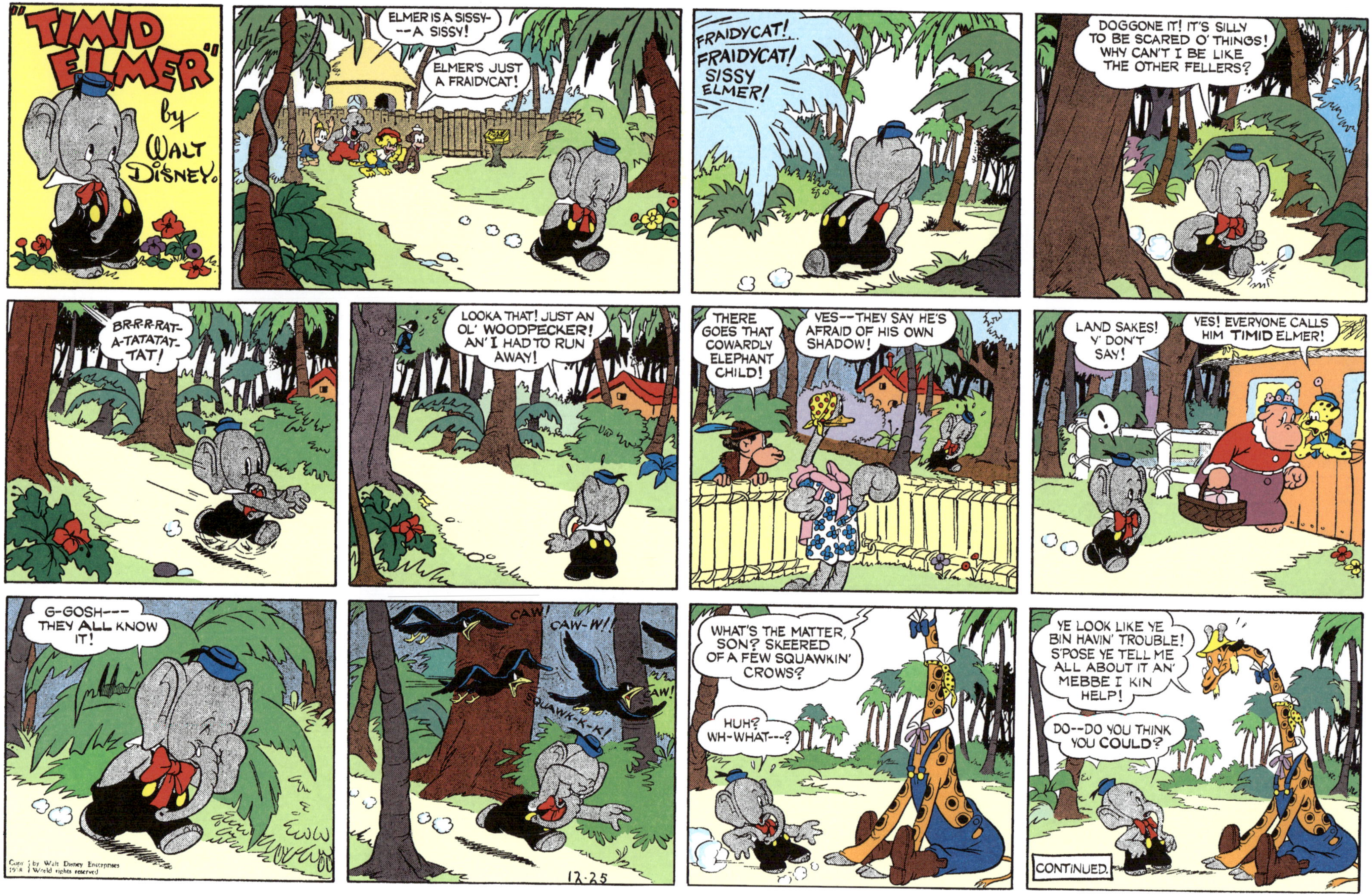
"TIMID ELMER"
by WALT DISNEY
ELMER IS A SISSY--A SISSY!
ELMER'S JUST A FRAIDYCAT!
FRAIDYCAT! FRAIDYCAT! SISSY ELMER!
DOGGONE IT! IT'S SILLY TO BE SCARED O' THINGS! WHY CAN'T I BE LIKE THE OTHER FELLERS?
BR-R-R-RAT-A-TATATAT-TAT!
LOOKA THAT! JUST AN OL' WOODPECKER! AN' I HAD TO RUN AWAY!
THERE GOES THAT COWARDLY ELEPHANT CHILD!
YES--THEY SAY HE'S AFRAID OF HIS OWN SHADOW!
LAND SAKES! Y' DON'T SAY!
YES! EVERYONE CALLS HIM TIMID ELMER!
G-GOSH--- THEY ALL KNOW IT!
Copr. 1938 by Walt Disney Enterprises World rights reserved
CAW!
CAW-W!
CAW!
SQUAWK-K-K!
12-25
WHAT'S THE MATTER, SON? SKEERED OF A FEW SQUAWKIN' CROWS?
HUH? WH-WHAT---?
YE LOOK LIKE YE BIN HAVIN' TROUBLE! S'POSE YE TELL ME ALL ABOUT IT AN' MEBBE I KIN HELP!
DO--DO YOU THINK YOU COULD?
CONTINUED.

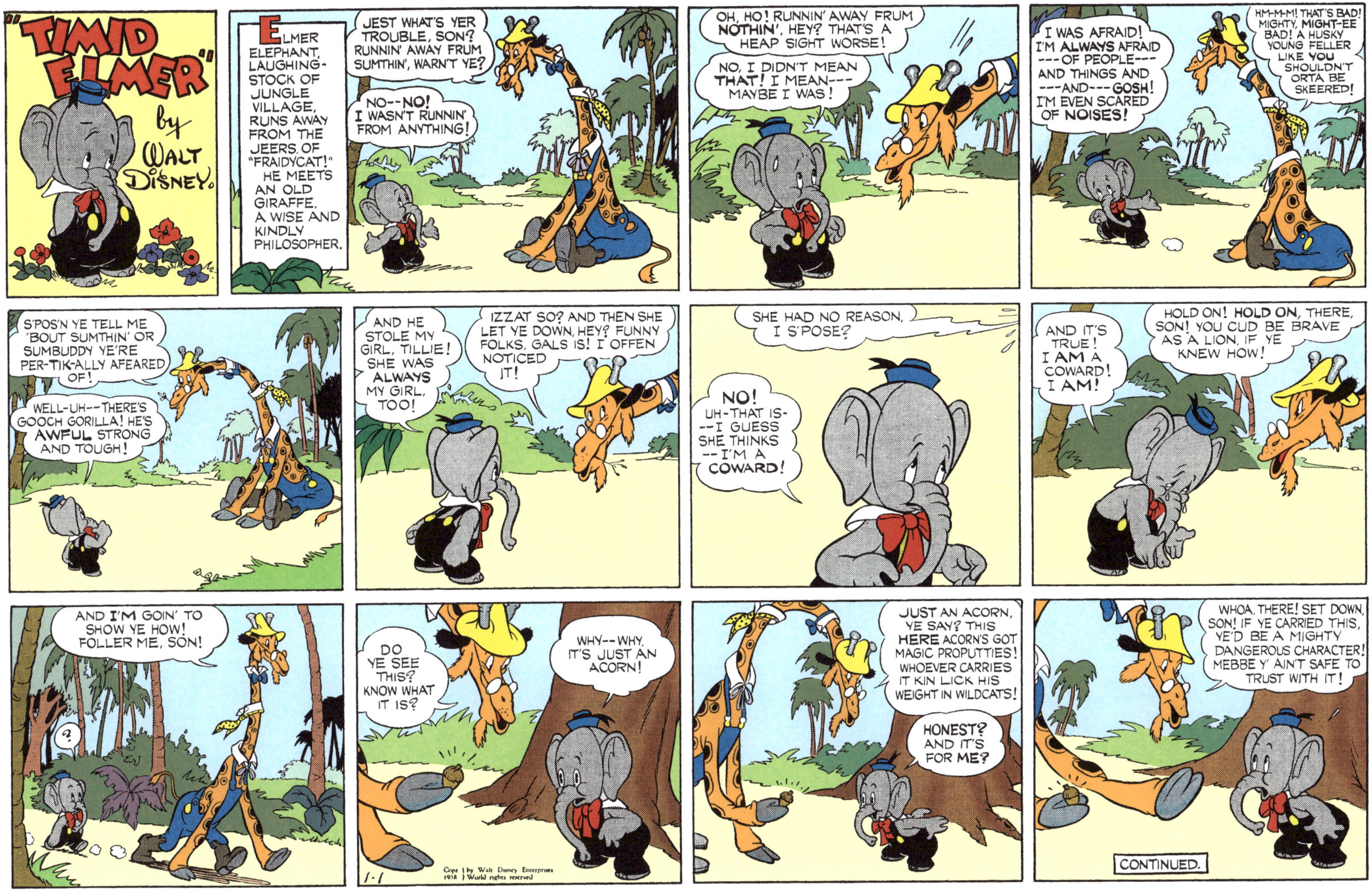

"TIMID ELMER"
by WALT DISNEY
ELMER ELEPHANT, LAUGHING-STOCK OF JUNGLE VILLAGE, RUNS AWAY FROM THE JEERS OF "FRAIDYCAT!" HE MEETS AN OLD GIRAFFE, A WISE AND KINDLY PHILOSOPHER.
JEST WHAT'S YER TROUBLE, SON? RUNNIN' AWAY FRUM SUMTHIN', WARN'T YE?
NO--NO! I WASN'T RUNNIN' FROM ANYTHING!
OH, HO! RUNNIN' AWAY FRUM NOTHIN', HEY? THAT'S A HEAP SIGHT WORSE!
NO, I DIDN'T MEAN THAT! I MEAN--- MAYBE I WAS!
I WAS AFRAID! I'M ALWAYS AFRAID ---OF PEOPLE--- AND THINGS AND ---AND---GOSH! I'M EVEN SCARED OF NOISES!
HM-M-M! THAT'S BAD! MIGHTY, MIGHT-EE BAD! A HUSKY YOUNG FELLER LIKE YOU SHOULDN'T ORTA BE SKEERED!
S'POS'N YE TELL ME 'BOUT SUMTHIN' OR SUMBUDDY YE'RE PER-TIK-ALLY AFEARED OF!
WELL-UH--THERE'S GOOCH GORILLA! HE'S AWFUL STRONG AND TOUGH!
AND HE STOLE MY GIRL, TILLIE! SHE WAS ALWAYS MY GIRL, TOO!
IZZAT SO? AND THEN SHE LET YE DOWN, HEY? FUNNY FOLKS, GALS IS! I OFFEN NOTICED IT!
SHE HAD NO REASON, I S'POSE?
NO! UH-THAT IS- --I GUESS SHE THINKS --I'M A COWARD!
AND IT'S TRUE! I AM A COWARD! I AM!
HOLD ON! HOLD ON, THERE, SON! YOU CUD BE BRAVE AS A LION, IF YE KNEW HOW!
AND I'M GOIN' TO SHOW YE HOW! FOLLER ME, SON!
?
DO YE SEE THIS? KNOW WHAT IT IS?
WHY--WHY, IT'S JUST AN ACORN!
Copr. by Walt Disney Enterprises 1938 World rights reserved
1-1
JUST AN ACORN, YE SAY? THIS HERE ACORN'S GOT MAGIC PROPUTTIES! WHOEVER CARRIES IT KIN LICK HIS WEIGHT IN WILDCATS!
HONEST? AND IT'S FOR ME?
WHOA, THERE! SET DOWN, SON! IF YE CARRIED THIS, YE'D BE A MIGHTY DANGEROUS CHARACTER! MEBBE Y' AIN'T SAFE TO TRUST WITH IT!
CONTINUED.

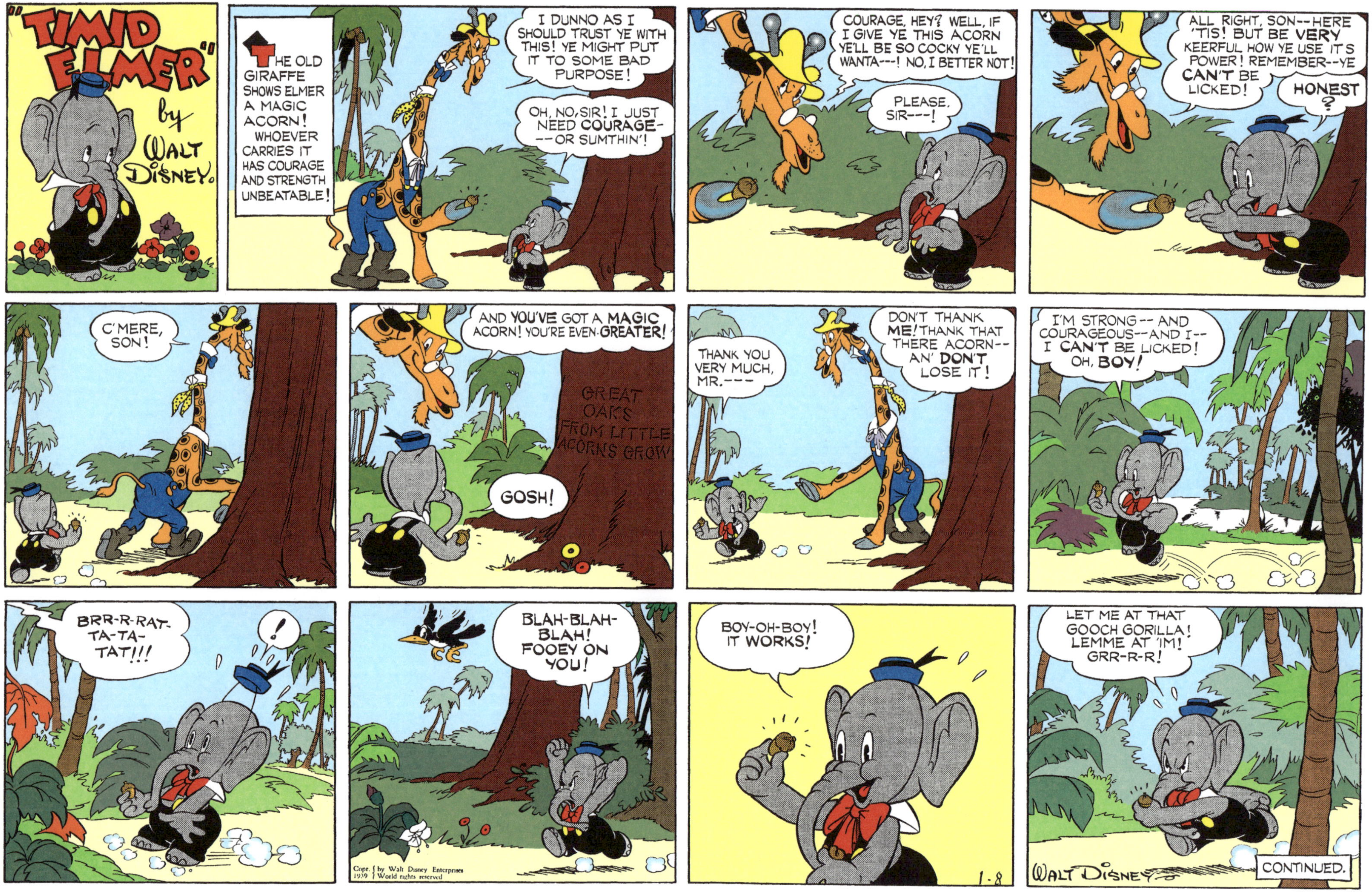

"TIMID ELMER" by WALT DISNEY.
THE OLD GIRAFFE SHOWS ELMER A MAGIC ACORN! WHOEVER CARRIES IT HAS COURAGE AND STRENGTH UNBEATABLE!
I DUNNO AS I SHOULD TRUST YE WITH THIS! YE MIGHT PUT IT TO SOME BAD PURPOSE!
OH, NO, SIR! I JUST NEED COURAGE- --OR SUMTHIN'!
COURAGE, HEY? WELL, IF I GIVE YE THIS ACORN YE'LL BE SO COCKY YE'LL WANTA---! NO, I BETTER NOT!
PLEASE, SIR---!
ALL RIGHT, SON--HERE 'TIS! BUT BE VERY KEERFUL HOW YE USE IT'S POWER! REMEMBER--YE CAN'T BE LICKED!
HONEST ?
C'MERE, SON!
AND YOU'VE GOT A MAGIC ACORN! YOU'RE EVEN GREATER!
GREAT OAKS FROM LITTLE ACORNS GROW
GOSH!
THANK YOU VERY MUCH, MR.---
DON'T THANK ME! THANK THAT THERE ACORN-- AN' DON'T LOSE IT!
I'M STRONG-- AND COURAGEOUS--AND I-- I CAN'T BE LICKED! OH, BOY!
BRR-R-RAT-TA-TA-TAT!!!
!
BLAH-BLAH-BLAH! FOOEY ON YOU!
Copr. 1939 by Walt Disney Enterprises World rights reserved
BOY-OH-BOY! IT WORKS!
1-8
LET ME AT THAT GOOCH GORILLA! LEMME AT 'IM! GRR-R-R!
WALT DISNEY
CONTINUED.

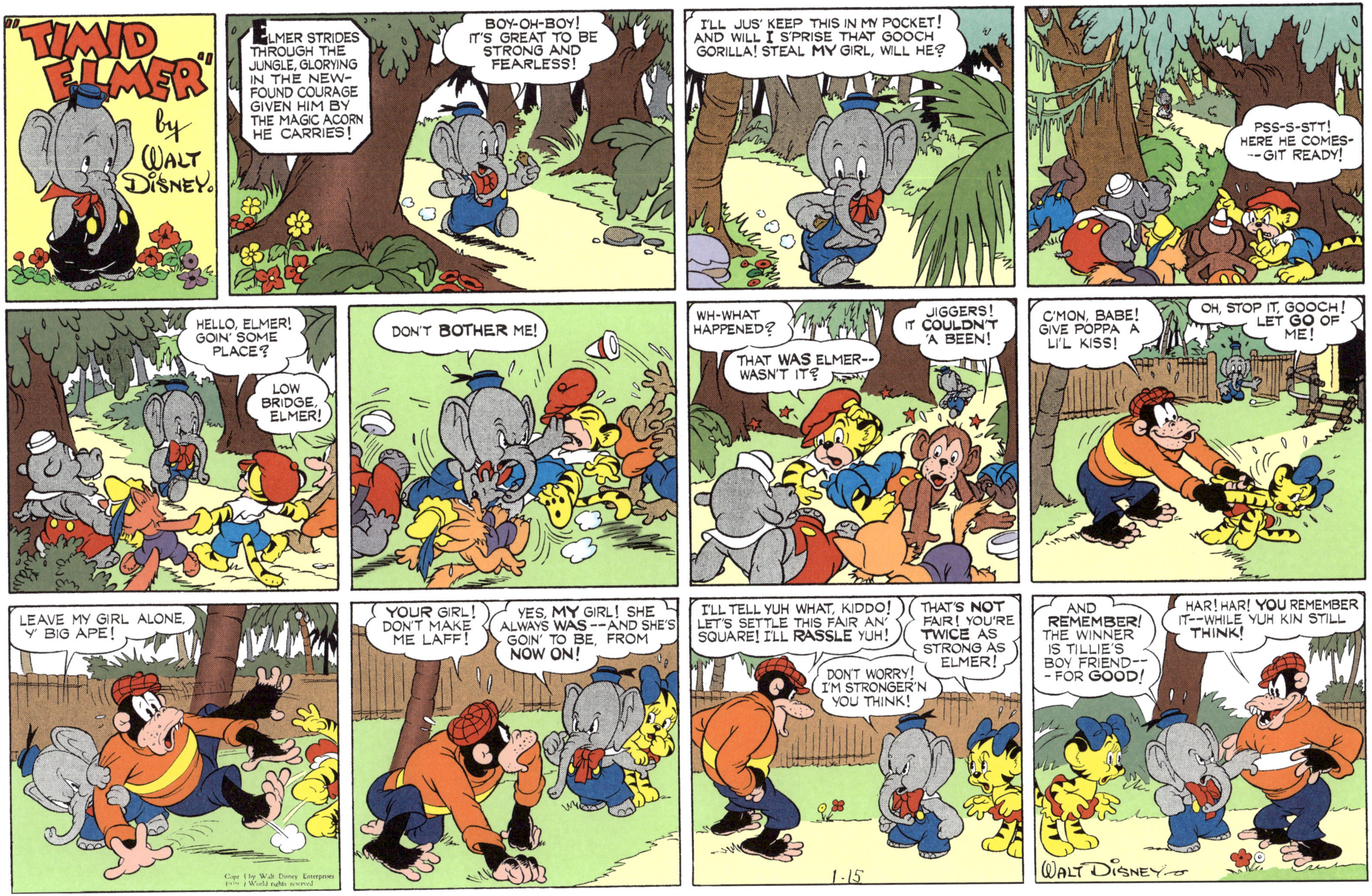

"TIMID ELMER"
by WALT DISNEY
ELMER STRIDES THROUGH THE JUNGLE, GLORYING IN THE NEW-FOUND COURAGE GIVEN HIM BY THE MAGIC ACORN HE CARRIES!
BOY-OH-BOY! IT'S GREAT TO BE STRONG AND FEARLESS!
I'LL JUS' KEEP THIS IN MY POCKET! AND WILL I S'PRISE THAT GOOCH GORILLA! STEAL MY GIRL, WILL HE?
PSS-S-STT! HERE HE COMES--GIT READY!
HELLO, ELMER! GOIN' SOME PLACE?
LOW BRIDGE, ELMER!
DON'T BOTHER ME!
WH-WHAT HAPPENED?
THAT WAS ELMER--WASN'T IT?
JIGGERS! IT COULDN'T 'A BEEN!
C'MON, BABE! GIVE POPPA A LI'L KISS!
OH, STOP IT, GOOCH! LET GO OF ME!
LEAVE MY GIRL ALONE, Y' BIG APE!
YOUR GIRL! DON'T MAKE ME LAFF!
YES, MY GIRL! SHE ALWAYS WAS--AND SHE'S GOIN' TO BE, FROM NOW ON!
I'LL TELL YUH WHAT, KIDDO! LET'S SETTLE THIS FAIR AN' SQUARE! I'LL RASSLE YUH!
THAT'S NOT FAIR! YOU'RE TWICE AS STRONG AS ELMER!
DON'T WORRY! I'M STRONGER'N YOU THINK!
1-15
AND REMEMBER! THE WINNER IS TILLIE'S BOY FRIEND--FOR GOOD!
HAR! HAR! YOU REMEMBER IT--WHILE YUH KIN STILL THINK!
WALT DISNEY

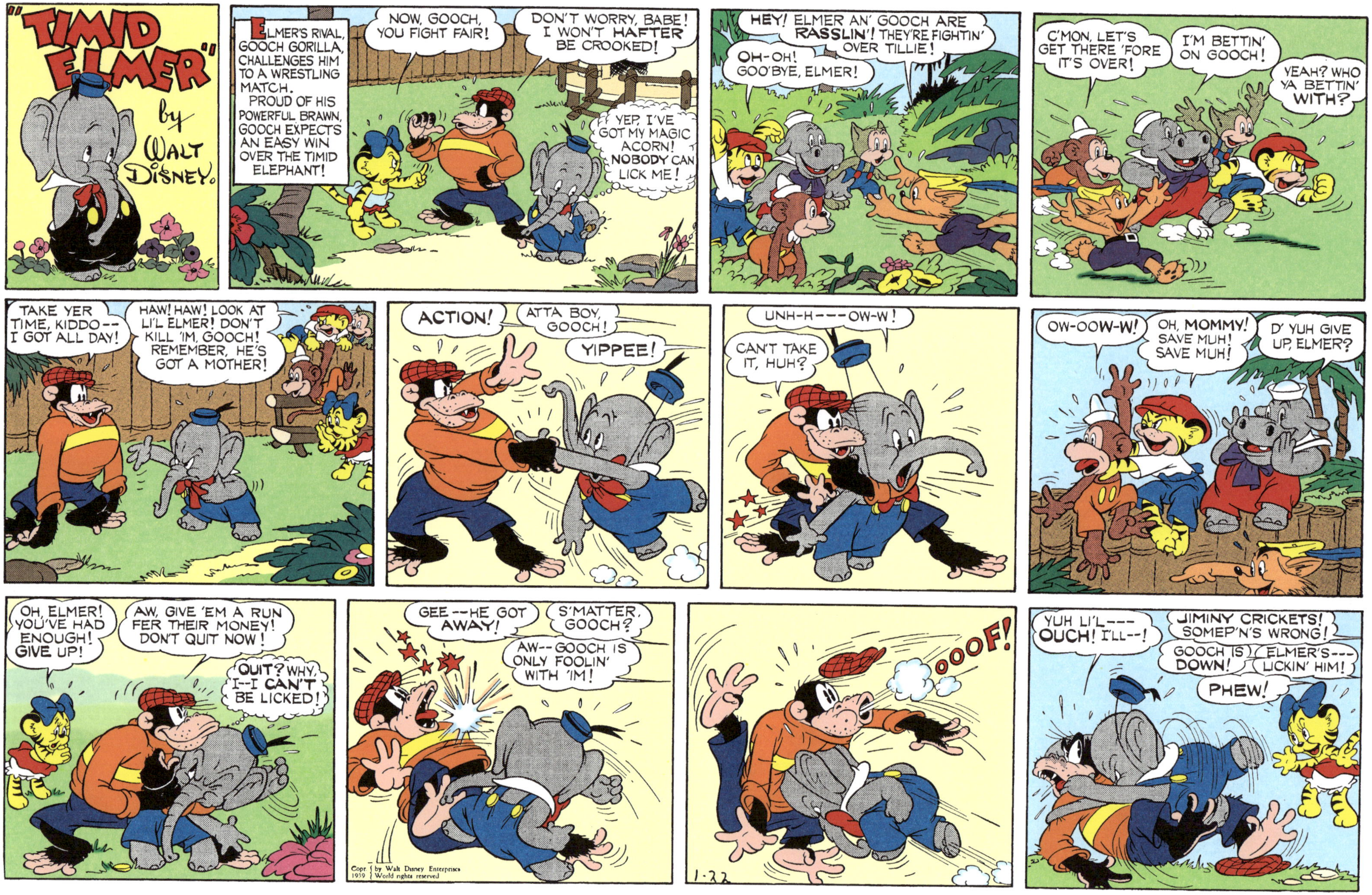
"TIMID ELMER"
by WALT DISNEY
ELMER'S RIVAL, GOOCH GORILLA, CHALLENGES HIM TO A WRESTLING MATCH. PROUD OF HIS POWERFUL BRAWN, GOOCH EXPECTS AN EASY WIN OVER THE TIMID ELEPHANT!
NOW, GOOCH, YOU FIGHT FAIR!
DON'T WORRY, BABE! I WON'T HAFTER BE CROOKED!
YEP, I'VE GOT MY MAGIC ACORN! NOBODY CAN LICK ME!
HEY! ELMER AN' GOOCH ARE RASSLIN'! THEY'RE FIGHTIN' OVER TILLIE!
OH-OH! GOO'BYE, ELMER!
C'MON, LET'S GET THERE 'FORE IT'S OVER!
I'M BETTIN' ON GOOCH!
YEAH? WHO YA BETTIN' WITH?
TAKE YER TIME, KIDDO-- I GOT ALL DAY!
HAW! HAW! LOOK AT LI'L ELMER! DON'T KILL 'IM, GOOCH! REMEMBER, HE'S GOT A MOTHER!
ACTION!
ATTA BOY, GOOCH!
YIPPEE!
UNH-H---OW-W!
CAN'T TAKE IT, HUH?
OW-OOW-W!
OH, MOMMY! SAVE MUH! SAVE MUH!
D' YUH GIVE UP, ELMER?
OH, ELMER! YOU'VE HAD ENOUGH! GIVE UP!
AW, GIVE 'EM A RUN FER THEIR MONEY! DON'T QUIT NOW!
QUIT? WHY, I--I CAN'T BE LICKED!
GEE--HE GOT AWAY!
S'MATTER, GOOCH?
AW--GOOCH IS ONLY FOOLIN' WITH 'IM!
Copr. 1939 by Walt Disney Enterprises World rights reserved
OOOF!
1-22
YUH LI'L--- OUCH! I'LL--!
JIMINY CRICKETS! SOMEP'N'S WRONG!
GOOCH IS DOWN!
ELMER'S--- LICKIN' HIM!
PHEW!

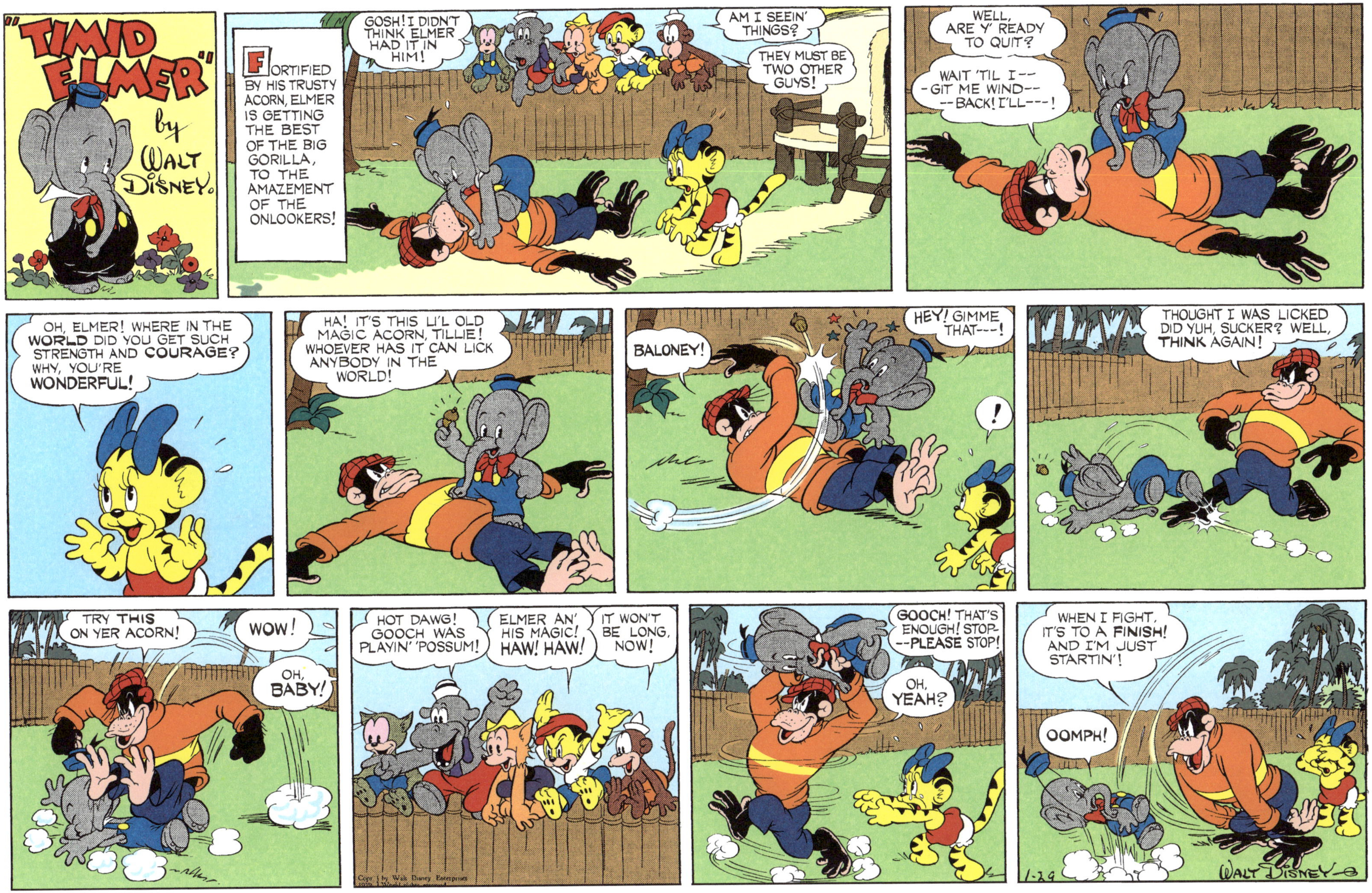
"TIMID ELMER"
by WALT DISNEY
FORTIFIED BY HIS TRUSTY ACORN, ELMER IS GETTING THE BEST OF THE BIG GORILLA, TO THE AMAZEMENT OF THE ONLOOKERS!
GOSH! I DIDN'T THINK ELMER HAD IT IN HIM!
AM I SEEIN' THINGS?
THEY MUST BE TWO OTHER GUYS!
WELL, ARE Y' READY TO QUIT?
WAIT 'TIL I-- -GIT ME WIND-- --BACK! I'LL---!
OH, ELMER! WHERE IN THE WORLD DID YOU GET SUCH STRENGTH AND COURAGE? WHY, YOU'RE WONDERFUL!
HA! IT'S THIS LI'L OLD MAGIC ACORN, TILLIE! WHOEVER HAS IT CAN LICK ANYBODY IN THE WORLD!
BALONEY!
HEY! GIMME THAT---!
!
THOUGHT I WAS LICKED DID YUH, SUCKER? WELL, THINK AGAIN!
TRY THIS ON YER ACORN!
WOW!
OH, BABY!
HOT DAWG! GOOCH WAS PLAYIN' 'POSSUM!
ELMER AN' HIS MAGIC! HAW! HAW!
IT WON'T BE LONG, NOW!
GOOCH! THAT'S ENOUGH! STOP- --PLEASE STOP!
OH, YEAH?
WHEN I FIGHT, IT'S TO A FINISH! AND I'M JUST STARTIN'!
OOMPH!
1-29
WALT DISNEY

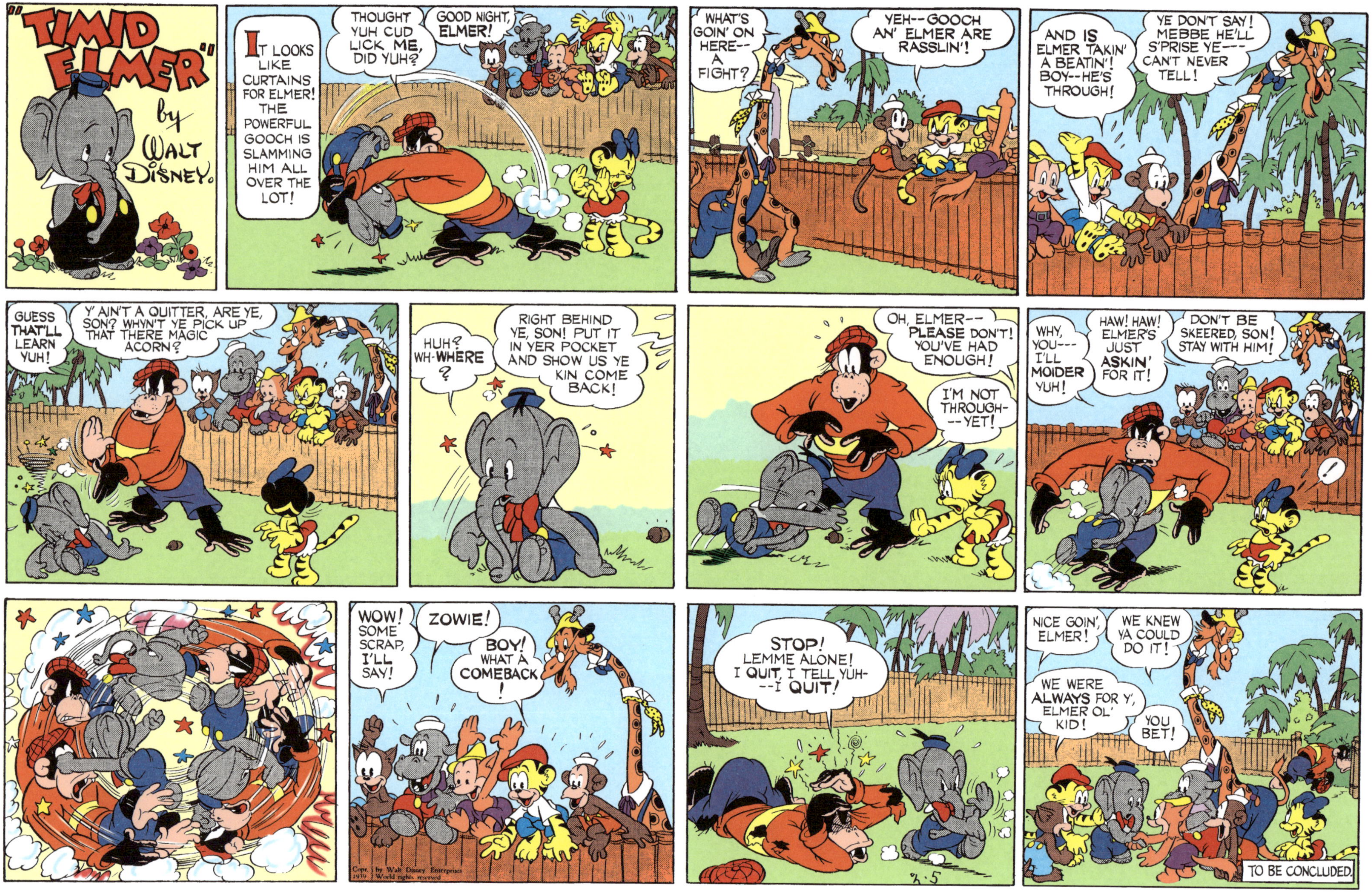
"TIMID ELMER"
by WALT DISNEY
IT LOOKS LIKE CURTAINS FOR ELMER! THE POWERFUL GOOCH IS SLAMMING HIM ALL OVER THE LOT!
THOUGHT YUH CUD LICK ME, DID YUH?
GOOD NIGHT, ELMER!
WHAT'S GOIN' ON HERE-- A FIGHT?
YEH--GOOCH AN' ELMER ARE RASSLIN'!
AND IS ELMER TAKIN' A BEATIN'! BOY--HE'S THROUGH!
YE DON'T SAY! MEBBE HE'LL S'PRISE YE--- CAN'T NEVER TELL!
GUESS THAT'LL LEARN YUH!
Y' AIN'T A QUITTER, ARE YE, SON? WHYN'T YE PICK UP THAT THERE MAGIC ACORN?
HUH? WH-WHERE?
RIGHT BEHIND YE, SON! PUT IT IN YER POCKET AND SHOW US YE KIN COME BACK!
OH, ELMER-- PLEASE DON'T! YOU'VE HAD ENOUGH!
I'M NOT THROUGH- --YET!
WHY, YOU--- I'LL MOIDER YUH!
HAW! HAW! ELMER'S JUST ASKIN' FOR IT!
DON'T BE SKEERED, SON! STAY WITH HIM!
!
WOW! SOME SCRAP, I'LL SAY!
ZOWIE!
BOY! WHAT A COMEBACK!
STOP! LEMME ALONE! I QUIT, I TELL YUH- --I QUIT!
NICE GOIN', ELMER!
WE KNEW YA COULD DO IT!
WE WERE ALWAYS FOR Y', ELMER OL' KID!
YOU BET!
TO BE CONCLUDED.

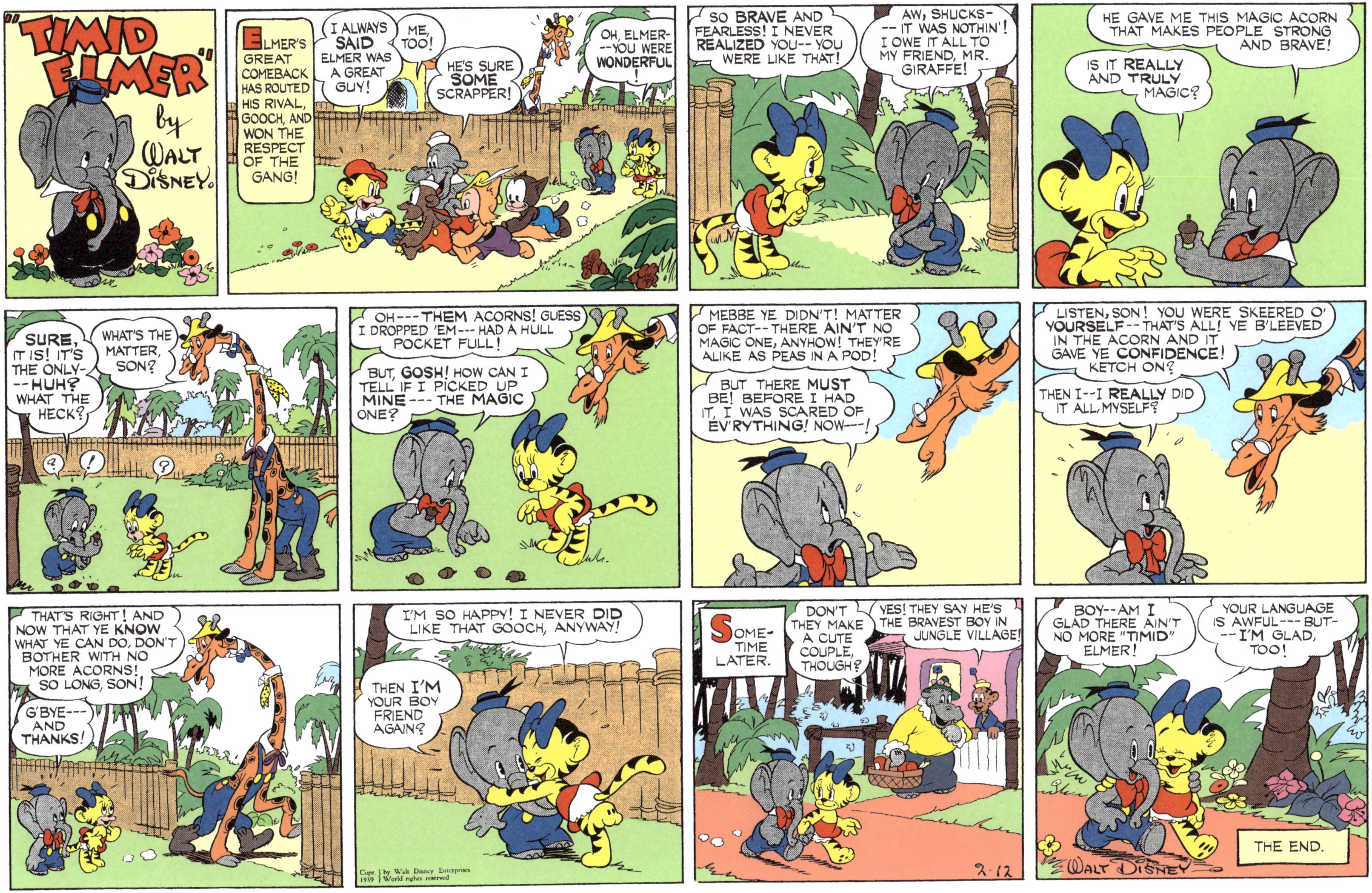
"TIMID ELMER"
by WALT DISNEY
ELMER'S GREAT COMEBACK HAS ROUTED HIS RIVAL, GOOCH, AND WON THE RESPECT OF THE GANG!
I ALWAYS SAID ELMER WAS A GREAT GUY!
ME, TOO!
HE'S SURE SOME SCRAPPER!
OH, ELMER--YOU WERE WONDERFUL!
SO BRAVE AND FEARLESS! I NEVER REALIZED YOU--YOU WERE LIKE THAT!
AW, SHUCKS--IT WAS NOTHIN'! I OWE IT ALL TO MY FRIEND, MR. GIRAFFE!
HE GAVE ME THIS MAGIC ACORN THAT MAKES PEOPLE STRONG AND BRAVE!
IS IT REALLY AND TRULY MAGIC?
SURE, IT IS! IT'S THE ONLY--HUH? WHAT THE HECK?
WHAT'S THE MATTER, SON?
?
!
?
OH---THEM ACORNS! GUESS I DROPPED 'EM---HAD A HULL POCKET FULL!
BUT, GOSH! HOW CAN I TELL IF I PICKED UP MINE---THE MAGIC ONE?
MEBBE YE DIDN'T! MATTER OF FACT--THERE AIN'T NO MAGIC ONE, ANYHOW! THEY'RE ALIKE AS PEAS IN A POD!
BUT THERE MUST BE! BEFORE I HAD IT, I WAS SCARED OF EV'RYTHING! NOW---!
LISTEN, SON! YOU WERE SKEERED O' YOURSELF--THAT'S ALL! YE B'LEEVED IN THE ACORN AND IT GAVE YE CONFIDENCE! KETCH ON?
THEN I--I REALLY DID IT ALL, MYSELF?
THAT'S RIGHT! AND NOW THAT YE KNOW WHAT YE CAN DO, DON'T BOTHER WITH NO MORE ACORNS! SO LONG, SON!
G'BYE---AND THANKS!
I'M SO HAPPY! I NEVER DID LIKE THAT GOOCH, ANYWAY!
THEN I'M YOUR BOY FRIEND AGAIN?
Copr. 1939 by Walt Disney Enterprises World rights reserved
SOMETIME LATER.
DON'T THEY MAKE A CUTE COUPLE, THOUGH?
YES! THEY SAY HE'S THE BRAVEST BOY IN JUNGLE VILLAGE!
2·12
BOY--AM I GLAD THERE AIN'T NO MORE "TIMID" ELMER!
YOUR LANGUAGE IS AWFUL---BUT---I'M GLAD, TOO!
THE END.
WALT DISNEY

ALSO FROM IDW AND THE LIBRARY OF AMERICAN COMICS

Thimble Theatre
POPEYE
CLASSIC NEWSPAPER COMICS
by BOBBY LONDON

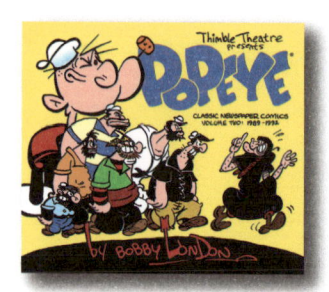

POPEYE
BY BOBBY LONDON

This two-volume set presents all of Bobby London's published strips plus his newly discovered final six weeks that have never before been printed!

"London here is the artist as smuggler: A creative type working around the system with the boot of the 'man' seemingly moments from planting itself firmly on his face."—*The Comics Journal*

EDGAR RICE BURROUGHS'
TARZAN
THE COMPLETE RUSS MANNING
NEWSPAPER STRIPS VOLUME TWO: 1969–1971

TARZAN
BY RUSS MANNING

Manning's run from 1967 to 1979 is considered the most accurate to the spirit of the original Tarzan novels and is reproduced from the ERB estate file copies.

EISNER AWARD WINNER!

Harold Gray's
Little Orphan Annie
VOLUME THIRTEEN
SPIES AND COUNTER SPIES
DAILIES AND COLOR SUNDAYS 1947–1948
America's Spunkiest Kid Meets the World's Greatest Cartoonist!

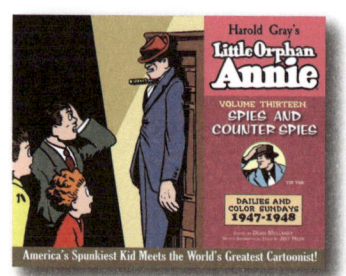

LITTLE ORPHAN ANNIE
BY HAROLD GRAY

Follow the exploits of the plucky orphan, her loveable mutt Sandy, and her adoptive benefactor Oliver "Daddy" Warbucks.

EISNER AWARD NOMINEE!

"One of the most impressive comic-strip collections ever produced."
—*The Washington Times*

Al Capp's
LI'L ABNER
THE COMPLETE DAILIES & COLOR SUNDAYS
EVIL-EYE FLEAGLE!
VOLUME EIGHT

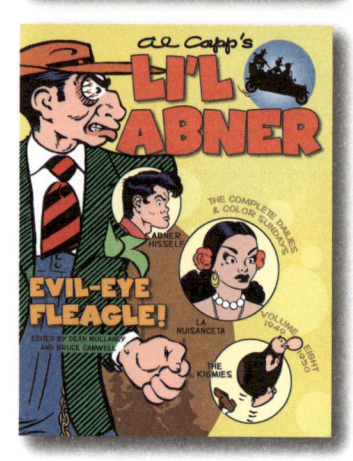

LI'L ABNER
BY AL CAPP

The strip that injected "Lower Slobbovia," "the double whammy," and "Sadie Hawkins Day" into our popular lexicon. This series is the first comprehensive archive of *Li'l Abner*, with the Sunday pages restored to their original pulchritudinous beauty.

HARVEY AWARD NOMINEE!

"Seeing Capp's strips reprinted in beautifully designed and hefty volumes, containing both dailies and Sundays, fulfills a longtime personal wish. This massive and important body of work will now steadily be accessible to yet another generation." —Denis Kitchen

AMAZING SPIDER-MAN
STAN LEE
JOHN ROMITA
1 THE ULTIMATE NEWSPAPER COMICS COLLECTION! 1977-1979

THE AMAZING SPIDER-MAN
BY STAN LEE & JOHN ROMITA

The wondrous wall-crawler's long-running newspaper strip with all Sundays in color and integrated with the dailies—just as they originally appeared in newspapers worldwide.

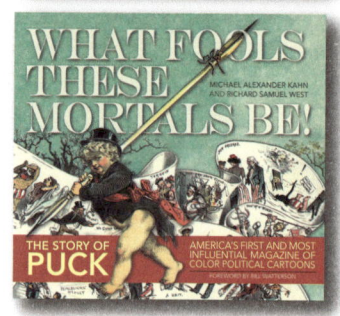

WHAT FOOLS THESE MORTALS BE!
MICHAEL ALEXANDER KAHN AND RICHARD SAMUEL WEST
THE STORY OF PUCK
AMERICA'S FIRST AND MOST INFLUENTIAL MAGAZINE OF COLOR POLITICAL CARTOONS

WHAT FOOLS THESE MORTALS BE!
BY KAHN & WEST

A lavish coffee table book devoted to the most important political satire magazine in American history, containing nearly 300 full-color plates.

EISNER AWARD NOMINEE!

"Richly illustrated and expertly curated ...[a] mesmerizing compendium."
—*The Wall Street Journal*

X-9
SECRET AGENT CORRIGAN
VOLUME FOUR: 1974–1977
AL WILLIAMSON & ARCHIE GOODWIN

X-9: SECRET AGENT CORRIGAN
BY WILLIAMSON & GOODWIN

Al Williamson's delicate line-work and Archie Goodwin's no-nonsense action made *Corrigan* arguably the last of the great adventure strips.

"One more in an amazing run of titles published by IDW under their Library of American Comics imprint."
—*The Christian Science Monitor*

CLIFF STERRETT
POLLY and HER PALS

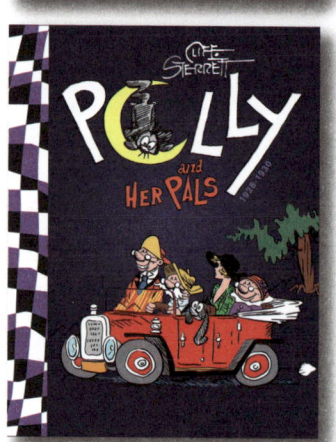

POLLY AND HER PALS
BY CLIFF STERRETT

Launching our oversized 12" x 16" Champagne Edition format, the groundbreaking surrealism of *Polly* is combined with the most detailed examination of Cliff Sterrett's life ever printed.

EISNER AWARD NOMINEE!

"The early years of newspaper comics produced a handful of acknowledged masterworks such as *Little Nemo* and *Krazy Kat*; this impressive collection makes a convincing case that Sterrett's creation should be added to that honor roll." —Gordon Flagg, *Booklist*

RIP KIRBY
THE FIRST MODERN DETECTIVE

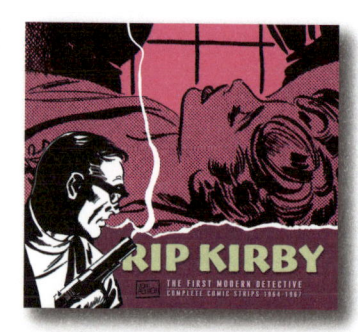

RIP KIRBY
VOL. 1-4 BY ALEX RAYMOND
VOL. 5-9 BY JOHN PRENTICE

Raymond eschewed the prevailing hard-boiled style and made Rip Kirby smart and sophisticated, full of '50s chic, but still a man's man...drawn in an equally modern style that influenced comics art for decades.

HARVEY AWARD NOMINEE!

"Raymond's art...set the template for the dramatic newspaper strips of the 1950s and beyond."—Gordon Flagg, *Booklist*

RED BARRY
"UNDERCOVER MAN"

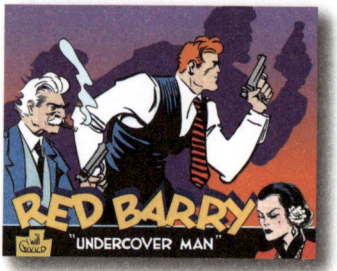

RED BARRY
BY WILL GOULD

One of the most visually innovative adventure strips of the mid-1930s, combining fluid brushwork and noir shadows (in bold blues and purples) with figures that were constantly in motion.

"The only detective strip...worthy of any consideration from my scholarly viewpoint."—*Anthony Boucher*

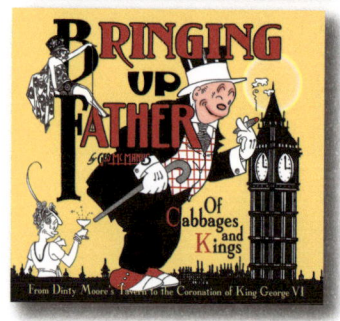

BRINGING UP FATHER
Of Cabbages and Kings
From Dinty Moore's Tavern to the Coronation of King George VI

BRINGING UP FATHER
BY GEORGE McMANUS

George McManus's funny gags, outlandish costumes, eye-catching artwork, and lush, Art Deco designs are all on display in this deluxe series, which features both daily strips and the spectacular Sunday pages reproduced large and in gloriously restored color. Edited by Bruce Canwell.

EISNER AWARD NOMINEE!

BEYOND MARS

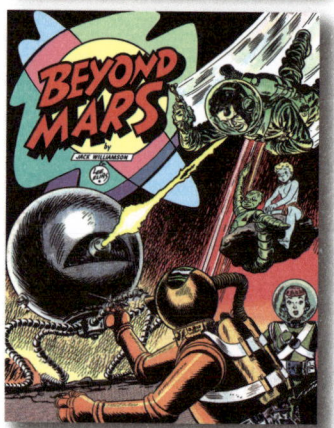

BEYOND MARS
BY JACK WILLIAMSON & LEE ELIAS

One of the rarest Sunday strips—it only appeared in a single newspaper! Written by Hugo Award-winner Williamson and beautifully drawn by Elias in a style clearly influenced by Milton Caniff and Noel Sickles. The story takes place 200 years in the future when "a new force—paragravity—has enabled men to live and breathe on the asteroids." Includes the complete series, all 161 Sundays from 1952-1955.

EISNER AWARD NOMINEE!

"THE LIBRARY OF AMERICAN COMICS HAS BECOME THE GOLD STANDARD FOR ARCHIVAL COMIC STRIP REPRINTS." — *Scoop*

PERCY CROSBY'S
SKIPPY
DAILY COMICS 1925–1927

Skippy
BY PERCY CROSBY

Skippy is the spiritual ancestor to *Peanuts*, *Calvin and Hobbes*, and just about every other kid strip ever created. This first-ever series to reprint Percy Crosby's legendary comics allows us to rediscover why America fell so in love with Skippy and his pals.

EISNER AWARD NOMINEE!

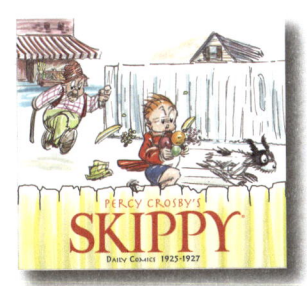

"The greatest children's comic strip ever."
—Michael Taube, *The Washington Times*

BLOOM COUNTY
THE COMPLETE LIBRARY
BERKELEY BREATHED

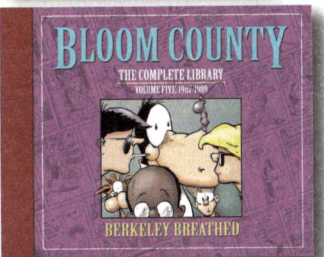

Bloom County
BY BERKELEY BREATHED

The Pulitzer Prize-winning strip transitioned from cult favorite to a phenomenon that entered and helped shape the American zeitgeist.

EISNER AWARD WINNER!

"*Bloom County*...seems like a bridge between *Doonesbury* and *The Simpsons* —with *The Daily Show* as a clear successor." —*Entertainment Weekly*

THE COMPLETE
DICK TRACY
THE MARAUDING DETECTIVE MEETS
MOON MAID
52 GANG
VOLUME 21:
1962–64
DAILIES & SUNDAYS

Dick Tracy
BY CHESTER GOULD

Gould introduced violence—blunt, ironic, and retributional violence—to the comics page. His intrepid square-jawed hero holds the line against crime in this incomparable morality play.

"It's time to build new bookshelves to welcome one of America's singular artistic achievements." —art spiegelman

Genius Animated
THE CARTOON ART OF
ALEX TOTH
DEAN MULLANEY & BRUCE CANWELL

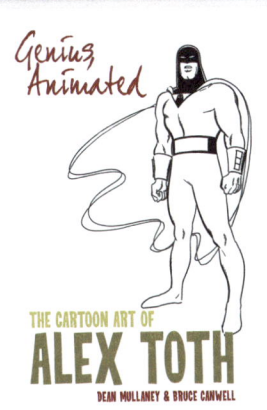

The Alex Toth Trilogy
BY MULLANEY & CANWELL

A three-part exhaustive illustrated biography of Alex Toth, one of the true giants in the history of comic books and animation. Includes more than 1,000 pages and dozens of complete Toth stories, many shot directly from the original art.

HARVEY & THREE-TIME EISNER AWARD WINNER!

"Nothing short of wonderful."
—*Los Angeles Review of Books*

"An astounding achievement...a game-changer.... Anyone with an interest in the medium should own and study this book. It's one of those."
— *The Comics Journal*

CARTOON MONARCH
OTTO SOGLOW & THE LITTLE KING

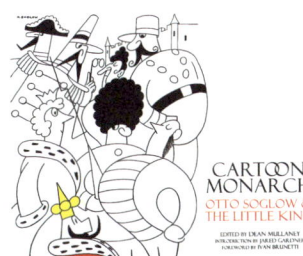

Cartoon Monarch
BY OTTO SOGLOW

A long-overdue look at the unique pantomime cartoons of Otto Soglow, who entertained millions for more than fifty years and whose influence remains current in the works of Chris Ware, Daniel Clowes, Ivan Brunetti, and others.

"An impressive examination...of this simple yet brilliant comic strip."
—Michael Taube, *The Washington Post*

SUPERMAN
The SILVER AGE DAILIES
1959–1961

Superman
BY JERRY SIEGEL, CURT SWAN, & WAYNE BORING

The Man of Steel's newspaper adventures ran for more than 25 years yet the vast majority of strips have never been reprinted. This series remedies that gap in the Superman mythos.

Archie
DAILY NEWSPAPER COMICS
THE SWINGIN' SIXTIES

Archie
BY BOB MONTANA

Archie, after conquering comic books, premiered as a newspaper comic strip in 1946. This series presents the most enduring classic stories from the '40s to the '60s.

EISNER AWARD WINNER!

"The best Archie book I've ever read."
—*Archie Comics Fan Forum*

FLASH GORDON
JUNGLE JIM

Flash Gordon & Jungle Jim
BY ALEX RAYMOND

For the first time, Alex Raymond's classic *Flash Gordon* and *Jungle Jim* are collected together in the oversized 12" x 16" Champagne Edition format that lets us see the strips as he originally intended. *Flash Gordon* is arguably the most famous science fiction comic strip of all time, but the real star of both strips is Alex Raymond's incredibly lush and lyrical artwork.

EISNER AWARD NOMINEE!

"This meticulously remastered and restored edition...will be the definitive edition for the ages." —Bud Plant

STEVE CANYON

Steve Canyon
BY MILTON CANIFF

The definitive edition of Caniff's famous flyboy featuring every Sunday in color.

"This collection, sharply reproduced from syndicate proofs, brilliantly shows off the hallmarks—cinematic storytelling, dramatic illustration, exotic locales, appealing characters, and snappy dialogue—that made Caniff one of comics' most highly regarded and influential artists."
—Gordon Flagg, *Booklist*

THE COMPLETE
TERRY AND THE PIRATES

Terry and the Pirates
BY MILTON CANIFF

Nothing short of the greatest adventure comic strip of all, featuring Terry, Pat, Connie, and Big Stoop, an array of unforgettable brigands, and a host of strong, alluring, and unforgettable women.

EISNER AWARD WINNER!

"All you could want in a comics collection."
—*Atlanta Journal-Constitution*

CANIFF
A VISUAL BIOGRAPHY
EDITED BY DEAN MULLANEY

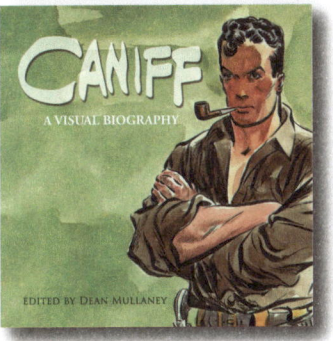

Caniff
BY DEAN MULLANEY

A visual biography of the artist known as "The Rembrandt of the Comic Strip." No comics artist has so heavily influenced his medium and no cartoonist has seen more imitators than Milton Arthur Paul Caniff. Produced with full access to the artist's extensive personal files.

EISNER AWARD NOMINEE!

"One of my favorite books of the year."
—Dan Nadel, *The Comics Journal*

SCORCHY SMITH
AND THE ART OF
NOEL SICKLES

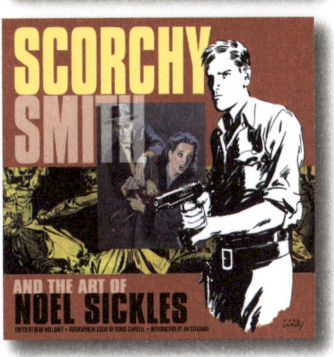

Scorchy Smith & the Art of Noel Sickles
BY MULLANEY & CANWELL

A comprehensive book that collects, for the first time, every Sickles *Scorchy Smith* strip, plus a 140-page biography and an examination of the full breadth of his decades-long career as one of America's foremost illustrators.

EISNER AND HARVEY AWARD NOMINEE!

"[An] almost embarrassing amount of riches." —*Comic Book Resources*

THE LIBRARY OF AMERICAN COMICS ESSENTIALS
Harry J. Tuthill's
THE BUNGLE FAMILY

THE LIBRARY OF AMERICAN COMICS ESSENTIALS
KRAZY KAT
Geo. Herriman

THE LIBRARY OF AMERICAN COMICS ESSENTIALS
TIM TYLER'S LUCK
LYMAN YOUNG & ALEX RAYMOND

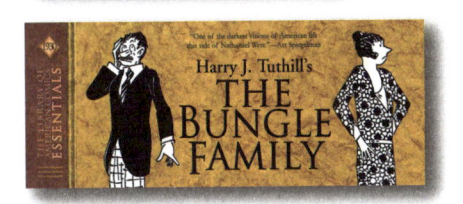

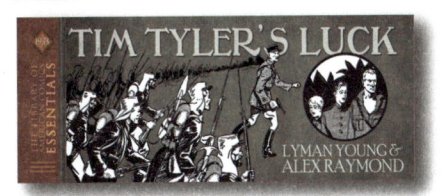

LOAC Essentials

An important series that collects, in yearly volumes, daily strips that are essential to comics history, such as *Baron Bean*, George Herriman's 1916 comedy; Sidney Smith's 1929 *Gumps* storyline that forever changed comics, the 1939 first time travel story in *Alley Oop*, and the first *Tarzan* dailies!

"Spotlight[ing] a classic comic strip over one full calendar year, complete with a short essay and at an affordable price. When it comes to old classic comic strips, the future looks bright."—*The Washington Times*

DON'T MISS THESE OTHER CLASSIC DISNEY NEWSPAPER COMICS...

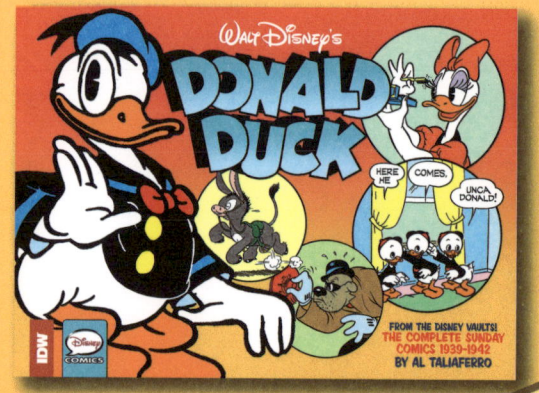

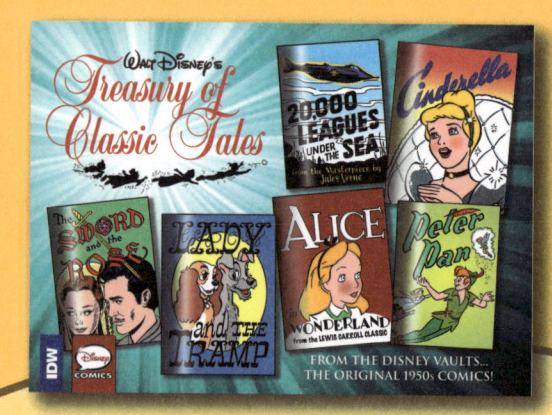

"The Library of American Comics [is] a reprint series that is becoming a national treasure."
— Mark Squirek, *The New York Journal of Books*

THE LIBRARY OF AMERICAN COMICS

The Library of American Comics is dedicated to preserving, in definitive editions, the long and jubilantly creative history of the American newspaper comic strip. The Library was created in 2007 and ushered in a new Golden Age of newspaper strip collections. While our production values are archival, the material we present is fresh and exciting. Each Library release frames the comics so readers can start turning pages and immediately begin to enjoy strips that may be decades or even a century old.

We invite you to visit us online at LibraryofAmericanComics.com

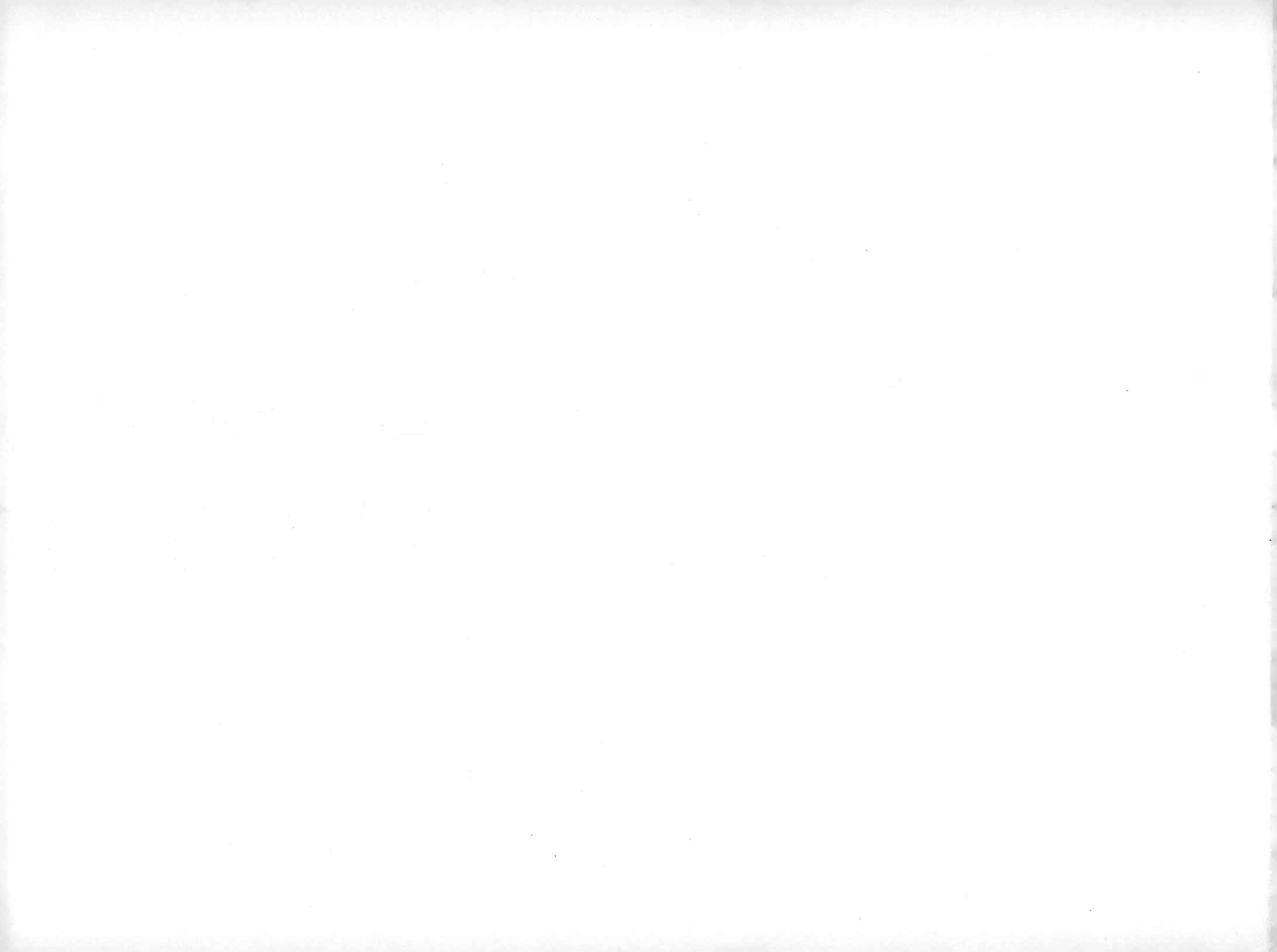

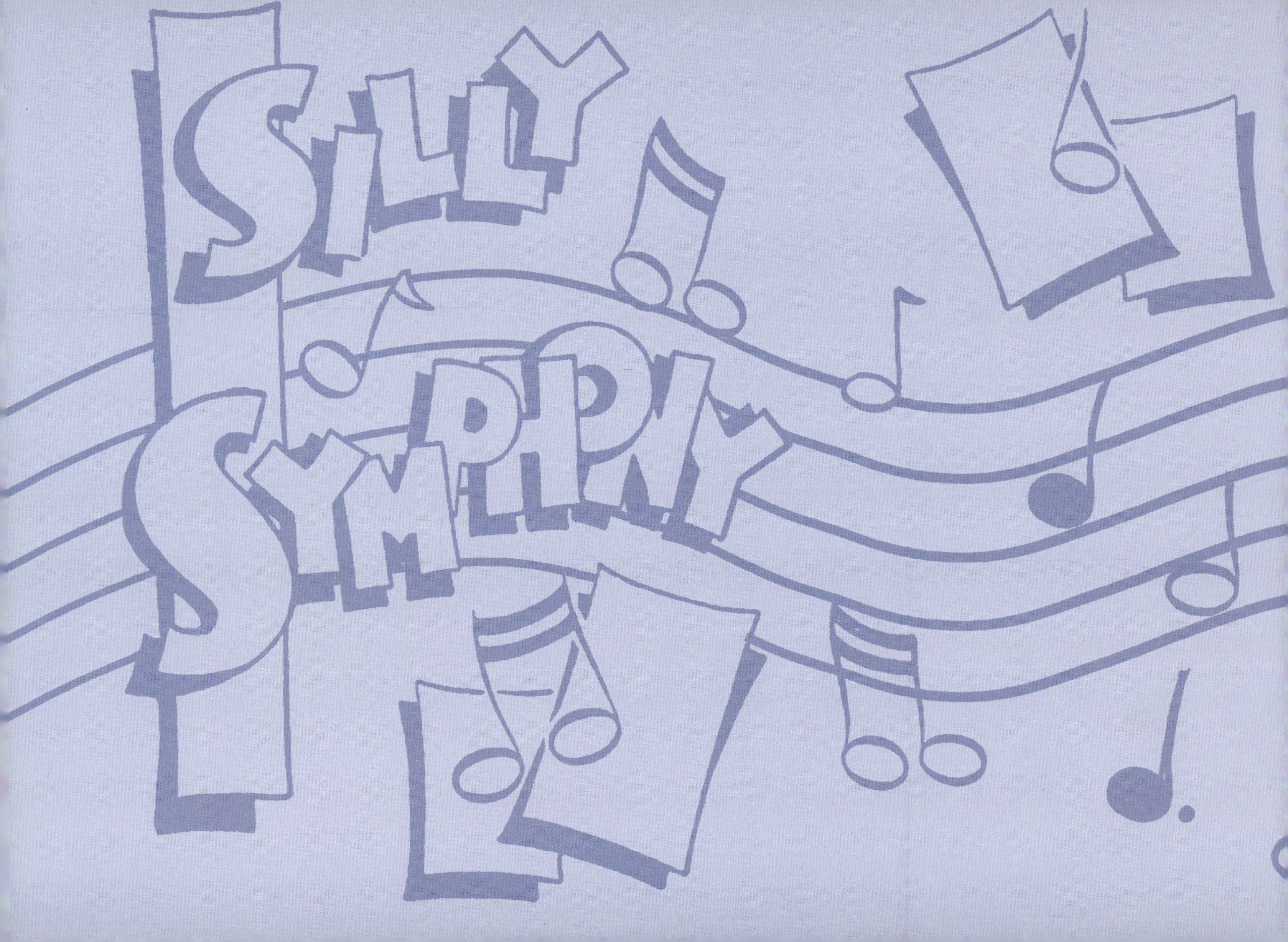
SILLY
SYMPHONY